EDEXCEL
A LEVEL
HISTORY

*ctive*Book included

Paper 3:
Mass media and social change in Britain, 1882–2004

Stuart Clayton
Series editor: Rosemary Rees

ALWAYS LEARNING

PEARSON

Published by Pearson Education Limited, 80 Strand, London, WC2R 0RL

www.pearsonschoolsandfecolleges.co.uk

Copies of official specifications for all Edexcel qualifications may be found on the website:
www.edexcel.com

Text © Pearson Education Limited 2016

Designed by Elizabeth Arnoux for Pearson

Typeset and illustrated by Phoenix Photosetting, Chatham, Kent

Produced by Out of House Publishing

Original illustrations © Pearson Education Limited 2016

Cover design by Malena Wilson-Max for Pearson

Cover photo/illustration © Getty/Duffy

The rights of Stuart Clayton to be identified as author of this work have been asserted by him in
accordance with the Copyright, Designs and Patents Act 1988

First published 2016

19 18 17 16

10 9 8 7 6 5 4 3 2 1

British Library Cataloguing in Publication Data
A catalogue record for this book is available from the British Library

ISBN 978 1 447 985402

Printed in the UK by CPI

Websites

Pearson Education Limited is not responsible for the content of any external internet sites. It is essential
for tutors to preview each website before using it in class so as to ensure that the URL is still accurate,
relevant and appropriate. We suggest that tutors bookmark useful websites and consider enabling
students to access them through the school/college intranet.

A note from the publisher

In order to ensure that this resource offers high-quality support for the associated Pearson
qualification, it has been through a review process by the awarding body. This process confirms
that this resource fully covers the teaching and learning content of the specification or part of
a specification at which it is aimed. It also confirms that it demonstrates an appropriate balance
between the development of subject skills, knowledge and understanding, in addition to preparation
for assessment.

Endorsement does not cover any guidance on assessment activities or processes (e.g. practice
questions or advice on how to answer assessment questions) included in the resource, nor does it
prescribe any particular approach to the teaching or delivery of a related course.

While the publishers have made every attempt to ensure that advice on the qualification and its
assessment is accurate, the official specification and associated assessment guidance materials are
the only authoritative source of information and should always be referred to for definitive guidance.

Pearson examiners have not contributed to any sections in this resource relevant to examination
papers for which they have responsibility.

Examiners will not use endorsed resources as a source of material for any assessment set by Pearson.

Endorsement of a resource does not mean that the resource is required to achieve this Pearson
qualification, nor does it mean that it is the only suitable material available to support the qualification,
and any resource lists produced by the awarding body shall include this and other appropriate
resources.

Contents

How to use this book

STRUCTURE

This book covers Paper 3, Option 39.2: Mass media and social change in Britain, 1882–2004 of the Edexcel A Level qualification.

You will also need to study a Paper 1 and a Paper 2 option and produce coursework in order to complete your qualification. All Paper 1/2 options are covered by other textbooks in this series.

EXAM SUPPORT

The examined assessment for Paper 3 requires you to answer questions from three sections. Throughout this book there are exam-style questions in all three section styles for you to practise your examination skills.

Section A contains a compulsory question that will assess your source analysis and evaluation skills.

> **A Level Exam-Style Question Section A**
>
> ***Study Source 10 before you answer this question.***
>
> Assess the value of the source for revealing the influence of the *Daily Herald* and the role of George Lansbury at the newspaper.
>
> Explain your answer using the source, the information given about its origin and your own knowledge about the historical context. (20 marks)
>
> **Tip**
> *It can help to structure your answer in the exam by using a pen to underline parts of the text that you will challenge or support with your own knowledge. This approach can also help you to avoid missing important points raised within the source.*

Section B contains a choice of essay questions that will look at your understanding of the studied period in depth.

> **A Level Exam-Style Question Section B**
>
> 'The role of technology was significant in improving public perception of the BBC's war coverage.'
>
> How far do you agree with this statement? (20 marks)
>
> **Tip**
> *Structure your answer with paragraphs that centre on ways in which technology was, and was not, significant, before reaching a supported judgement.*

Section C will again give you a choice of essay questions but these will assess your understanding of the period in breadth.

> **A Level Exam-Style Question Section C**
>
> How far do you agree with the opinion that the impact of government legislation was the most important factor affecting women's personal lives in the period 1882–2004? (20 marks)
>
> **Tip**
> *Make sure that you compare the impact of other factors with the impact of government legislation in each paragraph. Be clear about the criteria you will use to justify the comparative impact of each factor on women's personal lives.*

The Preparing for your exams sections at the end of this book contains sample answers of different standards, with comments on how they could be improved.

FEATURES

Extend your knowledge

These features contain additional information that will help you gain a deeper understanding of the topic. This could be a short biography of an important person, extra background information about an event, an alternative interpretation, or even a research idea that you could follow up. Information in these boxes is not essential to your exam success, but still provides insights of value.

> **EXTEND YOUR KNOWLEDGE**
>
> **Pioneering women in politics**
> Nancy Astor (1879–1964) was the first woman to take her seat in parliament, and she represented the Conservatives until 1945. Some see her as a controversial heroine because she gained her seat thanks to her wealthy husband, who held the seat until he was elevated to the House of Lords.
>
> Eleanor Rathbone (1872–1946) had been a suffragist. Her arguments in the House of Commons were crucial in changing Family Allowance payments to mothers rather than fathers in 1945.
>
> Ellen Wilkinson (1891–1947) was an inspirational MP for Jarrow. She organised the 1936 Jarrow March, which delivered a petition to parliament to highlight the suffering of this shipbuilding community. She also introduced the Hire Purchase Act 1938, which gave protection to people who bought goods on credit. Ellen also served as Minister for Education in Attlee's first post-war government. She raised the school leaving age from 14 to 15.
>
> Edith Summerskill (1901–80) was one of the first women to be trained as a doctor before becoming a Labour MP. She was a founder of the Socialist Health Association, which put forward arguments for a National Health Service.
>
> Barbara Castle (1910–2002) was a leading figure in Harold Wilson's Labour governments in the 1960s and 1970s. As Secretary of State for Transport (1965–68) she made seatbelts compulsory in new cars and introduced breathalysers to combat drink-driving.

Knowledge check activities

These activities are designed to check that you have understood the material that you have just studied. They might also ask you questions about the sources and extracts in the section to check that you have studied and analysed them thoroughly.

> **ACTIVITY**
> **KNOWLEDGE CHECK**
>
> **Mass media and popular attitudes to racial minorities in Britain**
> 1 Explain the difficulties of using film and television to explore the nature of race relations in the 1960s.
>
> 2 In your opinion, is there more evidence for film and television reflecting or moulding race relations?
>
> 3 Give examples of factors other than film and television that affected race relations in Britain in the 1960s.

Summary activities

At the end of each chapter, you will find summary activities. These are tasks designed to help you think about the key topic you have just studied as a whole. They may involve selecting and organising key information or analysing how things changed over time. You might want to keep your answers to these questions safe – they are handy for revision.

> **ACTIVITY**
> **SUMMARY**
>
> **The age of the press barons, 1914–36**
> 1 Create a graph with 'Degree of influence: 0-100%' on the vertical axis and 'Time: 1914-36' on the horizontal axis.
>
> 2 Plot a line that you feel best describes the impact of: Lord Northcliffe, Lord Rothermere, Lord Beaverbrook, George Lansbury/the *Daily Herald*. Give each person a separate line.
>
> 3 Once you have plotted all the lines, explain the overall trend for each line as well as any major peaks, troughs or turning points.
>
> 4 When you have done this, write a summary paragraph about the reasons why one newspaper proprietor could be judged to have been more influential than the rest. You could consider having a 'balloon debate' based on this task

Thinking Historically activities

These activities are found throughout the book, and are designed to develop your understanding of history, especially around the key concepts of evidence, interpretations, causation and change. Each activity is designed to challenge a conceptual barrier that might be holding you back. This is linked to a map of conceptual barriers developed by experts. You can look up the map and find out which barrier each activity challenges by downloading the progression map from this website: www.pearsonschools.co.uk/historyprogressionsapproach.

progression map
reference

 THINKING HISTORICALLY Evidence (6b)

The strength of argument
Answer the following questions about reportage on the Falklands conflict.

1 Read Source 9.

a) What is weak about this claim?

b) What could be added to it to make it stronger?

2 Read Extract 1.

a) Is this an argument? If yes, what makes it one?

b) How might this argument be strengthened?

3 Read Extract 2.

a) How have they expanded their explanation to make the claim stronger?

b) Can you explain why this is the strongest claim of the three sources?

4 What elements make a historian's claims strong?

Getting the most from your online ActiveBook

This book comes with three years' access to ActiveBook* – an online, digital version of your textbook. Follow the instructions printed on the inside front cover to start using your ActiveBook.

Your ActiveBook is the perfect way to personalise your learning as you progress through your A Level History course. You can:

- access your content online, anytime, anywhere
- use the inbuilt highlighting and annotation tools to personalise the content and make it really relevant to you.

Highlight tool – use this to pick out key terms or topics so you are ready and prepared for revision.

Annotations tool – use this to add your own notes, for example links to your wider reading, such as websites or other files. Or, make a note to remind yourself about work that you need to do.

*For new purchases only. If the access code has already been revealed, it may no longer be valid. If you have bought this textbook secondhand, the code may already have been used by the first owner of the book.

Introduction
A Level History

WHY HISTORY MATTERS

History is about people and people are complex, fascinating, frustrating and a whole lot of other things besides. This is why history is probably the most comprehensive and certainly one of the most intriguing subjects there is. History can also be inspiring and alarming, heartening and disturbing, a story of progress and civilisation and of catastrophe and inhumanity.

History's importance goes beyond the subject's intrinsic interest and appeal. Our beliefs and actions, our cultures, institutions and ways of living, our languages and means of making sense of ourselves are all shaped by the past. If we want to fully understand ourselves now, and to understand our possible futures, we have no alternative but to think about history.

History is a discipline as well as a subject matter. Making sense of the past develops qualities of mind that are valuable to anyone who wants to seek the truth and think clearly and intelligently about the most interesting and challenging intellectual problem of all: other people. Learning history is learning a powerful way of knowing.

WHAT IS HISTORY?

History is a way of constructing knowledge about the world through research, interpretation, argument and debate.

Building historical knowledge involves identifying the traces of the past that exist in the present – in people's memories, in old documents, photographs and other remains, and in objects and artefacts ranging from bullets and lipsticks, to field systems and cities. Historians interrogate these traces and *ask questions* that transform traces into *sources of evidence* for knowledge claims about the past.

Historians aim to understand what happened in the past by *explaining why* things happened as they did. Explaining why involves trying to understand past people and their beliefs, intentions and actions. It also involves explaining the causes and evaluating the effects of large-scale changes in the past and exploring relationships between what people aimed to do, the contexts that shaped what was possible and the outcomes and consequences of actions.

Historians also aim to *understand change* in the past. People, states of affairs, ideas, movements and civilisations come into being in time, grow, develop, and ultimately decline and disappear. Historians aim to identify and compare change and continuity in the past, to measure the rate at which things change and to identify the types of change that take place. Change can be slow or sudden. It can also be understood as progressive or regressive – leading to the improvement or worsening of a situation or state of affairs. How things change and whether changes are changes for the better are two key issues that historians frequently debate.

Figure 1 Fragment of a black granite statue possibly portraying the Roman politician Mark Antony.

Debate is the essence of history. Historians write arguments to support their knowledge claims and historians argue with each other to test and evaluate interpretations of the past. Historical knowledge itself changes and develops. On the one hand, new sources of knowledge and new methods of research cause *historical interpretations* to change. On the other hand, the questions that historians ask change with time and new questions produce new answers. Although the past is dead and gone, the interpretation of the past has a past, present and future.

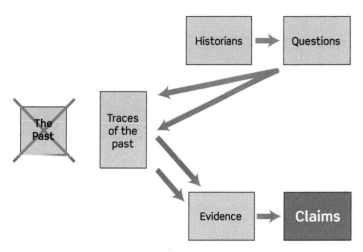

Figure 2 Constructing knowledge about the past.

THE CHALLENGES OF LEARNING HISTORY

Like all other Advanced Level subjects, A Level history is difficult – that is why it is called 'advanced'. Your Advanced Level studies will build on knowledge and understanding of history that you developed at GCSE and at Key Stage 3 – ideas like 'historical sources', 'historical evidence' and 'cause', for example. You will need to do a lot of reading and writing to progress in history. Most importantly, you will need to do a lot of thinking, and thinking about your thinking. This book aims to support you in developing both your knowledge and your understanding.

History is challenging in many ways. On the one hand, it is challenging to build up the range and depth of knowledge that you need to understand the past at an advanced level. Learning about the past involves mastering new and unfamiliar concepts arising from the past itself (such as the Inquisition, Laudianism, *Volksgemeinschaft*) and building up levels of knowledge that are both detailed and well organised. This book covers the key content of the topics that you are studying for your examination and provides a number of features to help you build and organise what you know – for example, diagrams, timelines and definitions of key terms. You will need to help yourself too, of course, adding to your knowledge through further reading, building on the foundations provided by this book.

Another challenge is to develop understandings of the discipline of history. You will have to learn to think historically about evidence, cause, change and interpretations and also to write historically, in a way that develops clear and supported argument.

Historians think with evidence in ways that differ from how we often think in everyday life. In history, as Figure 2 shows, we cannot go and 'see for ourselves' because the past no longer exists. Neither can we normally rely on 'credible witnesses' to tell us 'the truth' about 'what happened'. People in the past did not write down 'the truth' for our benefit. They often had clear agendas when creating the traces that remain and, as often as not, did not themselves know 'the truth' about complex historical events.

A root of the word 'history' is the Latin word *historia*, one of whose meanings is 'enquiry' or 'finding out'. Learning history means learning to ask questions and interrogate traces, and then to reason about what the new knowledge you have gained means. This book draws on historical scholarship for its narrative and contents. It also draws on research on the nature of historical thinking and on the challenges that learning history can present for students. Throughout the book you will find 'Thinking Historically' activities designed to support the development of your thinking.

You will also find – as you would expect given the nature of history – that the book is full of questions. This book aims to help you build your understandings of the content, contexts and concepts that you will need to advance both your historical knowledge and your historical understanding, and to lay strong foundations for the future development of both.

Dr Arthur Chapman
Institute of Education
University College London

Mass media and social change in Britain, 1882–2004

The British public became aware of Mandy Rice-Davies because of her connection with the 1963 Profumo affair, one of the great political scandals of the 20th century. Mandy was best friends with Christine Keeler, a model who had been sleeping not only with the British Secretary of State for War, John Profumo, but also with a Russian spy. Profumo was by no means the first senior politician to have an affair; the real scandal was that he got caught, lied about it in parliament and then had his lies exposed by the British press. The scandal led to a series of court trials that captured public attention. One trial dealt with Mandy's affairs with powerful figures such as Conservative politician Viscount Astor. When he denied the affair in court, she giggled and said, 'Well, he would, wouldn't he?'

SOURCE

1 The front cover of *Private Eye* magazine, published on 26 July 1963. The woman is model Mandy Rice-Davies. She had been the mistress of Peter Rachman, a landlord who became notorious for the exploitation of West Indian immigrants in the Notting Hill area of London.

1899–1902 – Britain fights and wins Boer War in South Africa — 1899–1902

1909 – Old Age Pensions paid to elderly poor for first time. Support for sick and injured workers starts in 1911 — 1909

1918 – Representation of the People Act gives women aged 30 and over right to vote — 1918

1926 – General Strike – 1.7 million workers stop work for nine days in May — 1926

1939–45 – Britain fights and wins Second World War against Germany and allies — 1939–1945

1961 – Contraceptive pill becomes available for first time in Britain — 1961

1973 – Britain joins the European Economic Community, forerunner of today's European Union — 1973

2003–11 – Britain fights alongside USA in Iraq War — 2003–2011

| 1888 | **1888** – Annie Besant organises first women's strike at Bryant and May's match factory |

| 1900 | **1900** – Labour Representation Committee formed. Renamed the Labour Party in 1906 |

| 1914-1918 | **1914-18** – Britain fights and wins the First World War against Germany and her allies |

| 1922 | **1922** – The BBC makes first radio broadcast
Irish Free State gains independence from Britain and is renamed Republic of Ireland in 1937 |

| 1929 | **1929** – BBC makes first television broadcast
Wall Street Crash in America ushers in Great Depression in Britain and world |

| 1948 | **1948** – Launch of NHS and free health care for all |

| 1967 | **1967** – Abortion Act legalises abortion through NHS during first 28 weeks of pregnancy |

| 1982 | **1982** – Launch of Channel 4 and satellite TV in Britain
Britain fights and wins Falklands War against Argentina |

Although such a comment does not seem unreasonable today, such a lack of public respect for the word of a member of the aristocracy shocked and entertained the public in the 1960s. Mandy's front-cover appearance and behaviour in court would have seemed very strange to the British public of 1882.

The 122 years covered in this book arguably saw the greatest change for the greatest number of people in British history.

- Women did not have a separate legal identity from their husbands in 1882, but by 2004 they had achieved full legal equality with men (although not as far as pay or career advancement were concerned). Most married women and mothers had no choice but to be housewives in 1882, but by 2004 they could consider having a career along with their family life.

- Most Britons in 1882 still lived in poverty, in unquestioning Christian faith and in deference to their social superiors. Even holidays and leisure pursuits were highly class specific in 1882, yet they were far more democratic by 2004. Britons also lived in an almost totally Caucasian society; Irish and Jewish communities were the only sizeable immigrant populations. By 2004, Britons were far wealthier, overwhelmingly secular, more liberal in their attitudes to sexuality, and far more likely to challenge authority figures. Eight percent of Britons were non-white; black and Asian communities in many towns and cities played a large part in the rise of a more multicultural Britain. Reasons for these dramatic changes include the impact of government legislation, two world wars and, above all, a large increase in general wealth.

A number of mass media and communications innovations were at the heart of these significant changes in British life.

- The huge expansion in radio ownership in the 1920s and 1930s led Britons to become a nation of listeners as well as readers. BBC radio broadcasts during the Second World War were a significant part of the home-front propaganda campaign.

- The rise of television in the 1950s and 1960s served as a powerful mirror and moulder of British social attitudes. For the first time the average Briton was exposed to satire that greatly undermined automatic deference to authority figures.

- All forms of mass media were opened to greater competition in the latter stages of the 20th century. This was largely the result of Margaret Thatcher's belief in the power of the free market to improve British productivity and creativity.

- The relationship between the government and mass media became increasingly important as political figures took far more interest in manipulating their media profile. Although this process gathered pace in the 1960s, its impact became truly apparent during the build up to, and aftermath of, the 2003 Iraq War.

The *Private Eye* cover not only suggests significant changes in British concepts of gender, sexuality, class and race, but also points towards the role of mass media in moulding and mirroring such ideas and experiences. It is the media's role in radical social change between 1882 and 2004 that is the key focus of this book

9

3.1 Changing patterns of women's lives within the family and in the world of work

KEY QUESTIONS

- How significant were the changes to women's personal lives in the years 1882–2004?
- To what extent, and why, did women's working lives change in the years 1882–2004?

KEY TERMS

Marriage bar
This was a rule, not always formalised, that existed from the 1870s to the1960s. It forced women to quit their jobs and become dutiful housewives as soon as they got married. It became almost universal in the last quarter of the 19th century and gradually faded out between 1945 and the mid-1960s. It was never applied in certain working-class jobs such as cotton weaving and lacemaking, where wives were accustomed to continuing to work until the birth of their first child.

Gendering
Unlike the male and female sex, which are biologically determined (excepting those who have undergone surgical sex realignment), gender is a social construct. 'Masculinity' and 'femininity' are not fixed in the same way as sex, and notions of what is considered 'normal' gender-specific behaviour have changed considerably throughout history. Gendering is the process of ascribing certain 'normal' behaviours to a particular sex. This can be a conscious process or subconscious one.

INTRODUCTION

If it were possible, an average British woman from 1882 would have a fascinating conversation with her great-great-granddaughter who reached adulthood at the start of the 21st century. They would both consider the same issues as important in their lives: family, friends, home life, health, work and income, but they would be amazed at the differences in how they each lived and thought about being a woman. Both women would agree that better housing from the 1930s onwards, and medical advances after the launch of the National Health Service in 1948, had greatly improved the quality of life for many women. They would also agree that long-term economic change and the impact of two world wars had increased the variety of female employment, particularly for married women following the gradual demise of the '**marriage bar**' after 1945. The great-great-grandmother would be impressed that women's wages as a percentage of men's had doubled from 40 to 80 percent. She would have been in one of the first cohorts of girls to receive state-provided elementary education, but she would have been amazed at the number of women studying at university (four women became the first to take their degrees in 1880 whereas 45 percent of all students were female in 2004). The two women might also reflect on the impact of government legislation on women's lives, with a range of laws passed to improve their domestic and working life. They would have an interesting debate about work, childcare, sex and marriage, and would probably not see eye to eye with many of each other's values. Life was materially harder for almost all women in the 1880s, but far more became expected of women in the second half of the 20th century. An increase in paid work was very rarely offset by a decline in their unpaid work as homemakers and mothers.

Mass media reflected the reality of women's lives but also played a large part in helping to construct dominant narratives of the way women ought to think and behave. Newspapers, cinema, radio and television all contributed to defining social norms and **gendering** a range of aspects of society, from emotions to employment. These powerful messages undoubtedly played a part in shaping the aims, expectations and self-perception of British women throughout the 20th century. In general, mass media began to depict a greater range of actions and attitudes as 'normal' for females, although older stereotypes continued to persist into the 21st century.

1882 – Married Women's Property Act enabled women to own and control property in their own right

1888 – Annie Besant organises first women's strike at Bryant and May's match factory

1894 – Local Government Act: married women have the right to vote in local elections and stand for election as municipal councillors

1918 – Representation of the People Act gives women aged 30 and over right to vote. Constance Markiewicz is first woman elected to parliament

1921 – First Marie Stopes' family-planning clinics

1882	1886	1888	1892	1894	1918	1920	1922	1928

1885 – Age of consent raised from 13 to 16 years

1893 – Women allowed to become factory inspectors

1919 – Nancy Astor becomes first woman to take her seat in parliament. Sex Disqualification (Removal) Act gives women the right to become jurors, magistrates, barristers and high-ranking civil servants

1928 – Universal suffrage for men and women aged 21 and over on equal terms

HOW SIGNIFICANT WERE THE CHANGES TO WOMEN'S PERSONAL LIVES IN THE YEARS 1882–2004?

Women, like men, cannot be seen as a single, homogenous group throughout this period. Women have lived dramatically different lives depending upon their family background, income, education and, increasingly after the Second World War, ethnicity. There is not space in this chapter to explore the varied impacts of key developments on a range of British women, we can only consider their most common, shared experiences, as wives, mothers and homemakers. While this focus could be seen as a gendered reading of history, it can be defended in that the vast majority of British women were brought up to define themselves according to these domestic roles. It was only with the rise of **second-wave feminism** in the 1970s that women began to challenge these powerfully reinforced social norms. Until then, the Victorian ideal of women as the 'Angel in the House' (see Source 1) remained a resilient cultural force that shaped women's lives. This was the ideal that the wife should remain in the private, domestic sphere to create the perfect refuge from the public sphere in which her breadwinning husband must toil.

KEY TERM

Second-wave feminism
This emerged in the 1960s and sought to overcome cultural and political inequalities. Second-wave feminists argued that the personal was the political (i.e. women should make unfair treatment in their personal lives a matter for political activism). They challenged structures and ideas that either deliberately or inadvertently reinforced the status of women as inferior to men.

SOURCE

1 From Coventry Patmore's narrative poem *The Angel in the House*, first published in 1854 and expanded until 1862. It became highly popular in the last quarter of the 19th century and its influence on views of the ideal woman lasted well into the 20th century. Patmore wrote the poem in honour of his wife, Emily.

Man must be pleased; but him to please
  Is woman's pleasure; down the gulf
Of his condoled necessities
  She casts her best, she flings herself.
How often flings for nought, and yokes
  Her heart to an icicle or whim,
Whose each impatient word provokes
  Another, not from her, but him;
While she, too gentle even to force
  His penitence by kind replies,
Waits by, expecting his remorse,
  With pardon in her pitying eyes;

And if he once, by shame oppress'd,
  A comfortable word confers,
She leans and weeps against his breast,
  And seems to think the sin was hers;
And whilst his love has any life,
  Or any eye to see her charms,
At any time, she's still his wife,
  Dearly devoted to his arms;
She loves with love that cannot tire;
  And when, ah woe, she loves alone,
Through passionate duty love springs higher,
  As grass grows taller round a stone.

1961 – Contraceptive pill becomes available

1969 – Divorce Act allows divorce to be granted after two years of separation if both parties want it, and after five years if one party wants it

1975 – Sex Discrimination Act establishes the Equal Opportunities Commission to enforce Equal Pay Act

1979 – Margaret Thatcher becomes first woman prime minister

| 1962 | 1966 | 1968 | 1970 | 1976 | 1978 | 2004 |

1967 – Abortion Act legalises abortion through NHS during first 28 weeks of pregnancy. Family Planning Act allows local health authorities to provide birth-control devices

1970 – Equal Pay Act prohibits different pay or working conditions according to gender. It comes into force in 1975

Matrimonial Property Act takes into account women's domestic work to ensure they get fair division of wealth in divorce

2004 – Civil Partnership Act allows homosexual couples to form civil partnerships and enjoy all legal benefits of being married

EXTEND YOUR KNOWLEDGE

Feminism

Feminists support women having the same rights and opportunities as men. There have been three main waves of feminism in Britain.

- First-wave feminism campaigned for property rights and a separate legal identity for married women as well as the right to vote in general elections. Key first-wave feminists included Emmeline Pankhurst and her daughters Sylvia and Christabel. Most women aged 30 or over gained the right to vote in 1918, and women could vote on an equal basis with men after 1928.

- Second-wave feminism was inspired by a series of books by female authors, such as Simone de Beauvoir's *The Second Sex* (1949), Betty Friedan's *The Feminine Mystique* (1963) and Germaine Greer's *The Female Eunuch* (1970).

- Third-wave feminism emerged in the 1990s and built on the foundations of the second wave. It continued to challenge cultural and political inequality but also sought to recognise the broader experiences of different types of women according to their class, ethnicity and sexuality.

Feminists today are divided over whether women should:

- continue to seek equality with men on a range of criteria largely created by a male-dominated world, or

- embrace essential differences between men and women and promote feminine-inspired virtues rather than seek an artificial and unhealthy equality.

The Married Women's Property Act 1882 and the end of couverture

Women in 1882 were almost entirely reliant on men in legal and financial matters. Girls from a young age were brought up with the aim of finding a good husband and being a dutiful wife and mother. The overwhelming majority of women got married before the age of 40, and spinsters were seen as an odd, pitiful minority. There were some powerful incentives to get married. The range of employment open to women was almost entirely limited to low-paid, often menial labour such as domestic service or unskilled factory work. Women had little representation in trade unions and were usually the first to be made redundant during a recession. There were no state pensions or unemployment benefits until they were introduced by a Liberal government between 1909 and 1911, so a single woman who lacked the means to support herself had two unenviable options:

- to go through the socially demeaning process of being judged worthy of 'outdoor relief' (the provision of food, clothing and sometimes money or housing paid for by local rates) by a panel of middle-class Poor Law Guardians

- to enter a workhouse in order to get shelter and food. The workhouses were designed to be worse than the housing that even the very lowest paid in society could afford.

However, until the 1870 and 1882 Married Women's Property Acts, marriage also meant that women lost their separate legal identity. To all intents and purposes, a husband could treat his wife as he might his children or any other of his possessions.

EXTEND YOUR KNOWLEDGE

The *Jackson* case (1891)

Perhaps the most dramatic case concerning the extent of a husband's legal control over his wife was *Regina v Jackson* (1891), better known as the *Clitheroe* case or the *Jackson* case. Mr Edmund Jackson brought the case against his wife Emily. Theirs was certainly an odd marriage. Emily had been living with her sister in Clitheroe, Lancashire, for nine years when, aged 42, she married Edmund without telling anyone in her family. Edmund brought Emily back to her sister's house on the evening of the wedding and then immediately departed for New Zealand (with the plan that Emily would follow shortly after). He spent the next eight months there.

Upon his arrival back in England, he hoped that they would set up home as husband and wife. However, Emily refused. Their correspondence had been full of terrible rows and now she wanted nothing to do with him.

Edmund hoped that the divorce court would restore his 'conjugal rights' over his wife. The term was not well defined in law but, as a minimum, it meant that the absentee partner would be compelled to live under the same roof as their husband or wife unless there was an acceptable cause for their absence. Until the Matrimonial Causes Act 1884, the absentee spouse could be imprisoned until they agreed to the court ruling. The 1884 Act meant that the partner who had been abandoned could demand an immediate divorce rather than waiting for two years as the divorce law stipulated.

The court did not have the authority to compel Emily to have sex with Edmund. But because a husband could not be charged with the rape of his wife, his success in the cohabitation case would, in practice, almost certainly result in Emily being raped. However, rather than let the legal process take its course, Edmund abducted Emily from outside church one Sunday and locked her up in his house.

Her family's attempt to use the law to have her released failed because the Court of Queen's Bench decided that a husband's right over his wife took precedence over habeas corpus (a writ requiring a person under arrest to be brought before a judge or into court). Emily's family immediately launched an appeal against this ruling and the case became national news. The Court of Appeal finally decided that the rule of personal freedom should take precedence over the common law right of a husband to command his wife: Edmund had no right to imprison Emily and she was released. The decision clearly defended the legal right of a wife to her personal freedom.

The 1870 and 1882 Married Women's Property Acts were important landmarks in overcoming domestic discrimination against wives. Before the Acts, wives were deemed to be 'feme covert' (literally hidden women) with no legal identity separate from that of their husband. This system, known as couverture, meant wives had no legal authority to own property or make a contract of any kind. The Acts undermined couverture: the 1870 Act because it allowed women to keep their own earnings from employment after marriage, and the 1882 Act because it allowed them to keep any property that they owned before marriage and to use it for their own commercial purposes if they wanted to. The Act was almost certainly more important in a legal than a social sense. Male members of the family supported the middle-class widows who had enough money or property to be affected by its provisions. The Act meant little to the mass of poor women who had to work, single or not, in order to avoid dependence on the Poor Law or workhouse.

Changes to women's personal lives as wives

Divorce and domestic abuse reform

Husbands at the start of 1882 were legally entitled to treat their wives in a way that would be considered appalling by their descendants in 2004. A wife might consider herself fortunate if her husband did not hit her too hard or too often. An 1895 City of London by-law made the beating of wives illegal between 10 p.m. and 7 a.m. because the noise kept people awake.

Between 1884 and 2004, divorce became easier to obtain and divorcee status became less of a stigma to affected women.

- Until 1857, a separate Act of parliament was required to obtain a divorce. The cost of this was beyond the means of all but the very wealthy. In 1882, there were just 289 divorces.

- The Matrimonial Causes Act 1923 ended the unequal terms on which a divorce could be requested. Between 1857 and 1923, husbands (unlike wives) could file for divorce on grounds of adultery alone. Wives had to prove extra faults, such as incest, abandonment or cruelty, in addition to adultery in order to gain a divorce. Other faults, such as insanity, desertion and drunkenness, were inadmissible grounds for divorce before a further Matrimonial Causes Act in 1937.

- It was not until the Divorce Reform Act 1969 that a couple could divorce without proof of any fault, and merely due to a breakdown in the relationship. This could be gained after a two-year separation if the decision was mutual, or five years if only one party wanted the divorce.

- The Matrimonial Proceedings and Property Act 1970 awarded a far higher share of the couple's wealth to the woman in the divorce settlement.

The 1969 and 1970 Acts resulted in a large increase in rates of divorce, from fewer than three in 1,000 marriages in 1965 to almost ten in 1,000 by 1976. It was not until the 2000 *White v White* judgement that the unpaid work of wives as homemakers was factored into the financial settlement of a divorce. Before then, the share of joint assets awarded to the less-wealthy spouse (overwhelmingly wives) was based on self-support needs rather than fair shares.

Divorce reform was an important part of increased female freedom between 1882 and 2004. The fact that the number of divorces rose after every Act suggests that many women were trapped in loveless or even abusive marriages before legislation gave them the realistic choice of separation. In 2004, there were 152,923 divorces, of which two-thirds were instigated by wives (105,177).

Various laws were also passed between 1882 and 2004 to prevent domestic abuse.

- The Domestic Violence and Matrimonial Proceedings Act 1976 offered victims a civil protection order (or injunction) against their abuser.

- The Housing (Homeless Persons) Act 1977 recognised that women and children in abusive homes often had nowhere else to go, and it gave them the right to state-funded temporary accommodation.

- It was not until 1991 that marital rape was criminalised. Before this, marriage implied consent and husbands could not be prosecuted for non-consensual sex with their wives.

- The Domestic Violence, Crime and Victims Act 2004 meant that police could arrest anyone suspected of threatening or carrying out domestic abuse. They did not need to leave a potential victim while they went to get an arrest warrant.

Domestic abuse remained largely inflicted by men on women at the start of the 21st century. However, there is strong evidence that few men are prepared to report female abuse to the police.

SOURCE The number of divorces in the UK from 1882 to 2002, and which party requested the divorce. Figures from the Office for National Statistics.

Year	Total number of divorces	Divorce granted on petition of husband	Divorce granted on petition of wife	Divorce granted on petition of both
1882	289	Not recorded	Not recorded	n/a
1902	601	361	240	n/a
1922	2,588	1,591	997	n/a
1942	7,618	4,000	3,618	n/a
1952	33,922	14,639	19,283	n/a
1962	28,935	12,769	16,059	107
1972	119,025	45,385	73,220	420
1982	146,698	41,761	104,349	588
1992	160,385	44,378	115,628	379
2002	147,735	44,771	102,796	168

The rise of the companionate marriage

As Coventry Patmore's 1854 poem *The Angel in the House* made clear (see Source 1), the ideal woman of 1882 was expected to be entirely subordinate to her husband. Although romantic notions of marriage existed, in reality most women had a few limited hopes for married life. The demarcation of men's public lives (work, pub or club) and women's domestic lives contributed to a clear double standard of acceptable behaviour for husbands and wives. J. Purvis (2000) describes how a working-class wife counted herself as fortunate if her husband did not keep back too much of his pay packet for 'spends' at the pub, did not 'bother' her too much for sex or was not a persistent womaniser behind her back.

A number of trends slowly began to change the idealised view of marriage. Increased knowledge of sex and contraception due to the work of post-First World War pioneers such as Mary Stopes (see page 15) led to a growth in the expectation of mutually fulfilling sex lives. Although the trend was far from universal, marriages increasingly became seen as a union of two individuals bonded by sexual love, rather than a traditional institution necessary for rearing children. Improvements in housing and the greater affordability of domestic leisure items increased the amount of time husbands spent at home with their wives and children. This helped to break down the male public sphere/ female private sphere divide, which had been a key assumption of the Victorian ideal. After both world wars there was an increase in media attention in relation to the maternal ideal of women. It was driven by official concern about population loss, and it helped to tone down, or displace, older, more rigidly patriarchal views of the ideal marriage.

Such developments did little to alter the share of household labour or other typical roles for husbands and wives. As men earned higher rates of pay, it made economic sense for many wives to ensure that their husbands remained fit and healthy for work. In practice, this sometimes meant that husbands had by far the best diet in the household well into the interwar period. In 1988, historian Professor Carl Chinn published a book called *They Worked All Their Lives*. It was a study of poor, urban women between 1880 and 1939, and it noted that in many urban households the men often ate alone after coming home from work. They expected their 'relishes' – extra items such as a kipper, chop or an egg – while poor women and their children survived on lots of bread, margarine and tea. He notes that this was a reflection of how tough mothers had to be to make ends meet in poor households. Changes in women's working lives, especially since the Second World War, have had some impact on the nature of marriage. The fact that more women work outside the home has led to an increase in the share of domestic work between husbands and wives (or cohabiting couples). A study of 1,000 adults in 2000 revealed that the average amount of housework done per week by men had increased from 10 minutes in 1960 to 50 minutes in 2000 (the same figures for women reduced from 110 minutes to 90 minutes in the same period). In 2004, it was far more likely to see men shopping, pushing a pram, cleaning or washing up than it was in the 1960s or 1970s. However, the vast majority of such duties continue to be performed by women, who are also in paid employment. Full-time house husbands remained a rare phenomenon at the start of the 21st century.

Taxation and the end of the composite tax system

In one narrow sense, couverture remained enshrined in British law until 1991. According to the composite (joint) tax system, a wife's income from savings was considered as part of her husband's income; joint interest earnings were processed as one 'composite' income. A single woman who earned less than the tax-paying income threshold would not be taxed on interest earned from her savings. However, the day after she married, a woman's income from all sources was added to that of her husband and their combined incomes were taxed as one income. As married women generally earned less than their husbands, women would, if taxed separately, pay less tax or even none at all. The system was clearly a triumph of administrative convenience over fairness to married women. The April 1991 Budget introduced the separate taxation of husbands and wives. It meant that married women would not pay tax on interest if they earned less than the tax-paying income threshold. Chancellor of the Exchequer John Major set out the benefits of the end of the composite tax system in his 1990 Budget Statement.

SOURCE

3 ▶ From Chancellor of the Exchequer John Major's Budget Statement, made in the House of Commons on 20 March 1990.

I wish to discuss a reform which was announced in the 1988 Budget and which comes into effect next month – independent taxation for women. There is too little understanding yet of what this change will mean, but it will fundamentally change the financial affairs of women. At present, the taxation of married women's income is wholly inconsistent with their role in society. In tax law, their income is still considered to belong to their husbands... Once independent taxation is implemented, there will be 14 million people, nearly one quarter of the population, who have savings income that does not merit taxation, but which will be taxed under present legislation. They include some 5 million married women with little or no other income of their own, 4 million pensioners, 2.5 million other adults, and 2.5 million children with small savings accounts, often funded with small gifts of money from grandparents, or savings from pocket money. There is no way out of this problem other than to abolish composite rate tax entirely. This I propose to do with effect from 6 April 1991, the earliest practicable date. From then on, tax will fall on those who should pay it, and will not fall on those who should not pay it... This change will significantly reduce the amount of tax paid by millions of married women, pensioners, children and others with small savings, and by removing the penalty of composite rate tax, it will play an important part in encouraging the savings habit.

The repeal of the composite tax system can be seen as a final chapter in a long struggle for women to gain fair treatment from the government in terms of taxes and benefits. Until 1978, the value of housewives' unpaid domestic work was not recognised by the state.

- The Unemployment Insurance Act 1920 stated that married women had to prove they were actively seeking work to claim unemployment benefits as set out in the National Insurance Act 1911 (Part II).

- The Anomalies Regulation 1931 added the further restriction that women had to prove they were able to do insurable work (only certain industries were covered by the scheme).

- The National Insurance Act 1946 classed non-working wives as dependents (like children) who could not claim unemployment benefits, even if they had worked before marriage.

This situation changed in 1978, when married women began to pay full National Insurance contributions while working and could claim full benefits when unemployed.

ACTIVITY
KNOWLEDGE CHECK

The Married Women's Property Act, the end of the composite tax system and other government legislation that affected women as wives

1 Explain why the Married Women's Property Act 1882 was an important turning point in the status of married women in Britain.

2 Produce a timeline of important government legislation that affected women as wives between 1882 and 2004.

3 How useful is Source 3 in understanding the significance of the end of the composite tax system in 1991?

Marie Stopes' family-planning clinics from 1921

Almost constant pregnancy continued to be a debilitating feature of many women's lives in the last 20 years of the 19th century. The Victorian working classes had large families, each with an average of more than six children in the 1860s gradually falling to nearer three children in the 1910s. A large family was in part insurance against high child mortality rates, partly to ensure means of support in old age (there were no state pensions before 1909), but largely because women did not have access to effective sex education or birth control. Organisations such as the **Fabian Women's Group** and the **Co-operative Women's Guild** began raising working-class female concerns about uncontrolled fertility some 20 years before the first family-planning clinic opened, but advances in birth control were hard fought and slow in coming.

Although male and female contraceptive devices were advertised at the start of the 20th century, information on how to use them was banned under the obscenity laws. These laws were introduced in 1857 to censor material that might corrupt the public, and they were greatly relaxed in 1959. The state was initially keen to limit access to such information. It wanted the birth rate to increase to ensure the strength of the empire and secure Britain's ability to wage future wars. The publisher of a 1923 family-planning leaflet with a medical diagram that demonstrated how to insert a cervical cap was successfully prosecuted under the obscenity laws because it was apparently unclear whether the finger inserting the cap belonged to the woman herself. Condoms were available but were relatively expensive, and men were reluctant to use any sort of birth control. Prevailing social attitudes meant that contraceptives were associated with sexual disease and prostitution, and men felt that a large family was proof of his virility. As a result, most women were forced to rely on the ineffective withdrawal method or, when this failed, an abortion, which remained illegal until 1967.

Marie Stopes was an important pioneer of birth control for British women. Her chief concern was not the empowerment of women as individuals but rather to ensure the birth of a 'better sort' of children for the good of the nation and empire. Stopes was a botanist by training and, inspired by Herbert Spencer's **Social Darwinism**, she became a **eugenicist**. She felt that the failure to raise 'the fittest' children in the next generation would lead to racial and political decline for Britain. Due to her own failure to conceive after three years of marriage, she was motivated to research all available literature on female sexuality. The lack of women's knowledge about their own bodies at the start of the 20th century would astound 21st-century women. As sex was not discussed, girls did not have the vocabulary to understand it themselves. One nurse recalled attending her first birth in the 1910s expecting the baby to come out of the navel. Stopes set out to dispel this ignorance through her 1918

KEY TERMS

Fabian Women's Group
The Fabian Society was established in 1883 as a socialist debating society. A key founder member was Edith Nesbit, who wanted to spread ideas about how to improve the social system. The Women's Group was set up in 1908 to lobby Labour MPs to support female suffrage.

Co-operative Women's Guild
Lady Alice Acland established the Co-operative Women's Guild (under a slightly different name) in 1883. Acland saw the potential for the co-operative movement to provide commercial opportunities for working class women. The Guild also aimed to provide education and constructive recreation for mothers and girls. It soon became politically active and lobbied MPs for reforms, including minimum pay for women and maternity benefits.

Social Darwinism
Charles Darwin set out his theory of biological evolution by natural selection in his 1859 book *On the Origin of Species*. From the 1870s, some thinkers sought to apply Darwin's theories to human social and economic problems. They argued that government policy ought to promote 'the strongest' (usually the wealthy) at the expense of 'the weakest' (usually the unrespectable working classes) for the good of the nation.

Eugenicist
Eugenics, from the Greek word for 'well-born', aims to promote the physical and intellectual quality of humankind through the control or manipulation of reproduction. 'Better' humans are encouraged to have more children and 'inferior' humans fewer. A eugenicist supports these aims and policies.

book *Married Love: A New Contribution to the Solution of the Sex Difficulties*. This became a bestseller and challenged the general reluctance to discuss sex in public. Stopes argued that women, as well as men, should enjoy sex within marriage.

EXTEND YOUR KNOWLEDGE

Marie Stopes (1880–1958)

Marie Stopes was born to parents who had met as a result of their love of science. This love was passed on to Marie, who went on to become the youngest person to gain a Doctor of Science degree, and the first female lecturer at Manchester University. She published a wide range of scholarly articles on pre-historic plants, and these articles are still studied by specialists today.

Stopes had two marriages. The first was annulled after three years in 1914 on grounds of non-consummation (she had not had sex with her husband). It was the failure of her first marriage that inspired her to write *Married Love*, a study of sex within marriage. Stopes argued that marriage should be an equal relationship between partners, and that women had sexual desires as well as men (women's desires being at their height during ovulation). The book was completed in 1913, but Stopes was unable to find anyone willing to publish it.

Stopes' second husband was a wealthy philanthropist who had already tried to open a birth-control clinic in Manchester. He paid a publishing company to print her book in March 1918. It was so successful that there were five editions in 1918 alone, and hundreds of thousands of copies were sold before the Second World War.

Stopes became a national figure and she sought to capitalise on this with further books and lectures on birth control. In 1919, she published *A Letter to Working Mothers on how to have healthy children and avoid weakening pregnancies*. This was a 16-page pamphlet that was distributed free of charge to women in poor areas of London. She also attempted to spread her views on marriage through the Church. However, her 1922 book *A New Gospel to All Peoples* was rejected by the Catholic Church, although the Church of England did approve the use of contraception by married couples in 1930.

Stopes attended the first ever meeting of the Eugenics Society in 1912 and became a fellow of the organisation in 1921. That year, due to the Eugenics Society's lack of emphasis on birth control, she also founded the Society for Constructive Birth Control and Racial Progress. She argued for the 'sterilisation of those totally unfit for parenthood' in order to perfect society through racial purification. In 1956, she even stated that one-third of British men should be sterilised, starting with the ugly and unfit. She had one son whose marriage she tried to prevent because she feared his fiancée would pass on her short-sightedness to her children.

SOURCE

4   From Marie Stopes' *Married Love: A New Contribution to the Solution of the Sex Difficulties*, published in 1918.

More than ever today are happy homes needed. It is my hope that this book may serve the State by adding to their numbers. Its object is to increase the joys of marriage, and to show how much sorrow may be avoided. The only secure basis for a present-day State is the welding of its units in marriage; but there is rottenness and danger at the foundations of the State if many of the marriages are unhappy. Today, particularly in the middle classes in this country, marriage is far less really happy than its surface appears. Too many who marry expecting joy are bitterly disappointed; and the demand for 'freedom' grows; while those who cry aloud are generally unaware that it is more likely to have been their own ignorance than the marriage-bond which was the origin of their unhappiness.

It is never easy to make marriage a lovely thing; and it is an achievement beyond the powers of the selfish, or the mentally cowardly. Knowledge is needed and, as things are at present, knowledge is almost unobtainable by those who are most in want of it. The problems of the sex-life are infinitely complex, and for their solution urgently demand both sympathy and scientific research. I have some things to say about sex, which, so far as I am aware, have not yet been said, things which seem to be of profound importance to men and women who hope to make their marriages beautiful...

In this country, in modern times, the old traditions, the profound primitive knowledge of the needs of both sexes have been lost, and nothing but a muffled confusion of individual gossip disturbs a silence, shamefaced or foul... In my own marriage I paid such a terrible price for sex – ignorance that I feel that knowledge gained at such a cost should be placed at the service of humanity. In this little book average, healthy, mating creatures will find the key to the happiness which should be the portion of each.

The success of *Married Love* made Stopes a national figure and gave her a platform on which to press forward with her campaign for birth control. She gradually helped to popularise birth control among the political establishment by freeing it from its association with fear of overpopulation and linking it instead to racial health. Birth control also became more popular with women due to its association with personal happiness, even where this was not in the interests of racial health. Stopes advocated four children as the ideal, but at lectures she drew attention to women who wanted contraception with fewer children because of difficult family lives or traumatic births.

On 17 March 1921, Stopes opened the Mothers' Clinic in Holloway, a working-class district in north London. It was the first to open in Britain and one of only a handful worldwide at that time. The clinic offered free birth-control devices, advice and education to married women supported by midwives. Stopes insisted that the midwives be kind, sympathetic and persistent in order to win the women's trust. Many women were reluctant to visit due to a stubborn association of birth control with sexual disease and prostitution, and even due to rumours of forced sterilisation at the clinics. Stopes was firmly against abortion and advice on how to induce miscarriages was not provided. She gradually opened a chain of such clinics across Britain. Branches opened in Leeds and Aberdeen in 1934, Belfast in 1936, Cardiff in 1937 and Swansea in 1943. The clinics were controversial and attracted public criticism from those who opposed birth control. Stopes even took prominent doctor and author Halliday Sutherland to court for libel in 1923. He branded her work as Germanic experimentation on the poor (she had studied in Munich for a while) in a post-war climate that was anti-German.

The use of birth-control clinics differed according to social class: middle-class women were far more likely to visit than working-class women. The latter would generally visit later in marriage after more pregnancies. By 1929, more than 10,000 patients had received advice, a figure that rose to 43,000 by 1945. Although this was an important step in the spread of birth control, a 1945 Mass Observation report found that the vast majority of women remained totally ignorant of measures they could take to prevent pregnancy. Although Stopes claimed in her first report on the Mothers' Clinics that there had been only 31 pregnancies from the first 5,000 women to seek advice, other birth-control groups challenged her statistics. The Cambridge Birth-Control Clinic found that around half of its patients had not actually used the methods taught at the clinic. In many cases this was because women did not have sufficient privacy at home or remained unsure of how to fit and remove the cervical cap (recommended to 80 percent of visitors).

The Marie Stopes Foundation went bankrupt in 1975 but was refounded a year later as Marie Stopes International by doctor and family-planning crusader Tim Black. By the 21st century, it provided access to advice, contraception, vasectomies and abortions in 38 countries around the world. Marie Stopes inspired a range of other birth-control organisations.

- In 1924, socialist-feminists Dora Russell and Stella Browne founded the Workers' Birth-Group.

- Five separate societies merged to form the National Birth-Control Council in 1930. Renamed the Family Planning Association (FPA) in 1939, its stated aim was that 'married people may space or limit their families and thus mitigate the evils of ill health and poverty'. It was not until the 1950s that the FPA began to offer family-planning advice to unmarried women. Even then, some clinics would not offer contraceptives to single women without a supporting letter from the family doctor or parish vicar. The FPA offered the contraceptive pill (see page 20) from 1961, and in 1974 it handed over the running of its 1,000-plus clinics to the National Health Service (NHS).

- From 1974, the NHS offered free contraception to all without any need for supporting letters or parental permission.

SOURCE 5 A poster produced by the Family Planning Association in the early 1970s.

Would you be more careful if it was you that got pregnant?

Contraception is one of the facts of life.
Anyone, married or single, can get free advice on contraception from their doctor or family planning clinic.
You can find your local clinic under Family Planning in the telephone directory or Yellow Pages.

The Health Education Council
78 New Oxford Street, London WC1A 1AH.

The impact of the NHS on women's lives from 1948

Until 1911, it was up to individuals to organise their own private insurance if they were to afford any health care. 'Friendly societies' were set up to help the poor afford basic medical care, but they were often so small that they could not afford to pay for members' hospital treatment. Some went bankrupt and left their members with no insurance at all. Membership of such societies involved paying a weekly subscription, something that was beyond the means of the poorest families. While Part I of the National Insurance Act 1911 provided state insurance to around 18 million workers by 1937, the wives, widows and children of poor workers were not covered by the Act and thus remained without a safety net. They were forced to rely on family, the local community or the rare sympathetic General Practitioner (GP) for treatment without charge. The vast majority of women chose to put up with chronic, and in many cases serious, medical conditions, many of which resulted from pregnancy and labour.

Doctors were shocked at the number of previously untreated medical issues that women came forward with once doctor's appointments were made free under the NHS in 1948. Varicose veins, infected piles and prolapsed uteruses were all painful conditions that were treated far more commonly after 1948. NHS managers might have been less shocked had they read the 1939 report *Working-Class Wives* by the Women's Health Enquiry. Based on the testimony of 1,250 married, working-class women, fewer than one-third were in good health while a similar number had severe, chronic conditions.

SOURCE

From Margery Spring Rice's *Working-Class Wives: Their health and conditions* published in 1939. Rice called for greater birth control and helped to set up the third family-planning clinic in Britain. She was a founder member of the Women's Health Enquiry and spent six years conducting research for the book.

If the mother has been 'really ill' she may be sent away by the hospital or under some insurance scheme... away from her home, away from the smell of inferior and inadequately prepared food, away from the noise and worry of her family, away to the sea... But if illness has been so severe as to merit this magnificent atonement, it has meant months probably of crippling indisposition which has added enormously to the burden of work, and robbed it of all that potential satisfaction that can be found in the fulfilment of her task. She has to let things slide, and she has slipped back so far that it will take months and months to catch up again even to her old standard of order and efficiency. This, in her own eyes, is probably the worst disaster that can happen – her own illness. Other disasters are bound to come in the ordinary course of family life; the sickness of a child – the unemployment of her husband... But if she can keep fit, she will meet the extra burden... she will augment the family income by going out to work herself, somehow or other squeezing her own house-work into shorter hours. It may be a little less efficient, but the compensation is that she will have a little more money for food, and can get better cooking utensils.

It may be said that, even granting that there is no exaggeration in the above account of the working-class mother's life, there is no ground for giving special consideration to her case as apart from that of the father and the children. That this in many respects is so, but it is abundantly clear from the accounts given by the women themselves in this investigation that they are subject to many hardships from which circumstance or they themselves protect their families. To begin with, the working mother is almost entirely cut off from contact with the world outside her house. She eats, sleeps, 'rests', on the scene of her labour, and her labour is entirely solitary... It is undoubtedly true that the mother will be the first to go without food. Husband and children must be clothed. She need not be; she need not go out, so it is not absolutely necessary for her to have an outdoor coat.

The NHS allowed many Britons to take advantage of scientific advances in combating disease. In the first 10 years of the NHS, the prescription of new antibiotics caused the almost total eradication of **puerperal fever** and saw the number of deaths from tuberculosis fall from 25,000 to 5,000 people per year. Increased funding for health care also helped. Over 300 inadequate cottage hospitals were closed in the 1960s. New centres of excellence with close ties with universities, such as Papworth Hospital's specialism in heart surgery near Cambridge, were founded. Childbirth had been a significant cause of death for young women well into the interwar period. In 1901, 4,400 women died due to childbirth complications or puerperal fever, a figure that had only fallen to 3,000 by 1924. In an article written for the medical journal *The Lancet* in May 1931, gynaecologist Blair Bell estimated that ten percent of women had been permanently disabled by childbirth. Better training for midwives and doctors, together with improved understanding of hygiene at home and in hospitals, had begun to reduce childbirth mortality before 1948, but the NHS accelerated this process. Mothers were entitled to free antenatal and post-natal care, and maternal death in childbirth fell from one per 1,000 births in 1949 to 0.18 in 1970.

Despite the positive impact of the NHS on women's lives, it is also important to note the limitations to this improvement. In her 1988 book *Out of the Doll's House*, journalist and historian Angela Holdsworth noted that the rise of the NHS led to the decline of informal, local support provided within a community of women. She noted the effort of women in the later 1980s to reverse this trend with the launch of **Well Woman Clinics**, self-help groups, and even health buses. She also notes how increased life expectancy has ironically increased the impact of chronic mental and physical health problems in the final years of many women's lives. Lastly, increased expectations of general health, together with free consultations, have led many women to visit doctors in the hope of medical solutions to non-medical problems. Holdsworth (1988) notes how marital or domestic problems and issues that stem from poverty or stress lead many women to never really feel well.

KEY TERM

Puerperal fever
Bacterial infection of the uterus following the birth of a child.

KEY TERM

Well Woman Clinics
GPs' surgeries, local hospitals and some private health organisations offer extensive health checks for women at these clinics, which are run by female doctors or nurses. They typically provide advice on contraception, gynaecological problems, breast disease, cervical smears and the menopause.

The NHS clearly contributed to a huge improvement in female health and an increased life expectancy for women, from 71 to 75 years, between 1950 and 1970 (for men, life expectancy rose from 66 to 70 years in the same period). However, it is important to note that improvements in diet and housing, as well as the decline in family size, also had a positive impact on female health. Between 1919 and 1940, four million homes were built to replace slum housing that was pulled down. By 1940, one-third of all houses had been built since 1918. The quality and sanitation of housing was much improved, with central heating, hot running water and indoor flushing toilets.

The impact of the contraceptive pill from 1961

In her 2015 television series *The Ascent of Women*, Dr Amanda Foreman argued that 9 May 1960 was the day when women's lives changed forever. This was the day when the US government approved the distribution and sale of the combined oral contraceptive pill. 'The Pill', as it became known in the English-speaking world, had been developed in the USA in the 1950s thanks to two women: Margaret Sanger and Katharine McCormick. Sanger was an American equivalent of Marie Stopes, and she persuaded wealthy philanthropist Katharine McCormick to provide $1 million funding for the necessary research and development costs.

A more relevant date for British women would be 4 December 1961, when Health Minister Enoch Powell announced that the Pill could be prescribed through the NHS at a subsidised price of two shillings a month. The number of women using the Pill increased from 50,000 in 1961 to 500,000 by 1964. The vast majority of these women were married. GPs generally only prescribed the Pill to older, married women until 1967.

From 1958, Lady Helen Brook ran a birth-control clinic that assisted unmarried women. In 1964, she set up her own Brook Advisory Centres to extend this service to single women between the ages of 16 and 25. The Family Planning Association enabled its branches to provide a similar service after the passage of the National Health Service (Family Planning) Act 1967. The FPA National Council made such a service compulsory for those branches that resisted the change in 1970. This empowered Local Health Authorities to give birth-control advice to women regardless of marital status. The Pill finally became available for free to all women on the NHS in 1974, when the NHS Reorganisation Act 1973 incorporated family planning into the NHS. Its use continued to rise sharply, reaching a peak of 28 percent of women aged 16–49 in the early 1980s before stabilising at 24 percent for the rest of the century. Conception rates for women aged 20–24 fell by 20 percent between 1976 and 1998, while the rates for women aged 30–34 and 35–39 increased by 62 and 82 percent respectively. This suggests that the Pill played a significant role in enabling women to prevent unwanted conceptions and delay motherhood.

EXTRACT

1 From historian Sue Bruley's book *Women in Britain Since 1900*, published in 1999. Here she gives her considered opinion on the impact of the Pill on British women.

Up until the introduction of the pill, birth control had mostly been the province of men, with the sheath and withdrawal the most common methods. The pill revolutionized contraception for women by giving them a totally reliable method which involved no messy jells or rubber and which left them in control. Millions of women, both married and unmarried, enjoyed these benefits. It soon became apparent, however, that the pill posed health risks to certain women and this issue was raised by feminists in the seventies. Increasingly, sex outside marriage was condoned between couples who showed any commitment to each other. Sex became a recreational activity with couples completely separating their sexual lives from any notions of family planning. Of course, there was a downside. The pill enabled casual sex without risk or consequences. Men, who could be as predatory as ever, undoubtedly exploited the introduction of the pill to persuade women to make themselves sexually available. The pill revolutionized women's control over their own fertility, but that in itself could not transform the power relationships between men and women. It may however have contributed to the growing feminist consciousness in the late sixties and helped to create a feeling among women that they must seek control over other aspects of their lives.

The Abortion Law Reform Act 1967

Abortion had been illegal since 1803 (it was punishable before this, but had not been clearly legally defined before the Act). Although the law went through a number of revisions, the Offenses Against the Person Act 1861 confirmed that abortion was illegal in all circumstances for women. The Infant Life Preservation Act 1929 meant that women could seek an abortion where it could be proven their life was endangered by pregnancy. Conditions such as tuberculosis, cancer, epilepsy and insanity were judged to be qualifying conditions, but there were many cases where the legality was unclear. Pregnant women who did not want to keep their babies faced the terrible choice between a risky illegal abortion or, in far fewer cases and if they were unmarried, of giving up their babies for adoption. Demographer David Glass has estimated that there were 68,000 illegal abortions in 1935. He adds that this is almost certainly a large underestimate of the total number of abortions as it does not factor in those carried out with home 'remedies'. The Abortion Law Reform Association (ALRA) was founded in 1936 to campaign for legal abortions for women suffering from economic, social and psychological as well as physical issues. In 1938, Dr Aleck Bourne drew attention to the negative consequences of a blanket ban on abortion. He carried out an abortion on a 14-year-old girl who had been raped by a soldier. Supported by ALRA, he successfully argued in court that, although her life was not in danger, her mental health would be irrevocably harmed by the birth of her attacker's child. A few abortions were subsequently granted on grounds of mental health, but it was not until 1967 that fundamental reforms were made to the law on abortion.

Dr David Steel MP pursued abortion law reform through the introduction of a Private Member's Bill (i.e. one that is put forward by an MP rather than by the government) in 1967. Although two previous Private Member's Bills had been defeated in 1965 and 1966, the nature of the debates clearly moved more in favour of abortion reform. Steel pressed for a change in the law by citing the harm done to British women by 'back-street' abortions. Such abortions, carried out by untrained people in unsanitary conditions at private homes, caused 40 maternal deaths and over 100,000 injuries in 1966 alone. With 262 votes in favour and 181 votes against the final bill, Steel successfully persuaded parliament to legalise abortion during the first 28 weeks of pregnancy. (This did not apply to Northern Ireland, where the pre-1967 abortion rules continued to apply.) A woman would now be able to get an abortion on the NHS if she was able to convince two doctors that she had good reason to have one. Reasons might include threats to the physical or mental health of the mother or existing children, or the likelihood of the foetus being born severely disabled. Some women complained about the need to gain clinical approval for a decision that should be any woman's right to make alone. However, such views were a small minority and 70 percent of the British public approved the measure. It is likely that many people's views had been shaped by the 1965 television play *Up the Junction,* which featured a hard-hitting home abortion scene, and by the birth between 1961 and 1964 of 364 children with serious deformities to mothers who had taken a sedative called Thalidomide. One significant change to the 1967 Abortion Act was made by the Human Fertilisation and Embryology Act 1990. Until 1990, an abortion could not be carried out if the child was 'capable of being born alive'. This rule stemmed from the Infant Life Preservation Act 1929. The 1990 Act meant that abortions could be carried out until just before birth under the clarified terms of the 1967 Act, rather than only up until 24 weeks (the time limit was lowered from 28 weeks due to advances in infant intensive care).

Since 1967, the rate of abortion for women in general, but particularly in those aged 20–24, has risen steadily, from eight abortions per 1,000 women to 19 per 1,000 in 2004. There were 185,415 abortions in 2004, with 95 percent of them justified on grounds of harm to the mental or physical health of the pregnant woman. A 2004 poll by *The Times* newspaper found that 75 percent of Britons thought abortion should be legal. A later poll exclusively of women found that 57 percent of women agreed that women should have right of access to an abortion while 19 percent disagreed.

ACTIVITY
KNOWLEDGE CHECK

Marie Stopes' family-planning clinics, the NHS, the contraceptive pill and the Abortion Law Reform Act 1967

1 Which is the more useful when considering changes in women's sexual lives: Source 4 or Extract 1? Explain your answer.

2 Explain why the creation of the NHS in 1948 had a particularly beneficial impact on women.

3 How useful is Source 6 in understanding how changes in health care affected women's lives?

4 Choose three examples of government legislation that you feel have made the biggest impact on married women in the period 1882–2004. Put your three choices in order of most to least important, and explain your choices and the reasons for their relative importance.

Changes to women's personal lives as homemakers

Domestic work

Second only to the demands of childbirth and child-rearing were those of housework. Although the range of chores would be familiar to women in 1882 and 2004, the time and effort required to achieve satisfactory results were generally far greater at the start than at the end of the period in question. At the start of the 20th century, an average woman rose at 6.30 a.m. and spent 13 hours on her feet before heading to bed at 10.30 p.m. As late as 1951, 20 percent of houses in England and Wales lacked piped water, and many jobs, such as scrubbing floors, carrying large buckets of water for washing, cooking and hand-washing clothes were extremely laborious. Most women had a weekly routine for domestic chores. Clothes were washed on one day and ironed on another. Rooms, windows or front steps were cleaned on other days and so on. Middle-class women were spared such physical labour until it became difficult to hire a single domestic servant in the late 1930s. At that time, working-class women became more reluctant to undertake such work as other forms of employment became available, as described below.

Cooking and providing light in homes became far easier with the introduction of gas as opposed to coal in the late 19th century. The supply of domestic electricity from the 1920s onwards made these things easier still. A related benefit was the decline of soot from domestic fires. The number of electricity consumers increased from 730,000 in 1920 to nine million in 1938. The share of homes with electricity increased from 32 percent in 1932 to 66 percent in 1938 (and 96 percent by 1961). This expansion was encouraged by the Electrical (Supply) Act 1926, which replaced a diverse range of voltages and networks with a Central Electricity Board and a National Grid. By 1934, the grid covered most parts of the country. However, use of electricity differed across the UK. Whereas homes in the south-east consumed an average of 861 kilowatt-hours in 1938, those in the north-east used only 386 kilowatt-hours. During the interwar period people in the north used a higher share of electricity for lighting rather than for labour-saving devices. Devices such as vacuum cleaners were slow to permeate working-class homes because women could not afford to purchase such expensive items, even on hire purchase.

SOURCE

The percentage of British homes that had a range of labour-saving devices in 1955, 1975 and 1995. Adapted from D. Murphy, *Britain 1914–2000* (2000).

	1955	1975	1995
Vacuum cleaner	51	90	96
Washing machine	18	70	91
Refrigerator	8	85	98
Freezer	n/a	15	79
Central heating	5	47	85
Dishwasher	1	2	12
Microwave oven	n/a	n/a	47

The lack of available domestic servants together with the rise of domestic appliances fostered the rise of a more professional, technical approach to housework. Aspirations of domestic perfection were clearly encouraged by magazines and advertising that strongly reinforced the gender division of domestic labour. The notion that women should be wholly responsible for washing, ironing, cooking and cleaning was still accepted uncritically by the vast majority of women in the early 1970s. In *Housewife*, Ann Oakley's 1971 study of female domestic life found that women saw housework as a major duty that they had no option but to fulfil. Historian A.H. Halsey noted in 1970 that while men did 172 minutes of unpaid work a day, women did 260 minutes. He concluded that the sharing of domestic labour was shifting, albeit very slowly.

SOURCE 8

The front cover of women's magazine *Red Star Weekly*, published on 16 April 1955.

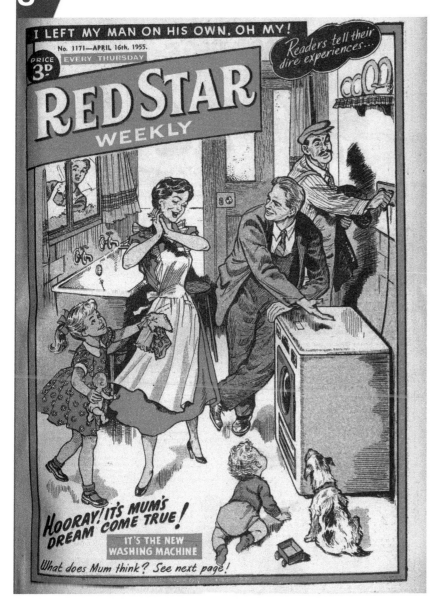

Motherhood

The ideal of motherhood was promoted by government policies, magazines and advertising throughout the 20th century, but it received a particular boost at times of concern over population growth and the health of the next generation. The shocking discovery that around one-third of volunteers for the 1899–1902 Boer War were unfit for active service fuelled official concern about the ability of working-class mothers to raise their children (note that the blame was placed on mothers themselves rather than poor diets or housing). Schools for Mothers, later renamed Infant Welfare Centres, opened in 1907 to provided lessons in cooking, feeding and hygiene. The huge loss of life during the First World War explains the timing of the 1918 Maternal and Child Welfare Act. This enabled local authorities to expand the range of services available to new mothers, especially through health visitors to check on the progress of mother and baby. National Baby Weeks were organised in 1917 and 1918 to promote motherhood skills. Some women tried to capitalise on the increased official attention to motherhood to press for greater assistance for mothers. Eleanor Rathbone MP (see page 26) maintained a campaign for family allowances throughout the interwar period, and then for the payments to be made directly to mothers. Official help only stretched so far. While crèches were set up to help female factory workers during the Second World War, they were deemed too expensive to maintain in post-war austerity Britain. The lack of adequate and affordable childcare facilities remained a major reason for the rise of part-time female employment after 1945.

A number of influential books also affected popular views on how mothers should raise their children. Sir Frederick Truby King's books, such as his *Feeding and Care of Baby* (1913), were popular during the interwar years. They recommended a highly strict regime, with limited cuddling and fixed four-hour feeding cycles no matter how much the baby cried. In the 1950s, the more progressive ideas of American paediatrician Benjamin Spock and British psychologist John Bowlby became highly influential. Bowlby argued that babies and toddlers needed their mother's continuous attention and severe psychological damage could occur if women neglected this duty. These views chimed with official concerns about the declining behaviour of children who had grown up during the more chaotic wartime period: mothers had a domestic responsibility to promote decent social relations. Many women suffered from the isolation that resulted from such full-time child-rearing duties. Novelist Margaret Drabble wrote newspaper articles in the 1960s that drew attention to this social problem. Her views fed into the rise of second-wave feminism that challenged assumptions that motherhood was the highest goal and fulfilment for British women. Since the 1970s, the percentage of women having children has fallen and the age at which they have their first child has risen considerably. Whereas 69 percent of women in 1976 had their first child when they were aged 20–29, this had fallen to 48 percent in 1998. In 1976, just 20 percent of women had their first child when they were 30–39. This had risen to 42 percent in 1998. Changes in women's working lives (discussed on page 28) are crucial in explaining this shift in female fertility.

ACTIVITY
KNOWLEDGE CHECK

Women's lives as mothers and homemakers

1 Find evidence for and against the notion that women's lives as mothers and homemakers became easier in the period 1882-2004. Create a table with two columns to organise your notes.

2 Use your contextual knowledge to rate the usefulness of Source 8 in assessing women's changing roles as mothers and homemakers.

The reasons for, and impact of, government legislation and shifts in attitudes to women's roles

There are a number of reasons that help to explain why governments passed reforms that benefited women between 1882 and 2004.

- A growing awareness among MPs (the vast majority of whom were men throughout the 20th century) of the unfairness of existing legislation towards women. This was due at various times to the impact of a particular legal case, to the influence of an MP's Private Member's Bill or to the increased representative voice of female MPs in parliament.

- The impact of women's pressure groups and their lobbying of MPs. Pressure groups in the 20th century owed much to the strategies (e.g. petitions, letter writing, marches and mass rallies) that originated with campaigners such as Josephine Butler. Her Ladies' National Association (formed in 1869) successfully lobbied for the repeal of the Contagious Diseases Act (that allowed the demeaning internal inspection of any woman suspected of being a prostitute) in 1886.

- Legislation has also had to evolve to keep up with, and reflect, important social and economic change.

Government legislation was generally of great benefit to British women between 1882 and 2004. Its provisions not only sought to improve living and working conditions, but also helped to set higher minimum standards of what was deemed acceptable in many areas of British women's lives. However, it is important to note the gap that sometimes existed between *de jure* and *de facto* legal change.

The impact of change in female participation in politics

Although the history of women's suffrage is not the focus of this chapter, it is important to note that increased female participation in local and national politics helped to shift attitudes towards women's personal and working lives. Women had a longer history of participation in local politics than in national politics. Widows and spinsters were allowed to vote in local elections from 1869 (and married women who met the property qualification could vote after 1894). Women had served on local education boards and as Poor Law Guardians in the late 19th century and as councillors after the Qualification of Women Act 1907.

KEY TERMS

De jure
According to the law.

De facto
The reality of what is happening in practice, regardless of what the law says.

A range of suffragist societies came together as the National Union of Women's Suffrage Societies in 1897 to campaign for the right to vote in national elections. Campaigners saw female suffrage as a fundamental right and an essential stepping stone to further progress in the quality of women's lives. The failure to gain the vote in 1897 led to the increasingly radical, and later violent, actions of the Women's Social and Political Union (WSPU) from 1903. These 'suffragettes' suspended their campaign for the duration of the First World War.

The scale of British women's contribution to the war effort was a key justification for the Representation of the People Act 1918, which enfranchised 8.4 million women aged 30 or over, and the Parliament (Qualification of Women) Act 1918, which allowed women to become MPs. It took another ten years for the young, female workers who sacrificed so much for the war effort to get the vote. The Equal Franchise Act 1928 finally enabled women aged 21 or over to vote on the same terms as men.

Although the number of women elected as MPs remained tiny, they made important contributions to social and welfare reforms. The Criminal Law (Amendment) Act 1922 (which removed some of the loopholes and possible defences used in cases of sexual activity with girls under the age of 16) and the Bastardy Act 1923 (which allowed children born before marriage to be recognised as legitimate after their parents' marriage) clearly reflected female concerns. There was a good deal of hostility in unsympathetic newspapers to votes for women aged 21–30, branded 'the flapper vote'. These women were deemed too emotional and irresponsible to use the right to vote with due caution. The National Union of Women Suffrage Societies (NUWSS) changed its name to the National Union of Societies for Equal Citizenship (NUSEC) to reflect the new focus of their campaigning. Their sustained and peaceful pressure secured the Equal Franchise Act 1928 far more quickly than if things had been left entirely in the hands of men.

However, there was no clear correlation between the right to vote and political advancement more generally. Although 8.5 million women over the age of 30 gained the right to vote in 1918, only 17 women stood as parliamentary candidates. Only one, Countess Constance Markievicz, was elected (as an Irish Republican she refused to take her seat in the Commons). The numbers of female MPs remained low until a steady increase after the 1997 general election.

There were a number of reasons for this failure to translate female majority in voting after 1928 (with 52.7 percent of total votes) into political advancement. Perhaps the most important were the structure and attitudes of the main parties. While organisations like the National Union of Societies for Equal Citizenship (NUSEC) were large and well run, they lacked the sort of expertise and local party machinery to help launch an effective 'Women's Party'. The NUSEC split up in 1928, largely over the issue of whether women should push for gender equality with men on men's terms or for the equal valuation of different gender roles. Eleanor Rathbone argued the latter and dismissed calls for equal roles and responsibilities with men as 'me too' feminism. She led the formation of the National Council for Equal Citizenship while her opponents formed the National Union of Townswomen's Guilds. Membership of both organisations fell throughout the 1930s. Although the main parties recognised the need to try to cultivate female participation, they were unwilling to risk losing a safe seat by selecting a female candidate. This reflected the ingrained male bias against female politicians, which they had to face at every stage of their careers. One pioneering female MP, Edith Summerskill, reflected that the House of Commons was 'like a boys' school which had decided to take a few girls'. With the exception of the 1928 franchise reform, both the Conservative and Labour Parties failed to promote specifically female issues. Female groups were incorporated into national organisations where they were outnumbered by men. Two Conservative women's groups joined the National Union of Conservative Associations, while Labour allowed four female representatives of the Women's Sections to sit on the main policy-making committee, the National Executive. Socialist women in particular faced a difficult choice between mainstream class campaigns, which often favoured working men over women, and fighting for female issues. In practice, many sacrificed fighting for female issues in favour of mainstream class campaigns.

Female politicians tended to focus on local, rather than national politics. There was a longer tradition of women serving on various local boards where they helped with social issues, such as health and education, which were seen as an extension of their domestic sphere of expertise. More practically, it was difficult for women to balance family life with the pressure for national politicians to be in Westminster. Despite this tradition and expertise, women only made up around five or six percent of local councillors between 1918 and 1939.

Having asserted themselves effectively during the war, women failed to press home possible gains in terms of female representation in parliament. In 1945 and 1955, there were just 24 females out of 630 MPs in the House of Commons; in 1974 the figure remained a lowly 23 out of 635 MPs. The same issues which had served as barriers before 1939 continued to apply, with the candidate selection committees as the most formidable. Women were rarely risked in safe seats and so had to overcome large opposition majorities to gain their seat. This meant that those women who did win a seat tended to have exceptional qualities. Once in parliament they stood a far greater chance of promotion to ministerial office (Harold Wilson's 1964 government contained seven of the 18 female Labour MPs).

The post-war generation of female MPs were more determined to be seen as well-rounded politicians rather than as simply advocates for women's issues. While a few women, such as Barbara Castle as Minister for Transport (1966–68) gained national prominence, the loss of cross-party cohesion weakened the advocacy of female rights in parliament after 1945. It took the growth of an extra-parliamentary women's movement in the 1970s to put female-specific issues back on the agenda. As Secretary of State for Employment, and later Secretary of State for Social Services, Castle was responsible for a range of significant legislation that affected women, including the Equal Pay Act 1970, pension reform and the introduction of child benefit. Although Margaret Thatcher, as the first woman to become prime minister (1979–90), is the most famous British female politician of all time, she did not use her authority to specifically assist women. In a speech on 26 July 1982 she admitted to not liking the forceful way some women in favour of women's rights talked and behaved. She also felt that the fight for women's rights had largely been won and should no longer be necessary. Although Thatcher may have been a female icon, such sentiments did little to endear her to many women.

EXTEND YOUR KNOWLEDGE

Pioneering women in politics

Nancy Astor (1879–1964) was the first woman to take her seat in parliament, and she represented the Conservatives until 1945. Some see her as a controversial heroine because she gained her seat thanks to her wealthy husband, who held the seat until he was elevated to the House of Lords.

Eleanor Rathbone (1872–1946) had been a suffragist. Her arguments in the House of Commons were crucial in changing Family Allowance payments to mothers rather than fathers in 1945.

Ellen Wilkinson (1891–1947) was an inspirational MP for Jarrow. She organised the 1936 Jarrow March, which delivered a petition to parliament to highlight the suffering of this shipbuilding community. She also introduced the Hire Purchase Act 1938, which gave protection to people who bought goods on credit. Ellen also served as Minister for Education in Attlee's first post-war government. She raised the school leaving age from 14 to 15.

Edith Summerskill (1901–80) was one of the first women to be trained as a doctor before becoming a Labour MP. She was a founder of the Socialist Health Association, which put forward arguments for a National Health Service.

Barbara Castle (1910–2002) was a leading figure in Harold Wilson's Labour governments in the 1960s and 1970s. As Secretary of State for Transport (1965–68) she made seatbelts compulsory in new cars and introduced breathalysers to combat drink-driving.

The Women's Liberation Movement

A number of developments outside parliament contributed to the broader political advancement of women. Feminist authors drew attention to the inequalities of a profoundly patriarchal society. Betty Friedan's *The Feminine Mystique* (1963) and Germaine Greer's *The Female Eunuch* (1970) are examples of feminist literature that became bestsellers in Britain. They argued that women would remain unfulfilled, second-class citizens unless they actively stood up to the male-dominated state of affairs. The success of the 1968 strike by the female employees at the Ford car factory in Dagenham (see page 31) attracted national attention and help to galvanise female activism. The National Women's Liberation Conference first met in Oxford in February 1970. Socialist and historian Sheila Rowbotham organised the meeting, to help set an agenda for 'women's lib'. The four key goals were equal education and opportunities, equal pay, free contraception and abortions on demand, and the universal provision of childcare for working women. Although disagreements over aims and tactics led to a fragmentation of the women's movement by the 1980s, a range of significant legislation had been achieved by then. This success owed a great deal to the sustained pressure of feminist activists in the 1970s.

Feminists did help to shift expectations about what was acceptable at work and in the home for many women despite the lack of popular activism. However, this took time, and in some areas of society there had been little change in attitudes towards women and sexual discrimination by 1979. In 1970, the *Sun* newspaper used a topless model for the first time, and by the mid-1970s the 'Page 3' feature had become a regular, yet controversial, feature of Britain's best-selling newspaper. Women's magazines, such as *Woman* or *Woman's Realm*, still focused primarily on traditional gender issues such as fashion, dieting, romance and the family. The most popular books for women in the 1960s and 1970s were fictional romances like those published by Mills and Boon. Only 10,000 women were active in the Women's Liberation Movement at its peak in the early 1970s. Children's toys in many ways reinforced gender stereotypes, as did children's reading books such as the *Janet and John* series (used in many primary schools to help children learn to read) and fiction such as *The Famous Five* stories. These were very popular children's books and included stories and pictures such as boys helping dad clean and mend the car, while girls worked in the home with their mother. In the less-academic secondary modern schools, subjects such as Physics, Chemistry, Woodwork and Metalwork were still seen as 'boys' subjects', while Cookery and Typing were considered 'girls' subjects'.

ACTIVITY
KNOWLEDGE CHECK

Political advancement and shifts in attitudes to women's roles

1 Create a timeline of women's political advancement. Provide details of each event on the timeline.

2 In what ways could women's political advancement be argued to have affected attitudes to women's roles?

3 'The rise of Women's Lib proves the failure of women's political advancement to secure real gains in women's lives before 1970.' How far do you agree with this statement?

TO WHAT EXTENT, AND WHY, DID WOMEN'S WORKING LIVES CHANGE IN THE YEARS 1882–2004?

In 1882, women were paid just 40 percent of the wage a man could expect for doing similar work. This reflected the limited range of low-skilled and oversupplied jobs they were able to gain. The situation was even more restricted for married women, where a 'marriage bar' forced most of them to give up work upon marriage. The 1901 Census recorded that while 61 percent of 15–24-year-old women worked, this reduced to 31 percent for 25–35-year-olds, and dropped even further for those aged 35 and over. There was something of a north/south divide in these figures. Work was considered more of a life occupation for women in the North, especially in towns dominated by the cotton industry, such as Preston, where women were often unionised and earned higher wages. In the South, with less industry and more domestic service, marriage was more clearly seen as an end to paid labour. The Census was unable to record the extent and variety of work carried out by women within the home. Childminding, taking in lodgers, washing or sewing, and completing small, repetitive tasks for '**sweated trades**', such as making matchboxes or covering tennis balls, were common, socially acceptable ways for women to make a little money. Part of the marriage bar logic was that men should be paid a 'family wage' to support their dependents including their wife. Even male trade unionists who joined women in their campaign for female workers' rights did so from a patriarchal standpoint. There was a clear assumption that a married woman's proper place was in the home and that the separate spheres of men's public and women's domestic life was the ideal.

There were also entrenched assumptions about work deemed suitable for men and women. Heavy or skilled work was reserved for men and more menial, repetitive work was reserved for women. Middle-class women could aspire to work as teachers, governesses or nurses, but until shortly before 1882 they were effectively barred from the professions. The Enabling Act 1876 had forced all medical schools to accept women. Women started attending a few English universities from the 1860s and by 1900 15 percent of students were female (this had risen to 23 percent by 1939). Most working-class women before the First World War worked in domestic service, with factory work and shop work lagging some way behind. There were important regional exceptions to this rule, such as in Lancashire where women made up 60 percent of the textile factory workforce. In such areas, which also included the potteries of Staffordshire and rope and sack-weaving factories of Dundee, women became prominent in local trade unions.

A Level Exam-Style Question Section C

How far do you agree with the opinion that government legislation was the most important factor affecting women's personal lives in the period 1882–2004? (20 marks)

Tip
Make sure that you compare the impact of other factors with the impact of government legislation in each paragraph. Be clear about the criteria you will use to justify the comparative impact of each factor on women's personal lives.

KEY TERM

Sweated trades
This refers to workers in industries who suffered from long hours, poor conditions and poor (often piece-rate) pay. The modern term 'sweatshop', that describes factories with poor working conditions, is derived from this term.

A range of factors combined to improve the range of occupations open to women and the pay they received for their work. Change would have occurred more slowly had it not been for the determined effort of some women to promote the greater equality between the sexes and to press for economic independence for women. Such arguments were advanced on many fronts, including calls for improved female education, the demand for equal voting and political representation rights, calls for employment law reform, and a large increase in female participation in trade unions and other direct-action groups. These campaigns not only shaped the legal and practical environment within which women worked, but, perhaps more importantly, fundamentally shifted male and female attitudes towards the employment of women. Although a huge amount of credit for these changes must go to pioneering female campaigners, organisers and professionals, women have also benefited from changes in the British economy and, more questionably, the impact of the two world wars. The dates when different advances were made perhaps gives the best clue as to the most significant reason for change in that area. Some arguments were won sooner than others. There are still key areas of women's work where total equality has yet to be achieved, for example pay (women in 2004 still only earned 80 percent of male wages in equivalent jobs) and senior promotions (the so-called 'glass ceiling': just 1.8 percent of new chief executive officers of large companies in 2004 were female).

The impact of direct action on women's roles

The 1888 Bryant and May matchgirls' strike

The working conditions of London matchgirls were among the worst in the country. Girls regularly worked 14-hour days for low pay in the presence of white phosphorus, a toxic chemical that was the active ingredient in matches from the 1840s until the 1910s. Many workers developed severe health problems such as 'phossy jaw', a condition that caused teeth, gums and the jawbone to rot away. The intense pain, disfiguration and noxious discharge caused by the rot brought misery. If the jawbone was not removed toxins spread through the body and caused a painful death by organ failure. The women and girls at the Bryant and May match factory in Bow, East London, were not members of a trade union, but 1,400 of them decided to strike on 2 July 1888. Four days later, the whole factory had ceased production. Conditions and pay had been appalling for decades, but the trigger for strike action was an article written by social activist Annie Besant.

SOURCE

9 From Annie Besant's article, 'White Slavery in London', published in the halfpenny weekly paper *The Link: A Journal for the Servants of Man* on 23 June 1888.

Bryant and May, now a limited liability company, paid last year a dividend of 23 per cent... The highest dividend paid has been 38 per cent. Let us see how the money is made with which these monstrous dividends are paid. The hour for commencing work is 6.30 in summer and 8 in winter; work concludes at 6 p.m. Half-an-hour is allowed for breakfast and an hour for dinner. This long day of work is performed by young girls, who have to stand the whole of the time. A typical case is that of a girl of 16, a piece-worker; she earns 4s. a week, and lives with a sister, employed by the same firm, who 'earns good money, as much as 8s. or 9s. per week'. Out of the earnings 2s. is paid for the rent of one room; the child lives on only bread-and-butter and tea, alike for breakfast and dinner, but related with dancing eyes that once a month she went to a meal where 'you get coffee, and bread and butter, and jam, and marmalade, and lots of it'; now and then she goes to the Paragon, someone 'stands treat, you know', and that appeared to be the solitary bit of colour in her life. The splendid salary of 4s. is subject to deductions in the shape of fines; if the feet are dirty, or the ground under the bench is left untidy, a fine of 3d. is inflicted; for putting 'burnts' – matches that have caught fire during the work – on the bench 1s. has been forfeited, and one unhappy girl was once fined 2s. 6d for some unknown crime. If a girl leaves four or five matches on her bench when she goes for a fresh 'frame' she is fined 3d., and in some departments a fine of 3d. is inflicted for talking. If a girl is late she is shut out for 'half the day', that is for the morning six hours, and 5d. is deducted out of her day's 8d. One girl was fined 1s. for letting the web twist round a machine in the endeavour to save her fingers from being cut, and was sharply told to take care of the machine, 'never mind your fingers'. Another, who carried out the instructions and lost a finger thereby, was left unsupported while she was helpless. The wage covers the duty of submitting to an occasional blow from a foreman; one, who appears to be a gentleman of variable temper, 'clouts' them 'when he is mad'.

But who cares for the fate of these white wage slaves? Born in slums, driven to work while still children, undersized because underfed, oppressed because helpless, flung aside as soon as worked out, who cares if they die or go on the streets, provided only that the Bryant and May shareholders get their 23 per cent.

Managers at the factory attempted to force employees to sign a statement that refuted the damaging article. When many refused to do so a ringleader was fired as a warning to the others. A campaign to reinstate this worker was the original cause for the strike, but the sense of empowerment and a unique opportunity for change quickly led to further demands. Top of the list was an end to the highly unfair system of fines that managers arbitrarily deducted from pay packets for a range of alleged infringements, from lateness to taking too long on a break. Such fines were common in factory work, domestic service and shop work. The Union of Shop Assistants and Clerks told a 1908 House of Commons Inquiry that mistakes in adding up bills, dating receipts or even addressing a customer as 'Miss' rather than 'Madam' all carried fines of up to 6 pennies (equivalent to about £15 today). That was a tough burden when weekly wages were only between 8 and 10 shillings (equivalent to about £250 today). Delegations from the match factory, impressed by her article, enlisted the help of Annie Besant on 6 July and MP Charles Bradlaugh five days later. Bradlaugh spoke in parliament on behalf of the women while Besant spoke at a number of strike meetings and helped to put the workers' case to the management. The resolution of the women, together with the mounting negative publicity, led to a settlement on 16 July. All of the key worker demands, including a separate room for meals to help prevent white phosphorus poisoning, were accepted. The **Salvation Army** continued to put pressure on Bryant and May to reform its production process. Between 1891 and 1901 it ran its own match factory in Bow that used less-toxic red phosphorus in its matches despite the higher production costs this entailed. In 1901, Bryant and May purchased this factory and announced it too would only use red phosphorus. A 1908 Act of parliament banned the use of white phosphorus in all matches produced after 31 December 1910.

> **KEY TERM**
>
> **Salvation Army**
> This combination of a church and charity was set up in London in 1865 by Methodist preacher William Booth. His aim was to help the poor, both spiritually and physically, or as Booth put it: soup, soap and then salvation.

The rise of female trade unionism and direct action groups

Female involvement in trade unions and other direct action groups grew in step with the growth of unionism as a whole. As with male union membership, growth was moderate before 1914 and received a dramatic boost during the First World War. By 1914, there were around 330,000 female trade unionists, some 220,000 of whom worked in the textile industry. With 32,000 members, the Co-operative Women's Guild was the largest exclusively female organisation before 1914. It campaigned for female suffrage, improved health care and encouraged industrial reform to assist women. Formed in 1894, the Women's Industrial Council also promoted education and legislation to support female workers. Its investigation of 117 industries before the First World War revealed widespread female exploitation and poor working conditions.

SOURCE 10 From a Woman's Trade Union League pamphlet distributed in 1909.

Would you like to iron a shirt a minute? Think of standing at a mangle just above the washroom with the hot steam pouring up through the floor for 10, 12, 14 and sometimes 17 hours a day! Sometimes the floors are made of cement and then it seems as though one were standing on hot coals, and the workers are dripping with perspiration. They are breathing air laden with particles of soda, ammonia and other chemicals! The Laundry Workers Union in one city reduced this long day to 9 hours, and has increased the wages 50 per cent.

Momentum against harsh, exploitative working environments built, with campaigns for better pay and conditions by the **Anti-Sweating League** and the National Federation of Women Workers (NFWW), both formed in 1906. Such pressure, spearheaded by NFWW leader Mary Macarthur, helped to persuade the Liberal government to pass the Trades Board Act 1909. Minimum rates of pay were established for workers in the clothing, lace-making, box-making and chain-making industries. The number of industries covered by the law was later extended. Regulatory boards were set up to investigate pay and working conditions. Weekly pay increased dramatically as a direct result, for example from 8 shillings to 12 shillings in lace-making and 8 shillings 5 pence to 13 shillings in box-making. The law gave employers six months to revise wages, but it also helped to make women more assertive in demanding fair pay. In Cradley Heath, Birmingham, with the support of the Anti-Sweating League, 700 chain-makers went on strike for ten weeks to successfully force the immediate implementation of a doubling of wages

> **KEY TERM**
>
> **Anti-Sweating League**
> This was a pressure group that existed between 1906 and 1909. It was formed specifically to campaign against the poor pay and conditions suffered in the 'sweated' industries, usually textile factories where employees' pay depended on how many items they produced (today we would call them sweatshops).

Despite these gains, it remained extremely rare for women to be paid the same amount as men, even in jobs where the work was identical. One important exception to the pay gap was clerical work, where unions accepted equal pay from 1912. Their acceptance of equal pay had far more to do with male fear of being totally replaced by women (who worked more efficiently in comparative tests) than feminist sentiments. The letter in Source 11 typifies the views of most male clerks to female demands for equal pay.

SOURCE

11 From a letter from a male clerk to the *Liverpool Echo*, written in 1911.

stereotype

above their station

> Your correspondent seems to think that the female clerk should receive the same wages as the male clerk for similar work. Surely this is a gross piece of audacity on the part of that small, but bombastic, section of clerical labour. Seeing that they are so fond of comparing the product of their labour as equal to that of the male clerk I would suggest that these intrepid 'typewriter pounders', instead of being allowed to gloat over love novels or do fancy crocheting during the time they are not 'pounding', should fill in their spare time washing out the offices and dusting same, which you will no doubt agree is more suited to their sex and maybe would give them a little practice and insight into the work they will be called up to do should they so far demean themselves as to marry one of the poor male clerks whose living they are doing their utmost to take out of his hands at the present time.

The demand for female industrial labour during the First World War, especially following the introduction of male conscription in January 1916, led many women to join trade unions for the first time. While female union membership increased by 160 percent between 1914 and 1918, there was little attempt to organise female industrial labour outside the National Federation of Women Workers (NFWW) and the Workers' Union (WU). Around 80,000 women joined the WU and formed a quarter of all members by 1918. Members of both groups organised a conference in 1915 called the Women's War Workers Committee. Its calls for equal pay for equal work, greater access to training and trade union membership were almost totally ignored. The only notable victory through direct action was in the 1918 Equal Pay strike by female bus and tram conductors, who demanded the same war bonus as male co-workers. Male trade unionists resented female employment and feared it would depress their wages after the war. They were greatly reassured by the Restoration of Pre-War Practices Act 1916, which allowed new female workers to be laid off to make way for men returning from war.

Trade unions became even more overtly prejudiced against female membership during the 'hungry' 1930s. As the Great Depression caused unemployment to hit three million in 1932, women came under pressure to forgo paid employment and see themselves as housewives and mothers. Female union membership fell from a high of 1.5 million in 1920 (around a quarter of all women workers) to one million in 1939, despite a three percent increase in female membership of the total workforce to 30 percent in the same period. In part this was because women took jobs in the non-unionised service sector, or on production lines in new industries such as car production, electrical products, chemicals and synthetic materials, where women did not have a tradition of unionisation. In older sectors with high female employment that were not in decline, such as teaching and shop work, unions called for the strict enforcement of the marriage bar. The Trades Union Congress (TUC) recognised that non-unionised women, as they could be hired more cheaply, were a greater threat to male wages than if they were unionised. It set up a Women's Conference in 1925 and then a Women Workers' Group in 1930 in a failed bid to attract more female members.

Although many unions rejected female membership or only accepted women on a temporary basis, the need for female help enabled some political progress at a national level. Margaret Bondfield, who had already been a suffragette and trade union activist before the war, served as part of the wartime Central Committee for Women's Employment. She was elected to the General Council of the TUC in November 1918 and this national profile paved the way for her to become a Labour MP in 1923. Despite the breakthrough of exceptional women such as Bondfield, most unions remained highly masculine environments until the 1980s, when several leading unions, such as UNISON, took deliberate steps to increase female representation at the highest decision-making levels. This was a reflection of a large increase in female trade union membership. Between 1970 and 1979 this increased from 2.6 to 3.8 million (or 24 to 30 percent of total membership). It was not until the early 2000s that women began to lead trade unions (the first female leader of the TUC was appointed in 2012).

The 1968 Dagenham Ford car factory strike and the fight for equal pay

The call for the same wages to be paid to women who did the same work as men was first advanced in the 1830s. This demand was subsumed within broader industrial campaigns for most of the 19th century but resurfaced in the 1880s. In 1888, Clementia Black, one of only three female TUC delegates, put forward a resolution for equal pay for equal work. The TUC ignored the motion for the patriarchal reasons outlined above. With great astuteness and impressive foresight, Beatrice Webb, a leading intellectual member of the early Labour Party, also rejected the demand of equal pay for equal work. She anticipated difficulties in proving the equivalence of female to male work in industries where roles were divided by gender. She instead recommended the introduction of a national minimum wage at different rates for different jobs regardless of gender.

With the exception of female clerks, the issue of equal pay remained an uphill struggle in all other areas of employment. The marriage bar, widely applied until the 1960s, fed the logic that women only needed money for extras rather than for the support of dependents. Winston Churchill personally intervened to overturn a 1943 Commons vote in favour of equal pay for female teachers (he was able to do this through the drastic step of threatening resignation should he not get his way). MP Maud Tate was furious with Churchill's decision to knock the momentum out of the equal pay campaign through the appointment of a Royal Commission on Equal Pay. Two years later, despite the opposition of three of the four women on the Commission, the Report stated that equal pay was only justified for the lower grades of the civil service. Even this limited recommendation was not acted upon, with the excuse of financial constraints after the Second World War. Many women in teaching, local government and the civil service were frustrated with the lack of support from MPs or trade unions. In 1951, the 'Equal Pay: When?' campaign was launched, with meetings, petitions, lobbying of MPs and the printing of badges with the campaign message. The campaign gradually worked, and equal pay was introduced by the London County Council in 1952 and extended nationally between 1954 and 1962. The success of women in these public sector jobs led those in private sector employment to question their acceptance of lower rates of pay.

A major reason for female success in a few public sector jobs was their ability to demonstrate that their work was exactly the same as male employees of the same grade. As Beatrice Webb predicted, this was far more difficult in many occupations. Even where women directly replaced men in factories, as happened during the two world wars, employers used two excuses to pay **substitute** and **dilutee** women less. A female substitute would only earn the full male wage if she was able to perform the task 'without additional supervision or assistance'. This was an arbitrary decision on the part of male supervisors. Dilutees were paid 'according to the nature of the work and the ability displayed'. The less-skilled nature of their work justified lower pay.

It was the unfair grading of pay, rather than a demand for equal pay, that led 168 women at the Ford factory in Dagenham, east London, to go on strike on 7 June 1968. A new pay system placed the female sewing machinists in the 'less skilled production jobs' category. Strike leader Rose Boland felt this was unfair because they were skilled workers, unlike the men in that category, every woman who worked on the car seat covers had to pass a skills test before being hired. Rose argued that this should entitle them to be placed in the 'more skilled production jobs' category, with a 15 percent higher wage. The strike stopped all production for three weeks and gained nationwide media attention after Barbara Castle, Secretary of State for Employment and Productivity, intervened in the dispute. Castle promised the women higher pay and new legislation to enforce equal pay (but not the regrading they actually demanded). Ford eventually agreed to increase the machinists' wages by seven percent, and then grade them as 'more skilled' a year later. Although the women returned to work, a court of inquiry ruled against the regrading. A further six-week strike was undertaken in 1984 to finally secure their status as skilled workers.

The machinists strike at Dagenham, together with a similar strike at the Ford assembly plant in Halewood, Liverpool, provided a catalyst for equal pay legislation. The National Joint Action Campaign Committee for Women's Equal Rights was founded by a range of female trade unionists in 1969. On 18 May that year, over 1,000 people attended an equal pay demonstration in Trafalgar Square. The need to mirror **European Economic Community** (EEC, the forerunner of today's European Union) laws is also cited as a further cause for new equal pay laws. Britain, in preparation for its successful 1973 bid to join the EEC, emulated Article 119 of its founding treaty, which called for equal pay between the sexes for equal work. However, it should be noted that the 1970–74 Conservative government proposed EEC entry as an economic solution, while major legislation

KEY TERMS

Substitute
Substitution was the direct replacement of men by women in skilled work. Unions were promised (in the Restoration of Pre-War Practices Acts 1919 and 1942) that the changes would be reversed at the end of hostilities.

Dilutee
Dilution was the employment of less-skilled women to do a skilled male job by breaking the work down into simpler, repetitive tasks

European Economic Community (EEC)
The Community was formed by six founding members in 1957 under the Treaty of Rome. It aimed to promote economic integration between member states. Britain joined the EEC in 1973. It was renamed the European Community in 1993 to recognise its aim of broader integration, not just economic. It was absorbed into the European Union by the 2009 Lisbon Treaty.

to promote gender equality in the workplace was passed by Labour governments before and after Conservative rule. The impact of direct action on women's working lives should not be underestimated.

SOURCE 12

Female sewing machinists at the Ford Motor Company plant in Dagenham who took strike action on 7 June 1968.

SOURCE 13

From an interview with representatives of the Ford machinists who went on strike in June 1968. They were interviewed for the *Guardian* newspaper shortly after their appearance at the Department of Employment and Productivity in London.

We're just cheap labour, like most other women. If Ford's [*sic*] would pay the right rate for the job, they'd get plenty of men machinists, they want us because it costs less. The strike is officially about upgrading our rate, but really it's about sex discrimination... It'll all be forgotten as soon as it's over... We want equal pay, we want equal rights, but women won't fight for them and we'd never get them. They haven't the time, they're too involved in their home lives. They'll go on settling for their smaller pay packets and a peaceful life. [Our husbands are] backing us all the time and most of them help with the housework at the weekends. Not like the women up North. It's a different world. They're completely at men's bidding and they'll never get their rights... The wives of other Ford workers who have been laid off are all against us. They say we do it just for pin money and why should their men's money be cut because of us? But we've as much right to a wage as anyone else.

ACTIVITY
KNOWLEDGE CHECK

The 1888 matchgirls' strike, the 1968 Ford car factory strike and women's direct action

1 Explain the causes and consequences of the 1888 matchgirls' strike and the 1968 Ford machinists' strike.

2 How far had the nature of women's direct action changed between 1888 and 1968? Explain your answer.

3 How useful is Source 13 in understanding women's direct action in the 20th century?

The impact of legislation on women's working lives

Legislation helped to promote gender equality in education (see page 36) and employment. However, this was not entirely a one-way process and there were some notable Acts during the two world wars that defended the patriarchal *status quo*. Just as significant were the legal loopholes in positive legislation that weakened the potential to improve women's working lives.

The Sex Disqualification (Removal) Act 1919 aimed to prevent the disqualification 'by sex or marriage from the exercise of any public function, or from being appointed to or holding any civil or judicial office or post, or from entering or assuming or carrying on any civil profession or vocation'. This enabled women, *de jure* if not *de facto*, to work in any profession even if married. On 23 December 1919, when the law came into effect, Ada Summers became the first female magistrate. It took three years to pass the Law Society examinations, so the first female solicitor, Carrie Morrison, was not admitted to the profession until 18 December 1922. A decade later, only 100 women had qualified in total as solicitors. Numbers remained very low until a steady increase from the mid-1970s (by 2004 almost 40 percent of all solicitors, and 30 percent of doctors, were female).

The impact of the National Service Act 1941

The impact of the two world wars on women's working lives has been a source of much debate among historians. General consensus is that the 1939–45 conflict had greater and more permanent effects than that of 1914–18. The greater scale of government intervention, popular mobilisation and shared sacrifices on the home front help to explain this difference. Women had volunteered for a range of roles to replace men who joined the armed forces during the First World War. Middle-class women volunteered as nurses but also undertook 'men's jobs' such as ambulance drivers, clerks in banks and insurance companies, and as agricultural labourers in the Women's Land Army. Working-class women continued to work in factories as before, and around 400,000 quit domestic service for factory work. Around 1.59 million women entered industrial work between 1914 and 1918, a million of whom worked in munitions. They also did 'men's jobs' such as bus conductors, carpenters, stokers (someone who feeds the furnace to operate a steam engine) and tool setters (someone who sets up machines in a factory and checks that they work properly). However, the Restoration of Pre-War Practices Act 1919 meant that fewer women were employed in 1919 than immediately before the war. Despite the experience of higher pay and greater independence in factory work, huge pressure from the media and government successfully forced women to return to pre-war roles. Employment exchanges (the forerunner of today's job centres) stopped a woman's unemployment benefit if she refused laundry work or domestic service. The interwar years saw the number of women in domestic service increase from 1.8 million in 1921 to 2.1 million in 1931.

Women were encouraged to volunteer for war service even before the outbreak of hostilities in September 1939. Some 80,000 volunteers worked in the re-formed Women's Land Army, while over a million women worked in a branch of the civil defence services, as Air Raid Precautions officers, in the fire service, and overwhelmingly in the Women's Voluntary Service (WVS). WVS workers performed tasks that ranged from assisting at canteens to helping organise evacuations. However, it was clear that voluntary schemes would not be enough to wage total war against Germany. Ministry of Labour propaganda campaigns for female workers had a limited impact, largely due to the pressure of domestic commitments. The March 1941 Registration for Employment Order meant that every woman aged 19–40 (50 by 1943) had to register their preference of war work at employment exchanges. The same month, Minister for Labour Ernest Bevin also introduced the Essential Work Order (EWO). Employers in industries covered by the EWOs could not sack workers and had to accept any worker sent to them by a labour exchange. Employees were not allowed to change jobs without permission. By 1944, 2.39 million women (compared to 6.18 million men) worked in industries covered by EWOs. The percentage of women who worked as engineers, in transport or the chemical industry rose from 14 percent in 1939 to 33 percent in 1945.

The National Service Act (No. 2), which came into force in December 1941, built upon earlier registration, with the conscription of all single, childless women aged 20–30 (19–40 from 1943) for war-related service. By 1943, 6.75 million women, 43 percent of all those aged 14–59, worked in industry or civil defence, with a further 500,000 serving in the armed forces. Women were given support rather than combat roles in either the Women's Auxiliary Air Force (WAAF), the Women's Royal Naval Services (WRENS) or – by far the largest – the Auxiliary Territorial Services (ATS). Married women, who made up 43 percent of this female workforce, struggled with the 'double burden' of work on top of all their domestic duties. The government recognised that a range of measures would have to be introduced to help women cope with this extra pressure. The introduction in 1940 of communal kitchens called British Restaurants took some of the pressure off cooking. The Ministry of Labour provided funds for local authorities to set up over 1,500 day nurseries by 1944. These cared for one-quarter of all children under the age of five while their mothers carried out war work. Reluctance to offer part-time work was eroded as gains in productivity by working mothers was noted. By 1944, 900,000 women held part-time jobs.

Unlike the years immediately after 1918, by 1939 there were women such as Nancy Astor and Eleanor Rathbone who had a good deal of parliamentary experience and were able to address specifically female issues. In recognition of the impact that the war had on women, female politicians abandoned strict party loyalty in favour of cross-party co-operation. In 1940, Astor set up the Women Power Committee to investigate and promote female-specific issues. In March 1941, Minister for Labour Ernest Bevin set up the Women's Consultative Committee to manage female participation in the war economy more effectively. This body contributed to the registration and then conscription of women for work in March and December 1941. The intervention of female MPs such as Maud Tate in debates about compensation for wartime injuries led to the introduction of equal compensation for men and women in April 1943 (women had previously received 7 shillings (35p) a week less than men). However, despite similar interventions in debates over work and pay, female MPs were unable to secure legislation that would have rewarded equal work between the genders with equal pay. Nevertheless, by 1945 male MPs were finally growing used to considering female issues more seriously. This undoubtedly influenced the range of social legislation passed by post-war governments.

The impact of the Equal Pay Act 1970

The Equal Pay Act 1970 aimed to enshrine in law the concept of equal pay for equal work. However, there were a number of loopholes that limited its impact. The most obvious flaw was that it did not cover women who worked in female-only occupations, only those whose work overlapped with male equivalents. For an unequal pay claim to succeed, women had to demonstrate at an industrial tribunal that the work they did was either broadly of equal value or rated at the same skill level as male employees. This would have been difficult had the law been implemented immediately, but it was only made compulsory for all businesses on 29 December 1975. This gave employers almost six years in which to implement work and pay-scale changes that highlighted differences between male and female work and justified the continuation of lower pay for women. Between 1976 and 1983, employers won 80 percent of unequal pay cases on the basis that the work performed by men and women was different and that the law did not apply. The Equal Pay (Amendment) Act 1983 attempted to close this loophole through the replacement of the term 'equal work' with 'work of comparable value'. This was also not straightforward to prove at a tribunal. The Dagenham machinists had to resort to strike action in 1984 after their second appeal for equal grading was defeated.

SOURCE 14

From a speech made in parliament by Dr Shirley Summerskill, the Labour MP for Halifax. The speech was made during the second reading of the Equal Pay Act on 9 February 1970. Summerskill was the daughter of pioneering MP Edith Summerskill and had been educated at St Paul's Girls' School and Somerville College, Oxford.

I believe that this Bill is one of the great Measures of social reform by which this Government will be remembered in the history books. It is another important milestone in the long struggle for women's rights which is far from concluded with this legislation. Ministers in successive Governments have resisted it. For years, parties have paid lip service to the principle of equal pay for women. But always the excuse has been that this is not the right time at which to implement it. Yet there has never been a more blatant case for the remedy of a social injustice.

To whom do we now owe credit for this piece of legislation which grants to women not a privilege but a basic human right? We should first be thankful that we have the important combination of a Labour Government and a woman Cabinet Minister bringing in this Bill... Second, we must acknowledge in this debate a group of women who played a very significant part in the history of the struggle for equal pay. I refer to that small group of women machinists at Fords [sic] who went on strike for their beliefs and their rights. I do not like strikes any more than anyone else, but those women had to take really forceful action to achieve this principle. Like the early pioneers for women's suffrage, they faced abuse, misrepresentation and ridicule, but they demonstrated their great industrial power and their vital role in the export drive, so that politicians and public alike were made to realise that working women are indispensable to the economy, and that nine out of ten of them are being exploited as cheap labour, a fact of which we should have been ashamed. But where the enemy is prejudice and custom, as in this case, those women at Fords showed that letters to the Press and conference resolutions are feeble weapons. Consultations and requests to employers over the years have been similarly ineffective. Only the present Government legislation can implement the principle of equal pay...

The implementation of the Bill will be long, complex and fraught with difficulties. I do not think that any of us underestimates them. Its opponents in all parts of society, those who are prejudiced against the whole Measure—whether they be directors, women themselves or even trade unionists—will do everything legally possible to find loopholes in its provisions. Great advantage will be taken of definitions—what they mean, whether they are too narrow or too wide. We must not underestimate the opposition that awaits the Bill. But the Government and those of us who support it must be vigilant in our determination to see that it works effectively and without evasion, and is strongly enforced.

The Sex Discrimination Act 1975 made it illegal to treat female job applicants or workers less favourably than males. Bella Keyzer had been a skilled welder during the Second World War but, following her dismissal at the end of the war, her applications to regain her old job were repeatedly turned down. The Act enabled her to take up her old job after 30 years of disappointment. It established the Equal Opportunities Commission (EOC) to promote gender equality, to act against sexual discrimination and to support the practical enactment of the Equal Pay Act. While the EOC did help to bring some cases of discrimination to court, in general it remained difficult and expensive for women to take legal action over sexual discrimination. The Employment Protection Act 1975 implemented a range of measures to improve workers' rights in general, but also made some special provision for women workers. The Act:

- made it illegal to sack women because they were pregnant

- gave women the right to six weeks' paid (and a further 23 weeks' unpaid) maternity leave

- gave women the right to take up their old job after maternity leave if they so wished.

The Employment Act 1978 closed a loophole that allowed firms with fewer than six employees to ignore these rules.

These Acts were a major advance for women in full-time employment, but they failed to address the vulnerability of the large number of women in part-time employment (by 1984, 82 percent of part-time workers were female). The Employment Protection Act 1977 extended the rights enshrined in the 1970 and 1975 Acts to all those working a 16-hour week, or eight hours after five years in the same job. The Part-time Workers (Prevention of Less Favourable Treatment) Regulations 2000 similarly sought to protect all part-time workers but had a particular impact on women because the majority of part-time workers are female. The regulations, enforced by the European Union, meant that employers had to treat part-time workers in the same way as those with full-time contracts.

By 2004, there were virtually no legal barriers to any form of female occupation. Informal barriers, such as sexual harassment, were increasingly challenged under the Sex Discrimination Act and women were beginning to gain more of the most senior jobs in a range of occupations. Between 1975 and 1996, the percentage of working-age women in employment rose from 60 to 71 percent. By 2004, women made up the majority of the British workforce.

Although legislation played an important part in this trend, it is important not to overlook the significance of changes in education and the British economy. The decline in 'men's jobs' in manufacturing since the 1980s and the growth of part-time jobs with flexible working hours in the public sector and service industry have favoured more 'feminine' work.

SOURCE 15

Changes in female employment between 1951 and 1981. From D. Murphy, *Britain 1914–2000* (2000).

	1951	1961	1971	1981
Percentage of workforce that are women	31	33	37	40
Percentage of 20–64-year-old women in workforce	36	42	52	61
Percentage of 20–64-year-old women employed part time	12	26	35	42
Percentage of married women in the workforce	26	35	49	62

KEY TERM

White collar
Someone who performs administrative, managerial or professional work, often in an office. The term was first coined in 1924 and referred to the typical colour of office workers' shirts. Manual labourers are often referred to as blue-collar workers as their overalls were usually blue.

The rise of female education was an important foundation for later gains in the workplace. Without literacy and numeracy, a whole swathe of **white-collar** employment would have remained a male preserve in the 20th century. A lack of university education had been a barrier to middle-class women entering the professions until the late 19th century. It was not until 1878 that the University of London became the first English university to allow women to take degrees. Cambridge and Oxford Universities opened colleges for women in 1869 and 1879, but did not allow them to graduate until 1920 (1948 for Cambridge). In 1910, just 70 girls with an elementary school background went to university in England and Wales (there were about 3,000 women at university altogether, which represented 15 percent of the total student population).The share of university students who were female increased from 15 percent in 1900 to 31 percent in 1970 and 42 percent in 1983. Access to higher education meant that the number of women who were medical students and trainee lawyers went from just a handful in 1900 to 60 percent in 2004. (But it should be noted that less than a quarter of judges and partners in legal firms, and just 28 percent of hospital consultants, were female.) While legal and educational advances promoted female access to the lower ranks of the professions, the practice of breaking through the 'glass ceiling' of promotion to senior roles was still in its early stages in 2004.

ACTIVITY
KNOWLEDGE CHECK

The National Service Act 1941, the Equal Pay Act 1970 and the impact of legislation on women's working lives

1 'As with war-related work between 1914 and 1918, the National Service Act 1941 had only a temporary impact on women's working lives.' How far do you agree with this statement?

2 How useful is Source 14 in understanding the significance of the Equal Pay Act 1970 on women's working lives?

3 Explain the relationship between government legislation and changes in women's working lives.

A Level Exam-Style Question Section C

How far can the Equal Pay Act 1970 be regarded as the key turning point in women's working lives in the period 1882–2004? (20 marks)

Tip
Make sure you offer clear criteria with which to judge the comparative impact of the stated event with other events that you put forward as potential turning points in the working lives of women.

EXTRACT

From Annette Mayer's conclusion to her book *Women in Britain 1900-2000* (2002).

For women, the most significant differences in 2000, compared with 1900, have been the opportunity to participate in politics, to exercise economic independence and to feel that their status within a community, whether at national or local level, is based on respect and recognition of them as men's equals.

EXTRACT

3

From Sue Bruley's book *Women in Britain Since 1900* (1999).

Many of the goals of 19th-century feminism are now accepted features of our society. Sexual segregation has been dramatically reduced. Almost all the formal barriers to gender equality have been removed and women enjoy full citizenship... Whilst agreeing then that some sort of gender convergence has occurred, it is important not to over-emphasise these changes as, fundamentally, we still have a gender system in which men are dominant. At present, what passes for equality is often assimilation of femininity into a male norm.

EXTRACT

4

From Brian Harrison's book *Finding a Role: The United Kingdom 1970–1990* (2010).

It was not fourth-phase feminism that produced the major emancipation involved in the growth of jobs for married women after 1945... The driving force lay in the combination of a tight post-war labour market whose industrial growth was powered by new technologies with little need for heavy labour, and with much need for a weakly unionized workforce flexible on hours and pay... Such gains did not come without losses. Society adjusted only slowly to the quietly gradual disappearance of the leisured woman: her many lubricating social and family roles had often gone unacknowledged in the past because unobtrusive and unpaid, yet her absence was soon felt. There were losses even for women themselves, especially as family and welfare structures adapted so slowly to rapid social change. These included stresses arising from women's enhanced freedom of choice.

THINKING HISTORICALLY Change (8a, b & c) (II)

Judgements about change

If two professionals were asked to track a patient's health over time, one might approach this task by measuring heart rate, weight and cholesterol, while the other professional might assess the patient's mental well-being, relationships and ability to achieve their goals. Both are valid approaches, but result in different reports. What is true in this medical case is true in historical cases. Measuring change in something requires: (a) a concept of what that something is (e.g. 'What is "health"?', 'What is an "economy"?'); (b) judgements about how this thing should be measured; and (c) judgements about what relevant 'markers of change' are (how we distinguish a change from a temporary and insignificant fluctuation).

Historians have differed in their accounts of the extent of change in the working and domestic lives of British women between 1882 and 2004 and debated the key turning points of change during that period.

Look at the short summaries of change in women's lives in Extracts 2, 3 and 4 and answer the following questions.

1 Do all three extracts agree on the extent of change that occurred in Britain between 1882 and 2004?

2 Do all three extracts agree in the chronology of change? (Do they see it happening in the same time periods and at the same pace?)

3 Do all three extracts agree in characterising change as (a) rapid, (b) dramatic and (c) impacting on women as a whole?

4 Do the historians all think the same issues are of equal significance in their account of change (for example, do they all focus on advances in health care)?

5 Generalising from these examples, to what extent do historians' judgements about change depend upon *what* historians decide to look at and *how* they decide to measure change?

SOURCE
16
From Jane Anger's pamphlet *Protection for Women*, printed in 1589. It is unclear who Jane Anger really was, or if this was her real name, but she wrote *Protection* to protest against an earlier pamphlet that insulted women.

The creation of man and woman at the first, he being formed of dross and filthy clay... God making woman of man's flesh, that she might be purer than he, does evidently show that women are more excellent than men. Our bodies are fruitful, whereby the world increases, and our care wonderful, by which man is preserved. From woman sprang man's salvation.

SOURCE
17
From J. Dod and R. Cleaver's *A godlie forme of householde government*, printed in 1612.

The dutie of the Husband is to get goods; and that of the Wife to gather them together and save them. The dutie of the Husband is to travel abroad, to seke living: and the Wives dutie is to keepe the house... The dutie of the Husbande is to be entermeddling and of the wife to be solitary and withdrawn. The dutie of man is to be skilful in talke; and of the wife, to boast of silence.

SOURCE
18
A 17th-century English pamphlet called 'The Good Housewife'.

THINKING HISTORICALLY Cause and consequence (6c)

Connections

Sources 16, 17 and 18 illustrate gender relations in early modern England.

Work in groups or individually and answer the following.

1 Read Source 16. How far might this be seen as similar to feminist views in the 20th century?

2 Read Source 17.

   a) What did Coventry Patmore say about the ideal woman in *The Angel in the House*?

   b) How is this similar to J. Dod and R. Cleaver's advice on ideal roles for husbands and wives?

3 Look at Source 18. How far would a late-Victorian or early 20th-century woman identify with the image of a good housewife presented in this pamphlet?

4 Make a list of other similarities between early modern and late-Victorian views about women and their relationship to men in society and the home. How far would the Victorian interest in early modern history have affected gender roles and stereotypes in the 1880s and 1890s?

5 Why it is important for historians to see these links across time and be able to explain how causal factors can influence situations much later in time?

ACTIVITY
SUMMARY

Changing patterns of women's personal and working lives

1 Create a graph with 'Quality of women's personal lives' on the vertical axis and 'Time' on the horizontal axis. For the years 1882–2004, plot a graph showing the key turning points (positive or negative) that affected women's personal lives. Be careful to reflect the degree of change that each turning point had.

2 Now add to the graph any key dates in government legislation affecting women that are not already on there.

3 Compare the line you drew for the quality of women's personal lives with the dates for government legislation. Does the line seem to be influenced more by legislation or other factors? Explain what this comparison tells you about the relative impact of government legislation on the quality of women's personal lives between 1882 and 2004.

4 Repeat steps 1–3 but with 'Quality of women's working lives' on the vertical axis of the original graph. Again, use the final graph to determine how legislation was the key factor that determined changes in women's working lives.

 WIDER READING

Bruley, S. *Women in Britain Since 1900*, Palgrave Macmillan (1999)

Holdsworth, A. *Out of the Doll's House: The Story of Women in the Twentieth Century*, BBC Books (1988)

Mayer, A. *Women in Britain 1900–2000*, Hodder & Stoughton (2002)

Purvis, J. *Women's History: Britain 1850–1945, An Introduction*, Routledge (2000)

3.2 Changing patterns of family leisure

KEY QUESTIONS

- How far did leisure change in Britain between 1882 and 2004?
- What were the most significant reasons for changes in leisure patterns between 1882 and 2004?

INTRODUCTION

Before the 1980s, leisure was seen as an unimportant area of historical study. However, more recent generations of historians have recognised that leisure is worthy of careful historical analysis. This is not only because Britons spent an increasing amount of time away from work throughout the 20th century, but also because the study of leisure sheds light on a range of important changes, from class and business structures to transport and media communications. Historian Jeffrey Hill (2002) has argued that leisure is more than just a useful window on important changes. He sees it as having played a significant role in forming people's lives and identities. For Hill, leisure activities serve as a key vehicle for individuals' understanding of themselves, their place in society and of powerful social forces in society itself. Just as gender is a socially constructed aspect of identity, so too are a range of other aspects, from nationality to class identity. From the messages imparted by mass media to the perspectives on everyday life afforded by holidays, leisure clearly has a huge potential to shape the way in which people see themselves and the world.

Leisure could simply be thought of as 'not work': something that is defined by time (a period away from work), money (you are not paid to do it, but most people earn the luxury of leisure by working) and usefulness (it is done for inherent pleasure rather than achieving something practical). However, this view of leisure as the opposite of work carries with it some distorting latent values. Most significantly, if work is time occupied by a function that you are paid to perform, then leisure becomes 'free time' where you are able to 'be yourself' and do 'useless' things. These assumptions have guided the thought of the British social elite concerned with the growth of ordinary workers' time away from work. They saw leisure as a problem. What would workers do with increased time away from work? How could workers be guided away from 'useless' activities that might bring out the worst in them, and towards edifying, useful activities?

There are some merits to this 'not work' (time, money and usefulness) approach to the study of leisure in British history. Different amounts of leisure time were available to people depending

1885 – John Kemp Starley launches 'Rover', the first commercially successful safety bicycle

1896 – Guglielmo Marconi patents the radio in Britain
First demonstration of moving images in Britain. First British fiction film made

1912 – British Board of Film Censors (BBFC) established

1922 – British Broadcasting Corporation (BBC) makes its first radio broadcast

1929 – The BBC makes its first television broadcast
Travel Association is established to attract foreign tourists to the UK

1936 – Regular television broadcasts begin from Alexandra Palace, London
First Butlin's holiday camp set up at Skegness

1938 – Holidays with Pay Act
Boeing 307 offers the first pressurised cabin. Frank Whittle's jet engine first demonstrated.

1947 – Transport Act nationalises railways and leads to creation of the British Transport Commission in 1948

| 1885 | 1915 | 1920 | 1925 | 1930 | 1935 | 1940 | 1945 |

on their social class, and this clearly affected their choice of leisure activities. In 1882, very few British people enjoyed significant amounts of time that were not spent either working or sleeping. The 'leisured classes' were the upper class who rarely, if ever, had to work. They either inherited their wealth or made money through rent on their land or, increasingly, profits and dividends from the ownership of commercial or industrial capital. Some middle-class workers, such as civil servants, enjoyed extended holidays. But, Sundays aside, the average industrial worker had fewer than six days off throughout the year. By 2004, a range of laws had been passed that meant most workers were entitled to a certain minimum time away from work, both annual days' leave and time off during the working week. To a large degree this has helped to facilitate the **democratisation** of British leisure pursuits: more people have more time to do a greater range of activities and hobbies.

Another factor that shaped class differences in leisure in late-Victorian Britain was income. It cost a lot more to enjoy polo or the opera than cheaper leisure pursuits such as football or **music hall**. The elite worried that ordinary people would develop tastes for leisure that were beyond their financial means, or that they would become defined by the consumption of cheap commercial products and activities, rather than genuinely 'being themselves'. The elite also tended to be protective of their privileges. Efforts to prevent the lower classes having access to the leisure pursuits of the elite are most evident in the exclusive membership requirements of sports organisations such as golf clubs. Professional cricketers, who were working class, had separate changing rooms from the 'gentlemen' (unpaid) players until the 1960s. Increases in average affluence, especially after the Second World War, and the impact of innovations in entertainment technology, have also democratised leisure to a large degree. Although polo and yachting are still beyond the financial means of most people, far more people of all backgrounds enjoy similar activities such as watching television or cycling.

A little further thought reveals that the mutually exclusive definition of work and leisure is misleading. What about the unemployed? What about housewives who, although not in paid employment, would strongly disagree that they spend their days in a leisurely fashion? What about professional sportsmen and women who spend their working lives doing activities that the vast majority of people look forward to doing after work? The impact of technology has increasingly blurred the boundaries of leisure and work. By 2004, large numbers of office workers were checking social media at work, while many people were dealing with work emails at home during what would once have been leisure time.

Several female historians and sociologists have contributed to a definition of leisure that helps to get around these problems. Margaret Talbot and Eileen Green among others have persuasively argued that the definition of leisure in opposition to work is a strongly male construction. They reject the idea of leisure as necessarily defined by a fixed time, but suggest it is more the quality, or impact on state of mind, of a particular experience. This could include chatting or relaxing rather than actively 'doing something'. Such a definition allows attention to shift away from traditionally male-dominated, communal, public leisure activities towards more private, individual enjoyment of leisure. This has become increasingly important in the study of post-1945 British leisure. Better housing and changes in entertainment technology have contributed to the increasingly domestic nature of leisure.

KEY TERMS

Democratisation
Change that promotes democracy. This is most obvious in relation to electoral systems, but the term can also be applied more generally to non-socially exclusive access to power or influence. In the context of leisure, it also refers to the process by which more people have equal access to a particular hobby or activity, thus reducing the class-specific identity attached to it.

Music hall
These were theatres dedicated to the performance of comedy, popular songs and variety acts. The entertainment acts themselves became collectively known as music hall. Music hall was hugely popular in Britain between 1850 and 1960.

1950 – Horizon Holidays offers the first overseas package holidays, taking students and teachers to camps in Corsica

1963 – Beeching Report (The Reshaping of British Railways) recommends the closure of 2,363 stations and 5,000 miles of track

1973 – Independent Broadcasting Authority Act allows the establishment of commercial radio stations in Britain

BOAC and BEA merge to form British Airways

1985 – Ryanair launched after the USA's 1978 Airline Deregulation Act promotes the growth of European budget airlines

| 1950 | 1960 | 1965 | 1970 | 1975 | 1980 | 1985 | 1990 |

1960 – Civil Aviation (Licensing) Act allows for the growth of non-scheduled flights

1967 – First colour television broadcasts begin

BBC Radio 1 launched and pirate radio banned

1977 – Apple launches the first mass-produced personal computer

1991 – Tim Berners-Lee creates the first website using his invention, the World Wide Web

HOW FAR DID LEISURE CHANGE IN BRITAIN BETWEEN 1882 AND 2004?

Entertainment in the home

The range and extent of entertainment in the home was not only affected by the rise of new technologies but also by the comfort of British houses and the structure of an average household. A lot of working-class (though not middle- or upper-class) accommodation in the 1880s had more in common with the slums of the current developing world than the worst accommodation found in Britain at the start of the 21st century. There was no central heating, so on cold evenings before retreating to bed families had to gather in the one room of the house that was heated by a coal fire. The ash and dust from the coal fire covered the surfaces in that room. There was no flushing toilet and no running water. Chamber pots were used during the night to spare a trip to a communal outdoor privy. There was no separate bathroom and family members would bathe every so often in a metal tub placed in front of the fire. The housing stock was ageing and damp in many slum areas, and drafty conditions made them even more uncomfortable if not unhealthy. With such conditions at home, it is unsurprising that there was little in the way of working-class domestic leisure in late-Victorian Britain. The overwhelming majority of their entertainment was public and communal in nature. This promoted segregation by age and gender in recreation. Working men tended to associate at the pub, women gathered at each other's homes or in the local community, and children played games such as 'hoops and sticks', marbles or 'kick the can' out in the streets. Middle-class families tended to be more private and self-sufficient in their recreation, with reading, musical recitals, parlour games such as 20 questions or tiddlywinks, and even the production of family newspapers, thanks in part to their greater domestic comfort.

The increase in the average size of Victorian families also enabled greater self-sufficiency in domestic entertainment. Working-class households tended to be larger and it was common for older children to help raise and entertain their younger siblings. While it was common for extended families to live together or very close to one another in Victorian Britain, growing rates of divorce, a declining birth rate and larger numbers of old people living by themselves shrunk the average household from 4.6 people in 1901 to 3.0 in 1961 and 2.4 in 1999. The rise of greater commercially generated and technology-based leisure provided a substitute for home-grown entertainment, especially with the rise of radio and television (see pages 59–60).

Local and national government had made efforts to improve housing since the mid-Victorian era. There was a concern that slums promoted crime and disease, and a lot of slum clearance (i.e. demolition) had been undertaken before 1918. A major improvement in urban living standards was achieved by the introduction of mains water and sewerage to homes. As late as 1899, only a quarter of houses in Manchester had flushing toilets compared to 98 percent by 1914. A series of Housing Acts in the early 1920s and 1930s promoted a great deal of better-quality house building. Historian Helen Meller (2003) has drawn attention to the remarkable statistic that 33 percent of all British houses in 1940 had been built since 1918. The New Town Act 1946 set up local corporations to build decent new housing in towns such as Corby in Northamptonshire, Milton Keynes in Buckinghamshire, Skelmersdale in Lancashire, Runcorn in Cheshire and Cwmbran in Monmouthshire. A lack of space in town and city centres also led to the accelerated construction of high-rise flats from the 1960s onwards. These had hot running water and extra living space. As a result of all this building, domestic comfort had dramatically improved by 2004. Central heating rather than open fires was in five percent of homes in 1960, but this increased to 50 percent in 1970 and 84 percent in 1991. With the new homes came not only indoor plumbing and gardens, but also increased demand for domestic goods, such as new furniture, which also helped to make domestic life more comfortable and attractive.

EXTRACT

From Brian Harrison's book, *Seeking a Role: The United Kingdom 1951–70* (2009). Harrison is Emeritus Professor of Modern British History at the University of Oxford and has published many books on British history from the 1790s to the present.

No end seemed in sight to material comfort's advance. By 1970 wall-to-wall carpets, electric blankets, double glazing, and central heating were extending within the home a year-long freedom of movement hitherto available only in the warmer months. One could move about freely instead of continually fending off draughts and huddling close to fires in the home's small heated area, periodically dashing out to a cold bedroom or an outside lavatory... Central heating had penetrated a majority of households by 1977... By the mid-1960s the home with a television had become for almost everyone what it had hitherto been for only a minority: a place comfortable enough and sufficiently stocked with the supermarket's bottled and canned beer to supplant the recreational and communal roles of the pub and cinema. The living room supplanted the bedroom as the room in the house on which the most was spent.

The rise of domestication provided far more opportunities for leisure in the home and for family-based recreation. A 1983 BBC survey found that 72 percent of the British public were at home on an average weekday evening while the percentage at home on a Sunday never fell below 61 percent. Improvements in housing meant that men began to enjoy drinking at home rather than at the pub. Sales of beer from off-licences increased from two percent of total sales in the 1960s to 20 percent in the 1990s. Pubs responded by trying to become more female and family-friendly. As discussed in Chapter 1, the domestic leisure situation is less clear-cut for women. Despite the rise of labour-saving domestic appliances, and the increased willingness of men to contribute to housework since the 1960s, higher standards of cleanliness meant that the amount of time dedicated to housework had not reduced very much. Sociological studies of domestic leisure have noted that men are able to enjoy domestic leisure with less of a sense of distraction than women, who often have a sense that there might be, or even ought to be, something else they could be getting on with at home. For children, the rise in separate bedrooms, a reduction in the accessibility of recreational space in towns and cities, and the impact of new technology have had the greatest impact on changes in their domestic leisure. There was an increasing sense of the importance of family leisure from the 1960s (the notion that a family that plays together stays together).

However, divorce, the rise of dual-earner families (which rose from 50 to 70 percent from 1979 to 1999) and the more solitary nature of computer-based games have served as hurdles to the achievement of this ideal.

Observational domestic leisure

Domestic leisure, aside from rest and relaxation, generally consists of some form of hobby performed in the home or garden. These can be categorised as observational, collection, creative or competition hobbies. Three major hobbies that do not fit neatly into these categories are cooking, gardening and DIY.

There has been great continuity in collection hobbies, with coin, card, stamp and memorabilia collecting appealing to a minority of Britons throughout the period 1882–2004. The rise in average disposable incomes has enabled more people (though still a minority) to indulge in collection hobbies to a greater extent.

There were some important changes in competition hobbies. Ancient board games such as chess and backgammon were more common in middle- and upper-class homes, but became more common in working-class homes following the mass production of cheaper sets. In some conservative and religious homes, card games were associated with gambling and viewed with distaste. However, card games such as cribbage (or 'crib') were highly popular among all classes. Bridge remained more of a middle-class interest, perhaps due to the greater time needed to master the skill of the game rather than just enjoying the fun. Board games grew in popularity as the modern classics familiar to us were invented. Monopoly was first sold commercially in 1935 (based on US game designer Lizzie Magie's 1904 'The Landlord's Game'). Sorry became hugely popular after its launch in 1934. Scrabble sold millions of sets after it was patented in 1948, as did Cluedo (1949), Risk (1959), Trivial Pursuit (1981) and Pictionary (1986).

The most popular observational hobby, before the mass ownership of radios in the 1920s, televisions in the 1950s and personal computers in the 1990s, was reading. Reading boomed in popularity in the last 20 years of the 19th century due to improved rates of literacy that resulted from compulsory elementary education from 1880 onwards. By 1914, 60 percent of the British population lived reasonably close to a public library. As Ross McKibbin (1998) has argued, what British people read was strongly determined by class, sex, and age.

Before the Second World War, women tended to enjoy the semi-realistic romantic fiction of the type produced by Mills and Boon (founded in 1908 with over 450 titles by 1939) or the more sensationalist 'erotic bloods', charged with scandal, revenge, jealousy and often murder. The erotic bloods carried on the tradition of the Victorian and Edwardian 'penny dreadfuls', which were cheap, sensationalist novels. Men tended to read crime and gang-related novels, whose stories lacked the personal and sexual relationships, or sports, hobby and technical magazines (there were 250 such magazine titles by 1950). Men and women alike were avid readers of newspapers. Boys and girls generally read highly gender-specific comics and magazines, with boys reading comics such as Adventure or The Wizard (1922–63 and 1970–78), and girls reading magazines such as Schoolgirl's Own (1921–36)

and The Schoolgirl (1922–40). One popular title that bucked this trend was the Children's Newspaper (1919–65), which aimed to keep both boys and girls abreast of the latest international and scientific news. Enid Blyton's highly popular novels from the 1940s, such as the Famous Five and Secret Seven series, also appealed to both boys and girls. However, strong gendering continued throughout the 20th century with Eagle (1950–69 and 1982–94), whose 'pilot of the future' Dan Dare was particularly popular with readers. There were also The Beano (1938–) and The Dandy (1937–2012) aimed at boys, and Girl (1951–64), Jackie (1964–93) and Bunty (1958–2001) aimed at girls. Although reading remained a popular hobby, time spent reading reduced due to the rise of radio, television and computer-based leisure.

Cooking, gardening and DIY

While more creative handicrafts such as knitting and sewing were traditionally seen as feminine activities, craft-based hobbies were promoted in magazines and newspaper columns as male activities in the late 19th and early 20th century. They were strongly approved of by social superiors, who saw the pursuit of woodwork, metalwork or general 'home improvements' as a way for the working man to retain personal fulfilment in the age of deskilled mass production. The term 'DIY' (do it yourself) had been used before the First World War, but only came into common usage in the 1950s. It was popularised as a way for men to avoid domestic **emasculation** and to fulfil the idealised role of the husband within the family. The rise of home ownership from 29 percent in 1950 to over 50 percent in 1970 fuelled demand for DIY materials. A 1970 survey of leisure activities listed DIY as the sixth most popular activity with 53 percent of those surveyed listing it as a regular hobby. In March 1969, Richard Block and David Quayle opened a hardware store in Southampton that became the first B&Q. By 2004, there were more than 300 B&Q stores across the country.

KEY TERM

Emasculation
The process by which a man is deprived of his male role or identity. Fears arose during the Second World War that men would feel emasculated by the rise of female workers in traditionally male industries.

Cooking was designated a female responsibility in the vast majority of British homes throughout the period 1882–2004. For many women during these years, cooking for the family was a domestic chore rather than a leisure activity. Improvements in cooking appliances helped to make cookery more of a leisure activity that women took pride in. These improvements included the increase of gas and electric cookers to replace coal-fuelled grates in the 1950s. There was also the rise of best-selling cookbooks with novel recipes. Since the early 1970s, Delia Smith has produced a large number of cookbooks and television shows that have contributed to this growth in cooking as a domestic leisure activity. Foreign holidays had an impact on the range of foodstuffs and recipes that featured in a typical diet. Trips to the continent promoted a taste for pasta, pizza and wine. In a similar way to DIY for men, cooking was promoted as a key way for women to fulfil the idealised role of the good wife and mother. More men also began to cook in the last two decades of the 20th century, a trend perhaps encouraged by the celebrity of chefs such as Keith Floyd and Gary Rhodes.

In a 1970 survey of leisure activities, gardening was second only to television viewing in popularity, with 64 percent of those surveyed listing it as a regular pastime. *Gardeners' Question Time*, first broadcast in 1947, catered for this mass hobby and inspired a wide range of subsequent radio and television programmes dedicated to gardening.

ACTIVITY
KNOWLEDGE CHECK

Entertainment in the home, 1882-2004

1 Summarise the key developments that have enabled greater domestic leisure.

2 Give examples of important observational domestic leisure (excluding television).

3 For what reasons did cooking, gardening and DIY gain in popularity as leisure activities in the 20th century?

4 How useful is Extract 1 in understanding changes in domestic leisure between 1882 and 2004?

Changes in excursions and holidays

The key changes hinted at in the introduction to this chapter are clearly demonstrated by the developments that took place in British holidays and excursions. Holidays became longer and involved more travel as there was more time available for them. More people enjoyed holidays due to greater average affluence. Also, possibly related to increased affluence, holidays became more individualistic rather than communal in nature. The extent to which holidays became less defined by, or revealing of, class is disputed. Despite these changes, there are clear continuities in the way British people have thought about holidays and relaxed their normal standards of behaviour when on holiday.

The origins of the modern holiday

The origin of modern holidays helps to explain the huge class differences in this aspect of British leisure in 1882. For the elite 'leisured classes', the first excursions for pleasure and self-improvement were 'grand tours' to the major cultural landmarks of continental Europe, principally found in France and Italy. A few 17th-century pioneers set out itineraries, but the tours really flourished in the 18th century The overwhelmingly young, aristocratic gentlemen on such a tour would be issued with letters of introduction to European nobility to facilitate their travel. The grand tours tailed off in the second half of the 19th century, due largely to the rise of the railway, which enabled those of a slightly lower social standing to explore the continent. In the 19th century, the upper classes also began to visit natural wonders and spa towns on the continent, thought to be conducive to good health. This was a reaction to the dirt and hectic pace of life in industrial urban Britain. Clean air and water were thought to restore the body, while inspirational vistas helped to calm the mind. The middle classes copied them and began to visit British equivalents

such as the Lake District and the spas in Bath and Harrogate. It was this desire for bracing, fresh air that led to the growth of seaside holidays for the well-off in the first half of the 19th century. The growth of railway and then coach transport made such excursions increasingly possible for a growing number of working-class Britons in the second half of the 19th century.

For the ordinary masses, before the advent of the day trip to the seaside, holidays did not usually mean travel. In medieval times, Holy Days were usually celebrations of saints' days. They were free from labour, and often involved a feast, fair or carnival. These local fairs and **wakes weeks** survived through custom and tradition even when many saints' days were no longer recognised as holidays by statute. However, the number of days given over to such celebrations was greatly reduced with the shift from an agrarian to an industrial economy in the 18th and 19th centuries. The Bank Holidays Act 1871 had increased the number of public holidays from four to six. So by 1882 there were just six public holidays including Good Friday and Christmas Day. Other holidays were at the discretion of employers. Apart from in areas where a week's break had been long established, such as the Lancashire Wakes Week or Fair Holidays in Glasgow, holidays did not usually extend to more than the odd day. Therefore, in the majority of working-class minds at the end of the 19th century, a holiday simply meant a break from work rather than also having the more modern connotations of travel and leisure.

KEY TERM

Wakes week
This regular summer holiday, especially common in the North of England, owed its origins to the celebration of the local church's patron saint's day. The night of prayer for the saint was called a 'wake' as people stayed up late to hold a vigil. Different industrial towns agreed to take their holiday week at different times between June and September. The practice died out in the 1990s largely as a result of standardised school holidays that were implemented by the Education Reform Act 1988.

Holidays before the Holidays with Pay Act 1938

There were two significant campaigns to reduce working hours that arose in the 19th century: the Eight-Hour Day movement and the Saturday Half Day campaign. While the Eight-Hour Day movement was bitterly resisted by employers, the Saturday Half Day campaign was gradually accepted due to the impact of the Factory Act 1850 that banned women and children from working in factories after 2 p.m. on a Saturday. As factory work could not be efficiently continued without these workers, men also benefited from the half day. This was voluntary on the part of employers and did not apply to non-factory workers. However, the half day came to be seen as of benefit to worker productivity and overall profitability. The Saturday half day made it possible for workers to cycle out into surrounding countryside, or even take a day trip to the seaside. Later campaigns for increased holidays with pay were a direct descendant of this first successful campaign for time away from work.

There had been signs before 1938 that more Britons wanted time away from home and work in the fresh air of the countryside. A number of clubs and societies were founded that helped to organise holidays for their members. The Co-operative Holidays Association, the Holiday Fellowship and the Workers' Travel Association all helped their members to save up and get to local resorts. The Youth Hostel Association, founded in 1929, had 80,000 members by 1939. The Ramblers Association (1935) also saw rapid increases in membership in the 1930s. A 'mass trespass' in Derbyshire in 1932 made national news and helped to inspire Britons to reclaim the land from private landowners for communal use. The movement gathered enough momentum to inspire the 1949 National Parks legislation, which set out the right to ramble along public footpaths across previously private land.

SOURCE 1

From the Annual Report of the Workers' Travel Association published in 1924.

Travel is the best means of achieving mutual understanding between the workers of all countries. Such understanding is only possible by mutual contact, by interchange of visits, by the study of languages and by an interest in the history, literature, art and social movements of other countries. [Our aim is] to provide for the healthy enjoyment of leisure; to encourage love of the open air; to promote social and international friendship; and to organise holidaymaking and other activities with these objects.

Before the 1950s there was no officially recognised system for measuring the number of British holidaymakers. Early pioneers of tourism studies based their estimates of travel to and from the UK on official migration statistics. In his 1933 study *The Tourist Movement*, Frederick Ogilvie saw 1929 as the peak year for travel with 692,000 foreigners holidaying in Britain and just over one million Britons going abroad. The vast majority of holidays of four days or more were taken within Britain, but the gap between foreign holidays and those taken in Britain closed rapidly in the 1990s. In his 1947 study *The Englishman's Holiday: a Social History*, John Pimlott estimated that the number of Britons who had enjoyed a week-long holiday had doubled from 7.5 million in 1927 to 15 million in 1937 (one-third of the population; several times this number had undertaken day trips to local resorts and attractions). Pimlott argued that a range of changes had brought about this expansion, from advances in transport (see pages 51–55) to the role of legislation, such as the Health Resorts and Watering Places Act 1921 that enabled local authorities to use locally raised taxes to pay for holiday advertisements.

The seaside visit, which comprised the vast majority of holidays undertaken by Britons between the wars, would have been very familiar to their parents' and grandparents' generation. Only the length of the trip and the numbers who went might have surprised them. As historian Edward Royale (1988) has highlighted, holiday locations within the UK were class-based. The better-off went to Lytham St Annes rather than Blackpool, Tynemouth not Whitley Bay, Llandudno not Rhyl, or Bournemouth not Margate. Even within certain resorts such as Scarborough, the upper and working classes used different parts of the town to enjoy the seaside. Sue Farrant has explained this hierarchy of resorts (with a special focus on resorts in Sussex) by drawing attention to the degree of investment and development by local authorities, differences in private investment in leisure facilities, the extent to which residential accommodation increased at the expense of more working-class boarding houses, and even the existence of private schools in particular resorts. By the 1880s, Brighton already boasted an ice-skating rink, a concert hall, several music hall theatres, and the Palace Pier. In 1911, it became the first local resort to establish a cinema with the Academy Picture Palace. Brighton's popularity grew, with many working-class Londoners taking advantage of rail links to the south coast. The Sunny South Special train service from Liverpool via Manchester and Birmingham added to the crowds at Brighton. Neighbouring Hove, in contrast, became more residential and self-consciously aimed to preserve its more exclusive social status. Between 1921 and 1923, Blackpool invested £1.5 million in its seven miles of promenade. By the mid-1930s the pleasure beach, with its tower and illuminations, drew over seven million working-class visitors each year.

The rise of the holiday camp and the first Butlin's (1936)

The rise of the holiday camp enabled more people to afford overnight trips to the seaside and other locations of natural beauty. The vast majority of the 200 camps catering for 30,000 visitors per week that had been created by 1939 were rather basic affairs. They did, however, enable many poorer families (those on less than £4 per week) to go away for the first time. Such camps remained popular throughout the Second World War and into the 1950s. However, 1936 saw the launch of the more luxurious commercial holiday camp that set a new bar for quality in this sector of the holiday industry. That year William Butlin launched his first camp in Skegness. His £100,000 investment in quality, all-inclusive dining and entertainment immediately attracted 100,000 visitors in each of the next three summers. The camp was used as troop barracks for the duration of the Second World War.

At £3 10 shillings for the week, his all-inclusive holidays were too expensive for many working-class families, and the majority of pre-war guests were middle class. In many ways, the camps fulfilled notions of the upper-class life they could only aspire towards: three cooked meals a day served by uniformed waiters, all-day child care to enable a truly leisurely time, access to a swimming pool, tennis courts and a host of entertainment. Butlin's camps also clearly tapped into a communal sense of fun and enjoyment that remained highly popular during and after the Second World War. The shared meals, singalongs and competitions such as tug of war and knobbly knees contests helped to create a friendly community of like-minded holidaymakers. The ability of the camp to host all of this entertainment under canvas roofs also helped to ensure a fun week despite the unpredictable nature of the British summer weather.

A 1950s poster advertising a Butlin's holiday camp.

The 1938 Holidays with Pay Act

Pressure from trade unions was a key reason for the passage of the Holidays with Pay Act 1938. The Trades Union Congress (TUC) had first passed a resolution calling for such legislation in 1911. It argued that many middle-class employees enjoyed paid leave and it was a clear social injustice that the same benefits did not apply to the working classes. Its lobbying of the Labour Party led to two bills that were defeated in parliament in 1925 and 1929 before the 1938 Act was finally passed. In addition to union pressure, a number of developments since 1929 help to explain the successful passage of the Act nine years later. The onset of the **Great Depression** led to a more sympathetic assessment of the working class by the elite. It became clear to the elite that idleness was not inherently desirable for workers, and it was also noted how ordinary people did not use the expanse of unoccupied time for socially corrosive activities such as excessive drinking or gambling. A degree of trust in workers was earned during those hard years and this helps to explain the reversal of fortune for paid holidays legislation. Indeed, many workers had gained annual paid holidays from their employees even before legislation made the phased introduction of such an arrangement compulsory. *The New Survey of London Life and Labour* noted in 1935 that more than half of the working population of London had annual paid holiday.

It also helped that the British economy looked to be in a healthier position in 1938 than in 1929. It was clear that industry could support the expense of paid holidays on a sustainable basis. A further development came from abroad. The International Labour Organisation, a branch of the **League of Nations** based in Geneva, passed a Convention on Holidays in 1936. This stated that workers should be entitled to six days of annual paid leave, not including public holidays or sick leave. The Convention was ratified by 54 countries (although 20 already had such legislation). Renewed union lobbying in light of the Convention led Prime Minister Stanley Baldwin to appoint a committee of enquiry chaired by Lord Amulree in 1937. His report was wholly sympathetic to union demands but raised concerns about the ability of resorts to cater for ever greater numbers of holidaymakers. The Holidays with Pay Act was an important step in the growth of leisure time. By 1952, 66 percent of workers had three weeks' paid annual leave. The adoption of the European Union Working Time Directive in 1998 meant that employers should offer workers four weeks' paid holiday each year.

KEY TERM

League of Nations
This was established after the First World War to promote international harmony and resolve disputes through discussion rather than violence. It was the forerunner of the modern United Nations, but it had far fewer members (most crucially the USA was never a member) and no armed force of its own.

SOURCE

3 From Lord Amulree's speech on Industrial Holidays to the Royal Society of Arts on 2 November 1938. A transcript of the speech was published in the Society's journal nine days later. Lord Amulree had trained as a barrister before becoming a Labour peer in 1929.

The Industrial Welfare Society, which speaks with authority on this subject… is of the opinion that when account is taken of the enormous annual loss caused to industry by sickness and voluntary absences, which are often due to physical and nervous strain, it may well be that holidays, with their beneficial effect on health, will result in gains that offset the immediate cost of the holidays to the employer.

It would be wrong, however, to pronounce in favour of or against holidays simply by reference to their effect on production… Too much mischief has been done in the past by treating workpeople simply as productive units, instead of as human beings. It is gratifying therefore to note that in the evidence tendered to the Departmental Committee by or on behalf of employers there was a recognition that the case for holidays rested on the broad ground of social justice… Not only was the holiday itself a good thing, with its opportunities of fresh air and exercise and mental relaxation, but it afforded something to look back upon and something to look forward to, each year, and so gave point and direction to what might otherwise have seemed an aimless existence…

The granting of holidays with pay to considerably larger numbers of persons than at present will raise other problems. Even now, during the holiday season, trains, coaches and excursion steamers are so overcrowded that travel, instead of being an exhilaration, becomes an exhaustion even to the point of physical injury. And when the destination is reached the overcrowding of lodgings and boarding houses is often so serious that a similar state of affairs elsewhere would be deemed insanitary [*sic*]. The difficulties of catering and the supply of public necessities are obvious to anyone who visits a popular seaside resort during the first weeks of August…

If we look into our own experience we shall realise how important our holidays and holiday experiences have been in forming the mental background against which we view life… Among the arts, which it is the aim of the Society to promote, we must not forget the art of living.

The impact of the Second World War on excursions and holidays

War reduced but did not entirely prevent British holidaymaking between 1939 and 1945. A huge swathe of coastline, from East Anglia to Land's End in Cornwall, was declared to be off limits to non-residents. This was to ensure security for preparations against a German invasion, which included the fortification and laying of mines on several southern beaches. As with Butlin's camps, several tourist attractions were requisitioned for military use. The government used a number of methods to prevent travel for pleasure to free up roads and railway for military and supply purposes. Petrol rationing between 1942 and 1950 reduced, but did not entirely prevent, the use of cars for holidays. A range of posters aimed to dissuade potential holidaymakers (see Source 4), and orders were given to prevent railway companies putting on additional trains at peak holiday times. The latter two measures were largely ineffective. Writer Vera Brittain observed in 1941 that the British were obviously determined to take a holiday no matter what the immediate circumstances were. Wakes Week in Lancashire (where most factory workers went to Blackpool) and 'Trip' week (to Weston-super-Mare) in Swindon continued throughout the war. The government tried, with some success, to promote 'Holidays at Home' in 1941–42, but it largely accepted that holidays *near* home were the best way to maintain worker morale and productivity. Some wartime developments inadvertently promoted the spread of holiday camps after 1945. The creation of prisoner of war camps, military barracks and workers' hostels provided the infrastructure for this post-war expansion.

EXTRACT

From Victor Middleton's *British Tourism: the remarkable story of growth*, published in 2005. Middleton had worked for the British Tourist Authority before becoming a Visiting Professor at Oxford Brookes University and the University of Central Lancashire. He is a founder fellow and former chairman of the UK Tourism Society.

Holiday camps flourished after the war... In a far-sighted deal when the war started, Butlin not only leased his existing two camps to the Navy for wartime purposes, but arranged for the other sites to be built for wartime use. These sites were designed to his overall specification, so that they were suitable for conversion to future holiday use and he leased them on the understanding that he could buy them back at the end of the war for 60 per cent of cost price... As a result he was in business very soon after the war with fully built operational holiday centres.

SOURCE

A poster produced by the Railway Executive Committee in 1941.

Holidays from the 1950s: the rise of the foreign package holiday

The most significant change in British holidaymaking since the Second World War has been the rise of the foreign package holiday, with the numbers of Britons taking a foreign holiday increasing dramatically from the 1970s onwards. One important consequence of this change was that domestic tourism, including holiday camps and seaside holidays, began to suffer from the added competition for business. Other significant impacts include changes in the British diet and sense of national identity.

SOURCE 5

The estimated number of holidays taken by the British population in Britain and abroad from 1951 to 2003. From Victor Middleton's *British Tourism: the remarkable story of growth*, published in 2005, figures published by the British National Travel Survey. All British holidays are four nights or more, but foreign holidays includes shorter trips.

	Britain (millions)	Abroad (millions)	Total (millions)
1951	25.00	1.50	26.50
1955	25.00	2.00	27.00
1960	31.50	3.50	35.00
1966	31.00	5.00	36.00
1971	34.00	7.25	41.25
1976	37.50	7.25	44.25
1981	36.50	13.25	49.75
1986	31.50	17.50	49.00
1991	34.00	20.00	54.00
1995	33.00	26.00	59.00
2000	28.00	30.50	58.50
2003	25.00	32.50	57.50

A number of factors account for this dramatic shift in holidaymaking. One key change was the growth of air travel (see page 54). The number of passengers on international flights from the UK increased from 887,000 in 1951 to just under 15 million in 1979. Another factor was the end of currency restrictions. Britons had only been allowed to take £50 on foreign holidays between 1966 and 1970. This was a rather desperate bid by the government to ease a **balance of payments** deficit. As the debate in the House of Commons to abolish the currency restriction suggests (Source 6), the limit on spending abroad fuelled the rise of package holidays where the cost of all flights, meals and accommodation were known before leaving the UK. There were restrictions on air routes as governments preferred 'scheduled flights' to charter flights because they flew at set times known in advance and were therefore easier to monitor. These restrictions also favoured the rise of package tour operators. Around 60 percent of those who took foreign holidays used tour companies such as Thompson Holiday Group, Clarksons, Horizon Travel, Global and Cosmos. Entrepreneur Vladimir Raitz's Horizon Travel was an early pioneer of package holidays. In 1950, he began offering all-inclusive trips for £32 10 shillings (about £850 in 2016) to a campsite in Calvi, Corsica to students and teachers (wartime restrictions that prevented members of the public travelling abroad were in force until 1952, but exceptions were made for educational purposes). At that time, a return flight alone to Nice in the south of France cost £70. Package holidays grew rapidly in popularity and within four years Horizon was offering similar trips to Majorca, Sardinia, Malaga and the Costa Brava. By 1969, six million Britons enjoyed holidays abroad. Whereas in 1971 only a third of Britons had been on a foreign holiday, by 1979 just over a third had not. Resorts such as Benidorm and Torremolinos in Spain became the most popular foreign destinations. British people were nervous of foreign travel and such resorts offered the familiar foods and comforts of home with far better weather.

As a result of caravanning (see page 53) and foreign holidays, the traditional British seaside holiday declined in popularity and holiday camps began to suffer by the mid-1960s. The share of holidays taken in domestic holiday camps was less than four percent, despite a £300,000 government campaign to promote 'holidays at home' in the late 1960s. The campaign was not helped by a shortage of decent hotels, something the government sought to address with the Development of Tourism Act 1969. The Act established the British Tourist Authority and worked with local tourist boards to double the quantity of international-class accommodation by 1973.

KEY TERM

Balance of payments
This is the gap between the total value of imports (goods coming into a country) and exports (goods leaving a country). If the value of exports exceeds imports then there is a balance of payments surplus; if the value of imports exceeds exports then there is a balance of payments deficit. Governments worry if the deficit is very large year after year. Loss of foreign currency reserves (used to buy imports) means they run the risk of not being able to pay existing debts. A lack of demand for sterling (used to buy British exports) causes the currency to fall in value.

SOURCE 6

From speeches made in the House of Commons during discussion of a motion to abolish the £50 foreign travel allowance limit on 30 June 1969.

Mr Kenneth Lewis MP: What this £50 is doing is to turn us into a nation of international trippers, because most people now, if they want to go abroad, have to go on a package tour, whether they like it or not. A large number of people, not only middle-class or rich people, but also ordinary chaps working in the docks in Liverpool, like to think that they can go abroad by themselves. They like to book in at a hotel, and not to have to take part in a package tour with a lot of other people, perhaps people whom they see day by day... They cannot do this because the £50 does not stretch to meeting the individual room charges of hoteliers compared with the charges hoteliers provide for people booking in groups of 30 or 40.

Mr Hector Hughes MP: I oppose this wrong-headed Motion on several grounds... First, we need the money at home. Secondly, our holiday camps need holiday workers and holiday makers. Thirdly, our hotels, both at the seaside and in the country, need visitors and money... We live in particular circumstances when such money as we have in Britain should be retained. The time may come when the authors of the Motion will have their way and we may pour money into foreign countries. Where are we to go? To dictatorships? To Spain? To Greece? No; I say we should keep our money at home and enjoy the advantages and the fruits of Britain. It is old-fashioned nonsense to say that we must go abroad for our education. We have at home all that we want. The other evening on television I had the advantage of seeing pictures of five countries. In our modern libraries there are books of a descriptive character. We have every advantage at home without pouring our money abroad into foreign countries. Butlins and other holiday camps offer not only education but enjoyment to people who want to stay at home.

Experience of foreign travel had some important effects on the British. In part, it might help to explain a decisive 'yes' vote in the 1975 referendum to stay in the European Economic Community. It also changed culinary tastes dramatically. Wine consumption more than doubled in the 1960s and again in the 1970s (up from 2.3 bottles per person per year to 12.6 bottles). Continental lager made up only three percent of the British beer market in 1960; by 1970 almost all pubs offered lagers such as Skol and Carling Black Label. Greek and Italian restaurants became popular, with exotic ingredients such as garlic, aubergine and fresh pasta. It would have been impossible to fool a British audience in 1977 into believing that spaghetti grew on trees, as an April Fool's report on *Panorama* did in 1957.

SOURCE 7

A popular TV comedy sketch from *Monty Python's Flying Circus* in 1972. Watney's Red Barrel was a popular bitter.

I've been on package tours several times and I'm fed up with being carted around in buses surrounded by sweaty mindless oafs from Kettering and Coventry in their cloth caps and their cardigans and their transistor radios and their 'Sunday Mirrors', complaining about the tea, 'Oh they don't make it properly here do they not like at home'. And then some typists from Birmingham with diarrhoea and flabby white legs saying 'Food's very greasy but we have managed to find this marvellous little place where you can even get Watney's Red Barrel and cheese and onion crisps.'

KEY TERM

Deregulation
This is the process by which rules and regulations governing trade and commerce are relaxed. The policy is most associated with the governments of Prime Minister Margaret Thatcher: in October 1979, all rules on currency exchanges were abolished.

Despite the collapse of several package tour operators in the mid-1970s, most notably Clarkson's in 1974 (the same year it had bought Horizon Travel), the sector recovered and continued to expand throughout the 1980s and 1990s. The 1990 EU Package Holiday Travel Directive offered financial protection and repatriation services to customers. This helped to avoid the loss of consumer confidence that resulted when 40,000 holidaymakers were stranded abroad (and many more lost their money without ever leaving the UK) following the mid-1970s tour operator collapses. By 2004, 46 percent of 43 million foreign holidays taken by Britons were taken with package tour operators. This represents a decline in the share of all foreign holidays from its peak of 56 percent (of 27 million foreign holidays) in 1994. The decline was largely due to the **deregulation** of air travel within the European Union in 1997. Cheaper flights offered by companies such as Ryanair (founded in 1985) and Easyjet (founded in 1995) meant more Britons could plan their own affordable holidays away from the typical package tour destinations.

Changes in excursions and holidays, 1884–2004

1 Summarise the main differences between holidays taken by Britons in 1884 and those taken in 2004.

2 Which decade would you argue saw the greatest change in British holidaymaking? Explain your answer.

3 Which source offers the more valuable evidence about changes in British holidaymaking: Source 3 or Source 6? Explain your answer.

WHAT WERE THE MOST SIGNIFICANT REASONS FOR CHANGES IN LEISURE PATTERNS BETWEEN 1882 AND 2004?

How far did changes in modes of transport affect British leisure?

The safety bicycle from the late 1880s

The safety bicycle was so named because its shape enabled the rider to place both feet on the floor while sitting on the saddle. This was far safer than the penny-farthing, where the rider had to step down from a considerable height when stopping. With the exception of recumbent bicycles (that are ridden in a reclined position), the safety bicycle was the prototype for all modern bicycles. It was based on designs that dated back to the 1860s, but the term was not coined until Harry John Lawson used the word 'safety' to describe his bicycle design in 1876. The first design sold in large numbers was the Rover, launched in 1885 by John Kemp Starley (whose company, renamed after its most successful model, went on to produce cars in the 20th century). It was lighter and cheaper than the tricycle, which was the other safer alternative to the penny-farthing. The fact that braking and stopping became easier, and the saddle was much easier to get on, made the safety bicycle far more popular than previous designs, especially with women. The 'step through' design from 1889 made it even easier for women in long skirts to ride a bicycle without the inconvenience or possible indignity of having to raise one leg over a waist-high bike frame. These advances in design fuelled the bike boom of the 1890s.

SOURCE

An advert for the Rover safety bicycle from 1889.

The bicycle, purchased second-hand or through hire purchase, enabled many working-class men to commute to and from work far more quickly than on foot. Middle-class men were far more likely to use bicycles to escape industrial towns and cities and enjoy the surrounding countryside (working-class men tended to see the countryside as impoverished rather than beautiful). Such men were also drawn to cycling clubs: by 1936 there were around 3,500 cycle clubs, the largest of which were the Cyclists' Touring Club and the National Cyclists' Union, with over 60,000 members. These clubs were sometimes overtly linked to the notion of 'self-improvement'. The National Clarion Cycling Club was founded in 1895 from five local clubs and took its name from a Socialist newspaper, *The Clarion*. It saw itself as spreading the virtues of socialist education and self-help as well as fresh air and fitness. Cycling groups became a familiar sight in the countryside in the 1920s and 1930s, something noted by author J.B. Priestly during one section of his 'English Journey' near Bradford in 1934.

The bike boom became the central focus of a broader debate on the legitimacy of sport for women and the types of sports clothing that could be worn to preserve female decency. Several magazines devoted a good deal of space to the argument between proponents of 'rational dress' for sport and those who saw sport as the enemy of femininity. As Elizabeth Linton argued in an 1896 edition of *Lady's Realm*, sport removed 'the faintest remnant of that sweet spirit of allurement which, conscious or unconscious, is woman's supreme attraction. Chief of all dangers attending this new development of feminine freedom is the intoxication which comes with unfettered liberty'. The *Rational Dress Society's Gazette* noted the hostility shown towards female cyclists as their confidence, strength and speed was associated with a loss of respectability and notions of 'free love'. Concerns were also raised about the dangers faced by lone female cyclists and even the risk of gynaecological damage caused to women by cycling. The bike boom drew a good deal of popular attention to female cyclists, but lower female wages meant that there were far more male cyclists until well into the 20th century. In a bid to protest against the spread of cycling on a Sunday, the Lord's Day Observation Society (founded in 1831 to campaign for activity on Sundays to be to restricted to prayer and churchgoing) recorded 125 female and 1,797 male cyclists ride past their base in Croydon one morning in 1904.

Increasing car ownership from the 1920s

The increase in car ownership in Britain has profoundly changed the life of its citizens. It has not only affected where they live and work, but it has moulded their leisure pursuits and, some historians claim, even the way they perceive themselves. Car ownership followed the trend of other consumer durables. It gradually trickled down from upper to middle classes between the wars and then exploded into a mass market in the 25 years after the end of austerity in the early 1950s. In 1904, there were only 9,000 private cars registered in Britain. Cars were prohibitively expensive and mechanically unreliable. Car ownership increased rapidly after the First World War, from 100,000 in 1919 to two million in 1939. Cheaper, smaller cars such as the Austin Seven launched in 1922 meant that motoring became affordable for the middle class. The average price of a car, adjusted for inflation, fell from £259 in 1924 to £130 in 1938. By 1939, around 1.4 million jobs were dependent on the motor industry. Motorists also benefited from large state subsidies for road transport. The Ministry of Transport (established in 1919) spent far more on road improvements than was collected in road tax until the mid-1930s. There were few restrictions on early motorists, and that also helped to popularise cars. Before the introduction of driving tests in 1934, anyone physically fit over the age of 17 was allowed to drive. A speed limit of 20 miles an hour was abolished in 1930. While a limit of 30 mph was introduced in built-up areas in 1934, some country roads had no speed limits until 1965. The trend for increased car ownership accelerated after the Second World War. The end of petrol rationing, more efficient production techniques and greater average incomes led car ownership to more than double between 1960 and 1970 from 5,650,000 to 11,802,000. Although motoring boomed as a leisure activity in and of itself, it remained an overwhelmingly male activity until late in the 20th century: in 1933, only 12 percent of all private driving licences were held by women.
By 1975–76, only 29 percent of women compared to 69 percent of men held driving licences. The increase in car ownership not only enabled trips for leisure outside the range or hours of public transport, it had a large impact on holidaymaking, especially the rise of caravan holidays in the 1960s and 1970s.

SOURCE
9
The number of motor vehicles registered in the UK, 1909–2004. Figures from the Department of Transport.

Year	Private cars	Motor cycles, scooters and mopeds	Public transport	Other types of vehicle including lorries	Total number of vehicles
1909	53,000	36,000	24,000	30,000	143,000
1920	187,000	228,000	75,000	101,000	591,000
1930	1,056,000	712,000	101,000	403,000	2,272,000
1939	2,034,000	418,000	90,000	606,000	3,148,000
1946	1,770,000	449,000	105,000	783,000	3,107,000
1954	2,733,000	977,000	97,000	1,443,000	5,250,000
1964	7,190,000	1,534,000	86,000	2,366,000	11,176,000
1974	11,917,000	918,000	96,000	2,711,000	15,642,000
1984	16,055,000	1,225,000	116,000	3,369,000	20,765,000
1994	20,479,000	630,000	107,000	4,015,000	25,231,000
2004	25,753,800	1,059,900	99,900	5,345,300	32,258,900

Private motorists were not the only road users to benefit from road improvements. Between 1929 and 1935, sales of bicycles increased from six to ten million, far outstripping the growth in car sales. Before the Second World War, buses were more important to the working class – they enabled people to commute from suburbs to their place of work and to enjoy day trips to the seaside. The number of passenger miles travelled by bus increased from 3.5 million in 1920 to 19 million in 1938. Buses overtook trams in passenger miles in 1932. By 1939, 37 million passengers were carried on long-distance bus routes. The same year, the Tour Operators Conference was launched to promote the vertically integrated service (transport, accommodation and sometimes meals and entertainment) offered by bus companies.

The growth of travel by bus and car at the expense of train and tram led to a shift in settlement. Houses and factories began to be built along roads rather than clustered around the urban nucleus of the train station. More people were able to live further out in suburbs rather than in the centre of towns. The divide between town and country began to blur as more people took advantage of improvements in transport to move from town centres to outlying areas. The populations of Blackburn, Bolton, Gateshead, Halifax, Manchester, Oldham, Salford, South Shields and Wigan all declined between 1911 and 1951.

Motoring also made weekend excursions to the surrounding countryside possible and opened up more remote parts of the UK to holidaymakers. Caravanning became so popular that the Caravan Sites and Control of Development Act 1960 had to be passed to regulate the location, planning and use of caravan sites. By the end of the 1970s, almost half the UK population had been on a caravan holiday. The caravan meant that people were able to visit parts of Britain such as Devon, Cornwall and Carmarthenshire, which as holiday destinations had previously been restricted to the wealthy few with second homes.

Car ownership impacted upon consumer habits as people could load up on greater quantities of groceries and other items in one big weekly shop. The rise of refrigerator ownership and a greater proportion of female employment also accelerated this trend.

The first purpose-built multi-storey car park opened in Blackpool in 1939. The increase in urban congestion in the 1960s led to the growth of out-of-town supermarkets, the first of which opened in Nottinghamshire in 1964 with a thousand car-parking spaces. It became highly successful under the ownership of Asda and spawned hundreds of imitators across the country. It could be argued that weekend shopping became something of a leisure activity in its own right, with increasingly affluent Britons able to browse for luxuries rather than spend the majority of their income on rent, utility bills and food.

The growth of air travel from the 1950s

Aircraft developed quickly after the first heavier-than-air flight on 17 December 1903. That day, Orville and Wilbur Wright flew 260 metres at Kitty Hawk, North Carolina in the USA. Planes captured British and worldwide attention in July 1909 when Louis Blériot became the first man to fly across the English Channel. He won a £1,000 prize from the *Daily Mail* for his efforts.

The First World War saw a rapid improvement in the design of aircraft and, by 1918, flight became a commercially viable option for travel. It remained expensive throughout the interwar years and was only affordable to wealthy businessmen. As a result, flight remained unprofitable, and four pioneering private companies had to be financially supported by the state. Imperial Airways was formed out of these companies in 1924. It was subsidised by the government to promote an image of British power and modernity rather than to make a profit. British Airways was set up as a private company in 1935, but this too had to be rescued with state financial assistance. In 1939 it merged with Imperial Airways to form the British Overseas Airways Corporation (BOAC). Civil aviation was nationalised between 1946 and 1947 following the Civil Aviation Act 1946. British European Airways was formed as a division of BOAC in 1946 (they merged to form British Airways in 1974) and was not privatised again until 1987. Scheduled flights within the UK began in the early 1930s but were slow to grow in popularity. Around 100,000 passengers enjoyed expensive return flights from the UK to Europe in 1939. Improvements in design, safety and economy led to a rapid growth in air transport after the Second World War.

Technological innovation drove the expansion of commercial flight. Increased capacity led to lower airfares and improved comfort led to increased consumer demand for air travel. The development of the first pressurised cabin (the Boeing 307) and of Frank Whittle's jet engine from 1938 made international air travel faster and more comfortable. BOAC's jet engine service to South Africa from 1952 halved the time of the same journey by propeller planes. The launch of jumbo jets in 1968 enabled even lower airfares to be offered due to the increased numbers of passengers per flight. The cost of a return flight from London to New York in 1969 was just a quarter of the price in 1949. This increase in capacity and the fall in price was a key reason why so many Britons were able to enjoy holidays in Greece and Spain from the 1960s onwards.

Governments had largely successfully maintained state monopolies on internal and international flights, the so-called 'scheduled flights'. The 1919 Paris Agreement stated that nations had sovereign rights over their airspace, so anyone who wanted to fly after 1919 had to have government approval. The **Chicago Convention 1944**, based upon an earlier convention between Britain and the USA, led to international agreement that 'scheduled traffic between two states is to be reserved for and shared by their own airlines'. The Civil Aviation (Licensing) Act 1960 undermined this overwhelming state control by enabling private airlines, such as British United Airways (1960–70), to apply to the newly established Air Transport Licensing Board for licences to operate air services. Non-scheduled flights increased at three times the rate of scheduled flights in the 1960s. This

SOURCE 10 Airport movements of cargo and passengers, 1925–95. From V. Middleton's *British Tourism: the remarkable story of growth* (2005).

Year	Terminal passengers	Air transport movements
1925	20,400	n/a
1930	44,600	n/a
1935	275,700	n/a
1961	13,793,000	449,000
1965	19,918,000	508,000
1970	31,606,000	607,000
1975	41,846,000	701,000
1980	57,823,000	954,000
1985	70,434,000	1,097,000
1990	102,418,000	1,420,000
1995	129,586,000	1,612,000

legislative change was crucial to the growth of package holidays as it enabled tour operators to operate their own air services. The other major legislative change that affected air travel after 1950 was the deregulation of the flight industry within the European Union in 1997. This enabled airlines to compete for any route within the EU, including those wholly within one state. Budget operators such as Ryanair and Easyjet soon undercut the prices of less cost-efficient state operators. By 2004, these highly price-competitive airlines offered much cheaper seats to a wide range of European destinations, greatly increasing the choice and potential for non-package holidays for most Britons.

ACTIVITY
KNOWLEDGE CHECK

The impact of changes in the means of transport, 1884–2004

1 Create a timeline of the key changes in transport that had an impact on leisure patterns in Britain.

2 Summarise the key ways in which bicycles, cars and planes affected leisure patterns in Britain.

3 'Technological innovation was the main reason why transport impacted on British leisure patterns.' How far would you agree with this judgement?

4 Which source tells us more about the impact of transport on British leisure patterns: Source 7, 8 or 9? Explain your answer.

KEY TERM

Chicago Convention 1944
The Convention on International Civil Aviation (to give the Chicago Convention its full title) set up the International Civil Aviation Authority in 1947 as an agency of the United Nations. Its aim was to co-ordinate and regulate international air travel. Key articles stated that scheduled flights needed the permission of states to cross their airspace, and that countries would agree to common standards of airworthiness for aircraft and pilots. Fifty-two countries signed the original agreement. It had been revised seven times by 2004, at which point it had 188 state signatories.

A Level Exam-Style Question Section C

How far do you agree with the opinion that changes in transportation were the most important factor affecting British leisure patterns from 1882 to 2004? (20 marks)

Tip

You should set out your overall answer as well as the other factors to be considered in the essay in your introduction. Examiners will expect you to focus on the stated factor in your first paragraph, which should typically form around a quarter to a third of your total essay.

EXTEND YOUR KNOWLEDGE

British railways in the 20th century

The First World War saw the state take control of railway operations from 120 different local companies. It became clear that the rail network ran more smoothly with fewer operators. The Railway Amalgamation Act 1921 forced all rail companies to merge into just four: Great Western Railway; London, Midland and Scottish Railway; London and North Eastern Railway; and Southern Railway.

The growth of railways encouraged 'ribbon development' before cars and buses became popular. The most famous example of this was the growth of 'Metroland', a series of suburbs north of London linked to the city centre by the Metropolitan Railway. From 1915 until its absorption by the London Passenger Transport Board in 1933, the Metropolitan Railway promoted Metroland as an ideal rural retreat from the congested, polluted centre. The poet Sir John Betjeman wrote a series of poems to celebrate the spirit of Metroland (he dropped the hyphen) and even created a Metroland documentary for the BBC in 1973. Other observers of the suburbs were less kind. Historian A.N. Wilson said that the Metropolitan Railway, rather than enhancing life in the town or countryside, merely blended the two together in one endless ribbon development.

The 'big four' struggled to compete with the growth of road transport, and in 1948 they were nationalised to create British Rail, an entity that survived until its privatisation between 1994 and 1997. The major change in train transport came as a result of two reports written by Dr Richard Beeching in 1963 and 1965. In these reports, Beeching recommended the closure of over half of all stations and almost a third of all track miles (around 5,000 miles in total) to make British Rail profitable. Track closures had begun before 1963 but dramatically accelerated in the mid-1960s. Many communities were cut off from the rail network as a result of the closures and left with no form of public transport. This furthered the demand for car ownership in the 1960s and beyond.

The impact of increasing affluence and reduced time at work

Falling prices, rising incomes

The expansion of global trade in the 19th century, and the British promotion of free trade in particular, led to a huge fall in the price of a range of commodities. British workers benefited from this trend between 1880 and 1900 in particular. Falling prices meant that their real wage rose by 40 percent in just 20 years. Social investigator Seebohm Rowntree estimated that the quality of life in York improved by 30 percent between 1899 and 1936, largely due to increases in **real wages**. An increase in the use of contraception, especially condoms, also meant that family sizes reduced during this period. By the late 1920s, British women

had 2.19 children on average (compared to 4.6 children in the 1880s). This meant that family incomes were shared between fewer people and therefore went further. Despite the economic difficulties of the interwar years, Britons on average enjoyed a 16 percent increase in their real wage as prices, especially for food, fell faster than wages.

KEY TERM

Real wages

A measure of income that takes into account the effects of inflation on purchasing power. Inflation is the average rise in prices of common consumer goods. If inflation was at two percent and nominal wages went up five percent, then real wages would have increased by three percent.

Not everyone benefited from this general trend and some areas suffered great poverty due to the decline of old industries that were the major local employers. For example, 62 percent of all shipbuilders were unemployed in 1932 compared to 20 percent of those who worked in car manufacturing. It is important to note that even the poorest in society were better off from 1909 onwards thanks to the introduction of state support for some of the most vulnerable. Over time, the amount of financial help offered, and the number of people who were eligible to claim state assistance, increased. Thanks to the expansion of social security and the welfare state more generally, although **relative poverty** existed in 2004, no one lived in the **absolute poverty** found in the slums of 1882.

KEY TERMS

Relative poverty

Somebody living in relative poverty does not have enough money to enjoy ordinary living patterns, customs and activities. Relative poverty is defined by the average standards of society and so can change over time as the average living standard rises or falls.

Absolute poverty

Someone living in absolute poverty does not have the fundamentals needed for survival, such as food, safe drinking water, decent shelter, health and sanitation.

Changes in working hours

The amount of time an average worker spent at work fell between 1882 and 2004. In addition to the rise of paid holidays discussed above, weekly working hours fell largely thanks to trade union pressure. From 1886, Tom Mann's Eight Hours League inspired his fellow trade unionists to build on the success of the Saturday half-day campaign and press for an eight-hour day during the working week. Such pressure led the average working week to reduce from 55 hours to 47–48 hours during the interwar years. The hard years of the Second World War contributed to demands for a further reduction in working hours, to 44–45 per week. This enabled workers to adopt a five-day working week. Many workers chose to work longer hours (with an average of 49 hours worked, for example, in 1955) but they were paid overtime rates for the 'extra' hours. Between 1951 and 1970, working hours fell from 44.6 to 40.3 hours, while those actually worked (including overtime) fell from 46.3 to 43.9. From 1998, the actual time spent at work was meant to be limited to 48 hours per week by the European Union Working Time Directive. However, Britain retained the right for most workers to opt out of the 48-hour week should they wish (they could not be sacked for refusing to opt out). Time away from work clearly provided more opportunities for leisure. As discussed above, an increasing proportion of this recreation time for men was spent at home rather than in communal, public activities.

It is important to note that these working hours figures are overwhelmingly for male industrial workers. Changes in the structure of the British economy, especially the decline of traditional industries and the rise of the service sector, have helped to encourage far more female, part-time and 'flexitime' work. By 1994, ten percent of male and 15 percent of female employees worked flexitime hours. Ironically, the growth of more time away from work fuelled the demand for more part-time and flexitime workers at weekends in the service and leisure industries. The weekend had been a time when dual-career households had been able to plan leisure activities. This shift in employment practice has made it harder for families to find time when they can all enjoy recreation together.

Changes in affluence

The historian Eric Hobsbawm called the period between the 1950s and early 1970s the 'golden era' of western capitalism. Even more so than before 1945, the rapid increase in real incomes fuelled higher material standards of living. Real disposable income rose 30 percent in the 1950s, 22 percent in the 1960s and 30 percent in the 1970s. The period is unique in British history in that profits, interest and rent declined as a share of national income, while average wages rose. Higher wages meant that people spent a smaller portion of their income on food, clothes and cigarettes and more on housing, motoring, consumer durables and entertainment. Home ownership increased from 29 percent of the population in 1950 to over 50 percent in 1970. Car ownership in the same period rose from 16 percent to 52 percent. By the early 1950s, consumer spending was back to what it was by the late 1930s. In 1957, Prime Minister Harold Macmillan was able to boast that 'most of our people have never had it so good'. Although there was a dip in real income in the 1970s (largely due to inflation caused by the high cost of oil), real wages surged ahead in the 1980s and 1990s, especially for higher income earners. The Gini coefficient is a single number between 0 and 1 used by economists to summarise the degree of inequality in income, with 0 representing a perfectly even distribution of income. The Gini coefficient for the UK was 0.25 in 1979 and had risen to 0.34 by 2004. While the rich could afford ever more extravagant forms of leisure, the change was less pronounced for those on lower incomes.

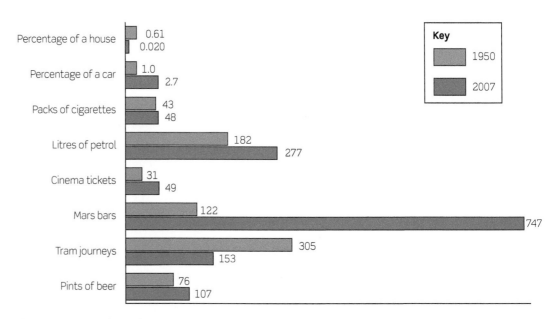

Figure 2.1 Comparison of what an average working-class man in Sheffield could buy with a week's pay in 1950 and in 2007.

SOURCE
11

The volume of household expenditure by purpose (excluding mortgage payments, water charges and council tax), 1971–2001 shown in index numbers. Index numbers show proportionate changes from a chosen base year (here it is 1971). To find the percentage change in expenditure in a given year after 1971 simply deduct 100 from the value. Figures from the Office for National Statistics.

	1971	1981	1991	2001
Food and non-alcoholic beverages	100	105	117	137
Alcoholic beverages and tobacco	100	99	92	88
Clothing and footware	100	120	187	344
Furnishings, household equipment and maintenance	100	117	160	262
Miscellaneous goods and services	100	121	240	336
Restaurants and hotels	100	126	167	193
Recreation and culture	100	158	279	545
Transport	100	128	181	246
Communication	100	190	306	790
Health	100	125	182	188
Education	100	160	199	255
Tourist expenditure abroad	100	193	298	699

ACTIVITY
KNOWLEDGE CHECK

The impact of changes in affluence and time spent away from work

1 Summarise the key data that supports the notion that the British, on average, became wealthier despite spending fewer hours at work in the 20th century.

2 Compare Sources 10 and 11. Which of these sources is more useful in understanding the impact of changes in affluence on changes in British leisure? Explain your answer.

Shops and shopping

The increase in disposable income and the rise of commercial television made invasive advertising a commonplace part of British life. The money spent on advertising rose threefold between 1947 and 1970. Shopping became a leisure activity in and of itself. New fashions, for example the miniskirt, were inspired by designers such as Mary Quant, who had their boutiques clustered around London's King's Road and Carnaby Street. They were made accessible to many by the mass production and sale of such designs in high streets across the country. From the mid-1960s, it was almost impossible to tell a young woman's class from the way she dressed. Barbara Hulanicki's fashion company Biba sold cheap clothes from her shops in London and across the country via mail order. The most famous model of the 1960s, Twiggy commented that while Mary Quant was for girls who were wealthy, Biba was for everyone. The clothes were given a lot of publicity in newspapers. This was partly due to the launch of colour sections in the papers after February 1962, and partly because of the work of a new breed of dashing photographer, including David Bailey, Brian Duffy and Terence Donovan. Mary Quant thought fashion attracted so much attention in the newspapers because it 'reflects what is really in the air': the growth of affluence, consumerism, the new confidence of youth and the changing role of women.

The first supermarket opened in St Albans in 1947, but it was the 1950 opening of Sainsbury's in Croydon that marked the permanent start of the supermarket era. The end of food rationing between 1951 and 1954 gave a boost to food sales. The rolling back of **Retail Price Maintenance** on groceries in 1956 and more generally in 1964 allowed supermarkets to flourish. They could take advantage of the size of their sales to slash prices and undercut smaller local shops. By 1959, there were 286 supermarkets, a figure that increased to 572 in 1961 and over 3,500 by 1971. The competition generated by this huge expansion led to the closure of 60,000 (or two-thirds of) local specialist grocers' shops between 1960 and 1990. There was also a reduction in the range and variety of local stores, with greater standardisation of chain stores. The growth of car ownership led to the growth of even larger supermarkets on the outskirts of towns and cities. While small-scale grocers

KEY TERM

Retail Price Maintenance (RPM)
This was an agreement between producers and vendors to set a minimum price for products. It was good for both parties as it avoided price competition and a loss of profit. At its height in the mid-1950s, it covered 44 percent of consumer spending on goods. The Restrictive Trade Practices Act 1956 undermined its use on grocery products. The Resale Prices Act 1964 virtually abolished RPM, except in cases where it was thought to be in the best interests of the public, such as books and medicines where RPM helped to maintain a socially desirable number of retail outlets. RPM was widely replaced with a recommended resale price.

and producers lost out, the consumer gained in terms of the average cost, quality and convenience of shopping in larger stores. To help make sense of the incredible choice (and the decline of personal service), the Consumer Association was founded in 1957 and launched its influential magazine *Which?* in the same year. A Ministry for Consumer Affairs, which aimed to protect consumers, existed (under slightly different official names) from 1972 until 1983.

Consumer credit

Credit cards were first used in Britain in 1966. Although debit cards had existed for a few years prior to this, Barclaycard remained unique until the launch of the Access card in 1972. The difficulty and social unacceptability of obtaining credit had been a major reason for the growth of hire purchase. The use of moneylenders by poor people was difficult to regulate and caused a great deal of harm in some cases – interest rates could be extortionate and physical force was sometimes used to intimidate local borrowers to pay up. The major breakthrough in ease of consumer access to credit began with the Consumer Credit Act 1974. This was largely based on the recommendations of the 1971 Crowther Report, which called for the repeal and replacement of all earlier legislation on moneylending and bank loans. The Act clarified the rights and responsibilities of lenders and borrowers and paved the way for an explosion of consumer borrowing in the 1980s and 1990s. Total UK personal debt rose above £1 trillion for the first time in July 2004, £55 billion of which was credit card debt. In that year the average Briton had debts of £1,302 on credit cards, £1,892 on unsecured personal loans and £812 on overdrafts and retail finance deals.

The impact of technology on leisure and entertainment between 1882 and 2004

Cinema in the early 20th century

A number of factors have affected the impact of cinema on the British. The first is the shift in its overall popularity: the greater the total audience for a film, the more likely it is to affect popular views. Cinema exploded in popularity during the First World War. *The Battle of the Somme* (1916) was seen by 20 million people in the first six weeks and remains one of the most viewed films in British cinema history. *The King Visits his Armies in the Great Advance* (1916) and especially *Hearts of the World: the Story of a Village* (1918) helped to cement the popularity of going to the cinema. The introduction of 'talkies' in 1928 further increased the popularity of going to 'the pictures', and cinema remained the most popular and important medium of popular culture in interwar Britain.

The number of cinemas increased from 3,000 in 1914 to almost 5,000 in the 1930s. The nature of cinemas changed too, from small venues that seated between 200 and 400 people to national chains of glamourous theatres that could seat up to 2,000. In 1950, four years after peak cinema attendance, the average person went to the cinema 28 times a year. This was more than in any other nation, including the US. The demand for escapism and restrictions on other forms of entertainment led to a boom

in cinema attendance during the Second World War. The most popular British films included *In Which We Serve* (1942) and *The Way Ahead* (1944), which showed the supreme fighting spirit of the navy and army, respectively, *The Gentle Sex* (1943) and *Millions Like Us* (1943) which explored wartime problems for women and workers, respectively. Popular American films about Britain included *Mrs Miniver* (1942) and *The White Cliffs of Dover* (1944). However, after record-high ticket sales of 1,635 million in 1946, attendance fell steadily until the late 1980s. Declining audiences meant that over half of the cinemas in the country were forced to close between 1955 and 1963. The most important reason for this decline was the rise of television (see page 60). It was not until the opening of state-of-the-art multiplexes (the first of which appeared in 1985 in Milton Keynes) that cinema attendance began to recover.

SOURCE
12 Total cinema admissions between 1935 and 2004. (There are no statistics available before 1935.) Based on data from www.launchingfilm.com.

Year	Total cinema admissions (millions)
1935	912
1946	1,635
1954	1,276
1964	343
1974	138
1984	53
1994	106
2004	171

The impact of cinema was also affected by who went most often. There were large variations in cinema attendance. The typical profile of a regular cinema-goer was young, urban, working class and, for those over the age of 19, female. In 1946, 69 percent of 16–19-year-olds went to the cinema once a week compared to 11 percent of over-60s. People in the North of England went on average almost twice as often as those in the South. This was probably because of income differences that enabled southerners to undertake more expensive activities such as participatory sport. Despite such differences, British audiences enjoyed remarkably similar films, especially comedies, musicals and crime thrillers. In all parts of the country, Saturday mornings were set aside for children, with age-specific films and cheap seats. These were hugely popular with children in the late 1940s and early 1950s, and their parents!

The content of films also affected the impact of cinema. There were somewhat patronising concerns about the potential impact of films on 'impressionable' audiences, and these were led by the conservative upper middle-class men who dominated the **British Board of Film Censors** (BBFC, established in 1912). However, the vast majority of cinema-goers saw films as a form of escapism. They appreciated the difference between real life and that depicted on screen and were unlikely to absorb moral values from films. The men at the BBFC did not see things that way; they saw it as their duty to protect Britons from bad language, sex and subversive ideas. The '43 rules' set out by the BBFC in 1917 had no official legal status, but most local authorities accepted them as laying down the law on which films were acceptable to show. Between 1928 and 1939, the BBFC banned 140 films and forced thousands more to edit their content. The Obscenity Act 1959 and Theatres Act 1968 led to greater permissiveness at the BBFC. By the early 1970s, the BBFC permitted films with much stronger violent or sexual content to be classified for release. Films such as *Get Carter* (1971), *A Clockwork Orange* (1971) *Straw Dogs* (1971) contained scenes of extreme violence, while *Last Tango In Paris* (1972), *Confessions of a Window Cleaner* (1974), and the *Emmanuelle* films (1974, 1975) contained nudity and sex. Some local authorities banned these films from their cinemas regardless of the BBFC classification.

KEY TERM

British Board of Film Censors

This organisation (known as the British Board of Film Classification from 1985) was established by the British film industry to pre-empt potentially more restrictive local government restrictions. The Cinematograph Act 1909 had empowered local councils to refuse permission to screen films on the basis of their content. The BBFC has in practice worked closely with the government, for example operating unofficial censorship during the Second World War.

The BBFC and the government were also concerned about the 'Americanisation' of cinema-goers. The First World War led to the collapse of the British film industry due to uncertainty over funding, disruption of production and the use of studios for government propaganda. So by 1925 only five percent of films shown in British cinemas were British-made. The Quota Act 1927 ensured that British films made up 20 percent of those shown by 1936. The British preferred the higher production quality of American films, and women in particular enjoyed the glamour of American heroes and heroines. Even before the Second World War, writers and journalists had noted youths dressing like gangsters and factory girls looking like actresses, using American slang such as 'Oh yeah?' and 'Sez you!'.

Improved production and acting, and the toning down of elite manners and accents, made British films more popular after the war. The 1950 Eady Levy (named after treasury official Sir Wilfrid Eady) gave a further boost to British film-making: a small charge on ticket sales created a fund to subsidise film-making in Britain. The 'New Wave' films of the late 1950s and 1960s, such as *Look Back in Anger* (1959) and *Saturday Night and Sunday Morning* (1960) were gritty films about working-class lives. They received critical acclaim, but most people preferred comedies such as the *Carry On* series and *James Bond* films. British film production collapsed in the 1970s and American films dominated once again. The number of British films made each year fell from 49 in 1968 to 31 in 1980. The key reasons for this were cuts in US investment in the British film industry and Conservative government cuts to the National Film Finance Corporation, one of the major British sources of investment.

Radio from the 1920s

Radio had a wider reach than cinema: between 1922 and 1939 the percentage of households with a receiver increased from one to 71 percent. By 1951, this figure had increased to 90 percent. The British Broadcasting Corporation (BBC), founded as a **quango** in 1927, had a **monopoly** on radio broadcasting in the UK until 1973. Two radio services were established: the National Programme and the Regional Programme. The latter was broadcast from six regions: the Midlands, London, the North, Scotland, the West, Northern Ireland, Wales (in order of when the first transmitter was set up). The National Service was also carried by regional transmitters as well as being broadcast from London by a longwave transmitter. Lord Reith, the first director-general of the BBC, explained how he saw the Corporation's role as a **public service broadcaster** (see Source 13).

KEY TERMS

Quango
From quasi non-governmental organisation, this is an administrative body outside the government, but whose members are appointed by the government.

Monopoly
The position of having no competition in a given trade or market.

Public service broadcaster
A radio or television company run to serve the public interest rather than for profit.

Empire Day
From 1901 this was a celebration of the British Empire held on 24 May, Queen Victoria's birthday. In 1958 it was renamed Commonwealth Day. Since 1973 it has been held on the second Monday in March.

SOURCE 13
From Lord Reith's autobiography, *Into the Wind*, published in 1949.

So the responsibility at the outset was conceived to carry into the greatest number of homes everything that was best in every department of human knowledge, endeavour and achievement; and to avoid whatever was or might be hurtful. In the earliest years accused of setting out to give the public not what it wanted but what the BBC thought it should have, the answer was that few knew what they wanted, fewer what they needed. In any event it was better to overestimate than underestimate. If another policy had been adopted – that of the lowest common denominator – what then?

Historians David Cardiff and Paddy Scannell have argued that the BBC enhanced a reassuring feeling of belonging to a national community. They claim that programmes such as the monarch's Christmas message (broadcast since 1932), anniversary programmes for New Year and **Empire Day**, acted as a set of symbols that helped to bind different classes into a more cohesive national identity. Radio certainly had an impact on British culture. At the start of the Second World War, the National and Regional Programmes were replaced with a single service, the Home Service. This was done to prevent enemy aircraft from using different regional broadcasts to aid navigation. As the war went on, more programming was restored to the regions due to the fear of concentrating all production in bomb-prone London. During the war, many radio programmes such as *Workers' Playtime* had been aimed at groups in factories to boost morale. After the war, radio programmes were targeted at listeners at home. In this way it promoted the domestication of leisure time. It also enhanced the existing feeling of national identity through its ability to give immediacy to an event and to reach out to the most remote parts of the country. Radio also broadened horizons: rather than 'listening in' for a particular programme, the working classes usually had the radio on all of the time, and sometimes listened to unexpected programmes.

The Light Programme, which replaced the wartime Forces' Programme in July 1945, with its mix of comedies and soaps such as *Mrs Dale's Diary* and *The Archers*, variety shows and famous personalities, remained by far the most popular channel, with around two-thirds of the 11 million daily listeners. Many of the daytime shows were aimed at women (a reflection of the clearly divided roles for men and women), with the most popular shows including *Housewives' Choice* and *Woman's Hour*. On Sundays, when the Light Programme broadcast shows dedicated to religious services, many of these listeners abandoned the BBC and tuned in to 'pirate' radio stations. Stations such as Radio Luxembourg and Radio Normandy had broadcast into Britain from beyond its shores since the 1930s. The Marine Broadcasting Offences Act 1967 banned pirate radio (although Radio Caroline ignored the ban). The BBC filled the gap for a pop radio station when it split the Light Programme into Radio 2 and Radio 1, the latter being its first channel specifically dedicated to pop music and a younger audience.

After the Independent Broadcasting Authority Act 1973, BBC radio had to compete with a range of UK-based commercial stations. Despite this, audiences for Radio 1 rose throughout the 1970s, with DJ Tony Blackburn's *Breakfast Show* attracting 20 million listeners. In 1967, the Third Programme, launched in September 1946, became Radio 3, while the Home Service became Radio 4. The Home Service catered for middlebrow tastes with news, plays and lectures, while the Third Programme was highbrow, with modern classical music and 'difficult' culture for the most highly educated listeners. The Third Programme attracted less than two percent of listeners.

The way in which radio affected domestic leisure differed depending upon the listener. Lord Reith was keen to promote active 'listening in', that is, tuning in for a particular programme, rather than 'tap listening', where the radio was simply left on all day as a background accompaniment to other daily activities. Middle-class households tended to listen in, while working-class families left the radio on all day. Children and adolescents tended not to see the radio as an activity in and of itself. Only 5.5 percent of teenagers surveyed in the 1930s listed radio as an activity they had enjoyed the previous evening. It is likely that they thought of the radio as a continuous background presence that they did not consciously have to pay attention to as opposed to there being no radio on in the home that evening. Unlike going to the cinema or a dance, listening to the radio was unexciting and unsociable. While radio helped to popularise particular songs, sporting events or entertainment shows, 'tap listening' in working-class homes suggests that radio only actively altered the allocation of domestic leisure time in middle-class homes.

Television from 1945

Of all mass media, television had the largest impact on British behaviour (before the rise of the internet). This was not only because of the programmes it brought to the masses, but also because the existence of the TV set itself profoundly affected the home dynamic and the use of leisure time. As Canadian academic Marshall McLuhan argued in his 1964 book *Understanding Media: The Extensions of Man*, 'the medium is the message'.

SOURCE 14

From Doris Lessing's autobiography *Walking in the Shade*, published in 1997. Lessing was a writer who here recounts her experiences of London in the early 1950s.

> Before, when the men came back from work, the tea was already on the table, a fire was roaring, the radio emitted words or music softly in a corner, they washed and sat down at their places, with the woman, the child... They all talked... And then... television had arrived and sat like a toad in the corner of the kitchen. Soon the big kitchen table had been pushed along the wall, chairs were installed in a semi-circle and, on their chair arms, the swivelling supper trays. It was the end of an exuberant verbal culture.

Television cannot really be considered a *mass* medium in Britain until after the Second World War. Moving pictures were not broadcast to televisions in British homes until 1929. Before 1939, the BBC only broadcast television signals to around 12,500 television sets in London. Television broadcasts were suspended during the Second World War and not resumed until June 1946. Sales of television licences did not really take off until the coronation of Elizabeth II seven years later. Four percent of households had a TV set in 1950, rising to 40 percent in 1955, 80 percent in 1960 and 95 percent in 1969. Following the launch of BBC2 in 1964, there were only three television channels. Given the scale of TV ownership, the potential audience for a popular programme was very large. Between 1977 and 1979, people on average watched 16 hours of television in the summer and 20 hours in the winter. Children and the elderly watched the most television, while women watched more than men. The Central Statistical Office recorded that watching television was one of the most popular leisure activities among all social groups. Men and women spent around 23 percent of their free time in front of the small screen, twice as much as people in Belgium, Italy or Sweden. The domestication of spare time that had begun with the radio blurred class divisions that had been reinforced by more public leisure pursuits such as dog racing (working class) or playing tennis (middle class). Now anyone could watch similar programmes from their own homes. As so many people saw the same programmes, the content of these shows formed an important part of the next day's conversations at school, work or home. The impact of television was further enhanced by the spread of broadcasts and reception in colour. BBC2 began colour broadcasts in 1967, with BBC1 following in November 1969. The percentage of colour television sets increased from 1.7 percent in 1970 to 70 percent in 1979.

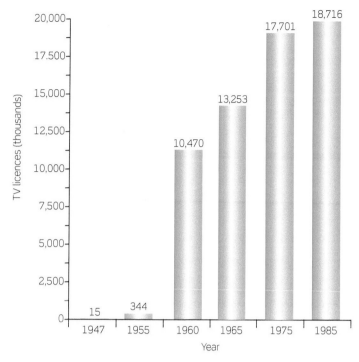

Figure 2.2 Sales of television licences from 1947 to 1985. Adapted from D. Murphy, *Britain 1914-2000* (2000).

The use of the internet for leisure from the late 20th century

The internet is a global network of computers linked by electronic cable and satellite relays. It all began on a much smaller scale. In 1969, an American military system called ARPANET linked just four computers. ARPANET allowed information to be shared instantaneously. The benefits of this were increasingly realised by the computer scientists who developed the network. By 1980, 213 computers were linked. In 1986, the US National Science Foundation launched NSFNet, a network of five supercomputers that could host information. Internet Service Providers (ISPs) began to provide software that allowed anyone with a computer to join this network via a telephone line. By 1988, 80,000 computers were linked. This figure had risen to 1.3 million by 1993, 9.5 million by 1996, and 19.5 million by 1999. In 1999, there were 153 million users worldwide, a figure that had increased to almost 1 billion by 2004. In the UK, the percentage of households with internet access rose from ten percent in 1998 to 50 percent in 2004. In 2004, over a third of households still had dial-up connections over a standard telephone landline rather than via a broadband connection. While the reduction in the cost of computers facilitated this increase, a major reason for this huge growth in usage was that the internet became much easier to use. This was thanks to the creation of the World Wide Web in 1990 by Tim Berners-Lee.

The internet and the World Wide Web have the potential to revolutionise patterns of family leisure. While the internet has already begun to change some aspects of leisure usage, it is too early to determine what the overall impact of the Web will be. Oxford University launched the Oxford Internet Institute in 2001 and now runs a Masters Degree course in 'The Social Science of the Internet'. Some academic studies, such as the 2002 study 'Internet use, interpersonal relations and sociability: A time diary study' by Stanford University social science professors N. Nie and D. Hillygus, suggested that increased internet usage has led to a decline in interaction with family members and a smaller social circle. Other studies, such as the 2002 study 'Is the internet changing social life? It seems the more things change the more things stay the same' by professor of psychology Tom Tyler, have concluded that the internet, far from damaging social relations, can improve them. Very few studies have specifically set out to determine the relationship between internet usage for leisure purposes and other leisure behaviour. Conclusions reached by researchers before 2004 were extremely tentative due to the limited widespread experience of the internet 's impact by that point in time. The Office for National Statistics only began to collect regular data on internet use in 2006. However, academic studies from 2004, such as a 'Internet Shopping Model and Customer Perceptions: A Study of UK Supermarkets' by Portsmouth University's M. Xu and M. Roberts, suggest that even activities that rapidly became common after 2004 were still highly limited during the final year of this study. While 74 percent of British adults shopped for groceries online in 2013, this figure was only 7.5 percent in 2004. **British Social Attitudes** surveys reveal that as late as 2002 over half of the UK population had never used the internet. By 2004, this had fallen to a tiny figure, but almost 80 percent of the population used the internet for less than five hours per month. It is fair to conclude that the impact of the internet on domestic leisure time, while highly significant for the 2010s and beyond, was negligible for the average Briton by 2004.

KEY TERM

British Social Attitudes

This is a survey conducted by the National Centre for Social Research. It has been carried out every year since 1983. It asks a representative sample of British people questions about social, political, economic and moral issues. The Centre has conducted surveys about internet usage since 1999.

SOURCE

15 From Ben Anderson and Karina Tracey's chapter 'Digital Living: The Impact (or Otherwise) of the Internet on Everyday British Life', from Barry Wellman and Caroline Haythornthwaite's 2002 book *The Internet in Everyday Life*. Anderson and Tracey both worked at Chimera, a research institute at the University of Essex, when they conducted this investigation.

In the interviews with Internet users one topic of discussion was the extent to which the Internet had an impact on the way interviewees spent their time and to what extent Internet use displaced other activities. Although this might appear a relatively straightforward question, informants found it extremely difficult to pin down any clear or explicit changes: 'It's difficult to say if it [the Internet] displaces one activity or another'.

The range of activities which were reported as possibly being displaced included watching television, spending time in the garden, reading newspapers, magazines and books, going to the supermarket, making telephone calls, going to the pub, doing nothing, writing letters, sleeping, playing computer games and typing on a typewriter. However, no one activity was mentioned by more than a handful of informants and even the heaviest of users felt that any displacement was marginal at best. One possible reason for this may have been the relatively low level of daily or weekly usage in the UK (between 1 and 3 hours per week) compared to the USA, although even those who spent as much as six hours per week using the Internet in the evenings couldn't pinpoint any major displacements... In addition, other factors have a significant influence on patterns of time-use. For example, during the summer months one respondent's television viewing, game playing and Internet usage were all displaced by spending time in the garden when the weather was good. Therefore it might be expected that changes in time use would not be significantly associated with a simple transition such as acquiring Internet access. It might also be expected that an analysis of patterns of changing time use would show that the acquisition of Internet access is having relatively little immediate impact on people's lives. If so we can conclude that conceptualizing the relationship between technological change and social change in terms of 'impact' or time-use 'substitution' may be over simplistic.

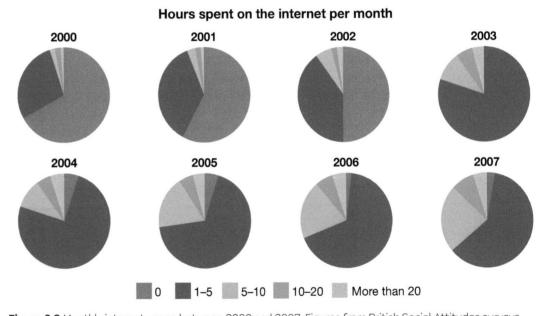

Figure 2.3 Monthly internet usage between 2000 and 2007. Figures from British Social Attitudes surveys.

SOURCE

16 Figures for internet usage by British adults in 2006 from the Office for National Statistics

16 million adults used the internet every day; this was 35 per cent of all adults. The percentages varied for different age groups: 63 (aged 16–24), 61 (aged 25–34), 63 (aged 35–44), 56 (aged 45–54), 37 (aged 55–64), 9 (aged 65 and above).

The percentage of adults who used the internet for the most popular web-based activities were 59 for finding information about goods and services, 58 for sending and receiving emails, 42 for services related to travel or travel accommodation, 30 for internet banking, 24 for playing or downloading games, images, films or music and 20 for reading or downloading newspapers or magazines.

EXTEND YOUR KNOWLEDGE

Tim Berners-Lee (born 1955)

Tim Berners-Lee was born in London where he went to Emanuel School. Having gained a first-class degree in Physics at Oxford University, he went to work at the European Organization for Nuclear Research (CERN). It was while he was working at CERN that he developed several crucial ideas that turned the internet from a tool for scientists into a global portal for education, entertainment and commerce. The first key idea was hypertext. Hyper is a prefix derived from Greek meaning 'beyond' or 'over'. Hypertext are words (or other symbols) that have an embedded link to other information *beyond* that which is immediately before you. This information (text, pictures, films and so on) is stored on computers across the world linked by the internet. The links to this information work thanks to two more ideas that he developed: Hypertext Transport (or Transfer) Protocol (HTTP) and Uniform Resource Locator (URL). HTTP is an instruction to a computer to find and display the information requested by clicking on a link. URL is the 'address' where this information may be found. Tim also created a simple computer language called Hypertext Mark-up Language (HTML) that allowed people to build their own web pages with hypertext links.

The ease and usefulness of the web page system has led to the rapid increase in their number since 1991. This could have resulted in chaos had it not been for another of Tim's ideas: a system of domain names, such as .com, .co.uk, .org, to organise web pages. Domain names allow search engines (which Tim originally called 'browsers') to find information in a useful fashion. All of these ideas came together in 1991 to create the 'World Wide Web'. This was initially a very grand name for just one website hosted on a single computer at CERN (which you can see online). However, the Web grew exponentially thanks to the growing sophistication of search engines, and the fact that Tim did not copyright his ideas: anyone could use them free of charge.

Tim has won many international awards for his work. He was named 'the greatest Briton' of 2004, to which he responded by saying not only how proud he was to be British but that it was fun to be British too.

The rise of the internet had not had a dramatic impact on the content of terrestrial television by 2004. Significant changes, such as the growth of lifestyle shows and reality television – for example *Big Brother* (Channel 4, 2000 onwards) and *I'm A Celebrity, Get Me Out of Here!* (ITV, 2002 onwards) – took place after the Broadcasting Act 1990 (see page 143) yet before the explosion of internet usage after 2002. It is worth noting that popular shows such as *Strictly Come Dancing* (BBC1, 2004 onwards) attracted an audience of 13 million, while around 9 million people still watched *EastEnders* and *Coronation Street* every week.

Only with regard to newspaper reading was there a recognisable shift away from old media by 2004 as a result of the internet. The key difference between early internet use and its use since 2004 has been the *interactivity* of use. Rather than merely using the Web as a source of information, people are now able to participate in the construction of web content by uploading their pictures, videos and blogs and by editing wiki web pages. Many people now use social networking sites such as Instagram, Facebook, Twitter and Snapchat to share information and keep in touch with an extended group of friends and contacts. As Tim Berners-Lee has pointed out, they *could* have done this from the very start of the Web; it is possibly the increased number of users and their familiarity with the Web that has led to this change in usage.

ACTIVITY
KNOWLEDGE CHECK

The impact of technology on leisure patterns, 1882–2004

1 For each of the following technologies, give statistical evidence of their impact on leisure patterns: cinema, radio, television, the internet.

2 How far is it possible to give qualitative evidence (i.e. measuring the experience) of the impact of those technologies on British people between the 1920s and 2004?

3 Rank the four technologies in terms of their overall impact on British people. Explain your rank order.

A Level Exam-Style Question Section C

How far were changes in mass media responsible for changes in British leisure patterns between 1882 and 2004? (20 marks)

Tip
As far as possible, you should aim to cover the whole of the period in question. In this particular case, you would be able to refer to typical patterns of leisure in late-Victorian Britain as a way of assessing the impact of early 20th-century innovations such as radio.

Change (7a)

Convergence and divergence

Changes in the means of transport, 1882–2004:

1885 First commercially successful safety bicycle launched	1922 Launch of the Austin Seven motorcar	1938 First pressurised cabin in aircraft and demonstration of jet engine	1963 Beeching report recommends closure of 5,000 miles of rail track	1985 Launch of Ryanair

Changes in legislation relevant to excursions and holidays, 1882–2004:

Health Resorts and Watering Places Act 1921	Holidays with Pay Act 1938	Caravan Sites and Control of Development Act 1960	End of currency restrictions for British holidaymakers 1970	Deregulation of flights within the European Union 1997

1 Draw a timeline across the middle of a landscape piece of A3 paper. Cut out ten small rectangular cards and write the above changes on them. Then place them on the timeline with transport events above the line and legislation events below. Make sure there is a lot of space between the changes and the line.

2 Draw a line and write a link between each change within each strand, so that you have four links that join up the changes in the *transportation* part of the timeline and four that join the *legislation* changes. You will then have two strands of change: *transport and legislation.*

3 Now make as many links as possible across the timeline between changes in transportation and changes in legislation. Think about how they are affected by one another and think about how things can link across long periods of time.

You should end up with something like this:

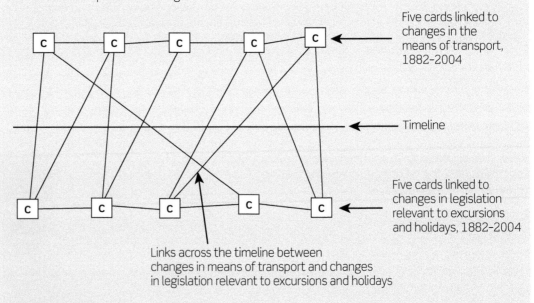

Five cards linked to changes in the means of transport, 1882–2004

Timeline

Five cards linked to changes in legislation relevant to excursions and holidays, 1882–2004

Links across the timeline between changes in means of transport and changes in legislation relevant to excursions and holidays

Answer the following:

4 How far do different strands of history interact with one another? Illustrate your answer with two well-explained examples.

5 At what point do the two strands of development converge (i.e. when do the changes have the biggest impact on one another)?

6 How useful are the strands in understanding changes in holidays and excursions, 1882–2004?

ACTIVITY
SUMMARY

1 Create timelines for the key changes that took place in each of the following factors that affected British leisure between 1882 and 2004: time away from work; affluence; government legislation; the role of private business/entrepreneurs; transportation; entertainment technology.

2 Using the timelines:

a) consider the ways in which one factor affected or combined with other factors to impact upon British leisure patterns

b) rank the factors in importance of their overall contribution to changes in leisure patterns.

 WIDER READING

Blackshaw, T. *The Routledge Handbook of Leisure Studies*, Routledge (2013)

Hill, J. *Sport, Leisure and Culture in Twentieth-Century Britain*, Palgrave (2002)

Middleton, V. *British Tourism: the Story of Remarkable Growth*, Elsevier (2005)

Thompson, F.M.L. *The Cambridge Social History of Britain 1750–1950 Volume 2*, Cambridge University Press (2008), Chapter 6

3.3 The age of the press barons, 1914–36

KEY QUESTIONS

- Who exercised the greater influence: Northcliffe or Beaverbrook?
- How influential was Lord Rothermere in the period 1922–36?
- How influential was the *Daily Herald* in the period 1914–36?

INTRODUCTION

The years 1914–36 saw great change in both British journalism and politics. 'New journalism', improvements in the production and distribution of newspapers, and the rise of mass literacy prompted a rapid increase in circulation figures. Millions of people who would not have bought a daily newspaper at the end of the 19th century began to buy titles such as Lord Northcliffe's *Daily Mail* or Lord Beaverbrook's *Daily Express*. The Representation of the People Acts of 1918 and 1928 completed a century-long change in suffrage from only two percent of men before 1832 to all men and women over the age of 21 by 1928. Many men, who had grown to positions of influence before these great changes, feared the influence that mass journalism might have in the new era of mass politics. Yet those such as Northcliffe and his brother Lord Rothermere, who rose to prominence during this period, believed they had an opportunity to affect mass politics through their command of mass journalism. The key question is the extent to which those fears were justified and those opportunities realised.

The journalistic context

Without several important changes in journalism before 1914 there would not have been an 'age of the press barons' between 1914 and 1936. Before the industrial revolution, newspapers could only be printed and distributed on a limited basis. The first titled newsletter, *Corante* (launched in 1621), and the first daily newspaper, the *Daily Courant* (launched by Elizabeth Mallett in 1702), were both a single sheet of news only available in London. While this limited their reach, the comparatively cheap and simple technology used to produce them enabled sufficiently educated people from humble backgrounds to set up and run independent newspapers. A lot of early journalism was radical in nature: it sought to attack excessive government control and promote social change. Political parties fought back by subsidising sympathetic newspapers. Until the mid-19th century, governments placed a 'stamp duty' on paper in an attempt to squeeze poor, radical papers out of business. Between 1853 and 1861, these 'taxes on

---

1896 – Alfred Harmsworth, later Lord Northcliffe, publishes first edition of the *Daily Mail*

1904 – *Daily Mirror* refounded as first national daily newspaper to use photographs on a regular basis

1911 – Launch of the *Daily Herald* (replaced by the *Sun* in 1964)

1915 – *Daily Mail*, owned by Lord Northcliffe, accuses government of mismanagement during the shell crisis

1896	1900	1904	1908	1910	1912	1914	1916

1900 – Arthur Pearson launches the *Daily Express*

1908 – Harmsworth purchases the *Times*

1914 – Defence of the Realm Act introduces censorship for the duration of the First World War

The *Daily Herald*, under George Lansbury since 1913, takes anti-war, pro-conscientious objector, stand

1916 – *Daily Mail* takes a stance against conscription

Lord Beaverbrook, with a secret controlling interest in the *Daily Express*, uses the newspaper to undermine Asquith and support Lloyd George as prime minister

knowledge' were repealed. However, this did not represent victory for the free press, as some radicals had hoped. Lower production costs encouraged successful businessmen to invest in newspapers. At the same time, new industrial printing presses meant that start-up costs were beyond the means of all but the rich. Depending on the political views of the businessmen proprietors, almost all newspapers launched between 1861 and 1910 were affiliated to either the Conservative or Liberal Party and did not challenge the established political order.

Industrialisation also led to a revolution in transport and communication, which greatly increased the potential market for newspaper sales. Successful proprietors began to buy rival newspapers to expand their own sales. The use of images, investigative journalism and news agencies all caused newspaper sales to gradually expand. The 'new journalism' from the 1880s accelerated this trend. William Thomas Stead was particularly influential with the changes he ushered in at the *Pall Mall Gazette*: catchy headlines, shorter paragraphs, interviews and more human interest stories were all key ingredients in the subsequent success of the *Daily Mail* and *Daily Express*. The growth towards mass markets and narrow ownership of newspaper chains did not begin with the press barons; they merely saw the opportunity to exploit these trends and push them to their limit. Although the establishment vilified Northcliffe and Beaverbrook for ruining a **'golden age' of journalism**, the reality is that they represented a continuation of some important late 19th-century trends. Their real innovation, and the real cause of their demonisation by some, was to separate the commercial press from political parties and government.

The press barons accelerated an existing trend towards the more concentrated ownership of newspaper chains. Between 1921 and 1939, the percentage of provincial evening press titles owned by one of the 'big five' proprietors (Lords Northcliffe, Rothermere, Beaverbrook, Kemsley and Camrose) rose from eight percent to 40 percent. At the same time, the number of towns with a choice of local newspaper fell from 24 to 10. The final journalistic development was the rise of the national daily newspaper. Between 1918 and 1936, sales of national titles overtook those of local dailies for the first time. The increased reach and volume of sales for national papers increased their potential to affect national views, a fact that politicians in the period became increasingly aware of.

> **KEY TERM**
>
> **'Golden age' of journalism**
> This is not a term used by historians to describe journalism during the years 1860–1900, but at the turn of the 20th century it was certainly used by the elite who looked down on 'new journalism'. Compared to the serious, academic tone of earlier newspapers, written by gentlemen for gentlemen, elite critics such as Matthew Arnold thought the *Daily Mail* and *Daily Express* were 'feather-brained'.

The political context

A number of important political issues dominated the period 1914–36, several of which the press barons hoped to influence through their dominance of mass journalism. The First World War was not over in a matter of months as many politicians had hoped. The longer the war lasted the more men and materials were needed to press for victory. At the same time, greater regulation of people's private lives and control over information were required to keep the war effort going on the Home Front. A loss of morale or production could have led to defeat. Such demands did not sit easily with the political values of the Liberal Party or its leader and prime minister in 1914, Herbert Henry Asquith. Traditional Liberalism had stood for Free Trade, *laissez-faire* ('let it be') economic

1917 – *Daily Herald* supports Bolshevik Revolution in Russia

1922 – Lord Northcliffe dies. His press empire is bought by his brother, Lord Rothermere (Harold Harmsworth) Lansbury loses proprietorial and editorial control of *Daily Herald*

1928–29 – Newspaper circulation war: Lord Rothermere takes on the Berry Brothers press for provincial newspaper sales

1936 – Abdication Crisis: Edward VIII quits throne in order to marry American divorcee Wallis Simpson

1918	1920	1922	1924	1928	1930	1934	1936

1920 – Kamenev telegram discredits *Daily Herald*

1924 – *Daily Mail* prints the 'Zinoviev Telegram', damaging Labour Party's reputation four days before a general election

1931 – Lord Rothermere's clash with Baldwin; Lord Rothermere's support for Moseley and the BUF

1936 – Daily sales of national newspapers climb towards ten million while those of provincial newspapers fall towards 28 million from a high of 41 million in 1921

Total war
War without any limitation on the degree of damage inflicted on civilians or non-military infrastructure as a means to victory. Such fighting often requires the dedication of the whole nation's resources to defeat the enemy.

policies and the defence of personal freedoms against the creeping power of the state. Asquith, like most members of his Party, had hoped to fight and win the war without having to sacrifice such cherished goals. However, by mid-1915 it was becoming increasingly clear to those at the front that more intervention and more state control would be required to fight a '**total war**'. Some Liberals, most significantly the highly respected Chancellor of the Exchequer David Lloyd George, were far more receptive to the idea of state intervention than those loyal to Asquith. It was this division that afforded the press barons their first opportunity to influence political decision-making since the outbreak of the war.

Arguably one of the most important consequences of the First World War was the decline of the Liberal Party and the rise of the Labour Party as chief rival to the Conservatives. The Labour Party (rebranded in 1906 after six years as the Labour Representation Committee) had only been formed in 1900. It had done modestly well in the pre-war general elections, but it was very much the junior party to the Liberals before 1918. Yet, in the 1923 election, Labour gained more votes than the Liberals for the first time and, in 1924, Ramsay MacDonald became the first Labour prime minister. Labour became the largest parliamentary party in May 1929 and MacDonald became prime minister for the second time. The press barons were concerned about the rise of Labour and sought to use their influence to counter the rise of socialism in Britain. In 1906, in its first profile of the Labour Party, the *Daily Mail* stated that Labour's aims 'must of necessity conflict with the organisation of industrial enterprise' due to its 'campaign of class hatred and plunder'. In essence, the barons were afraid that a Labour government would use state intervention to gag their newspapers and introduce taxes to confiscate their wealth.

EXTEND YOUR KNOWLEDGE

The rise of the Labour Party and the failure of the far left, 1914-36
The emergence of the Labour Party is of huge significance in understanding the aims and motives of the press barons. Lord Rothermere (see pages 75-80) saw himself as anti-socialist and a guardian against a party which, in his eyes, represented a threat to Britain. The strength of such hostility is largely explained by clear class interest in the preservation of the *status quo*. The popular daily newspapers competed for influence over the same demographic as the increasingly powerful Labour Party.

Unlike the Liberals, Labour emerged united at the end of the war. There had been splits in 1914 over war support, but in 1917 Labour ministers in the wartime coalition resigned and the party was reunited. The war also led to a huge growth in trade union membership. This was significant as the unions funded the party from membership fees and provided the vast bulk of party membership. Thanks to union backing, Labour, unlike the Liberals, ran a successful local political machine and fielded a similar number of candidates to the Conservatives in the 1922, 1923 and 1924 elections.

In 1922 and 1923, the *Daily Mail* had suggested every man's house and every woman's belongings would be at risk if people voted Labour as it would be tantamount to voting for Bolshevism (Russian Communism). The reality was that the Labour Party rejected communism, and the Communist Party of Great Britain (CPGB) remained tiny with only one MP in 1924 and 1935, and two in 1945. With a maximum 0.4 percent of the vote, it is clear that British voters also rejected communism, and this was largely due to the traditions and strength of the trade union and Labour movements. This home-grown socialism was far more practical than the ideological, revolutionary socialism advocated by communists. The CPGB gained some support due to the role of Soviet Russia (the only communist state) in defeating Nazi Germany. However, the CPGB had clearly placed the needs of Moscow ahead of Britain. Until Hitler attacked Russia in June 1941, the party had followed Soviet orders to oppose the war (a highly cynical Nazi-Soviet Pact for peace had been agreed in August 1939). The only way forward for the CPGB was in a few inner-city councils, and through 'entryism' into the Labour Party – communists would conceal their true loyalties and infiltrate the Labour Party to try to steer national politics further to the radical left.

WHO EXERCISED THE GREATER INFLUENCE: NORTHCLIFFE OR BEAVERBROOK?
The irresistible rise of Lord Northcliffe

Alfred Harmsworth was ennobled as Lord Northcliffe in 1905. He had enjoyed a meteoric rise in wealth, status and fame in a short space of time thanks to his insight into the potential of 'new journalism' to capture a huge, lucrative readership. He began his journalistic career with the production of a school magazine before moving on to work for a range of London newspapers, as well as the special interest magazines *The Cyclist* and *Wheeling*. By the age of 19 he was editor of *Youth* magazine. Within two years of this appointment, he had earned over £1,000 through the sale of two books, *All About Railways* and *One Thousand Ways to Earn a Living*. He invested these savings into the titles that were to facilitate his fortune: *Answers to Correspondents* (launched in 1888) and *Comic Cuts* (1890). By 1893, *Answers to Correspondents* sold over one million copies each week and his magazine company, Amalgamated Press, had become the largest in the world. Harmsworth recognised that people, in his words, wanted 'less British Museum and more life' and he used this formula when he broke into the daily newspaper market.

SOURCE

1

From Philip Gibbs' book *The Pageant of Years: an Autobiography*, published in 1946. Gibbs was appointed as literary editor at the *Daily Mail* in 1902. He went on to become one of only five official war correspondents during the First World War.

The New Journalism had arrived, and the *Daily Mail* under Alfred Harmsworth for whom I worked was its founder and pioneer. There were violent critics of this new type of journalism. They thought it vulgar, trashy, and lacking altogether in the dignity of the old-time Press. But Alfred Harmsworth knew what he was doing, and did it with genius. He knew that a public had grown up which took an intelligent interest in things not previously considered part of newspaper chronicles. Food; fashions; the drama of life in low places as well as high; sport of all kinds; the human story wherever it might be found; the adventure of science as it affected everyday life. Harmsworth knew that women's interests had been left out mainly from the old fashioned newspapers, and he knew that here was an enormous field for increasing circulation. He scorned the deadly dullness of the newspaper Press which had preceded him, with its long and dreary reports of political speeches, its portentous leaders, its blindness towards the little things of everyday life and their infinite variety.

With his earnings from Amalgamated Press, Harmsworth bought the *Evening News* in 1894 and the *Daily Mail* a year later. It was the *Mail* that truly made his name and fortune. Harmsworth had a clear vision for the *Mail*: he personally wrote the early taglines 'the busy man's daily journal' and 'the penny newspaper for one halfpenny'. It was targeted at lower middle-class workers such as clerks and office workers and, from February 1896, it pioneered a women's page (this was only published following 65 test runs). It was not only the eye-catching headlines, photographs and human interest stories that boosted sales – Harmsworth invested in a range of new production facilities that reduced his costs. He bought new presses that could print, fold, cut and count the number of papers, something that enabled him to attract new advertising revenue through the creation of net sales certificates. In 1902, he created a Manchester office to boost sales in the North and moved his print operations in London to Carmelite House, where his new presses led to a 35 percent saving on production costs. This enabled him to sell the *Mail* at half the cost of other daily papers. Sales rose from 397,213 in March 1896 to 989,255 by January 1900. He made further savings in 1905 by investing in 3,100 square miles of woodland in Newfoundland (now part of Canada) to feed his own paper mills.

The huge success of the *Mail* allowed Harmsworth to launch the *Daily Mirror* in November 1903. This was pioneering in that it was conceived and launched as a newspaper run exclusively by women for a female readership. Although poor sales figures meant that all of the female journalists were sacked and the paper's focus broadened with more pictorial content after just a year, this was a clear example of his willingness to try risky innovations. He also purchased the *Observer* in 1905 (although this was sold only seven years later) and, in March 1908, *The Times*. *The Times* had a long, illustrious history as the newspaper of choice for the informed, influential classes. Yet its thorough reporting of parliamentary debates lost favour at the start of the 20th century. By 1914, readership had fallen to around 40,000. Harmsworth cut the price to one penny and sales recovered to a healthier 145,000. The mass circulation *Mail*, and the highly influential *Times*, gave Harmsworth (Lord Northcliffe after 1905) a significant national platform to promote his views and attack those he disagreed with. Like him or loathe him, it was simply not possible for politicians to ignore the Northcliffe press.

Lord Northcliffe's stance on conscription

Northcliffe had some strident views on a range of issues, and this was significant as he clearly saw his papers, especially the *Mail*, as a vehicle for his political views. He exercised tight control over editorial decisions at the *Mail*, although he allowed for more independence of viewpoint at *The Times*. He could be highly critical of politicians whom he felt were doing a less effective job of running national affairs than he might have done. He had always had an interest in politics. His criticism of elected politicians might have stemmed from his failure to win a seat as a Conservative MP for Portsmouth in the 1895 general election. Northcliffe felt that for too long politicians had been allowed to act without reference or regard for popular will, and he saw his press empire as a way to hold government to account more effectively than had been possible previously.

Northcliffe had first experienced the ability of his press to influence national politics during the Boer War (1899–1901). The *Mail* had been critical of the Conservative conduct of the war, and the publication of negative stories was thought to have played a part in their landslide defeat by the Liberals in the 1906 election. Northcliffe continued to feel a duty to alert the nation to ineffective foreign policy, especially its lack of readiness for what Northcliffe saw as an inevitable war with Germany. In 1910, the *Mail* conducted a publicity stunt where men dressed as German troops marched through the streets of London. The 'invasion of 1910' was just one episode in a whole string of stories about the mounting naval and imperial threat that the Germans posed.

Northcliffe weighed in on several issues during the First World War. He was initially opposed to sending British troops to fight on the continent, but when it became clear this would happen he styled the *Mail* as the soldiers' friend and advocate. He sent 10,000 free copies to the front each day, paid soldiers for their war stories, and ran a 'Soldier's Friend' column with information, messages, advice and features relevant to troops. He also ensured that sensationalised stories of German atrocities in Belgium and northern France featured prominently. However, while he was keen to support the war, several visits to the front, together with dispiriting private information from a range of correspondents, led Northcliffe to become increasingly intolerant of war leaders. He felt trapped between a duty to report the truth and the necessity of backing a government in a time of national crisis. Despite some graphic early reporting of British casualties (such as the **Amiens dispatch**) and a campaign against excessive censorship, it was not until the spring of 1915 that the *Mail* really broke rank with the government.

KEY TERM

Amiens dispatch
Until the publication of this report in *The Sunday Times* on 30 August 1914, reporting from the front had been generalised and overwhelmingly upbeat. This article, under the headline 'Fiercest Fight in History: Heavy Losses of British Troops' gave a more accurate account of the British retreat at a series of battles in late August 1914. The report described a broken army in retreat with seriously injured troops. The government censor, the Press Bureau, had approved the article and its chief, F.E. Smith, was forced to resign. The *Mail* later printed whole articles that clearly showed which parts of its reports had been censored.

Lord Northcliffe's criticisms of some conduct of the First World War

The Shells Scandal of 1915, the creation of a War Cabinet and the attack on Kitchener

British failure at the battles of Neuve Chapelle (10–12 March 1915) and Aubers Ridge (9 May 1915) led Sir John French, commander-in-chief of the British Expeditionary Force, to complain to *The Times*

war correspondent Colonel Charles à Court Repington about a shortage of explosive shells as the key reason for defeat. Repington sent a letter that contained French's views (without naming him) to *The Times*, published on 14 May 1915 under the headline 'Need for shells: British attacks checked: Limited supply the cause: A Lesson From France'. The letter went on: 'We had not sufficient high explosives to lower the enemy's parapets to the ground… The want of an unlimited supply of high explosives was a fatal bar to our success.' Although this criticism put pressure on Asquith, his announcement on 19 May that he would dissolve the Liberal government and form a new coalition was precipitated far more by the resignation of First Sea Lord Admiral Fisher four days earlier. Political factors also played a large part in the decision. Asquith felt the need to promote greater unity in national leadership, while Andrew Bonar Law, Conservative leader, welcomed the coalition as a way to escape backbench criticism for his lack of opposition during the political truce. The planned restructuring of the government did not bring the Shells Scandal to a close.

On 21 May, the *Mail* published a direct attack on the leadership of Secretary for War, General Kitchener, written by Lord Northcliffe himself. The editorial headline that day read 'The Tragedy of the Shells – Lord Kitchener's Grave Error'. Kitchener is most famous today as the face of the 'Your Country Needs You' poster. He was highly popular with the British public in 1915, largely due to his daring exploits as a general in the late 19th century.

SOURCE 2

From Lord Northcliffe's editorial published in the *Daily Mail* on 21 May 1915. Northcliffe was driven by his fear of British defeat due to poor leadership and by his anger at the repeated wounding of his nephew Vyvyan on the Western Front.

In the dark days when Lord Haldane… showed signs of renewed tinkering with the Army, the 'Daily Mail' suggested that Lord Kitchener should take charge of the raising of the new troops. Lord Kitchener at once saw the size of that part of his job, and that part of the work was done as well as anyone could do it… We have never liked, and the public have never liked, Lord Kitchener's use of his own name, instead of the King's, in connection with those armies; and the public has greatly disliked some of the advertising methods employed by Lord Kitchener, but it has pardoned him in the urgent need of the moment, and the soldiers are there. How many, nobody knows… What we do know is that Lord Kitchener has starved the Army in France of high-explosive shells… It has never been pretended that Lord Kitchener is a soldier… Lord Kitchener is a gatherer of men, and a very fine one too… Nothing in Lord Kitchener's experience suggests that he has the qualifications required for conducting a European campaign in the field… The admitted fact is that Lord Kitchener ordered the wrong kind of shell… He persisted in sending shrapnel, a useless weapon in trench warfare. He was warned repeatedly that the kind of shell required was a violently explosive bomb which would dynamite its way through the German trenches and entanglements and enable our brave men to advance in safety. The kind of shell our poor soldiers have had has caused the death of thousands of them. Incidentally, it has brought about a Cabinet crisis and the formation of what we hope is going to be a National Government… It is to be hoped that Lord Kitchener, with proper and necessary assistance, will remain at the War Office, though when compulsory service comes his sphere of usefulness will, of course, be greatly diminished. That Compulsion is coming, and coming soon, is proved by the extremities to which Lord Kitchener is reduced… Men of 40 should not be used until the recruiting powers of the country are exhausted.

Study Source 2 before you answer this question.

Assess the value of the source for revealing Lord Northcliffe's stance, and the impact of the *Daily Mail*, on the conduct of the First World War.

Explain your answer using the source, the information given about its origin and your own knowledge about the historical context. (20 marks)

Tip

The key to success is clear judgement about the value of the source. Consider the limitations of the source as well as its usefulness. Use your contextual knowledge to expose where the source might be misleading or exaggerating. Use the provenance and tone of the source to inform your judgement about its overall reliability.

Although Northcliffe believed Kitchener had to go, the attack backfired. Circulation dropped overnight from 1,386,000 to 238,000 copies (although sales quickly recovered). Members of the London Stock Exchange burned copies of the *Mail* and *The Times*, and advertisers cancelled their bookings. Kitchener remained as Secretary for War until June 1916 when his Russia-bound ship hit a German mine near the Orkneys and sunk with the loss of 600 lives. Despite this, Northcliffe was pleased with overall developments. He blamed Asquith's sluggish leadership for the wretched conditions experienced by another of his nephews, Vere, in Gallipoli (see below). He was hopeful that the coalition, finally formed on 25 May, would prosecute the war with more vigour. He was also pleased that Lloyd George was appointed to the newly created position of Minister for Munitions. Although they increasingly disagreed on war strategy (see page 72), Northcliffe rated the energy of Lloyd George and saw him as the only viable replacement for Asquith. The production of shells increased from 70,000 in May 1915 to over a million in July 1916.

Criticisms of the Gallipoli campaign of 1915–16 and the Food Crisis

The *Mail* kept up pressure on Asquith and the coalition government over the conduct of the Gallipoli campaign. The failed naval attack on Turkey (a German ally) had been the main reason for Admiral Fisher's resignation, and an article by Keith Murdoch (father of future press baron Rupert Murdoch) accused the government of using censorship to hide the mistakes made by incompetent military leaders. The *Mail* began a crusade against what it called the 'Hide-the-Truth' papers that went along with official government information. The *Mail* also attacked the 'recruiting muddle' and pressed for conscription. Men had been encouraged to volunteer but had not been drafted into the armed forces by law as had happened in France and Germany. The edition published on 16 August 1915 came with a 'manifesto' in support of conscription, for readers to sign and post to the government. The halfway house tactic of creating a 'National Register' to assist voluntary recruitment was criticised in the *Mail* for its lack of compulsion over 'slackers'. This pressure, together with the failure of the Derby Scheme (a late 1915 effort to boost recruitment led by the Earl of Derby), eventually bore fruit with the Military Service Act in

January 1916. The Act conscripted unmarried men between the ages of 19 and 40, but not before a further change in government in which Northcliffe also played a part.

The *Mail* had criticised the 23-man War Cabinet for being too large and unwieldy. It called for a 'war council' to prosecute the conflict more efficiently. It was especially critical of the mounting 'food crisis', which it believed was entirely due to the 'wait and see Asquith government' (a reference to his inaction as wartime prime minister), and called for strict rationing to be introduced. Asquith, Kitchener and others who appeared to block any initiative were referred to as 'limpets' who clung to power but let down the 'magnificent men' at the front. However, although *The Times* played a crucial part in the final demise of Asquith's leadership, there would have been no change in government in December 1916 without the actions of Lloyd George and Bonar Law.

Asquith's resignation and the rise of Lloyd George

Following Kitchener's death Lloyd George had been appointed as Secretary for War, a role he had successfully stripped of effective power during the preceding year. He wanted to chair a small War Council as a way to regain influence over the generals at the front. Asquith initially rejected the idea but was pressed with similar demands by Bonar Law on 3 December, who said he would be unable to restrain Conservative opposition unless such a change was enacted. Asquith finally agreed to a War Council under his leadership. However, an article published in *The Times* on 4 December, together with declarations of loyalty from leading Liberal and Conservative members of the Cabinet, led him to renege on his decision. An editorial entitled 'Towards Reconstruction' can be seen as a deliberate attack on Asquith. It suggested that Asquith only agreed to the change from a position of weakness and would only serve as a figurehead in the Council. The article had been written anonymously by *Times* journalist Geoffrey Dawson, using information almost certainly provided by Sir Edward Carson, a highly articulate, forceful Conservative MP. To many at the time it appeared that Lloyd George had been the source for Northcliffe's words. Lloyd George had already been criticised for being the alleged source of a well-informed article in *Reynold's News* (a popular left-wing Sunday newspaper). Asquith's abrupt change led Lloyd George and Bonar Law to resign. Without their support, Asquith resigned on 5 December. He anticipated that no one but him would be able to form a government and, with his authority strengthened, he could get rid of the rebels. The king initially offered the premiership to Bonar Law. Asquith refused to serve under him or under fellow Conservative and former Prime Minister Arthur Balfour. The position was then offered to Lloyd George, who was able to form a government on 7 December with the backing of influential members of both the Conservative and Labour parties. Asquith was shocked, but in the event those Conservative ministers who had pledged to support him put patriotic duty ahead of narrow political preference. The *Mail* celebrated the change of government with the banner 'The Paper that is Combing Them Out'. It also printed photographs of the outgoing ministers with labels that pointed out their key faults. Asquith's label simply read 'Wait and see'.

A collection of correspondence relating to the downfall of the Asquith government in December 1916. Although such letters were private, MPs kept copies of the letters they sent, with the understanding that such correspondence could be made public if the need arose.

Asquith to Lloyd George, 4 December 1916: Such productions as the first leading article in today's 'Times' showing the infinite possibilities for misunderstanding and misrepresentation of such an arrangement we discussed yesterday, make me at least doubtful of its feasibility. Unless the impression is at once corrected that I am being relegated to the position of an irresponsible spectator of the War, I cannot go on.

Lloyd George to Asquith, 4 December 1916: I have not seen the 'Times' article. But I hope you will not attach undue importance to these effusions. I have had these misrepresentations to put up with for months. Northcliffe frankly wants a smash. Derby and I do not. Northcliffe would like to make this or any other arrangements under your Premiership impossible. Derby and I attach great importance to your retaining your present position – effectively, I cannot restrain, nor I fear influence Northcliffe.

Lytton Strachey (Editor of *The Spectator*) to Asquith's wife Margot, December 1916: Your husband's speech was splendid but I think he made a very great mistake in letting the world know, even though it was true, that what determined his action was the leading article in the 'Times'. Honestly that does not seem to me to be the way to keep the Harmsworth Press or newspapers in general in order. There is nothing that a newspaper likes so much as to be told that it has brought down a powerful Ministry. It feeds its vanity, and what is worse, gives the public in general a wholly exaggerated belief in its powers. What Northcliffe wants above all things is to create prestige for himself and to make himself dreaded by politicians. There was always danger from this kind of attitude and it has been increased a hundred-fold by recent events. I hear whispers of the Harmsworth 'terror' on all sides.

How far did Lord Northcliffe support Lloyd George as prime minister, 1916-22?

Despite his respect for Lloyd George, Northcliffe had a strained relationship from the start with the new prime minister. Lloyd George was horrified by the number of casualties sustained during the Battle of the Somme (July–November 1916) and wanted to divert men and resources to support campaigns on other fronts in Greece, the Balkans and Mesopotamia. Northcliffe remained convinced that the only way to defeat Germany was through the destruction of their main armed force on the Western Front. He sent a series of letters, entitled 'News From the Home Front', to Commander-in-Chief Sir Douglas Haig in which he described his ongoing duel with the politicians. A famous *Mail* headline on 13 October 1916 read 'Ministerial Meddling Means Military Muddling'. Northcliffe maintained his faith in the generals until early 1918. The death of his nephew, Vyvyan, together with a series of gruelling battles in 1917 helped to sway his views more in line with Lloyd George. However, even this tentative rapprochement was undermined by severe disagreements over the end of the war and the following peace settlement.

Northcliffe wanted an unconditional German surrender followed by a harsh settlement. He set out his views in an article called 'From War to Peace' on 4 November 1918. These were soon referred to as Northcliffe's '13 Points' with reference to US President Woodrow Wilson's '14 Points' on the peace settlement. Northcliffe hoped for a place on the official British delegation to the Paris Peace Conference. He felt he had earned this position through his work for the government as head of the British War Mission to America (May–December 1917), where he successfully raised financial support, and as Director for Propaganda in enemy countries (February–November 1918). He had been so effective in the latter role that the Germans produced a 'hate medal', which depicted Northcliffe and his toxic writing. Even after the Treaty of Versailles had been signed, Northcliffe kept up public pressure in support of French claims to a colossal sum in reparations. Lloyd George thought him a 'damned scoundrel' and deliberately fed inside knowledge on negotiations to the *Telegraph* to undermine *The Times*.

EXTRACT

1 From 'Harmsworth, Alfred Charles William, Viscount Northcliffe (1865–1922)' by Professor D. George Boyce, published in the *Oxford Dictionary of National Biography* in 2004. Professor Boyce has a Chair in the Department of Politics and International Relations at the University of Wales, Swansea and has written extensively on politics and the media.

Northcliffe sought political power, and used his independence from the political parties, which subsidized and suborned newspapers, to pursue his aim as self-appointed tribune of the people. This pleased neither politicians nor political journalists. It also missed the point that Northcliffe was essentially a great newspaperman, who exercised a profound influence on popular culture. This is not to deny that Northcliffe exercised a certain kind of political power; when conditions were right, when governments were weak, or politicians made vulnerable for other reasons, then the Northcliffe press could and did exert influence on the workings of high politics. Contemporaries in the political world seemed to fear him; but it was hard to judge the extent of their fear, for it was always useful for politicians to have as their stock-in-trade the argument that press power was too great and that press lords were over-mighty subjects.

SOURCE

4 Lord Northcliffe (in the fur coat) with former Prime Minister Arthur Balfour (to Northcliffe's right) helping to haul the Wright Brothers' plane into position for a demonstration flight, Pau, France, 1909.

ACTIVITY
KNOWLEDGE CHECK

Lord Northcliffe's influence on British politics, 1916–22

1 Summarise the key reasons why Lord Northcliffe came to enjoy such prominence in the British media.

2 In what ways, and for what reasons, did Northcliffe undermine Asquith's government during the First World War?

3 How far is it fair to say that Northcliffe treated Lloyd George in the same manner as he treated Asquith?

4 Evaluate the usefulness of each extract in Source 3 to a historian who wants to know about the role of Northcliffe in the downfall of Asquith.

5 How far does the gap between the date of writing and the events described undermine the value of Source 1 to a historian who wants to understand the influence of Lord Northcliffe on journalism?

Beaverbrook's undermining of Asquith and support for Lloyd George

There were a number of similarities between Northcliffe and Max Aitken (called Lord Beaverbrook from December 1916): both were self-made men from outside the traditional establishment. Aitken was born in New Brunswick, Canada, then part of the British Empire, in May 1879. Through a series of acquisitions and mergers in the cement, energy and finance sectors he became a millionaire by the age of 30. Both men were interested in politics and sought to influence developments through newspaper ownership. Aitken travelled to Britain in 1910 to carve out a role of national prominence. He succeeded in his ambition through his gradual acquisition of the *Daily Express* (he invested £25,000 in January 1911 and secretly gained a controlling interest with a further £17,500 investment in November 1916) and through his close personal connection to Andrew Bonar Law, Conservative Party leader from 1911–21 and 1922–23. Bonar Law was born in the same area of Canada. This connection paved the way for a deep and sincere friendship that even extended to Aitken taking care of Bonar Law as he lay dying from throat cancer in 1923. Both Aitken and Northcliffe developed political enemies and thought that they could do a better job of running national affairs. However, whereas Northcliffe failed to become an MP and subsequently preferred to conduct his influence from outside government, Aitken became a Conservative MP in December 1910 and relished his role on the inside as a political go-between. Although he remained a backbench MP until his appointment to the Cabinet as Minister of Information and Head of the Duchy of Lancaster in February 1918, Aitken enjoyed regular access to the political elite due to his connection with Bonar Law and his influence over the *Daily Express*.

The key events of Asquith's fall from power have been outlined above. However, the role of Beaverbrook in those events remains controversial. A significant reason for this is that one of the best sources of information on the political intrigue of early December is Beaverbrook himself. In 1928 and 1932, he published two volumes entitled *Politicians and the War* in which he described and analysed the events leading up to Lloyd George's accession to power. He was in regular contact with Bonar Law (through friendship) and Lloyd George (through his work at the War Office for the Canadian government) and served as a go-between for the two men. It is his role as a go-between that has attracted controversy. Beaverbrook made notes on the events as early as January 1917 but edited these during the intervening years as he gained access to a wider range of information, including private letters from Asquith to two mistresses. He also got a range of people, including Lloyd George, Bonar Law, Churchill and others involved in the events, to check his drafts and offer comments before publication. Significantly, however, he did not offer the same privilege to Asquith and his supporters. In his 1972 biography of Beaverbrook, historian A.J.P. Taylor points out how the draft gradually changed to promote the 'heroic' role of Bonar Law and diminish his own role in the proceedings. Taylor is not convinced by the changes and labels Beaverbrook 'the Kingmaker' in the relevant chapter.

EXTRACT 2

From A.J.P. Taylor's biography *Beaverbrook*, published in 1972. Taylor was a highly respected academic historian; he also became a friend of Beaverbrook (here referred to by his surname Aitken) following Taylor's very positive review of his historical books.

Some great change was impending in British politics during the winter of 1916–17. Northcliffe voiced dissatisfaction with Asquith in his newspapers, but his agitation was ineffective only because the dissatisfaction was so widespread. In this sense Northcliffe provided the driving force behind the political upheaval. He had no clear idea what would emerge from it. This was Aitken's doing. Aitken did not cause the storm. He did not foresee it. When it began to blow, he took advantage of it and turned it in a particular direction. He appreciated this himself. When asked in 1934: 'What is the biggest thing you have ever done?', he replied: 'The destruction of the Asquith Government which was brought about by an honest intrigue. If the Asquith Government had gone on, the country would have gone down'... Aitken himself hoped from the first to bring down Asquith, presumably with the idea of putting Bonar Law in his place. Lloyd George was primarily concerned to shake off Robertson's control [Robertson was Chief of the Imperial General Staff, a key role linking the Army and government]. But he also wanted effective strategic control of the war, and this turned him implicitly against Asquith almost without his knowing it. Bonar Law was willing to support Lloyd George against Robertson but had no inkling that this might grow into a move against Asquith... Aitken was pushing both Bonar Law and Lloyd George into a crisis neither wanted.

A.J.P. Taylor sees Beaverbrook as key to Asquith's downfall as he was the one who 'gave the wheel another shove' after proceedings had stalled with Asquith's initial rejection of the War Cabinet idea on 1 December 1916. He urged Lloyd George to threaten resignation unless his ideas were adopted. At the same time he also passed on details of the scheme to the *Express* and the *Daily Chronicle*. In his books, Beaverbrook makes it seem as if Bonar Law had been the driving force behind the plot to unseat Asquith. In fact, Bonar Law was perfectly happy with the initial agreement on 3 December. He only gave his full support to Lloyd George following Asquith's abrupt rejection of this agreement. In reality, the only plotter who had consistently worked to bring about Asquith's downfall was Beaverbrook. Even with this wily determination, however, Beaverbrook would have failed had Asquith not made the blunder of rejecting the original War Cabinet proposal based upon supposed Conservative Cabinet support, which subsequently vanished. Beaverbrook's enemies also blamed him for engineering the split that began the demise of the Liberal Party. Once again, it would be fairer to say that Asquith had the opportunity to maintain party unity had he not refused to serve under Bonar Law, Balfour or Lloyd George.

A Level Exam-Style Question Section B

To what extent was Lord Beaverbrook the chief cause of the downfall of Asquith's government in December 1916? (20 marks)

Tip

Start by analysing the extent to which the stated factor did contribute to the downfall of Asquith's coalition government. You should reflect on the issues with the evidence available for this analysis. Then move on to consider the comparative significance of other factors, such as the role of the Northcliffe press and the aims of David Lloyd George.

Beaverbrook's involvement in the abdication of Edward VIII

As the Prince of Wales, Edward had developed a playboy reputation throughout the 1920s. His father, George V, despaired of Edward's unsuitable behaviour. He hoped that his far more steady and serious younger son Albert, known to his family as Bertie, would inherit the throne and, in time, pass it on to his charming granddaughter Elizabeth. Edward inherited the throne on 20 January 1936 but was soon embroiled in an affair that led to his abdication 327 days later. Edward had fallen in love with an American divorcee, Wallis Simpson. They spent more and more time together despite the fact that her divorce hearing from her current husband was not due to be held until 27 October. At that time it was not permitted for a divorcee to marry in church while their previous spouse was still alive. Edward would have to break that rule to marry Mrs Simpson, something which the Head of the Church of England thought was unacceptable. It was largely for this reason that Prime Minister Stanley Baldwin opposed the marriage. He insisted that Edward could either marry Mrs Simpson or remain king, but he could not do both. Edward was convinced he had found a workable solution: a **morganatic marriage** would make them man and wife but would deny Mrs Simpson and her children any royal titles or privileges. The sticking point for Baldwin and the vast majority of the establishment was the issue of marriage of any sort to a divorcee. Added to this, there were lots of rumours in elite circles about Mrs Simpson's affairs, including one with powerful Nazi Joachim von Ribbentrop. Other rumours circulated about the sexual control that Simpson held over Edward. Such was the perceived seriousness of the situation that her telephones and, as it emerged in 2013, Edward's telephones were bugged by the government. Edward wanted to make an appeal directly to the British people via a radio broadcast on 3 December. Baldwin blocked this as he said that such a private appeal was an unconstitutional breach of the government's advice to the monarch. A week later, despite Mrs Simpson's willingness to withdraw from the marriage so that Edward could remain king, Edward announced his abdication. He became known as the Duke of Windsor, and his younger brother Albert became King George VI. Edward married Mrs Simpson in June 1937. His sympathy for Nazi Germany ensured that he remained a controversial figure even after his abdication.

KEY TERM

Morganatic marriage
A marriage between a couple of unequal social rank. The titles and privileges of the higher-ranked individual (usually the husband) do not pass to the spouse or their children. The term derives from the Latin term meaning the 'morning gift' provided by a husband to his wife to sustain her in the event of his death. The implication is that the morning gift is the only part of the husband's possessions the wife will be entitled to in such a marriage.

Beaverbrook played a small role in these events, which unfolded in the last months of 1936, although his enemies exaggerated his part. He was not a friend of Edward's and had only met him a few times before the abdication crisis. His first role in the crisis was to permit the publication of news about Mrs Simpson's divorce trial in October 1936. This was despite the request for privacy from Mrs Simpson's solicitor, an old friend of Beaverbrook. Despite stories in foreign newspapers, the British press had entirely ignored the increasingly public relationship between Edward and Mrs Simpson. Until the story finally broke at the start of December, this was the only reference to Mrs Simpson in print. The king invited Beaverbrook to Buckingham Palace on 16 October 1936 and requested privacy for Mrs Simpson from then on. The only reason for the divorce's newsworthiness was her connection to Edward, and this could lead to speculation about the sexual nature of their relationship. Beaverbrook visited Rothermere and the proprietor of the *Daily Chronicle* (a left-leaning daily newspaper with a circulation of around 400,000) to pass on the king's wishes. In mid-November, Edward telephoned Beaverbrook, then in New York, to inform him of his desire to marry Mrs Simpson and to ask for advice. Beaverbrook sailed back to England and informed the king that he would allow his papers to support the idea of a morganatic marriage. Privately he hoped for a delay to the marriage so that Edward would stay on the throne and hopefully lose interest in Mrs Simpson. A.J.P Taylor claims that Beaverbrook played a part in persuading Mrs Simpson to go to the south of France and withdraw from the marriage. His key motive was the strength of the Empire – he feared the effects that the abdication would have on the ability of the monarchy to bind the Empire together. Only the *Daily Express* and the *Daily Mail* supported the marriage, with all other national dailies opposed to it.

Beaverbrook's critics insisted that the *Express* had been used as part of his ongoing campaign against Baldwin. There is no question that Beaverbrook loathed the prime minister. Upon Baldwin's retirement in May 1937, he wrote a scathing article for the *Express* entitled 'Mr Baldwin is Always Right' in which he pointed out every occasion where Baldwin had changed his stance on national policy. However, Beaverbrook had been brought into the crisis by the king and had little contact with him following the meeting in mid-November. It is clear that the king acted according to what he thought was best for him and Mrs Simpson throughout, and was only marginally influenced by the positive press in the *Express* in early December. As Edward said in the radio broadcast he was allowed to make on 11 December, 'You must believe me when I tell you that I have found it impossible to carry the heavy burden of responsibility and to discharge my duties as king as I would wish to do without the help and support of the woman I love.'

HOW INFLUENTIAL WAS LORD ROTHERMERE IN THE PERIOD 1922–36?

The impact of Lord Rothermere's newspaper empire, its expansion, and the newspaper war of 1928–29

Lord Rothermere (Harold Harmsworth) was usually characterised as the dull, plodding relation to Alfred's charismatic genius. It is certainly true that whereas his younger brother had an intuitive flair for talent spotting and for anticipating the next big thing, Harold had a more meticulous, measured approach to business. One of the major factors in the early success of the Harmsworth press was the combination of Alfred's dynamism and Harold's business acumen. Harold had an uncanny ability to predict the profitability of a new enterprise, and that only abandoned him on occasion as he grew older. This gulf in temperament helps to explain their different relationship to their newspapers. Whereas Alfred was determined to use his newspapers to champion his causes, Harold saw them in a more detached sense, purely as a business interest. When Alfred died in 1922, Harold bought his brother's stake in Associated Newspapers for £1.6 million. Although he retained ownership of the *Mail*, the *Evening News*, the *Daily Mirror*, the *Weekly Dispatch*, the *Sunday Pictorial* and a number of local papers in Glasgow, his lack of emotional attachment to the press was made immediately apparent when he sold *The Times*. His business brain was revealed by a series of newspaper acquisitions and sales that he made throughout the 1920s and 1930s, some of which triggered a 'newspaper war' from 1928 to 1929.

Many of Rothermere's business and political interests were closely tied up with Lord Beaverbrook. He advised Aitken on the launch of his newspaper empire and always conveyed a sense of belief in him. He was also one of the two sponsors for Aitken's elevation to Lord Beaverbrook in December 1916. Their association blossomed in 1918 following the death of Rothermere's eldest son Vyvyan. This, on top of the death of his middle son Vere in 1916, drove Rothermere to the point of mental breakdown. Beaverbrook took Rothermere under his wing and coaxed him back to a still rather gloomy normality. Their business relationships became entwined in late 1922 when the Daily Mail Holding Trust bought 49 percent of Beaverbrook's stake in London Express Newspapers (he received 80,000 Daily Mail Trust shares as part of the deal). Rothermere hoped that this would ensure that competition between the *Mail* and the *Express* would never reach damaging levels. Beaverbrook bought the Hulton Press in 1923 and sold every title except the *Evening Standard* to Rothermere, who promptly sold most of them on at a profit of £1.8 million. Despite this apparent generosity, Beaverbrook gradually waged a circulation war against the *Mail*. He used the dividends from his investment in the *Mail* to build up the presses and distribution at the *Express,* and even offered huge wages to poach top *Mail* journalists. On 28 October 1928, he told the Conservative Party chairman, 'I shall go back to New Brunswick and retire a failure if I don't succeed in killing the *Daily Mail*.' Beaverbrook made a few changes, such as putting news headlines on the front page rather than adverts like the *Mail*. Thanks to the changes, his investments and above all the higher quality of the writing, the *Express* overtook the *Mail* as the highest circulation national daily in the 1930s. From only 40,000 in 1919, sales rose to 1.7 million in 1930 and 2.3 million in 1937.

Perhaps in response to the growing threat to his national newspapers, Rothermere sought to break into the regional press. Until he founded Northcliffe Newspapers Ltd in 1928, the Berry Brothers, Lord Kemsley and Lord Camrose had largely dominated this sector. This appeared to be a poor business move to many at the time, especially after the Berry Brothers strongly resisted this encroachment. In what became known as the newspaper war, both the Berrys and Rothermere used promotions and giveaways to boost local circulation, even if this resulted in damaging financial losses. Rothermere's titles won the contest in Gloucester,

Staffordshire, South Wales and Hull, while the Berrys clung on in Newcastle. In a bid to end this ruinous war, the Berrys agreed to leave Bristol, while Rothermere only set up one further paper in Derby, cancelling proposed titles in Cardiff, Sheffield and Aberdeen. By 1929, Rothermere was the proprietor of 14 daily and Sunday newspapers and had major holdings in three other newspaper empires. Although Northcliffe Newspapers Ltd was merged into Associated Newspapers in 1932, this did not signal a failure. The regional branch of Rothermere's press empire (handed over to his son in 1937) went on to be among the most lucrative in the following decades.

Lord Rothermere's influence, including support of revisions to First World War treaties

Revisions to First World War treaties

Rothermere shared many domestic political interests with Beaverbrook but also developed his own connections with Hungary and Germany. Rothermere became interested in the plight of Hungary after the First World War, following a meeting with Austrian princess Stephanie Hohenloe. He had taken an interest in Eastern Europe before this due to his gloomy prognosis for the spread of communism and his view of the region as a powder keg for future wars. The Treaty of Trianon (1920) had stripped Hungary of two-thirds of its pre-war territory, including the overwhelmingly Hungarian-populated Transylvania to Romania. Hohenloe's reports of the anger in Hungary led Rothermere to write and print two articles that called for a revision of the Treaty of Trianon. In 'Hungary's Place in the Sun', published on 11 June 1927, he argued that the territorial clauses in the Treaty were 'some of the worst frauds that have ever taken place in the public life of Europe'.

The Hungarians were ecstatic about the support and Rothermere was overwhelmed by the popular response. He received over 200,000 letters of thanks and, most incredibly, the offer to become the King of Hungary. His son Esmond was met by huge welcoming crowds when he went to receive an honorary doctorate for his father from a Hungarian university. Although Rothermere was laughed at for his sympathies, the *Mail* continued to print pro-Hungarian articles until the outbreak of the Second World War. Aside from his huge popularity in Hungary, nothing was achieved and Hungary remained without its confiscated territory.

'Squandermania'

Beaverbrook masterminded and spearheaded a public attack on what he branded '**squandermania**'. In 1921, Rothermere threw his weight behind this attack as President of the Anti-Waste League, a group that also sponsored sympathetic Conservative candidates at a number of by-elections. He was gloomy about the economic outlook and forecast that the government must stick to an annual budget of £800 million to avoid catastrophe. He provided substantial financial assistance to the League and this enabled them to win by-election seats in Dover, Hertford and Westminster St George in 1921. That year he also published a book called *Solvency or Downfall? Squandermania and its*

Story, a collection of all the articles on the subject printed in his *Sunday Pictorial* in 1919 and 1920. The book was dedicated to his surviving son Esmond as 'the first anti-waste MP'. The book repeatedly demanded that the government abandon planning, cut spending and privatise publicly owned assets. The combined press and political pressure contributed to the decision to abolish the Ministries of Shipping, Munitions and Food, and the lifting of public controls on a range of activities. However, there is no doubt that the onset of a severe recession in the period 1920–22 also prompted a swift reduction in government expenditure to ensure a balanced budget (the cut in spending was known as the 'Geddes Axe' after Chairman of the National Expenditure Committee, Sir Eric Geddes). Once government spending dipped to £800 million in 1922, Rothermere quit the League and left it impotent. Together with Beaverbrook, he returned his support to the Conservatives following their rejection of Lloyd George in October 1922.

KEY TERM

Squandermania
Beaverbrook used this phrase to pour scorn on what he saw as excessive peacetime government spending on projects that required too much government interference.

Lord Rothermere's clash with Stanley Baldwin in 1931

Rothermere and Beaverbrook were hostile to communism and viewed the rise of the Labour Party with unease. On 25 October 1924, the *Daily Mail* ran the headline 'Civil War Plot by Socialists' Masters: Moscow Orders to Our Reds, Great Plot Discovered Yesterday, Paralyse the Army and Navy'. The article exposed a telegram supposedly sent by Grigory Zinoviev, leader of the **Comintern**, to the Communist Party of Great Britain, which praised Labour's policy of recognising Soviet Russia. Despite the fact that the *Mail* had known of the letter since 15 September, the story was published just four days before the general election so that it would have the maximum impact on Labour support. The telegram was exposed as a fake in 1928. Written by White Russian enemies of communism, the letter found its way into the Foreign Office thanks to the combined efforts of British Intelligence and the Conservative Central Office. The true version of events was finally confirmed in the 1960s. Following a landslide Conservative victory in the 1924 election, Beaverbrook sent a telegram to Rothermere stating, 'I congratulate you most heartily on your magnificent victory. You have made the new Baldwin ministry. Now control it if you can.' Rothermere certainly tried. In a letter to a Conservative MP in 1929 he wrote: 'I cannot make it too abundantly clear that, under no circumstances whatsoever, will I support Mr Baldwin unless I know exactly what his policy is going to be, unless I have complete guarantees that such policy will be carried out if his party achieves office, and unless I am acquainted

KEY TERM

Comintern (1919–43)
An abbreviated term used to refer to the Communist International. This was an organisation that advocated communism for the whole world and supported action that worked towards communist revolution.

with the names of at least eight or ten of his most prominent colleagues in the next Ministry.' Baldwin read the letter out at a Conservative meeting in June 1930, together with his reaction: 'A more preposterous and insolent demand was never made on the leader of any political party. I repudiate it with contempt, and will resist that attempt at domination to the end.'

Neither Rothermere nor Beaverbrook was able to control Baldwin, despite the flow of generally unfavourable press directed towards him. They grew to despise the Conservative leader and blamed his lacklustre 'Safety First' campaign for losing to Labour in the 1929 general election. Beaverbrook in particular hated the way Baldwin had briefly raised the prospect of **protectionism** as a way to boost the British economy but without linking this to **Imperial Preference**. As a Canadian, the Empire was particularly close to his heart. In December 1929, having failed to win Baldwin to his cause, he helped to launch the Empire Crusade Register, a fund for a new political party, with £25,000 of his own money. Rothermere also contributed £5,000 due to his diehard attachment to British rule in India, which at that time was under the threat of Mohandas Gandhi's liberation campaign. He was far less attached to Imperial Preference as he saw tariffs on food imports as a 'stomach tax'.

KEY TERMS

Protectionism
The use of import taxes (tariffs) to make foreign goods more expensive than domestic ones. This protects domestic producers from foreign competition but increases the cost of imports, including food items.

Imperial Preference
This called for free trade (a rejection of tariffs) within the British Empire, with tariffs imposed on imports from outside the Empire. Beaverbrook referred to Imperial Preference as 'Empire Free Trade'.

The United Empire Party (UEP) was briefly launched in February 1930 before its permanent launch on 3 April 1930. It existed purely to promote Empire Free Trade as a way for Britain to escape the worst effects of the Great Depression (a collapse of global trade triggered by a crash on the US stock market in October 1929). Beaverbrook was the major driving force behind the Party. He spoke at meetings across the country and used the *Express* to give a lot of coverage to the cause, even when this led to a dip in sales figures. On 15 January 1930, Rothermere's *Sunday Pictorial* hailed Beaverbrook as the next prime minister. Beaverbrook thought for a while that his campaign was bearing fruit, but Baldwin broke a promise to hold a party referendum on food import tariffs. Beaverbrook decided to throw his support behind UEP candidates who stood against Conservatives at a series of by-elections in 1930 and 1931. Their victory at West Fulham in May 1930 and South Paddington in October 1930, and the split of the vote that allowed a Labour victory at East Islington in February 1931, greatly angered and concerned Baldwin. He realised he had to act to preserve Conservative unity, and for this reason went on the attack against Beaverbrook and Rothermere. The context of his attack was yet another by-election contest, this time in St George's, Westminster, in March 1931. He was particularly provoked by an article by 'Editor' (Rothermere) published in the *Mail* that questioned his ability to lead the Conservatives based on the alleged fact that he had squandered the fortune left to him by his father.

SOURCE 5

From a speech made by Stanley Baldwin to Conservative Party members at the Queen's Hall on 17 March 1931.

The papers conducted by Lord Rothermere and Lord Beaverbrook are not newspapers in the ordinary acceptance of the term. They are engines of propaganda for the constantly changing policies, desires, personal wishes, personal likes and dislikes of the two men. What are their methods? Their methods are direct falsehood, misrepresentation, half-truths, the alteration of the speakers' meaning by publishing a sentence spare from the context, such as you see in these leaflets handed out outside this hall; suppression and editorial criticism of speeches which are not reported in the paper... I have no idea the name of the gentleman ['Editor']. I would only observe that he is well qualified for the post he holds. The first part of the statement is a lie and the second part of the statement by its implications is untrue. The paragraph itself could only have been written by a cad. I have consulted a very high legal authority and am advised that an action for libel would lie. I shall not move in the matter, and for this reason: I should get an apology and heavy damages. The first is of no value, and the second I would not touch with a barge pole. What the proprietorship of these papers is aiming at is power, and power without responsibility – the prerogative of the harlot throughout the ages.

This contest is not a contest as to who is to lead the party, but as to who is to appoint the leader of the party. It is a challenge to the accepted constitutional Parliamentary system. That is why Liberals and Socialists alike resent this interference with the liberty of a political party just as much as we do, because it may be their turn tomorrow to suffer from what we have to suffer today.

SOURCE 6

A cartoon by Leonard Raven Hill published in *Punch* magazine in 1930. It shows Lord Rothermere and Lord Beaverbrook with their 'catch': Leo Amery. Amery was a Conservative MP who had been Colonial Secretary in Baldwin's government from 1924–29. He set up the Empire Marketing Board and was a 'diehard' for colonial rule in India. Although he was sympathetic to the UEP he never joined.

THE UNITED EMPIRE ANGLERS.

LORD ROTHERMERE. "GOT ANY BIG ONES?"
LORD BEAVERBROOK. "I'VE NOT ACTUALLY LANDED ANY; BUT AMERY'S NIBBLING AGAIN."

It was widely perceived that Baldwin had triumphed against his press baron rivals; certainly his leadership of the Conservatives was never challenged again, as it had been in 1930. His candidate, Duff Cooper, defeated the UEP candidate at the by-election and this marked the beginning of the end of Empire Free Trade. Two weeks later an agreement signed between Baldwin and Beaverbrook, which the latter referred to as the Stornoway Pact, pledged the Conservatives' agreement to pursue the use of tariffs and quotas to promote British agriculture. While some tariffs were introduced at the British Empire Economic Conference held in Ottawa in 1932, this was far from the full implementation of Empire Free Trade. The issue failed to excite the British electorate and there was just one more dismal by-election defeat for a UEP candidate at East Fife in early 1933. Although Beaverbrook claimed some success, in reality it was a near-total defeat. The defeat was less acute for Rothermere, but only because he had only ever been a lukewarm supporter of Empire Free Trade.

Lord Rothermere's support for Oswald Mosley and the British Union of Fascists (BUF)

Rothermere, far more than Beaverbrook, became sympathetic towards the extreme right, although he was only prepared to go so far with this support. Oswald Mosley had been a promising Labour MP before he became disillusioned with the lack of innovation in tackling the economic crisis. He founded the New Party to promote his own ideas at the 1931 election, but he only gained 0.2 percent of the vote. After this abysmal result, he became disillusioned with democracy itself. In 1932, he formed the British Union of Fascists (BUF), with the aim of emulating the Italian dictator Benito Mussolini. Members were easily identified by their black-shirt uniforms. The BUF was openly racist and anti-Semitic, yet Rothermere initially pledged support. He invested £70,000 in a cigarette company whose proceeds would fund the BUF. It is likely that G. Ward Price, chief reporter at the *Mail* and a good friend of Mosley, helped to arrange the funding. At the height of his support, on 15 January 1934, the *Mail* ran an article by Rothermere with the headline 'Hurrah for the Blackshirts'. At this time employees were known to turn up at work in black shirts. Rothermere ended this association after a violent rally at the Kensington Olympia on 7 June 1934 where a large number of fights broke out between blackshirts and communists, who had infiltrated the gathering. Rothermere and Mosley both blamed the threats of Jewish advertisers to cancel contracts with the *Mail* for disassociation, but the timing suggests that the press baron was more concerned with connections to thuggery. Events proved Rothermere's decision to be sound. In October 1936, a BUF march through East London, an area home to many Jewish and Irish immigrants, turned into a violent clash that became known as the Battle of Cable Street. The struggle against fascism in the Second World War made Mosley and the BUF even more unpopular. Mosley was imprisoned for three years and the BUF was banned. He was released in 1943, at which point he was deemed not to be a threat to the war effort.

EXTEND YOUR KNOWLEDGE

Lord Rothermere's relationship with Adolf Hitler

Lord Rothermere developed a controversial relationship with Nazi leader Adolf Hitler. He first met the future German Führer on 14 September 1930 and prophesised his leadership over two years before he was appointed chancellor in January 1933. The *Mail* regularly ran positive pieces about the rebirth of Germany under Hitler and his heroic role in standing up to communism. In March 1934, Rothermere even wrote an article calling for colonies stripped from Germany after the First World War to be restored; Hitler sent one of many letters of thanks for this support. Just as with the BUF, Rothermere grew more cautious of his association with Hitler following a violent episode on 30 June 1934, when over 400 of Hitler's enemies were murdered in what became known as the Night of the Long Knives. Rothermere maintained cordial relations with Hitler but began to inform the British government of any intelligence gained from this friendship. He was made to look foolish in September 1939 when the European war he publicly predicted would not break out was unleashed by Hitler's invasion of Poland.

SOURCE

7

Oswald Mosley giving a speech at a British Union of Fascists rally in East London c1935. The growing size of such rallies was one reason for the 1936 Public Order Act that banned political uniforms and military-style organisations.

SOURCE

8

An editorial comment published in the *Spectator* magazine on 19 January 1934. The *Spectator* was, and still is, a right-wing journal aimed at an educated, informed readership.

Monday's 'Daily Mail' is not entirely negligible. It is quite true that the 'Daily Mail' is little read by people who think; it is equally true, as the 'Manchester Guardian' demonstrates with the aid of a number of telling quotations, that previous nostrums [an ineffective medicine made by a quack] of Lord Rothermere's, such as the United Empire Party, have been ignominious fiascos. But the Blackshirts, like the 'Daily Mail', appeal to people unaccustomed to thinking. The average 'Daily Mail' reader is a potential Blackshirt ready-made. When Lord Rothermere tells his clientele to go and join the Fascists some of them pretty certainly will. There is little sign of the British Fascists becoming a danger, but they may quite well become a nuisance. But nothing Lord Rothermere can say will help them so much as dictatorship-talk from the Left. Meanwhile, Lord Beaverbrook, it is interesting to observe, launches the slogan, 'Empire Ever, Nazi-ism Never'. 'Nazi-ism' in this sense appears to include Fascism of all brands.

ACTIVITY
KNOWLEDGE CHECK

The influence of Lord Rothermere and Lord Beaverbrook on British politics, 1922–36

1 Explain how far you think Beaverbrook influenced the abdication of Edward VIII in 1936.

2 Give reasons why there was a 'newspaper war' from 1928 to 1929. Explain the significance of these events for the British press.

3 List Rothermere's foreign and domestic political goals and add a judgement about the extent to which he succeeded in each goal.

4 Which is the more useful source in understanding the political influence of the press barons in the 1930s: Source 5 or Source 8? Explain your answer.

A Level Exam-Style Question Section B

'Lord Rothermere failed to achieve his political aims.'

How far do you agree with this judgement? (20 marks)

Tip

Each paragraph should focus on one particular political aim. Consider the order in which you deal with each aim. A good essay will offer a progression of comparative judgements with regard to his aims. You might also consider which of his aims were of greatest significance when making an overall judgement about the extent of his success or failure.

HOW INFLUENTIAL WAS THE *DAILY HERALD* IN THE PERIOD 1914–36?

The role of George Lansbury

George Lansbury was born on 21 February 1859 and spent virtually his whole life based in the East End of London. Although he was not raised in poverty, he witnessed the effects of slum housing, poor education and health care, and low and intermittent wages on the people of the East End. He became a devout Christian and, having become disillusioned with the slow, ineffectual pace of Liberal reform, became a socialist in 1889. Lansbury joined the Social Democratic Federation in 1892 and stood unsuccessfully at a series of by-elections before ploughing his considerable energy into local politics in Poplar. He served on the board of Poor Law Guardians and helped found a school and a farm to provide more effective support for the poorest in the area. Lansbury joined the Independent Labour Party in 1903 and was among the most left-wing of this broad coalition of trade unionists, disillusioned Liberals and socialists. He finally became an MP in 1910, winning the Bow and Bromley seat and became well known for his unflinching support for female suffrage. He was once ordered to leave the House of Commons for shaking his fist at Asquith and branding him as 'beneath contempt' for his reactionary views on the subject. In October 1912, Lansbury resigned his seat in order to fight a by-election on the suffrage issue. He lost his seat and in April 1913 he was sent to Pentonville Prison for his opposition to the '**Cat and Mouse Act**'. It was shortly after his release from prison that his nine-year editorship of the *Daily Herald* began.

Lansbury's tenure as proprietor and editor of the *Daily Herald* had an unpromising start. His journalistic experience was limited to writing for a local Liberal monthly 'The Coming Times' between 1885 and 1895 and his contributions to the early *Daily Herald*. The newspaper, only launched in April 1912, had gone bankrupt in June 1913. Lansbury then bought it from the official receivers for £100. Despite this, Lansbury enjoyed some remarkable success before passing ownership over to the TUC and the Labour Party in 1922. There were a number of reasons for this success.

- Lansbury recognised that left-wingers of all shades would have to stand together if they were to offer effective opposition to the right-wing forces that dominated Britain. This was true nowhere more than in the media, where the Northcliffe press was so dominant. Until the *Daily Herald* (which emerged from a strike pamphlet called *The World* printed by the London Society of Compositors in January 1911) there was no left-wing daily newspaper. The divisions within the left were made apparent by the appearance of two newspapers in quick succession: the *Daily Herald*, followed six months later by the *Daily Citizen*. Whereas the *Citizen* was the official mouthpiece of the Labour Party, the *Herald* before Lansbury had attacked Labour MPs and union leaders just as often as right-wing figures. Charles Lapworth, the editor before Lansbury, had ensured that the newspaper supported all strikes, even unofficial ones. Headlines such as 'Lead on you Labour leaders if you don't want to be run over!' were typical of Lapworth's critical view of anyone who co-operated with the capitalist system. Lansbury did not like the personal attacks and encouraged a broader range of opinion, even if this led to a lack of overall editorial clarity. This inclusive approach became more important when the *Citizen* collapsed, never to rise again, in June 1915. Lansbury saw it as the *Herald*'s duty to speak for the left-wing as a whole, not just one section.

KEY TERM

Cat and Mouse Act
This was how the British public referred to the officially titled Prisoners (Temporary Discharge for Ill-Health) Act 1913. The Act allowed for the release of prisoners who neared death as a result of their hunger strikes against their treatment as common, rather than political, prisoners. Once they had recovered their health outside prison, the former prisoners were rearrested to serve the remainder of their sentence. It was felt that the government was playing with these prisoners in the way a cat plays with its prey.

- The growth in circulation was also due to the quality of writing and hugely powerful, popular cartoons by Australian Will Dyson. Whole front pages were regularly given over to his cartoons, which regularly savaged capitalists through their depiction as 'Fat', an obscenely obese figure. Several contributors were famous authors or went on to become famous: H.G. Wells, Hilaire Belloc, Aldous Huxley, Siegfried Sassoon, Robert Graves and G.K. Chesterton, to name a few. The newspaper had made a name for itself from the start through reports about the far higher loss of life for women and children in third class than first or second class aboard the *Titanic*. Lansbury himself was proud of the *Daily Herald*'s status as a 'rebel organ'.

SOURCE 9

An advertisement poster for the *Daily Herald*, celebrating its high circulation, created by artist Tom Purvis in 1935. Purvis was also well known for his designs for London and North East Railway that advertised British holiday destinations.

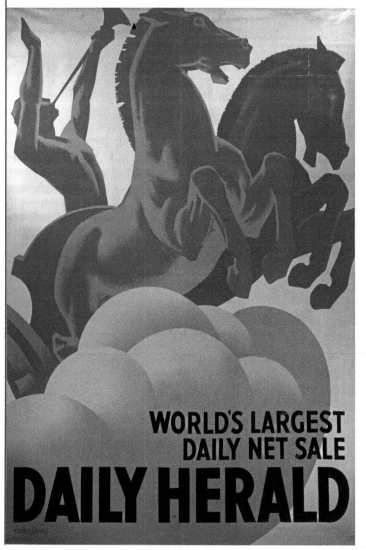

WORLD'S LARGEST DAILY NET SALE
DAILY HERALD

SOURCE 10

From George Lansbury's autobiography *My Life*, published in 1928.

Alone in the British press we denounced the scandals connected with the sinking of the *Titanic*, and forced the Government to institute an inquiry which in turn we proved was, from first to last, a more or less whitewashing affair. Our presence among the daily Press forced journals with much bigger circulations to mention at least the fact that, to the eternal discredit of those concerned, the cry which sounded loudest was 'First-class passengers first'...

Although at all times we never knew one day from another how to pay our bills, we started funds to assist unemployed marchers from the provinces. It could be said of us that whenever a strike took place we were in its midst... Without the *Daily Herald*, and the influence which a daily paper published in London gives, we should have hopelessly failed. Those who think a newspaper is judged only by its circulation, or that its influence is confined to those who boast of millions of readers, are not aware that the most influential among Tory papers are those with small circulations. In this matter quality counts as well as money...

Nobody has yet discovered how to compete with the octopus Press, and the money lords who now control it. Insurance schemes, stunts, huge advertising all cost no end of money; money which has never been available either for me or any other Labour press manager or editor. I think we must continue to do our best with what means we possess until the growing intelligence of the masses turns their minds away from the poisonous trash poured out against them in the insidious form of news propaganda by those who use the Press today to keep things as they are... Our work has not failed: on the foundations we have built with so much effort and sacrifice will one day arise a great Press devoted, not to the spread of half-truths and lies, but to the single propaganda of truth.

A Level Exam-Style Question Section A

Study Source 10 before you answer this question.

Assess the value of the source for revealing the influence of the *Daily Herald* and the role of George Lansbury at the newspaper.

Explain your answer using the source, the information given about its origin and your own knowledge about the historical context. (20 marks)

Tip

It can help to structure your answer in the exam by using a pen to underline parts of the text that you will challenge or support with your own knowledge. This approach can also help you to avoid missing important points raised within the source.

The *Herald* and the significance of its editorial stance on the First World War, conscientious objectors and the Russian Revolutions

The *Daily Herald* and the First World War

Popular demand for war stories led to a collapse in circulation figures for the left-wing press; their right-wing rivals simply had more money and more reporters to facilitate better war reporting. On 3 October 1914, just a couple of months after the outbreak of the First World War, the *Daily Herald* went weekly and, until its restoration as a daily paper on 31 March 1919, was known simply as the *Herald*. Lansbury was a pacifist and had published the headline 'War is Hell' in July 1914 when fighting broke out between Austria and Serbia. However, the Labour movement as a whole was divided in its attitude to the war. The majority accepted that it was Britain's moral duty to stand up to German militarism and defend democratic values in Europe, while a minority of pacifists rejected any British involvement from the outset. Ramsay MacDonald resigned as Labour leader due to his pacifism, and his replacement Arthur Henderson served in the Cabinet from May 1915 until August 1917. The tone of the *Herald* reflected this division. Until Christmas 1914, the newspaper concentrated on the social and economic impact of the war, with campaigns for the care of soldiers' wives and children, and against the impact of rising prices. It was especially critical of those who profiteered from the war. Once the government had addressed these issues, the increasingly grim stories of suffering at the front led the *Herald* to become *the* anti-war journal. It continued to expose social injustice on the Home Front. Its most famous headline, 'How They Starve at the Ritz' on 24 October 1917, published the menu and details of a huge banquet enjoyed by a *Herald* reporter. This at a time when Britain had only six weeks' worth of food due to the impact of German submarine warfare.

The *Herald* and conscientious objectors

In May 1915, the *Herald* launched a discussion about what peace terms would be acceptable from Germany. The extent to which the paper was out of step with popular opinion was revealed by the overwhelming majority of responses from its readers to Lansbury, which called for no negotiated peace whatsoever. This did not prevent the *Herald* answering the Northcliffe-owned *Evening News'* NO! campaign to tentative German peace proposals in December 1916 with its own YES! poster campaign. The *Herald* offered unswerving support for conscientious objectors (men who refused to take any part in the armed forces following the introduction of conscription). While the *Mail* branded these 16,000 men '**conchies**' and 'slackers', the *Herald* offered support and reported their trials sympathetically if they were arrested (there was even a police raid on a *Herald* dance party and help had to be given to several men 'on the run' to evade arrest that night). Lansbury was pelted with missiles and subject to personal verbal assaults when he attended an anti-conscription rally in late 1915. He argued that 'no man should be conscripted by hunger or by pressure, but all who want the war carried on should take their share of the risks and sacrifices involved in war'. At a meeting with Lloyd George after the war in January 1919, Lansbury pleaded for the release of those conscientious objectors still in prison. The men were released a short time after this meeting.

The *Herald* and the Russian Revolution

Lansbury and the vast majority of the Labour movement welcomed news of the 1917 February Revolution in Russia (see page 84). The downfall of the autocratic Tsar (emperor) had been a progressive hope for over a century. The *Herald* helped to organise a huge rally at the Royal Albert Hall on 31 March with 12,000 packed inside and a further 5,000 unable to gain entry. Lansbury made a hugely popular speech in which he set out his attitude towards the revolution. Such fulsome praise for an event that ultimately led Russia to cease hostilities with Germany, together with its subversive suggestions to British troops, attracted the government's anger.

SOURCE 11

From a speech by George Lansbury to a crowd of 12,000 socialists who gathered at the Royal Albert Hall on 31 March 1917 to celebrate the fall of the Russian Tsars.

We have met here to celebrate one of the great historical events in the history of the world... It is a great and glorious thought that you gather up all the work of the men and women and the boys and girls of Russia who have given all they had to give for Russian liberty. This triumph has come, friends, because for the first time... working-class soldiers have refused to fire on the workers. To me, comrades, that is the greatest lesson of all... When the working-classes of all nations refuse to shoot down the working-classes of other countries, Governments won't be able to make wars any more. This war would end tomorrow if the troops on all sides marched out into No Man's Land and refused to fight any longer... To the young men – if there are any here; to the young women – there are many here – I want to say this: it is fine to cheer these other people; a finer thing still is to emulate and follow their example.

The impact of the 1920 Kamenev telegram

In September 1920, the *Daily Herald* was embroiled in a scandal surrounding allegations of its work for, and funding by, the communist regime in Russia. The scandal was triggered by the publication of eight telegrams in *The Times* that had been intercepted and deciphered by British intelligence. One telegram, from Communist Party leader Lenin to Leonid Kamenev (the Communist Party boss in Moscow and a member of the Party's powerful Central Committee), caused particular outrage among British enemies of socialism. Despite his seniority within the Communist Party, Kamanev had been sent to London on 8 July 1920 to lead a Russian trade delegation for two months.

SOURCE 12 A telegram sent from Lenin to Kamenev, written on 20 August 1920. The telegram had been encrypted using a device called MARTA. British intelligence had cracked the code and could read all encrypted correspondence.

It is hardly likely that we shall capture Warsaw soon. The enemy there has built up strength and is attacking. Obviously, Lloyd George is deliberately dividing up the roles with Churchill, using pacifist phrases to conceal the real policy of the French and Churchill and duping the Henderson-and-Co. fools. Do your utmost to bring this home to the British workers; write articles and theses for them yourself, teach Marxism concretely, teach them to make use of the leftward swings of the Hendersons, teach them agitation among the masses—that is your main task. Lloyd George has been duping us with pacifism and has helped Churchill to land assistance for the Poles in Danzig. That is the essence of the matter.

Kamenev had also sent telegrams to Lenin in which he described £40,000-worth of funding for the *Daily Herald*, smuggled into Britain in the form of diamonds and platinum, with a further instalment of £10,000 to follow. Telegrams from other Bolsheviks based in London suggested that they were 'making use of the *Daily Herald* for purposes of information and agitation' and that the funds were justified by their view that the paper 'acts as if it were our organ'. British intelligence was also aware of £25,000-worth (about £850,000 in 2016 terms) of paper given to Lansbury by a Bolshevik agent in Sweden while he was en route to Russia in January 1920. On 10 September 1920, a headline in the *Daily Herald* openly stated, 'Shall we accept £75,000 of Russian money?' For Lansbury, the dilemma was not so much about being paid by foreign revolutionaries (from whom he felt no strings were attached to the payment), but about taking money from such an impoverished state. In order to understand the significance of the telegrams and why they caused such outrage when a selection was published in *The Times*, it is necessary to understand the backdrop of Anglo-Russian relations and domestic tension that followed the First World War in Britain.

In October 1917, under their pre-revolutionary name of the Bolshevik Party, the communists had seized power from more liberal, moderate revolutionaries who themselves had deposed the last Russian Tsar six months earlier. A civil war soon erupted between the Bolshevik Reds and their assorted domestic enemies, the Whites. The leaders of the former Allies (Britain, France, the USA and Japan) immediately backed the Whites. The Bolsheviks had signed a separate peace agreement with the Germans in March 1918, and were refusing to return huge amounts of money lent to Russia by governments and private institutions before the October Revolution. The British were also alarmed at reports of Bolshevik support for rebellious movements in northern India, then the 'jewel in the crown' of the British Empire. Between November 1918 and early 1920, the British government spent £100 million (around £28 billion in 2016 terms) on military support for the Whites, including the deployment of British troops in Russia until 5 April 1919.

The Reds gained the upper hand in the civil war and the possibility emerged of using the Red Army to export communist revolution to other countries. Poland had only recently been reconstituted as a separate state by the Treaty of Versailles and was determined to safeguard its independence. War broke out for control over the neighbouring states of Belarus and Ukraine. The war initially went well for the Poles, but by July 1920 the Reds had pushed into Poland. Despite its desire to seal a trade deal with Russia, the British government threatened to send arms to Poland unless the Red Army stopped at the Curzon Line, the Russo-Polish border agreed at Versailles. The Bolsheviks rejected this, but the Labour Party launched a campaign against sending arms to Poland. The *Daily Herald* helped to establish the 'Council of Action' in early August 1920 to prevent the loading of military aid to Poland. While no further arms were dispatched, this was not quite the victory claimed by Lansbury. Lloyd George was reluctant to send further aid, and Polish victory at the Battle of Warsaw in mid-August made such support unnecessary. In the treaty that formally ended the war in March 1921, the Poles gained a border east of the Curzon line.

Lloyd George must have seen the publication of the telegrams as a successful compromise. He had to placate a storm of anti-Bolshevik feeling in the Northcliffe press and from members of his Conservative-dominated Cabinet, such as Churchill and Lord Curzon. The telegrams served as a public excuse to 'expel' Kamenev from Britain on 11 September 1920. In reality, although he accused Kamenev of a 'gross breach of faith' for his interference in British domestic affairs, Lloyd George knew he was due to leave Britain the next day anyway. He allowed other Bolsheviks known to be engaged in espionage to remain in London, partly because this helped British intelligence to gather information on Russian activities, and partly because it helped to pave the way for the Anglo-Soviet Trade Agreement, finally signed on 16 March 1921. Russia was a key supplier of the raw materials that British industry required in order to help escape economic recession in the early 1920s. British concerns were directly reflected in a clause in the trade agreement, which stated as a condition of trade 'no interference in any way in the politics or internal affairs of the country'.

SOURCE

13 From the minutes of meeting with the Soviet trade delegation on 10 September 1920, where David Lloyd George presented his reasons for expelling Kamenev from Britain.

He... subsidised a newspaper, not merely hostile to the Government... This is a newspaper whose very objective it is to attack the institutions of this country, which every day is trying to sow strife... to create unrest, and to spread discord... It is a great mistake to think an old Government like ours is so utterly inept that men can do anything they like without its being discovered. Our machinery is fairly efficient.

The Conservative and Northcliffe press attacks on Bolshevism are explained by tense industrial relations in the years that followed the First World War. Trade unions had supported the war at the outset, but anger over profiteering and wages failing to keep up with inflation led to a huge number of strikes in 1917–18. While the Clydeside shipbuilders had been in the vanguard of industrial action during the war, a 'Triple Alliance' of miners, transport and rail workers were perceived as the key threat both before and after the war. Yet the government's worst fears failed to materialise when the transport and rail unions failed to go on strike in support of the miners – 15 April 1921 was branded 'Black Friday' by those on the left such as the *Daily Herald*. The paper, always supportive of strikes, was seen as a threat to national stability and economic recovery. On 13 May 1919, the government published a secret War Office enquiry on whether British troops were becoming union members and whether they would help to break strikes in case of emergency. On 9 July 1919, the government also published an instruction for bundles of the *Daily Herald* destined for troops to be burnt with as little attention as possible. Circulation figures had risen to around 400,000, so the paper's influence was far from negligible.

Despite this surge, readership figures for the *Daily Herald* fell back to nearer 200,000 by 1922, a year when the paper made losses of £80,485 (around £15 million in modern money). Lansbury, for so long reluctant to be bound to one element of the Labour movement, was forced to give proprietorial and editorial control of the *Daily Herald* to the Labour Party and the TUC. From 1922 until its resale to the commercial Odhams Press in 1930, the *Daily Herald* served as the official newspaper of the Labour Party. Divisions within the Party continued to be reflected in the paper thanks to new editor Henry Hamilton Fyfe (especially the letters page, which greatly angered Party leader Ramsay MacDonald). But it lost some of its charm when Lansbury finally quit the paper in 1925. Under commercial ownership the *Daily Herald* began to mirror its rivals in the Rothermere and Beaverbrook press, with giveaways and political news reduced from 12 to two of its 20 pages.

ACTIVITY

KNOWLEDGE CHECK

The importance of the *Daily Herald*, 1914–36

1 Explain the reasons why George Lansbury had such an impact on the *Daily Herald* from 1914 to 1922.

2 Summarise the *Daily Herald*'s attitude to the First World War and the Russian Revolution.

3 Explain why, and with what significance, Lloyd George published the Kamenev telegram in August 1920.

4 How useful is Source 13 in understanding the importance of the *Daily Herald* in Britain between 1914 and 1922?

THINKING HISTORICALLY Cause and consequence (7a & b)

Questions and answers

Questions that historians ask vary depending on what they think is important. It is the questions that interest us that define the history that is written. These questions change with time and place. Different historians will also come up with different answers to the same questions, depending on their perspectives and methods of interpretation, as well as the evidence they use.

Below are three historians who had different areas of interest.

Ross McKibbin	A.J.P. Taylor	Stephen Koss
• A social and political historian who specialises in the history of the Labour Party • He is interested in the ways that social identities shape political allegiance	• A political historian and biographer who was fascinated by British history • He was interested in the Liberal politicians and the British press	• A biographer and specialist in 19th- and 20th-century European diplomatic history • He was interested in leading statesmen and British foreign policy

These are some key events in the age of the press barons:

The publication of the first edition of the *Daily Mail*	The fall of Asquith as prime minister	The newspaper circulation war
The Defence of the Realm Act 1914 introduces censorship for the duration of the First World War	The Kamenev Telegram	The *Daily Mail* supports the Blackshirts
The Shells Crisis	The Zinoviev Telegram	The Abdication Crisis

Work in groups of between three and six.

1 Which of these events would have been of most interest to each historian? Explain your answer.

2 Each take the role of one historian and devise a question that would interest them about each of the events.

3 Discuss each event in turn. Present the questions that have been devised for each historian and offer some ideas about how they would have answered them.

4 For each event, decide as a group which question is the most interesting and worthwhile of the three.

Answer the following questions in pairs.

5 Identify the different ways that each historian would approach writing an account of the rise of Lloyd George as prime minister.

6 In what ways would McKibbin and A.J.P. Taylor differ in their explanations of the significance of the Kamenev and Zinoviev Telegrams? What would be the focus of their arguments?

Answer the following questions individually.

7 All three historians may produce very different accounts and explanations of the same piece of history. Of the three historians, whose account would you prefer to read first? Explain your answer.

8 Do the differences in these accounts mean that one is more valid than the others?

9 Explain why different historians write different historical explanations.

10 Explain why different explanations of the same event can be equally valid.

ACTIVITY
SUMMARY

The age of the press barons, 1914–36

1 Create a graph with 'Degree of influence: 0–100%' on the vertical axis and 'Time: 1914–36' on the horizontal axis.

2 Plot a line that you feel best describes the impact of: Lord Northcliffe, Lord Rothermere, Lord Beaverbrook, George Lansbury/the *Daily Herald*. Give each person a separate line.

3 Once you have plotted all the lines, explain the overall trend for each line as well as any major peaks, troughs or turning points.

4 When you have done this, write a summary paragraph about the reasons why one newspaper proprietor could be judged to have been more influential than the rest. You could consider having a 'balloon debate' based on this task.

WIDER READING

Lee Thompson, J. *Northcliffe: Press Baron in Politics, 1865–1922*, John Murray Ltd (2000)

Postgate, R. *The Life of George Lansbury*, Longman, Green & Co. (1951)

Richards, H. *The Bloody Circus: The Daily Herald and the Left*, Pluto Press (1997)

Taylor, A.J.P. *Beaverbrook*, Hamish Hamilton (1972)

Taylor, S.J. *The Great Outsiders: Northcliffe, Rothermere and the Daily Mail*, Weidenfeld & Nicholson (1996)

3.4

Wireless and the war: propaganda, information and entertainment, 1939–45

KEY QUESTIONS

- What were the most significant impacts of BBC war reporting, 1939–45?
- How successfully did the BBC broadcast to the home front?
- What was the impact of British and enemy propaganda broadcasts?

INTRODUCTION

The Second World War was a 'total war' – it drew upon the efforts and resources of the whole country to fight a determined, powerful enemy on many fronts to the bitter end. Even before war was officially declared on Germany, on 3 September 1939, political leaders and powerful figures in mass media realised that the control and use of information would be a vital part of the war effort. Not only would censorship be critical to prevent information of any use reaching the enemy, but propaganda would play a vital part in the maintenance of public morale. It was feared that if morale failed, the war would not be waged on the home front with the intensity required to secure victory. No one understood this better than Winston Churchill. His speeches as British prime minister were felt to be fundamental to public morale during the darkest days of the Second World War. However, the war was also a struggle of ideas: Nazi Germany was a young dictatorship (only six years old in 1939) that claimed the British and French democracies had become tired, decadent and ripe for replacement. The British government faced the difficult task of promoting the virtue and vitality of a modern, free democracy while controlling information in a fashion that some regarded as dictatorial. Despite some serious issues in the first months of the war, a remarkably effective balance was struck. This was in large part due to the increasingly smooth working relations between the armed forces, a range of government ministries and key figures in the mass media. Although the BBC took time to adjust, it came to play a leading role in the national war effort.

WHAT WERE THE MOST SIGNIFICANT IMPACTS OF BBC WAR REPORTING, 1939–45?

The impact of broadcasts from the front

Problems with news reporting early in the war

Despite some careful preparation before the outbreak of the war, the BBC did not get off to a good start as a news broadcaster. Many MPs, the popular press and members of the public were

1936 – Public Relations Division of the BBC establishes Listener Research Section

1938 – 3 January: BBC launches its first foreign language broadcast service in Arabic

27 September: BBC's European Service starts, with broadcasts in French, German, Italian, Spanish and Portuguese by September 1939

| 1936 | 1937 | 1938 | 1939 |

1939 – BBC monitoring established to keep government informed of developments revealed by foreign broadcasts. BBC Listener Research Section expanded and renamed Listener Research Department

1 September: German invasion of Poland triggers mass evacuations from urban areas. The BBC closes National and Regional Programmes and launches Home Service. Television broadcasts stop

4 September: Ministry of Information founded and starts work the next day

highly critical of both news coverage and entertainment provision. Such criticism was deserved, yet at the same time it was not entirely fair for a range of reasons.

The BBC had seen itself as a news broadcaster rather than a news gatherer, and it had an understanding with the press that it would not release news before it had appeared in print. With the exception of coverage of the May 1926 General Strike and the September 1938 Munich Crisis, there had only been one news bulletin a day at 6 p.m. So the BBC received a lot of press criticism when, on 25 August 1939, it introduced more bulletins that broadcast news yet to appear in print. At this time the BBC had only two reporters: Richard Dimbleby and David Howarth. The BBC relied on news agencies such as Reuters, foreign broadcasts and official government communications for the content of its bulletins. Plans had been made to improve this situation in anticipation of a large demand for broadcast news in the event of war.

The BBC, like many other organisations in Britain, expected war with Germany to open with a hugely destructive aerial assault on British towns and cities. Around 600,000 casualties were expected. The likely destruction of printing presses and means of distribution would lead to greater reliance on broadcast news. As a result, the BBC was placed on a war footing on 1 September 1939.

- Twenty-eight percent of its staff were evacuated from London to Wood Horton Hall near Evesham, Worcestershire, and others were sent as far afield as Bristol, Caernarvon and Glasgow.

- The two pre-war channels – the Regional Programme and National Programme – were closed and replaced by a single Home Service. This broadcast on just three transmitters pointing north and south in an attempt to prevent German planes using the signals as an orientation guide.

- The **BBC Board of Governors** was reduced from seven governors to two, to ensure swift decision-making.

- The number of news bulletins was increased to ten each day.

Reporting during the 'Phoney War'

There was a flurry of national action. Some 834,000 children, 500,000 mothers and 103,000 teachers were evacuated from urban centres to rural areas, and gas masks were issued which had to be carried at all times. However, the feared onslaught did not materialise for another eight months. In Britain, this period of inactivity became known as 'the Bore War' (a pun on the Boer War of 1899–1902), but the American term 'Phoney War' came to displace this original name in popular memory. By January 1940, two-thirds of those evacuated had returned home and very few people carried their gas masks around. Despite a huge demand for news, there was little to report due to a total lull in fighting between the defeat of Poland on 6 October 1939 and the rapid overrun of Scandinavia and Benelux in April 1940. News bulletins quickly became repetitive and were soon cut to seven a day. The press criticised the bulletins as gloomy and a mockery. At a Cabinet meeting, Winston Churchill mentioned his loathing of the 'unrelieved pessimism' of the BBC news, while Labour leader Clement Attlee referred to 'very wide criticism of broadcasting' in parliament on 26 September 1939.

KEY TERM

BBC Board of Governors
This existed from 1927 until 2007 when it was replaced by the BBC Trust. It was a group of 12 people who appointed the BBC's director-general, approved general strategy and policy, dealt with serious complaints, and compiled an annual report into the performance of the Corporation. The chairman of the board was a government appointment and the Board itself was answerable to parliament.

1941 – 10 May: Blitz ends
1 June: clothes rationing introduced

18 December: National Service (No. 2) Act requires all men and women aged 18–60 to be recruited to some form of National Service

1942 – 26 January: first US soldiers (GIs) arrive in Britain
1 July: petrol no longer available for private motorists

1944 – 27 February: BBC launches General Forces Programme to replace Forces Programmes and Overseas Service

| 1940 | 1941 | 1942 | 1943 | 1944 |

1940 – 10 May: Neville Chamberlain resigns as prime minister. Winston Churchill takes control of all-party coalition government. Some unemployment benefits cut

9 July–31 October: Battle of Britain

7 September: start of the Blitz (Cardiff, Plymouth, Birmingham and Liverpool bombed before start of Blitz proper)

1943 – 29 July: women aged 19–50 recruited for work in aeroplane and munitions factories; men can choose to work in coal mines rather than perform military service

December: men are selected for mines by fortnightly ballots

The lack of news was exacerbated by the reluctance of the armed forces to pass on information about its activities. In theory, the Ministry of Information (see page 98) should have coordinated the dissemination of all news. In practice, it was as reliant as the BBC on the willingness of the armed forces to share information. Their reluctance was understandable at a time when there was almost no good war-related news to report.

The course of the war turns, April 1940

The Phoney War came to a sudden end between April and June 1940, when German forces overran and defeated Denmark, Norway, Belgium, Luxemburg, Holland and, most shockingly, France, which capitulated within a month of the opening of hostilities. The British Expeditionary Force (BEF) retreated to the Belgian coast before a highly successful evacuation enabled 338,000 troops (123,000 of them French) to escape from Dunkirk between 27 May and 4 June. Until the German attack on the Soviet Union in June 1941 forced an unofficial alliance against the Nazis, Britain (or rather the British Empire) had no option but to hold out alone. There was a widespread and genuine fear of invasion and possibly defeat. In these circumstances the government and the armed forces were reluctant to release demoralising news. However, this led to some embarrassing episodes and severe criticism of the BBC.

- On the evening of 16 March 1940, the Luftwaffe (German Air Force) raided the naval base at Scapa Flow, Orkney. At seven o'clock the next morning, the Admiralty asked the BBC not to broadcast the news, despite the fact that German radio had carried reports of the raid during the night (the *Auslandsrundfunk* or Foreign Radio Section had broadcast in English since 1933). French radio had also reported the raid by mid-morning, so lots of British people knew about the events before the BBC finally broadcast the news at 1 p.m.

- German broadcasts also got the scoop on the resignation of Minister for Defence Leslie Hore-Belisha on 6 January 1940, as well as the formation of a new British Cabinet on 10 May 1940. This was because, although the information had been made public, the Ministry of Information prevented reporting until a set time in Britain.

- A BBC report on British determination to fight on in Norway following the attempted landing at Narvik in April 1940 was criticised in the press when it emerged that the decision to withdraw troops had been taken the day before. However, the BBC was not made aware of this decision, so the report gave a false impression of the likely success of the raid.

- There was also anger at the 'soft peddling of bad tidings' in the initial BBC reports of the disastrous Dieppe raid on 18 August 1942, when British and Canadian forces suffered 907 deaths and 4,000 casualties fighting a well-defended German position. The BBC reports had understated casualties and made the raid sound successful.

EXTEND YOUR KNOWLEDGE

The BBC before 1939

The reasons for the BBC's lack of success as a wartime broadcaster in the early stages of the Second World War stem from its first years of existence. The British Broadcasting Company Ltd was founded in November 1922 after pressure from a wide range of private radio entrepreneurs for a licence to broadcast. All private broadcasts had been banned shortly after they had started in late 1920 for fear of interference with military and official communications. It was felt that broadcast technologies were too important to be left in the hands of private businessmen. Politicians also feared that total governmental control of broadcasting would restrict freedom of expression and promote dictatorship. Additional pressure to reform the new Company in the mid-1920s came as a result of the lack of funding secured through the sale of licence fees and BBC wireless sets – people simply made their own or bought cheaper alternatives. The success of the BBC in reporting the May 1926 General Strike (all newspapers were forced to close due to strike action apart from an official government paper) cemented political support for the BBC's long-term financial security.

On 1 January 1927, a Royal Charter founded the British Broadcasting Corporation. The BBC's output would be controlled by an independent quango, the Board of Governors, and only occasionally by parliamentary legislation. The BBC would be funded by the sale of licence fees rather than taxation. This ensured that the BBC was free from direct governmental control and the demands of advertisers who preferred cheap, tacky shows that appealed to a mass audience, such as those being produced in the USA. The BBC was to be run in the public interest rather than for profit. Despite this, the potential power of the new rival worried those who worked for profit in the newspaper and entertainment industries. Powerful press barons insisted that the BBC should not be allowed to broadcast news before it had appeared in print, a stance that was reaffirmed by the Newspaper and Periodicals Emergency Council in October 1939. The General Theatre Company banned its performing artists from making appearances on the BBC in 1933.

Despite these restrictions, the BBC did make some innovations before 1939 that served as a basis for important wartime work. An Empire Service began broadcasts in 1932 (renamed the Overseas Service in November 1939); a News Department was founded in 1934; a Listener Research Department was launched in 1936; an External Broadcast Service began in 1938; broadcasts in foreign languages began with Arabic in January 1938, followed in September 1938 with the launch of the European Service.

The improvement of BBC news and war reporting, 1941–44

The BBC's provision of news improved for a range of reasons. The organisation recognised the need to respond to competition from enemy propaganda and invested more time and energy into monitoring public feedback. The leadership of the BBC changed, as did the corporation's relationship with government ministries. Perhaps above all, the improvement in the war situation meant that the armed forces gradually became more willing to share information with the BBC and to have more accurate news broadcast, even if the news was bad. Fear of the impact of potentially demoralising information was gradually replaced by trust in the British public's capacity to endure tough times.

Between July and September 1940, during the Battle of Britain, the Luftwaffe fought the Royal Air Force (RAF) for the aerial supremacy required to enable a successful invasion of Britain (or at least to attempt the forced acceptance of surrender). Although the RAF finally won, the Luftwaffe conducted massive bombing raids on several British cities. In what was immediately referred to as 'the Blitz', London was bombed on 7 September and for a further 57 consecutive nights. Towns and cities including Southampton, Bristol, Cardiff, Liverpool, Manchester, Hull, Coventry and Plymouth, suffered terrible damage and a huge number of casualties. Around 40,000 people died as a consequence of the bombing, with two million houses destroyed. Clearly the government and the BBC could not deny the bombing, but there was a lack of specific detail in news about the Blitz. Bulletins referred to 'a district of London' or 'some casualties'. According to Mass Observation reports, members of the public accepted the wisdom of not specifying casualty figures due to its draining effect on morale. They also understood that references to specific bombsites could provide valuable information to the enemy. There were reports from people in some provincial towns and cities that said they felt overlooked by the focus on London's Blitz. However, such coverage was not always welcome – just an hour after a broadcast about the king's inspection of bomb-damaged Plymouth four months previously, the city was bombed yet again.

While the British public were obviously aware of the aerial threat at home, they were not aware of the extent of the threat posed by German submarines and aeroplanes on British merchant shipping in what became known as 'the Battle of the Atlantic'. By December 1941, 875 British, Allied and neutral ships (some 3,297,000 tonnes) had been sunk in UK waters and in the Atlantic. Despite this level of loss, a combination of the bravery of merchant seamen, improvements in the defence of Atlantic convoys and the success of efforts to grow domestic food meant that Britons, unlike many Russians, Chinese and Greeks, did not face the horrors of starvation. The British were made aware of the sacrifices of the merchant navy (see Source 5 on page 98) and knew food was relatively scarce due to rationing on the home front, but the seriousness of the Battle of the Atlantic was censored until convoys and radar technology helped to overcome the worst of the submarine threat in late 1942.

An upturn in the course of events enabled the BBC to report more accurate, positive news in programmes such as *American Commentary* and *Russian Commentary*, which regularly attracted audiences of six million and four million, respectively. *American Commentary* had run fortnightly since 1930 to meet the public interest stimulated by the rise of Hollywood. In 1940, it sought to explain the policy of isolationism. The show was broadcast weekly from April 1941 and messages of sympathy for Britons during the Blitz were hugely popular. By 1945, Alastair Cooke had became the most popular correspondent, providing insights into the American view of key events such as Hitler's declaration of war on the USA on 11 December 1941 (which brought the USA into the war as a British ally), the British and American landings in North Africa in November 1942, and in Sicily in July 1943. Cooke's reports conveyed the reassuring message that the USA was a mighty power and a fearsome ally. They also satisfied British curiosity about US culture and politics. From July 1942, Moscow-based correspondent Alexander Werth's *Russian Commentary* gave the Russian point of view on key events such as the Soviet annihilation of a huge, elite German force at Kursk in July 1943, and the subsequent battles that pushed the invaders back into German territory by January 1945. *Russian Commentary* broadcast celebrations of Stalin's birthday and anniversaries of the October Revolution and the May Day parade in Moscow. The popularity of all things Russian was reflected in the huge audiences for an all-star radio production of Tolstoy's *War and Peace* in 1943. Although the Americans had the higher profile on BBC radio, the Russians – thanks to their determined struggle against the Nazis from June 1941 – were the most popular ally in Britain until the end of the war.

The appointment of A.P. Ryan as head of the restructured News Division in September 1942 (he had previously been controller of the Home Service) contributed to a change in the ethos of war reporting. He forcefully argued that effective news provision should keep the public as fully aware of (and stirred up by) military operations as possible, as far as this was compatible with security. He was fortunate in that the longest-serving Minster of Information, Brendan Bracken, shared the same view. The department rapidly trained reporters and put together a talented team of foreign correspondents who were seen within the BBC as the elite members of the organisation. Improvements in organisation and manpower certainly enhanced the quality and popularity of news reporting. Even before the huge advances that accompanied the launch of *War Report* on 6 June 1944 (see page 93), reporters such as Edward Ward paved the way for future success when he recorded (on acetate discs) and sent despatches from Finland following the Soviet invasion in November 1939. Closer to home, BBC reporter Charles Gardner vividly described a dogfight over the Kent coastline on 14 July 1940. His commentary divided opinion, with some praising his energetic, engaging style and others criticising his coverage of a lethal encounter as if it were a sports event: 'There are three Spitfires chasing three Messerschmitts now. Oh boy! That really was grand! I've never seen anything as good as this. The RAF fighters have really got those boys taped.'

SOURCE 1

From a confidential report by the BBC Listener Research Section, Programme Division on Charles Gardiner's commentary, written in late July 1940.

In view of the controversy aroused by this broadcast, the Listener Research Department addressed an urgent enquiry to (a) a group of 220 Honorary Local Correspondents, and (b) a group of industrial welfare workers recommended by the secretary of their professional society as being likely to report especially intelligently on the radio reactions of large groups of manual workers. A questionnaire was sent out on Friday, 19th July: by midday on Tuesday, 23rd July, 166 completed replies (76% of those sent out) had been received from Local Correspondents and 30 (75% of those sent out) from welfare workers...

There can be no doubt that this broadcast was enormously appreciated, that it gave a great fillip [boost] to morale, (though there is no evidence that morale was in any way shaky beforehand), and that most Correspondents believe that the public would welcome more such items if broadcast... There is an appreciable amount of feeling that the 'football style' was only justified, if at all, by its complete spontaneity... Judged from the point of view of effect on morale the broadcast was thoroughly justified, but this success does not necessarily mean that further exactly similar broadcasts would be equally successful, partly because the law of diminishing returns is bound to operate, and partly because doubts will arise if commentaries are confined to successful battles. With that caution, the evidence is overwhelming that the appetite for first-hand accounts that are known not to be doctored is enormous, and the presentation of good material in first hand forms is a superb tonic for morale.

The following extracts from replies typify points of view that the investigation has brought to light.

1. 'At the works on Monday it was the main topic for discussion.' (Almost all the men and women in workshops.)

2. 'This commentary did more to dispel gloom and the idea of German supremacy than all the talks so far broadcast with the object of keeping up our morale.' (Chief Engineer, Radio Relay Co, East Anglia.)

3. 'It may go a long way to clear the doubt from a lot of people's minds about our pilots taking on the odds they are doing as quite a few think the reports are cooked.' (Midland working class housewife.)

4. 'On two occasions recently bombs were dropped on civilians in this vicinity and people were saying "where are our fighters?" as there were no signs of them. Such broadcasts can be used by some of us to answer such questions.' (Edinburgh businessman.)

Recordings on disc were sent in from submarines, ships, planes, docks, factories and bombed cities, and were used in the programme *War Commentary*, which ran from October 1939 through to June 1944, and regularly attracted seven million listeners. Robin Duff captured the horror of the German shelling of Dover in September 1940 (German guns in France fired 2,000 shells on Dover and it became known as 'hellfire corner' for the duration of the war). Godfrey Talbot replaced Richard Dimbleby as the North Africa correspondent in October 1942. His first reports captured the dramatic advance of the Eighth Army and he even recorded a speech by Montgomery to the troops on 23 October 1942, before the decisive Battle of El Alamein. Despatches from North Africa at this point still took two days to get on the air. Wynford Vaughan Thomas impressed listeners with his 'live' recording of a Lancaster bomber raid over Berlin on 5 September 1943. Frank Gillard, with his mobile recording truck 'Berlinda', covered some of the most important battles in North Africa and Italy, including El Alamein and Monte Cassino, as well as the liberation of Rome on 5 June 1944. The use of vivid description, personal accounts and eyewitness interviews brought the war situation home with an immediacy previously unknown by the British public. The personalisation of bulletins was furthered by newsreaders using their own names from June 1940. On 7 December 1941, Yorkshireman Wilfred Pickles ended his first bulletin with what became his catchphrase 'and to all in the North, good neet' (all BBC newsreaders had been anonymous and posh-sounding before these changes). A February 1941 Listener Research Survey found that two-thirds felt the BBC news was now 'one-hundred per cent reliable', with only one in 1,200 describing it as 'completely unreliable'.

War reporting comes of age: D-Day and beyond

The public and the government both knew that the duration, and even the overall outcome of the war, hinged on the success or failure of the Allied assault on the German-held French coast. The BBC recognised the magnitude of D-Day through the extensive preparations to cover the events as they happened. In March 1943, BBC engineers were 'embedded' in opposing sides for a huge simulated battle in Oxfordshire and the Thames Valley, codenamed 'Exercise Spartan'. The reporters used 'Midget' mobile recording devices to capture the sounds of battle, eyewitness commentary, the reporters' own descriptive accounts and documentary narrative before transmitting it all to Broadcasting House. The material was then edited and turned into a news report within a few hours. The results greatly impressed the Secretary of State for War and the commander-in-chief of the Home Forces. The fact that the BBC were trusted to attend these secret manoeuvres reveals the extent of the trust that had developed between the armed forces and the BBC by 1943. Although formal communications between the BBC and War Office had been established under Major R.S.P. Marchioness in January 1940, by January 1943 an Army Broadcasting Liaison Committee held weekly meetings. The success of 'Spartan' further increased co-operation. BBC reporters were trained alongside the infantry who took part in the D-Day landings, including assault courses, tank recognition and live ammunition drills. When the reporters went to cover the real fighting they were not outsiders – they were more like part of the team. The extent of this was tragically demonstrated by the fate of reporters Guy Byam and Kent Stevenson, who went missing in action. The success also prompted the permanent formation of a War Reporting Unit to co-ordinate all of the different elements of material transmitted from the front.

SOURCE

BBC reporter Stanley Maxted uses a 'Midget' portable recording device at Arnhem in June 1944.

On the morning of 6 June 1944, a break in the weather allowed over 5,000 vessels to deliver 160,000 British, US and Canadian troops to attack five beaches in Normandy. Casualties were relatively light, apart from one of the beachheads. Operation Overlord was a success but hard fighting followed as the Germans sought to contain the Allied forces. Not until US forces broke through to the south of Caen was the route to Paris opened up and France liberated by late August. By October, a series of famous victories enabled the British and Americans to reach German territory. It was not until 7 May 1945 that the Germans finally agreed to an unconditional surrender. All of these dramatic events were covered by *War Report*, aired each night at 9 p.m. for 11 months following D-Day. Two hundred and thirty-five editions of the programme, using over 1,500 separate despatches, were broadcast in total. There were between ten and 15 million listeners every day, all eager to hear the latest dramatic developments at the front. Stormy seas delayed the dispatch of mobile transmitter units to France until 18 June. Before then, reports could be 'telediphoned' to Broadcasting House. This involved large numbers of women listening to recorded reports and typing them up for the censor to inspect before they were broadcast. The speed of the advance meant that more powerful transmitters had to be sent in order for the signal to reach London. Recording transmitters Mike Charlie Nan and Mike

Charlie Peter were powerful enough to broadcast over 100 live transmissions, some of which were relayed live around the world. One of the transmitters found a permanent home at Chateux Creully near Bayeaux. One live broadcast broke the news of the capture of a huge number of Germans during the Reichswald Offensive in February 1945.

By May 1945, BBC journalists and engineers had largely spearheaded a huge revolution in war journalism. The immediacy and vibrancy of the programmes helped to bridge a divide that had existed between civilians and those at the front throughout the First World War. This was not just in terms of a sense of the danger of combat, but also the songs, the slang and the jokes that became common currency between troops and public alike. This togetherness was promoted by the launch of the Forces Programme in January 1940 (see page 102). It was maintained by the replacement of Forces Radio and the Overseas Service with General Forces Radio in February 1944, which – for the first time in four-and-a-half years – meant that listeners at home and overseas heard exactly the same programmes.

> ### A Level Exam-Style Question Section B
>
> 'The role of technology was most significant in improving public perception of the BBC's war coverage.'
>
> How far do you agree with this statement? (20 marks)
>
> **Tip**
>
> *Aim to set out a range of contributing factors and offer a strong overall judgement in your introduction, then support this with comparative judgements about each factor throughout the essay.*

ACTIVITY
KNOWLEDGE CHECK

Reporting the war

1 What evidence exists for early dissatisfaction with the quality of war reporting by the BBC?

2 Outline the key developments in war broadcast journalism from 1939 to 1945.

3 List the reasons for the improvement in war reporting between 1939 and 1945. Support each reason with one piece of evidence.

Churchill's speeches on the BBC and his relationship with the Corporation

EXTEND YOUR KNOWLEDGE

Churchill before 1940

Winston Churchill was voted number one out of the hundred Best Britons in a national poll of 2002. This was undeniably due to his performance as wartime prime minister. However, he had a long and controversial career before 10 May 1940, as demonstrated by the timeline below.

- 1874 – Born to a powerful aristocratic family at their stately home, Blenheim Palace near Oxford. His father Randolph was a leading Conservative statesman and his mother Jennie was the daughter of an American millionaire.

- 1900 – Having served as a cavalry officer and come to national attention as a war correspondent, he entered parliament as Conservative MP for Oldham.

- 1904 – He switched to the Liberal Party in support of Free Trade (the rejection of tariffs on imports).

- 1910 – As Home Secretary (1910-11) he was unfairly rumoured to have ordered troops to attack striking coal miners in the Welsh town of Tonypandy.

- 1915 – As First Lord of the Admiralty (1911-15), he inspired and drove forward a disastrous plan to launch a naval attack on Turkey (an ally of Germany). Churchill resigned following the failure of the plan.

- 1924 – Churchill rejoined the Conservative Party. As Chancellor of the Exchequer (1924-29) he took the costly decision to rejoin the Gold Standard at the pre-war value of the pound. The overvalued currency caused exports to suffer.

- 1926 – Churchill took an extremely hostile stance against strikers during the General Strike of May 1926.

- 1929-39 – Churchill's 'wilderness years'. He stood for vigorous defence of empire and rearmament as opposed to the appeasement of Germany.

- 1936 – Churchill backed the 'wrong side' during Edward VIII's abdication crisis. Against the will of the government he encouraged the king not to abdicate when he wanted to marry American divorcee Wallis Simpson. He was shouted down in the House of Commons when he tried to defend the king and it appeared that his political career was over.

How far did Churchill see the Second World War as the BBC's finest hour?

In September 1939, it was not at all certain that Winston Churchill would emerge as one of the most important factors in the maintenance of Britain's war effort and British morale in particular. What was perhaps more certain was the rather uneasy relationship he would have with the BBC for the duration of the war. Churchill had a long and controversial career before his appointment as First Lord of the Admiralty in September 1939, but the following episodes serve as an important backdrop to his often tense relationship with the BBC. Churchill had always been hostile to socialism. During the May 1926 General Strike, Churchill saw the strikers as socialist criminals who were using illegal actions to hold the constitutionally elected government to ransom. He launched and ran a government newspaper called the *British Gazette* to put forward his strident views and thought that the BBC should emulate his tone and perspective. When it would not comply he even advocated commandeering the corporation. John Reith (later Lord Reith), first director-general of the BBC, was adamant that the BBC should retain its impartiality and not serve as a mouthpiece for the government. Reith was happy to broadcast the facts, but he insisted that the newly formed corporation should maintain a completely impartial editorial stance on the events, despite his personal hostility to the strikers. Churchill felt that this was tantamount to support for the strikers and became convinced that the BBC was a hotbed of socialists and communist sympathisers. On a personal level he hated Reith, whom he referred to as 'old Wuthering Heights' (Reith was 6 feet 4 inches tall).

Churchill's controversial career, which included in his words 'ratting' on (behaving dishonourably towards) the Conservatives before 're-ratting' on the Liberal Party, left him with few political allies. As a result he was not offered any position of power between 1929 and his appointment to the War Cabinet in September 1939. His biographers refer to this stretch of his career as his 'wilderness years' – he was still a famous statesman but he was perceived as a nonconformist at best, and an anachronistic (outdated) warmonger to less charitable observers. The BBC's policy, once it decided to allow political talks after 1928, was to invite each political party to recommend a speaker in strict rotation in order to maintain its impartiality. As Churchill was out of favour with the political establishment until the outbreak of war, he was not selected to speak on political programmes. He was in fact invited to talk on the radio on a number of occasions in the 1930s, but he turned them all down because the programmes were on non-political topics such as 'Great Escapes' or 'Great Lives'. What Churchill was desperate to talk about was the need to preserve British control over India. In December 1929, he offered £100 to the BBC to talk for 30 minutes on the subject, but was politely rebuffed. When he was finally allowed to contribute to a debate on the future of Indian rule in 1935, he was disappointed by the lack of air time. Churchill felt deliberately marginalised (excluded) by the BBC and never forgave Reith in particular. He blamed the director-general's membership of the political establishment for his lack of national exposure. It must have given Churchill some delight to shunt Reith from Minister for Information to Minister for Transport in his first Cabinet in May 1940. At the time Churchill described the BBC as 'an enemy within the gates, doing more harm than good'. It is telling that in Churchill's monumental six-volume history *The Second World War*, written between 1948 and 1953, there are fewer than ten references to the wartime role of the BBC.

Churchill's radio speeches

Churchill's most important speeches were delivered in light of adverse events.

- The withdrawal of the BEF from France was turned into a miraculous escape. ('We shall fight on the beaches'.)

- The fall of France and the start of the Battle of Britain became an opportunity for the British to demonstrate their pluck and resolve alone in 'War of the unknown warriors'.

- The onset of the Blitz was an occasion to impress the world with the British ability to 'take it' in his speech 'Every man to his post'.

The Ministry of Information observed that following the fall of France on 17 June 1940, 'unless there is a strong lead from the prime minister defeatism was certain to gain ground and there would be serious division between the government and the people.' Its Home Intelligence Department wrote a report on 19 June called 'Public Opinion on the Present Crisis'. It concluded that Churchill's speech 'Their finest hour' was 'considered courageous and hopeful, giving bad news quite frankly' (see Source 4 for an extract of the speech).

Mass observation diaries make reference to the electrifying, fortifying power of Churchill's words, especially during the dark days of threatened invasion and Blitz terror, but there was only one officially monitored response to one of his speeches. It was difficult to organise detailed feedback, as Churchill's speeches were set up and broadcast according to unpredictable events and his pressurised timetable, rather than planned and advertised in advance. It was only because the Listener Review Service was set up in readiness for a programme which Churchill's speech replaced at 9 p.m. on 15 February 1942 (just after the fall of Singapore) that there is even one detailed record of the impact. Despite the difficulty of this speech, Churchill still received a 62 percent approval rating. The fact that 77 percent of the population gathered to listen to his speeches between 1940 and 1941 does provide strong evidence that they were felt to be of great importance.

There are a few reasons why it is surprising that Churchill is so famous for his radio speeches. He hated talking into a microphone (although he did propose having one installed in the House of Commons to record key speeches and so avoid having to repeat them later) and was often tired when he had to repeat speeches for the radio. Some of his most famous speeches may have been read by BBC actors but opinions on this differ. Lastly, he only gave 49 broadcasts as prime minister between 1940 and 1945.

SOURCE

From a letter written by MP Harold Nicolson to his wife Vita Sackville-West on 19 June 1940. Nicolson was an admirer of Churchill.

> How I wish Winston would not talk on the wireless unless he is feeling in good form. He hates the microphone, and when we bullied him into speaking last night, he just sulked and read his House of Commons speech over again. Now as delivered in the House of Commons, that speech was magnificent, especially the concluding sentence. But it sounded ghastly on the wireless. All the great vigour he put into it seemed to evaporate.

Churchill spoke less frequently on the radio after 1942, partly because the change in British fortunes no longer necessitated his morale-boosting speeches, but also because he preferred to appear in cinema newsreels. That medium enabled him to be seen energetically carrying out the business of war leadership. He did not have to take a break from it to painstakingly prepare a speech. (Unlike most later politicians, Churchill wrote and revised all of his speeches himself. He was bad at ad-libbing (speaking without prior preparation).) The changing nature of the war meant that, rather than having the sole task of steeling the nation for survival, he had to compose longer and more complex speeches that set out how the war was to be won.

However, despite all of these impediments, his speeches still retain their power for modern listeners. His use of slightly outdated language, together with everyday slang, his alternately **resolute or lilting cadence** and oratorical devices, made him a master of public speaking and of the English language. Churchill went on to win the Nobel Prize for Literature for his six-volume book, *The History of the Second World War* in 1953.

KEY TERM

Resolute, lilting cadence
Cadence is the total effect of the rhythm, changing tone, pattern and flow of speech. Lilting refers to a rising and falling tone, while resolute refers to the determination and conviction conveyed by his speeches.

SOURCE

4

From Churchill's House of Commons speech on the war situation, 18 June 1940.

> What General Weygand called the 'Battle of France' is over. I expect that the battle of Britain is about to begin. Upon this battle depends the survival of Christian civilisation. Upon it depends our own British life and the long continuity of our institutions and our Empire. The whole fury and might of the enemy must very soon be turned on us. Hitler knows that he will have to break us in this island or lose the war. If we can stand up to him all Europe may be free, and the life of the world may move forward into broad, sunlit uplands; but if we fail then the whole world, including the United States, and all that we have known and cared for, will sink into the abyss of a new dark age made more sinister, and perhaps more prolonged, by the lights of a perverted science. Let us therefore brace ourselves to our duty and so bear ourselves that if the British Commonwealth and Empire lasts for a thousand years men will still say, 'This was their finest hour.'

The nature of censorship

Churchill, propaganda and censorship

Aside from his speeches of 1940–41, Churchill was himself an inspiration for propaganda. He was personally very popular. According to the British Institute of Public Opinion (BIPO) polls of 1940–41, while half the public approved of the government as a whole, Churchill's personal approval rating hovered between 87 and 88 percent (and never dipped below 78 percent for the duration of the war). He became heavily identified with possibly the most famous propaganda campaign of the war, 'V for Victory'. The slogan was the idea of the BBC Belgian Service employee Victor de Laveleye. He recommended the slogan as V was the first letter of victory in English and French (*victoire*), and the Flemish word for freedom (*Vryheid*). In large part due to Churchill's adoption of the V sign, it began to be scrawled on walls throughout Nazi-occupied Europe and helped to encourage resistance.

Churchill had far less impact on censorship. In October 1941, he wanted the *Sunday Pictorial* newspaper to be closed following its attack on ineffective ministers. Home Secretary Herbert Morrison was able to persuade the Cabinet to veto the proposal for fear of appearing concerned by freedom of speech. The Cabinet agreed that the government should censor facts but not opinions. Churchill also opposed the screening of the 1941 film *Ships With Wings* because of the large number of British casualties it portrayed. The film gained the approval of First Sea Lord, Sir Dudley Pound, who said that the Navy could take such films and far worse. Churchill also wanted the 1943 film *The Life and Death of Colonel Blimp* banned for undermining the reputation of British officers. The Ministry of Information passed the film and it was a huge hit. Churchill said of the 1943 film *San Demetrio London*, 'Pray who is responsible for this dastardly film? It must be stopped'. Once again, the film, based on the true story of a rescue mission for a torpedoed fuel tanker, got official approval.

ACTIVITY
KNOWLEDGE CHECK

Churchill's radio speeches, 1939–45

1 Outline the key reasons why Churchill had an uneasy relationship with the BBC.

2 What issues, could it be argued, limited the impact of Churchill's radio speeches on the British public?

A Level Exam-Style Question Section B

Assess the impact of Churchill's radio speeches to the British war effort between 1939 and 1945? (20 marks)

Tip
The best answers will not lose sight of the focus on Churchill's radio speeches. Consider planning your answer around areas in which his speeches did have a major impact, areas where they had a more modest impact, and areas where they cannot be judged to have had any real impact whatsoever. This will help to maintain focus and make your answer a sustained comparative judgement.

Powers on paper

The government could, in theory, have asserted total control over the distribution of all information within Britain. There were some suggestions in the 1930s that the government would at least assume power over the BBC in the event of war. Yet, while there were some significant controls on what mass media could say, an effective, largely voluntary system was created thanks to a good deal of co-operation. Above all, after an ineffective start to the war, the government successfully gave the appearance of allowing relative freedom of expression during the implementation of significant censorship and propaganda. The press had been subject to Defence Notices since 1912. These were a list of topics on which newspapers were advised not to report. The Ministry of Information (see page 98) issued these throughout the war and, in March 1940, its Press and Censorship Bureau began to hold daily 'Guidance to the Press' meetings, to help newspapers avoid prosecution. Only two newspapers, including the communist *Daily Worker*, were prosecuted under the legislation, and both were only suspended for a short period rather than banned outright. The *Daily Mirror* was also threatened with prosecution in March 1942, following the publication of cartoonist Philip Zec's '"The price of petrol has been increased by one penny" – Official' (see Source 5). Similarly, with regard to the BBC, the government reversed their pre-war plans to control the Corporation. This was in part because of the trust acquired through co-operation, but also because of the efforts of director-generals such as Sir Frederick Ogilvie (1938–42) to resist greater government encroachment on its independence. Behind the scenes, however, almost all shows were scripted, and these had to be approved by a censor before broadcast.

SOURCE 5

Philip Zec's controversial cartoon '"The price of petrol has been increased by one penny" – Official.' was published in the *Daily Mirror* on 6 March 1942.

The Ministry of Information

A Ministry of Information had existed during the First World War. Its only task was to censor information that could harm domestic morale or provide valuable information to the enemy. The Committee of Imperial Defence, formed in 1902, drew up plans in 1936 for a new department that would handle all government publicity and propaganda as well as censorship in the event of war. Pre-war ambitions for the new ministry proved too large for it to handle in practice. By 9 October, responsibility for publicity and censorship had reverted to the service departments of ministries with relevant specialisms. The Ministry of Information merely retained the ability to set censorship policy and to provide and distribute information common to all ministries. The War Office, Army and Admiralty also ran their own censorship operations. The lack of effective co-ordinating power and the clashes that resulted from overlapping spheres of responsibility led the Minister for Information, Sir Walter Monckton, to submit his resignation four times in the first month to Home Secretary Sir John Anderson. Anderson was concerned about potential press criticism and refused his resignation three times because Monkton was very well regarded. Contemporaries initially referred to it as the 'Ministry of No Comment', and one former minister believed 'there [was] no place in the British scheme of government for [the Ministry]'.

Thanks to the stern leadership of Sir John Reith as Minister for Information (January–May 1940) and Brendan Bracken's successful tenure of the role (July 1941–July 1945), the Ministry gradually found its feet and fulfilled more of its pre-war allotted roles. Three divisions were established (the Press and Censorship Bureau, Home Publicity and Foreign Publicity), which eventually had 2,950 staff in the UK and 3,600 overseas. The Ministry also took sole responsibility for foreign propaganda when the Political Warfare Executive was brought under its control in March 1942. The Home Intelligence Division of the Home Publicity division undertook a Wartime Social Survey. Its investigators became known as 'Cooper's Snoopers', named after the third Minister of Information, Duff Cooper.

The Ministry increasingly provided publicity support for other areas of government through its General Products division, which covered photographs, broadcasting, the Crown Film Unit, campaigns, exhibitions, religion and publications. The government was careful not to appear to **monopolise** book production. Historian Valerie Holman (2008) has highlighted how 'the Ministry of Information paid a small fee [to private publishers] for lending their imprint to books that the government wanted to see in print, but did not want the public to see as official propaganda'. This was once again designed to distance British freedom from Nazi dictatorship. However, the Ministry also published its own books – *Battle of Britain* sold 4.8 million copies by December 1941, with *Bomber Command* selling a further 1.25 million. Other titles included *Assurance of Victory* (December 1939), *How to Keep Well in Wartime* (February 1943) and *Make Do and Mend* (September 1943). Interestingly, the poster for which the Ministry is best known today, 'Keep Calm and Carry On', was never used during the war. The vast majority of the 2.5 million posters were pulped in April 1940 when the German onslaught failed to materialise and the paper was needed elsewhere.

KEY TERM

Monopolise
To obtain exclusive possession or control over something, usually a commodity, trade or service.

ACTIVITY
KNOWLEDGE CHECK

Government censorship, 1939–45

1 Explain why the British government was keen to avoid the appearance of excessive censorship.

2 Give examples of measures taken by the government to avoid this.

3 Explain the role of the Ministry of Information between 1939 and 1945.

HOW SUCCESSFULLY DID THE BBC BROADCAST TO THE HOME FRONT?

The number of radio licences sold in the UK had increased from 1.5 million per year in 1925 to nine million in 1939. This meant that 73 percent of all homes in Britain had legal radio. There were some stark regional variations within this average, with Wiltshire and Dorset at 90 percent, Wales at 64 percent, northern Scotland at 42 percent, and Counties Fermanagh and Tyrone in Northern Ireland at 25 percent. Even so, this meant that the BBC had huge potential to influence the everyday lives and morale of the British public. The potential influence of the BBC was boosted by the rapid expansion of the Corporation. The number of employees increased from 4,899 in 1939 to 11,417 by 1945 (and this was despite the fact that 200 employees left the BBC in 1940 to join the armed forces). The number of transmitters increased from 23 to 138 during the war. The purchase of the hugely powerful Aspidistra transmitter from the USA in 1942 even enabled the BBC to broadcast to German submarines in the mid-Atlantic. On 6 June 1944, 28 million people (80 percent of the whole population) heard King George VI's broadcast on D-Day. Although even the most popular shows attracted far fewer listeners, the potential power of broadcasting was clearly appreciated by BBC executives and the government alike. The question was how successfully would the BBC use this opportunity to cement the appeal of radio.

'Make-do and mend': the role of government ministries, their advice and information

A key development during the war was the shift in radio listening from homes to public spaces such as cafes, train stations and factories. This shift was brought about partly by new patterns of life, for example the large numbers of women who entered the factories or people who bedded down in public shelters after the onset of the Blitz. It was also reinforced by the fact that, when private radios broke, replacement parts were very difficult to obtain so people had to listen to broadcasts in public places. An appreciation of this shift led to a change in the orientation of programming, from private, intimate enjoyment to public information and entertainment. The major issue on the home front, apart from the need to maintain morale, was to give practical advice and information to cope with the difficulties presented by wartime conditions. Problems centred around health and safety, levels of production and coping with rationing.

The BBC did not achieve the appropriate tone with its advice and information at the start of the war. The broadcast of government instructions and regulations, together with exhortations to self-improvement, were felt to be nagging and patronising. One listener lamented the fact that the wireless had become bullying rather than companionable. It is no coincidence that the BBC began to be referred to as 'Aunty' at the start of the war due to its fussy interference. There were some popular campaigns before the appointment of Brendan Bracken as Minister for Information in July 1941, but he had a clear vision of how the BBC could broadcast advice and information in a more palatable fashion. Rather than demand action, the public should be encouraged to provide ideas to be discussed. Bracken felt that if explanation and education were provided for the public then they would be happy to make sacrifices and take on an equal share of the overall burden.

The context of rationing

Britain's population had boomed during the 18th and 19th centuries and the nation relied on imports of food to avoid starvation. Eighty percent of all fruit, 70 percent of cereals, cheese and sugar, and half of all meat was imported thanks to the merchant navy. An obvious German strategy was to sink as many supply ships as possible. In addition, a lot of processed and canned food was diverted to feed the armed forces. The need to save fuel for military purposes contributed to the decline in transport for fresh food from abroad.

A Ministry of Food had overseen rationing to cope with a similar situation in the First World War and served as a precedent in 1939. Planning for a wartime food strategy had begun in 1937 and the Ministry was fully operational on the outbreak of war. Petrol was rationed immediately, with sugar, butter and bacon following on 8 January 1940. Rationing was then gradually extended to cover cheese, eggs, milk, tea, jam, biscuits, canned fruit, meat and, on 1 June 1941, clothing. Every family in Britain was issued with one of 15 million ration books (even the Royal Family had one), which contained coupons to exchange for rationed goods. Women (who almost exclusively did the family shopping in the 1940s) signed up at a grocers, a butchers, a clothes shop and so on, and the shopkeeper would be issued with the necessary quantity of whatever was available to supply his registered customers. The coupon price was fixed at the same price in every shop in the country, but the volume of any rationed good available could go up or down depending on available stocks. A typical weekly ration for one adult would include 225 grams of sugar, 100 grams of bacon and margarine, 50 grams of butter, tea and cheese, three pints of milk, and one egg. Lord Woolton, Minister of Food from 1940 to 1943, oversaw the preparation of over 200 feeding stations in London (where they were called the Londoners' Meal Service) and other cities before the onset of the Blitz. These were the forerunner of the 2,160 highly popular British Restaurants (launched as 'Community Kitchens' but renamed at Churchill's request in March 1941 because he felt the original name sounded

too socialist). These were where workers could get a cheap, nutritious, hot meal. Woolton also organised free school meals for 650,000 children and free milk for 3.5 million children. He became a household figure, largely thanks to a series of propaganda campaigns aimed at avoiding shortages.

'Dig for Victory' and other campaigns

Each ministry had a public relations unit, increasingly supported by the Ministry of Information, which worked very closely with the BBC. One of the most successful campaigns, launched in October 1939, was called 'Dig for Victory'. The message was simple: Britain simply had to produce more food to feed itself to avoid shortages or starvation. The campaign clearly had a significant impact – 600,000 new allotments were cultivated, helping to produce over a million tonnes more fruit and vegetables per year, and 7,000 'pig clubs' fed waste to pigs. Posters such as Source 7 were widely distributed. The message was reinforced daily on the Home Service through *The Kitchen Front*, a highly popular five-minute programme that attracted between five and seven million listeners every morning. According to historian Hugh Chignell, this short show represented the best example of the BBC working extremely closely with government ministries. The show offered tips on how to make the most of available food, with a 'dish of the week', including the recipe for **Woolton Pie**. From June 1942, the programme regularly carried tips on how to save fuel, a message also conveyed in 'Fuel Flashes' that followed the six o'clock news. It also gave a regular slot to the first radio doctor, Charles Hill, who became famous for his regular references to 'digestive problems'.

KEY TERM

Woolton Pie
The pie was named after Lord Woolton, Minister of Food from 1940 to 1943, and was designed by the head chef at the Savoy Hotel to make the most of widely available domestic vegetables. It consisted of potatoes, parsnip, cauliflower, swede, carrots, oats and spring onions with potato pastry and grated cheese topping. It was not well liked by the public.

There were other significant campaigns, which involved the collaboration of the Ministry of Information and other ministries.

- The Squander Bug campaign was led by the National Savings Committee and helped to promote economising throughout the war.

- Make-Do and Mend gave tips to housewives on how to be stylish despite the onset of clothes rationing. The Ministry of Information released a booklet with this title in 1943.

- Several campaigns with the War Office, the Ministry of Production and the Ministry of Aircraft Production aimed to recruit women for the forces or for industrial war work.

- Lots of publicity was given to the role of 'roof spotters', who were trained to spot enemy aircraft and let workers in factories know when it was safe to return after an air-raid warning. In May 1941, 300 roof-spotter clubs joined together to form the National Association of Spotters Clubs.

- There were several health campaigns with the Ministry of Health, such as 'anti-sneezing' and 'keeping fit'.

SOURCE 6

From Minister of Health Ernest Brown's introduction to the Ministry of Information book *How to Keep Well in Wartime*, published on 1 February 1943.

DURING three years of total war the nation's stubborn good health has been invaluable to our war effort. Even so, as a nation we are still losing about 22 million weeks' work each year through common and often preventable illnesses such as colds and influenza, dyspepsia, biliousness, neurasthenia, rheumatism, boils and other septic conditions. This is calculated to be equivalent to the loss of 24,000 tanks, 6,750 bombers, and 6,750,000 rifles a year, not to mention the pain and inconvenience we suffer as individuals. We cannot expect, whatever we do, to wipe out this loss completely, but we can all do something to reduce it. And now that we are at the turning point of the war it is more than ever important that we should do everything we can to keep fit – fit to hasten victory and to tackle the tasks that lie beyond. But to maintain vigorous health calls for conscious effort from each one of us. In this little book Dr. Clegg has set out the simple safeguards, the common sense rules, and the good habits which we can make part and parcel of our daily lives. By doing so we shall both help ourselves to health and help to keep the nation fighting fit.

SOURCE 7

A poster produced by the Ministry of Food in support of the Dig for Victory campaign.

Your own vegetables all the year round ...
if you
DIG FOR VICTORY NOW

Radio was not the only mass media used to get across campaign messages that were vital to the war effort. The Film Division of the Ministry of Information negotiated an agreement with the head of the Cinematograph Exhibitioners' Association, Sir Joseph Ball, to set aside ten minutes for government films before each show began. The Crown Film Unit, absorbed within the Ministry of Information in April 1940, produced a range of short films such as *London Can Take It!* (1940), which received huge praise in Mass Observation feedback. Historian Mark Connelly (2010) has argued that such films profoundly shaped the public response of other blitzed towns and cities. People saw the Londoners' resolve and adopted this as their behavioural norm in the wake of an air raid.

ACTIVITY
KNOWLEDGE CHECK

The role of information and advice, 1939–45
Construct a table like the one below.

Home front problem that needed tackling	Direct action taken by the government (such as legislation)	Examples of propaganda campaigns to help overcome problems	Evidence for the impact of propaganda campaigns

Use the information in this section to complete each column.

Popular light entertainment and its impact on morale

The BBC under Reith was prejudiced against light, trivial, popular entertainment. It encouraged listeners to tune in for particular programmes rather than adopt 'tap-listening', with the radio always on as background noise. On 'Reithian Sundays', sober, religious programmes were broadcast throughout the day. Many people chose to tune in to foreign broadcasts such as Radio Luxemburg and Radio Normandie to hear popular music instead.

Despite criticisms in the press, especially over the justification of the licence fee, the BBC stuck to its mission to give the British public a little better than they thought they would want. However, the outbreak of the war forced the BBC to substantially revise its attitude to preferred listening habits and the balance of light broadcast entertainment. The BBC now needed to attract an audience and do its best to maintain national morale. In a statement in September 1939, the BBC said that its key role was to provide 'entertainment to keep people in good heart in the difficult days ahead'. The pressure to entertain was never more keenly felt than in the first months of the war. As a result of the Emergency Powers Act 1939, the government was able to enforce a nightly blackout (every night until 17 September 1944), and to close all theatres, cinemas and sports venues. Although this was logical (such large crowds would be highly vulnerable to German bombs), it caused a lot of boredom and resentment, especially when the Phoney War dragged on until April 1940. The government caved in to widespread criticism and most public entertainment venues had reopened by the end of September 1939. However, a Mass Observation report that month recorded that half of the public were dissatisfied with the BBC, particularly the thrice daily organ recitals. The public found programmes such as *The Land We Defend*, which was intended to boost national pride, condescending and dull. Similar programmes such as *Forever England* also marginalised listeners in Wales and Scotland. If the BBC was to stop people tuning in to more entertaining broadcasts from Germany, it simply had to become less patronising and more responsive and popular.

A huge step forward in this respect was the launch of the Forces Programme on 6 January 1940, which was made up of 90 percent light entertainment. Director-general Frederick Ogilvie visited the British Expeditionary Force (BEF) in France and heard first hand how most troops preferred the local Radio Fécamp to the BBC Home Service. Ogilvie decided that the BBC had to emulate the mix of popular music, variety acts and sport that made the rival station so popular. The music department was ordered to 'lighten' its output, with fewer chamber music recitals in particular. The volume of classical music broadcast by the BBC remained fairly constant throughout the war, but this was largely because the total output increased so much. As a percentage of air time, classical music fell from 17 percent in 1938 to just under nine percent in 1942. Although the Forces Programme was broadcast with servicemen and women in mind, members of the public now had a choice of two domestic stations. While important announcements and speeches were broadcast simultaneously on both channels, there was usually a real choice in listening. The Forces Programme soon gained 60 percent of listener share, and 90 percent of all listeners aged 16–20.

Variety: the spice of life?

The variety, music and talks departments of the BBC produced a range of incredibly popular shows that helped to maintain morale. The most popular show had actually started before the war broke out: *It's That Man Again* (or *ITMA*, as it was always referred to) was a comedy vehicle for Tommy Handley. The show centred on Handley's supposed jobs, such as mayor of seaside town Foaming-at-the-Mouth, or Minister of Aggravation and Mysteries at the Office of Twerps, and the odd characters he worked with. The show was always topical and provided the nation, civilians and servicemen and women alike, with a range of popular catchphrases (for example, washerwoman Mona Lott's drearily delivered line, 'It's being so cheerful as keeps me going'). Fourteen million people listened to the show each week. The ITMA tour of military bases in January 1944 was hugely popular. Other popular shows included the American comedy-inspired *Hi Gang!* and the traditional British variety shows *Band Waggon*, *Music Hall*, *Saturday Night Variety* and *Happidrome*. The latter show inspired a spin-off film in 1943 and a nationally popular song 'We Three'. Such shows were greatly aided by the General Theatre Company's decision in April 1940 to lift the ban on its stage artists working for the BBC.

Other shows were aimed at specific groups but ended up having far wider appeal. *Ack-Ack Beer-Beer* was aimed at anti-aircraft gunners, barrage balloon and searchlight operators, but had widespread appeal. *Music While You Work* was broadcast to 4.5 million workers in over 8,000 factories each day at 10.30 a.m. and 3 p.m., times at which research had suggested worker productivity flagged. A further 2.5 million listened to the show at home, a

reflection of the popularity of the Wynford Reynolds band's spirit-rousing music.

Ernest Bevin, Minister for Labour and National Service, recognised that for many, conscription to war-work was a severe imposition on life plans. He said that 'the BBC is a factory for entertainment and education, and must be regarded as one of the vital services'. A meeting between Bevin and director of variety John Watt in May 1941 led to the creation of *Workers' Playtime*, *Factory Canteen* and *Works Wonders*. Workers themselves provided the entertainment in the latter two programmes. This was certainly an improvement on earlier scripted shows aimed at workers such as *My Day's Work*, *Go To It* and *We Speak for Ourselves*, which were thought to be stereotypical and **tokenistic**. The most surprising success of the war was *The Brains Trust* (January 1941 onwards). This involved questions from the public being put to three resident and two guest experts. By 1944, it had gained a weekly audience of 40 percent of all domestic listeners and was judged a national institution by the popular press. Something that listeners did criticise was the avoidance of political discussion on the programme – throughout 1943 and 1944, more people wanted to hear about William Beveridge's post-war plans for a welfare state.

> **KEY TERM**
>
> Tokenism
> The practice of doing something without real interest or feeling, but with only the minimum effort necessary to avoid complaints.

Although light entertainment clearly helped to sustain morale on the home front and in the armed forces, the war situation was the key determinant of morale. The collapse of France in June 1940 was a profound shock. That month, Mass Observation recorded pessimists to optimists in a ratio of 2.33 : 1. When this was not followed by a German invasion in July this ratio fell to 0.26 : 1. Even at the height of the Blitz, 80 percent of those polled by BIPO believed in a final British victory.

Public attitudes to the BBC

The monitoring of public opinion

Unlike in the US, where strong commercial pressures led to intensive listener research, the public service ethos of Reith's BBC meant that there was no need to monitor ratings or change programming to cater for the masses. The BBC did have some feedback mechanisms before 1936, such as the large volume of letters it received from listeners (50,000 between 1922 and 1927 alone) and 'preference polls' conducted by newspapers such as the *Daily Express* from 1927. It was thanks to the drive of a new BBC director of public relations, Sir Stephen Tallents, and his appointment of the thorough, energetic Robert Silvey as listener research officer that audience research began in 1936 and expanded significantly in 1939. The value of such research became apparent early in the war. A survey of November 1939 revealed that only 16 percent of working people were home for lunch at noon, whereas 57 percent were home at 1 p.m. This led to the midday news being scheduled an hour later and a huge increase in listeners, up to 13 million by the end of the year.

This deliberate effort to reach a mass audience was clearly a major shift in BBC ethos. By December 1939, Silvey had turned a weekly General Listening Barometer into a daily survey of listener habits and satisfaction. Silvey also set up a network of 2,000 'local correspondents' who returned monthly questionnaires and, from 1941, 'listener panels' who filled in weekly questionnaires about recent programmes.

A number of different measures of morale were open to the government and BBC chiefs.

- Mass Observation: this was a project launched in 1937 by Tom Harrison and Charles Madge that recorded the thoughts, observations and conversations of a representative sample of Britons. Around 500 volunteers were asked to keep a diary about their everyday lives. It was turned into a consumer survey in the early 1950s but reverted to its social research function in the 1980s.

- BIPO (Gallup Polls): the American George Gallup founded this information-gathering business in 1935. Its British offshoot, the British Institute of Public Opinion was founded in 1937. Although its methods inspired a range of imitators later in the century (for example AGB in 1962, and MORI in 1969), Gallup was the only polling company available during the Second World War.

- Ministry of Information Wartime Social Surveys: these were conducted by the Home Intelligence Division to monitor morale and assess the impact of government policy from July 1940 until the end of the war.

ACTIVITY
KNOWLEDGE CHECK

The significance of popular light entertainment and public attitudes to the BBC

1 Explain why the BBC was criticised for its poor provision of popular light entertainment at the start of the Second World War.

2 Explain how and why the BBC overcame this perceived failure in its broadcasting to the home front.

3 Summarise the ways in which the BBC became more highly attuned to public opinion about its broadcasting.

WHAT WAS THE IMPACT OF BRITISH AND ENEMY PROPAGANDA BROADCASTS?

Germany calling! Germany calling! The role of Lord Haw Haw

How William Joyce became Lord Haw Haw

The Nazis had recognised the power of propaganda from the foundation of the party in 1919. Hitler himself had run party propaganda in the early days, but Josef Goebbels took the role in 1930. When the Nazis came to power in 1933, Goebbels was appointed to head the newly created Ministry of Propaganda and Popular Enlightenment. He was instrumental in Nazi efforts to indoctrinate the German population and wasted no time in launching a wide range of propaganda to undermine the national resolve of enemy nations to withstand the armed onslaught. The greatest hindrance to the success of such propaganda against Britain was the lack of fluent English speakers to make persuasive, effective broadcasts. Goebbels was fortunate to receive the help of William Joyce from August 1939 until the end of the war.

EXTEND YOUR KNOWLEDGE

William Joyce (1906–45)

William Joyce had a strange life, neatly summarised by journalist Ludovic Kennedy who pointed out on the occasion of Joyce's reburial in 1987 that he had been born in America, lived in Germany, died as a British traitor but was an Irishman from Connemara all along.

Joyce was born in 1906 in New York to an Irish father and English mother. The family moved to Ireland in 1909 where Joyce stayed until he left to pursue his university education in England. There, he quickly became associated with a right-wing group called the English Fascisti, before joining Oswald Mosley's British Union of Fascists (BUF) in 1932. He quickly rose to prominence within the BUF and acquired the nickname 'Mighty Atom' for his short stature but powerful oratory. By 1934, he had become director of propaganda and deputy leader of the BUF. Joyce parted company with the BUF in 1937 to found his own group, the National Socialist League. Here he could give full vent to his virulent anti-Semitism.

Mosley was arrested as a Nazi sympathiser under Defence Regulation 18B in August 1939. After a tip-off that he himself was also to be arrested, Joyce fled to Germany with his fellow fascist and second wife Margaret Collins. He initially worked for Nazi 'black propaganda' but soon made the move to overt 'white propaganda' (see page 107), where his talents could be utilised to their full extent. In September 1939, his show, *Views on the News*, which always began with the words 'Germany calling! Germany calling!', began regular broadcasts to Britain. A *Daily Express* journalist, Jonah Barrington, wrote an article mocking his accent (and the accents of other Nazi broadcasters) as the 'Haw Haw, dammit-get-out-of-my-way' upper-class drawl style of English. This quickly led to Joyce being known to British listeners as Lord Haw Haw.

He became a naturalised German citizen in 1940 and went on to win the German War Merit Cross. In April 1945, he was captured at Flensburg (close to the town of Zeesen where he had broadcast from) and he was taken to London to face charges of high treason. Joyce claimed that, as he had been born in the US and was now a German citizen, he could not be found guilty of treason against Britain. However, when he had applied for a British passport, in order to aid his study and work in the UK, he had claimed to be born in Ireland (which was part of the UK at the time of his birth). On those grounds, he was found guilty and hanged at Wandsworth Prison on 3 January 1946.

The impact of Lord Haw Haw on Britain

At a time when many found the BBC broadcasts to be dull and patronising (see page 102), it was no wonder that many people tuned in to listen to Haw Haw on Radio Hamburg. Many people publicly claimed to listen to Haw Haw for entertainment. Newspapers such as the *Daily Mirror* (in its Cassandra column) and the *Daily Mail*, which ran an anti-Haw Haw campaign, encouraged this. The BBC was concerned about the loss of audience and its Listener Research Department conducted a thorough survey into the Haw Haw phenomenon in the autumn and winter of 1939–40.

SOURCE 8

A list of the reasons why people tuned in to listen to Lord Haw Haw. The information, based on 34,000 interviews and 750 questionnaires, was printed for confidential use in a report in March 1940.

Why do people listen to Hamburg?	Thought to be one of the chief reasons by (%)
Because his (Lord Haw Haw's) version of the news is so fantastic that it is funny	58
Because so many other people listen to him and talk about it	50
Because people are amused at his voice and manner	38
Because they like to hear the German point of view	29
Because they hope to get more news	26
Because his anecdotes make people laugh	26
Because he is a good broadcaster	15
Because the BBC news is so dull	9
Because he is so clever	6

Several comedians, most famously Arthur Askey, did Haw Haw impersonations as part of their routine, and a whole show at the Holborn Empire music hall was simply called 'Haw Haw'. Despite the apparent humour with which Haw Haw was treated by comedians and the national press, the scale of his impact on Britain alarmed the government. The government estimated that six million regularly tuned in to Radio Hamburg, with a record audience of 18 million at the time of the fall of France in June 1940. A December 1939 Mass Observation report on 'Why we are Fighting' revealed that 17 percent agreed with Haw Haw's view that the conflict was the fault of an international Jewish conspiracy. The Ministry of Intelligence was concerned enough about Haw Haw's influence to launch its own 'Report on opinion and morale' in March 1940. This presented different and, for the government, more worrying reasons for tuning in to Radio Hamburg. In the BBC report, 58 percent claimed in public to listen to Haw Haw because they thought he was funny, but this dropped to 15 percent in private. More people tuned in because he seemed to have access to accurate news before the BBC. For example, the loss of Arras and Amiens to the Germans was broadcast 12 hours before the BBC, something that led people to suspect the Corporation was working with the government to hide information. People did not listen exclusively to Radio Hamburg, but saw it as a way of getting a balanced view of events in addition to the BBC news. The report also showed that people listened in the hope of getting tip-offs on future German actions – Haw Haw would sometimes name parts of towns or individual schools that were scheduled for bombing. His information was taken seriously by many due to his seemingly uncanny knowledge of life in Britain (see the role of rumour on page 105). Joyce not only aimed to spread fear and demoralise British workers, he attempted to exploit genuine resentments and divisions that he knew to exist within the country.

SOURCE 9

From a broadcast by William Joyce on 29 August 1940.

We have learned with horror and disgust that while London was suffering all the nightmares of aerial bombardment a few nights ago, there was a contrast between the situation of the rich and the poor which we hardly know how to describe. There were two Londons that night. Down by the docks and in the poor districts and the suburbs, people lay dead, or dying in agony from their wounds; but, while their counterparts were suffering only a little distance away, the plutocrats and the favoured lords of creation were making the raid an excuse for their drunken orgies and debaucheries in the saloons of Piccadilly and in the Cafe de Paris. Spending on champagne in one night what they would consider enough for a soldier's wife for a month these monied fools shouted and sang in the streets, crying, as the son of a profiteer baron put it, 'They won't bomb this part of the town! They want the docks! Fill up boys!'

One option discussed to deal with Haw Haw was to jam German transmissions, as the French government had done. However, this was not carried out, partly in light of the French experience. The French interpreted the jamming as a sign that the Germans were broadcasting accurate news that the government wanted hidden from the public, something which led to a consequent loss of trust in official French radio. The Political Warfare Executive was also keen to avoid jamming in case the Germans retaliated in kind and undermined the valuable work being carried out by Sefton Delmer's 'black propaganda' (see page 106). As a result, Joyce was free to broadcast to Britain until the fall of Hamburg and his capture in late April 1945.

Historian Angus Calder has drawn attention to the sinister effects of rumours on the home front, a common problem for populations forced to endure a state of siege. One famous rumour had it that Haw Haw knew that the clock in Darlington Town Hall ran two minutes slow. A Ministry of Information investigation found that many warnings and stories attributed to Haw Haw had not originated with him. The government fought against the demoralising effects of such rumours by issuing the famous poster 'Careless Talk Cost Lives' (see Source 10), by introducing a £50 fine for spreading rumours and with a July 1940 campaign called 'What do I do…?'

SOURCE 10

'Careless Talk Costs Lives', one of the most famous posters issued by the Ministry of Information. The characters on the back row are Adolf Hitler and Head of the German Airforce, Herman Goering.

These measures alone were not enough to counter established listening habits (Haw Haw's broadcasts often provided the basis for gossip and chat in the workplace the next day). The BBC was asked to broadcast a popular programme at the same time as Joyce's *Views on the News*, to tempt people away from Radio Hamburg. The result was one of the BBC's greatest success stories: *Postscript to the News. Postscript* was a talk programme at the height of its popularity when delivered by the writer and poet J.B. Priestley. Ten million people listened to his talks which followed the nine o'clock news each Sunday, and they grew to love his homely warmth and gentle encouragement. Haw Haw's influence began to decline, not only because of Priestley's success but because the British gained confidence in the accuracy of BBC news and in the prospect of victory throughout 1942. Haw Haw lost all credibility following the Allied successes from D-Day onwards. His last broadcasts consisted of slurring, drunken abuse hurled at everyone and everything.

ACTIVITY
KNOWLEDGE CHECK

The impact of Lord Haw Haw

1 What evidence exists that Lord Haw Haw's influence was greater than that suggested by the press?

2 How effective were British efforts to undermine the influence of Lord Haw Haw?

THINKING HISTORICALLY   Change (8a, b & c) (I)

Imposing realities

Look again at Source 10. Imagine that the two women depicted have the following conversation:

Woman 1: 'I hear that the "Blitz spirit" is actually a myth carefully constructed by the government.'

Woman 2: 'You mean our ability to pluck victory from the jaws of defeat thanks to our teamwork, good humour and stiff upper lip are no more than a fiction generated by official propaganda? Well I never!'

Answer the following questions:

1 Explain why the conversation would not have happened.

The shape of history is imposed by people looking back. People who lived through the 'history' did not always perceive the patterns that historians identify later. For example, some people living through the industrial revolution may have understood that great change was taking place, but they would not have been able to understand the massive economic, social and political consequences of industrialisation.

2 Consider the British home front during the Second World War.

   a) Who would have made the decision as to whether the Blitz spirit was a myth or not?

   b) Could anybody have challenged this decision?

   c) Explain why someone living through the war would have been unable to make a judgement about the state of British morale.

3 Why might judgements about British morale have changed since 1945?

4 What does Source 10, in connection with the above conversation, tell us about the structure of history as we understand it?

The dark arts of propaganda: the impact of Sefton Delmer

Sefton Delmer played an important yet unsung part in Britain's propaganda effort. He was born to Australian parents in Berlin in 1904 and was only allowed to speak German for the first five years of his life. His family moved to England when he was 13, but he never lost his slight German accent. His fluency in German facilitated his appointment in 1927 as Berlin correspondent for the *Daily Express*. In Berlin he gained the acquaintance of high-ranking Nazi Ernst Rohm, and that enabled him to become the first British journalist to interview Hitler. He spent some time with the Nazi leader, including flying the length and breadth of Germany with him on an election campaign in 1932. His time in Germany gave him a keen insight into the Nazi mindset as well as the German national character.

Delmer returned to Britain at the outbreak of the war and initially worked as an announcer on the BBC's German Service. However, his previous experience led the Political Warfare Executive (a secret organisation formed in August 1941 to conduct psychological warfare against the Nazis) to appoint him to the political intelligence department of the Foreign Office. His job was to co-ordinate and broadcast 'black' propaganda to German troops and civilians. Black propaganda pretended to originate from within the enemy country itself. It aimed to subtly demoralise the enemy by sowing discord between different sections of society and by planting misinformation among other accurate news. Delmer referred to demoralising misinformation as 'dirt' and real news as 'cover'. He said that the secret to successful black propaganda was the formula 'dirt, cover, cover, dirt, cover, cover'.

Gustav Seigfried Eins

Delmer's first success came with the broadcast of *Gustav Seigfried Eins* (from May 1941 to October 1943), run by a fictional character known as 'Der Chef' (The Boss). The show was broadcast at seven minutes to each hour during the afternoon and evening and began with a call from GS1 (Gustav Seigfried is the German phonetic alphabet for GS) to a range of other GSs, such as GS18 or GS76. This was not only designed to keep Nazi code-breakers busy, but also to give the impression that there was a wide network of anti-Nazi radio operatives inside Germany. Delmer crafted the character of 'Der Chef' to have the greatest possible impact. He was a senior Prussian former army officer, which automatically commanded a degree of respect in German listeners. He was anti-communist, anti-Semitic, a huge patriot and fan of Hitler personally and of the German Army, characteristics all designed to ingratiate him with the target audience. He was also critical of the Nazis and of the impact of the war on the German home front. These criticisms were shared by many Germans and struck a chord with privately grumbling listeners.

Sefton Delmer's masterpiece: Soldatensender

The purchase of one of the most powerful transmitters in the world (called 'Aspidistra', from the USA at the cost of £165,000) in 1942, enabled Delmer's team to target German U-boat crews in the Atlantic. The black propaganda radio station Deutsche Kurzwellensender Atlantik (or Atlantiksender) became highly popular among U-boat crews, due to the high proportion of popular music (around half of all programming) that was broadcast 24 hours a day, together with 90 percent accurate German news. One favoured piece of 'dirt' was to include interviews with 'sailors' who had gone on leave only to find out that their wives or girlfriends had been cheating on them with foreign workers while they had been away risking their lives. Atlantiksender even had its own wartime sweetheart, 'Vicky', to stir up feelings of longing and isolation.

From December 1943, another black propaganda radio station Soldatensender Calais built upon the success of Atlantiksender with its similar appeal to German troops stationed throughout France. Other methods used to give the impression of a genuine German station included the use of diaries and letters confiscated from German prisoners of war (POWs) to provide the basis of celebratory greetings to real soldiers, and the live transmission of Hitler's speeches relayed from real German stations. The broadcasts were so convincing that the Americans and press in neutral countries believed they were actual German broadcasts.

SOURCE

11 From a pamphlet called 'Dangerous Enemy Propaganda: Warning Against the so-called "Soldatensender Calais" by Lieutenant Herbert Schwan.' It was distributed to German Army officers in February 1944.

Within our army command area a camouflaged enemy radio has been heard in recent weeks which broadcasts under the name of "Soldatensender Calais". The manner in which the enemy propaganda operates must be described as highly dangerous as it is not recognisable as enemy propaganda by the unsuspecting. The enemy radio mixes genuine and invented news and... achieves a very considerable degree of credibility with uninitiated listeners. An example: "A reassuring message for all fathers has been received from the administrative authority for Children's Evacuation Camps. It reports that deaths from diphtheria have decreased from 548 to 372 per week. There is every reason to hope that despite the shortage of doctors and medicines the number of deaths will be kept down. End of item. That is all." This factual sounding item, which is, of course an invention from start to finish, sticks like a poisonous barb in the minds of soldiers with children in such a camp... Instructional talks must be given to those who listen to the station despite the fact they have recognised it as enemy radio and are doing so from boredom or a hunger for sensations.

The work of the station was reinforced from May 1944 with the distribution of a newsletter to German soldiers at the front called 'News for the Troops'. The newsletter and the station carried identical news, both cover and dirt, and as preparations for D-Day came to fruition they were designed to lead Germans into traps and mistakes. The loss of Calais to the Allies in September 1944 led to the station being rebranded as Soldatensender West. As the Allies advanced, the station became progressively more critical of Hitler's war leadership. Although morale would already have suffered due to mounting defeats, the supposed accuracy of casualty rates encouraged mass surrender. One-and-a-half million German soldiers were taken prisoner between D-Day and April 1945 in western Europe. During the final assault on Germany, Aspidistra's power enabled it to 'intrude' on local radio broadcast frequencies. The Nazis attempted to prevent the confusion this caused in the civilian populations of cities such as Hamburg and Leipzig by broadcasting warnings about Allied impersonation of local networks, but the black propaganda team easily countered this by issuing exactly the same warnings in its transmissions.

The impact of 'black propaganda' on Germany

The best evidence for the impact of British propaganda, both white and black, on the German home front is provided by Nazi secret police reports, which consistently suggest that there was a highly positive view of the British throughout the war, despite Nazi propaganda efforts to demonise them. Older people knew stories about the decent treatment of German POWs during the First World War and hoped that their sons were safe in British captivity after June 1944. German Christians believed that Britain would win the war because its government had not attacked the Church as the Nazis had done. Even at the height of the RAF bombing of German cities, there was no evidence of hatred against the British people as a whole, and Churchill was seen as a man of ability. Nazi leaders deplored this 'ambiguity' and 'objectiveness'. Propaganda Minister Goebbels largely failed in his self-appointed mission to make the Germans hate the British. Although the subtle spread of negative information weakened German morale, this must be put in the context of increasing shortages, the urban devastation wrought by aerial bombardment and news of mounting losses on all fronts from mid-1943. It is fair to conclude that British propaganda was made far more effective by the cumulative effect of these desperate circumstances on German civilians.

ACTIVITY
KNOWLEDGE CHECK

The impact of Sefton Delmer

1 Explain the difference between 'white' and 'black' propaganda. Why might Soldatensender Calais be referred to as 'grey' propaganda?

2 Give examples of the impact of Delmer's work on the German capacity to wage war.

ACTIVITY
SUMMARY

Propaganda, information and entertainment, 1939–45

1 Create a graph with 'British public morale' on the vertical axis and 'Time' on the horizontal axis. For the years 1939–45, plot a graph showing the average change in morale throughout the war.

2 Now add the key dates in the development of the war, either on the home front or the fighting front. Also add key dates in the development of information and the provision of entertainment.

3 Compare the line you drew for British morale with the developments in the war you added afterwards. Does the line seem to be influenced more by actual events or changes in information and propaganda (or neither)? Explain what this comparison tells you about the relative impact of information and propaganda on British morale during the Second World War.

WIDER READING

Gardiner, J. *The Blitz*, HarperPress (2011)

Gardiner, J. *Wartime Britain 1939-1945*, Headline Review (2005). Both Gardiner books give a highly readable account of life on the home front driven by eyewitness anecdotes.

Jenkins, R. *Churchill: A Biography*, Macmillan (2001). This is huge, but Part Five provides an excellent account of Churchill's war years.

Kenny, M. *Germany Calling: A Personal Biography of William Joyce*, New Island Books (2004)

Mackay, R. *Half the Battle: Civilian Morale in Britain during the Second World War*, Manchester University Press (2003). Provides lots of valuable evidence about public morale.

Nicholas, S. 'The People's Radio: the BBC and its Audience 1939–45' in Hayes, N. and Hill, J. (eds) *Millions Like Us? British Culture in the Second World War*, Liverpool University Press (1999). Gives a clear and thorough guide to the impact of key changes within the BBC.

The MOI Digital project at the School of Advanced Studies, University of London provides a wealth of information on the Ministry of Information, its role in censorship and propaganda, and its relationship with other ministries and the BBC – www.moidigital.ac.uk

The PsyWar website hosts the collected works of Sefton Delmer as well as a large number of interesting articles about his black propaganda – www.psywar.co.uk

3.5 Media in the sixties: satire, image and social change

- How far did satire undermine authority figures during the sixties?
- How far did film and television mould or mirror British attitudes to social issues?
- To what extent were the 'swinging sixties' more image than reality?

INTRODUCTION

'The sixties' have come to be understood as shorthand for a whole host of ideas that together formed a decisive break with the past. Liberalism, sexualisation, youth rebellion and consumerism are thought to have sloughed off the oppressive, more formal culture of previous decades. Iconic images of the Beatles, the Rolling Stones and pop culture, mods, rockers and hippies, the Campaign for Nuclear Disarmament (CND), protests against the Vietnam War and the black civil rights movement in the United States all suggest a youthful, rebellious energy that broke with tradition. However, these impressions are based not on a detailed study of history books but on sounds and images largely generated by mass media.

The question at the heart of this chapter is the extent to which film and television faithfully reflected real life, or whether they generated their own distorted version of reality. This question is further complicated by the fact that media images and messages helped to mould as well as mirror social attitudes and behaviour. Commentators who dislike or mistrust mass media have tended to exaggerate its influence on the way British people live and think. Apologists for mass media promote the notion that people know the difference between real life and what is portrayed on screen. They argue that levels of wealth, changes in the law, education and employment have all had a far greater impact on British society. The truth is almost certainly between these two positions: the impact of film and television on public attitudes to government, monarchy, the Church, race, sex and social inequality cannot be ignored, but it certainly varies in respect of each issue.

The changing nature of mass media in the middle of the 20th century further obscures the assessment of its impact on British society. In 1945, mass media comprised newspapers, radio and cinema. Television was still in its infancy in 1945, and BBC TV broadcasts did not resume until 1946 (having been suspended at the outbreak of the Second World War in September 1939). The BBC enjoyed a monopoly on TV broadcasts until 1955 and on radio until 1973. Cinema was still a major source of news as well as entertainment thanks to the newsreels that

1948 – Nationality Act enables all 'citizens of the UK and Colonies' to have freedom of movement and settlement within the Commonwealth

SS *Windrush* arrives at Tilbury Docks in London

1959 – Obscene Publications Act allows serious works of art to use 'obscene' words and images

The Second Vatican Council, the first since 1870, begins to revise Catholic worship and teaching

1962 – Commonwealth Immigrants Act

First Hindu Temple opens in UK

Colour supplements first appear in Sunday newspapers

| 1948 | 1954 | 1958 | 1959 | 1960 | 1961 | 1962 |

1954 – Television Act allows creation of commercial Independent Television (ITV) in 1955

1958 – Nottingham and Notting Hill race riots

1960 – Geoffrey Fisher becomes the first Archbishop of Canterbury to visit the Pope since the Reformation

Lady Chatterley's Lover trial allows publication of 'pornographic' novel

1961 – Suicide Act means those who fail to kill themselves will no longer be prosecuted

preceded films. The newsreels were usually less than ten minutes long and were highly deferential towards leading figures of authority. A decline in cinema attendance led to the demise of the newsreel format. After a peak of 1.6 billion admissions in 1945–46, cinema audiences plunged to under a third of this figure by the mid-1950s. This collapse was almost entirely due to the rise of television, which soon emerged as the main provider of news and entertainment. Newspapers had to respond to the increased competition from TV for advertisement revenue after the launch of commercial television in 1955. Several contemporary commentators feared that such competition would drive a vulgar 'race to the bottom' to attract the largest possible audience. They wondered how far a retreat from the public service ethic in broadcasting would affect television shows and their influence on British values.

HOW FAR DID SATIRE UNDERMINE AUTHORITY FIGURES DURING THE SIXTIES?

Satire and changing attitudes to government

The crucial difference between earlier forms of **satire** and that inspired by a handful of Oxford- and Cambridge-educated comedians in the early 1960s, was the intended audience. Whereas the satirical prints of the 18th century were intended for an elite audience, TV satire of the 1960s was designed for a mass audience.

Every generation looks back with rose-tinted glasses at the quality of politicians 'back in their day'. An inspection of Mass Observation diaries or early polls quickly reveals that, with a few exceptions, most politicians have been seen as self-seeking and untrustworthy. While millions of listeners tuned in to hear William Beveridge's social welfare proposals, most people did not trust political promises of post-war improvements. However, despite this low threshold of respect for politicians, there are grounds to argue that 'the sixties' made life far more difficult for the political class. The 1960s satire boom undoubtedly poked fun at the public posturing of politicians and helped to increase interest in their private lives. It is not so clear whether 1960s satire was also responsible for increased coverage of parliamentary proceedings, the rise of investigative journalism or the cult of celebrity, which also affected the depiction of the elite and undermined popular **deference** towards them.

The context of increased mass media access to politicians

News reports on television and by the press shifted from a broadly deferential tone at the start of the 1950s to a questioning one at the start of the 1960s. Some legal changes help to account for this shift. In 1944, the BBC agreed that it would not discuss any issue that was due to be debated in parliament within the next 14 days. Winston Churchill defended the **14-Day Rule** as it stopped parliamentary debates being influenced by the 'expressions' by persons who had not the status or responsibility of Members of Parliament'. However, by 1056, BBC and ITV journalists had grown frustrated with the Rule. For instance, the inability to discuss the first successful testing of a hydrogen

KEY TERMS

Satire
Satire is humour that makes fun of people, usually those who are famous. It pokes fun at their failings and vices, and has been a prominent feature of British humour for a long time.

Deference
An almost automatic, unquestioned respect for social superiors.

14-Day Rule
This rule meant that television programmes were not allowed to discuss any issues scheduled to be discussed in parliament within the next fortnight.

1963 – Publication of John Robinson's *Honest to God* causes religious controversy. Sales reach 300,000 copies

1965 – Murder (Abolition of the Death Penalty) Act passed

First Race Relations Act establishes the Race Relations Board

1968 – Second Race Relations Act establishes Community Relations Commission

Enoch Powell makes 'rivers of blood' speech

Theatres Act abolishes censorship of plays on stage in UK

1963	1964	1965	1966	1967	1968	1969

1964 – BBC2 launched

Pilkington Committee Report made public on television

Sun newspaper launched

1967 – BBC Radio 1 launched and pirate radio banned

First colour television broadcasts begin

Sexual Offences Act legalises homosexual acts between men over 21, in private, in England and Wales (not in Scotland until 1980 or Northern Ireland until 1982)

1969 – Audience of around 500 million worldwide watches Charles' investiture as Prince of Wales

Divorce Act allows divorce to be granted after two years of separation if both parties want it, and after five years if one party wants it

bomb for two weeks in 1957 was much criticised. A government report concluded that contemporary coverage of debates would increase interest in parliament, and the Rule was greatly relaxed. It was finally abolished in 1958.

Political parties virtually ignored television until the mid-1950s. The huge increase in television ownership before Elizabeth II's coronation in June 1953 (with 500,000 sets sold the week before) led to TV cameras being admitted to party conferences from 1955. In 1955, Anthony Eden became the first prime minister to speak to the nation on live TV. In 1958 he also became the first to be interviewed by a journalist on television.

SOURCE 1

From *The News Interview: Journalists and Public Figures on the Air* by Steven Clayman (2002). Robin Day was a television journalist who is regarded as having transformed the television interview and helped to change the relationship between politicians and television during the 1960s. The interview described took place on 23 February 1958.

... news interviews became more adversarial, and the independent companies abandoned the BBC practice of submitting lists of questions in advance to ministers, who would then give rehearsed answers. 'Unscripted' interviews became the order of the day. ... Perhaps the key interview during this period was Day's interview with then-Prime Minister Harold Macmillan which flatly departed from the previous deferential style with which senior politicians had been treated. One newspaper described it as 'the most vigorous cross-examination a Prime Minister has been subjected to in the public.' While the interview got mixed reviews in the press, it struck a chord with the viewing public and Macmillan himself found that surviving Day's most aggressive cross-questioning gave him enhanced credibility with the electorate.

Both Labour and the Conservatives began to employ public relations experts in the 1960s to maximise the use of media coverage for electoral gain. The battle for votes was increasingly fought by getting messages across at a national level, something that undermined the importance and vitality of local constituency work. During the 1964 election, only eight percent of British electors attended local election meetings and only three percent participated in local campaigning. The image of national politicians clearly began to matter more due to the impact of television. Politicians such as future Labour leader Michael Foot complained that politicians were increasingly like film stars trying to boost their ratings.

TV satire: *That Was The Week That Was*

The launch of *That Was The Week That Was* (also known as *TW3*) in November 1962 represented the pinnacle of the 'satire boom'. This boom had its origins in mildly subversive humour during the Second World War, which paved the way for the hugely influential satirical 1960 stage show *Beyond the Fringe*. Comedians such as Peter Cook and Dudley Moore used their success on stage to spearhead the satire boom on television in the early 1960s. *TW3*, presented by David Frost, built on *Beyond the Fringe* with its combination of current affairs satire and stand-up comedy. At its peak, it had 12 million viewers a week and was said to empty

many pubs late on Saturday night when it was screened. Reginald Bevins, the postmaster general who oversaw broadcasting, tried to have *TW3* stopped. It was Prime Minister Harold Macmillan who prevented this (even though he was the target of many jokes), as he recognised the damage that would be done by attacking such a popular programme.

Despite its short run of two series, *TW3* did help to substantially erode deference to politicians by encouraging the British public to mock and laugh at them. Peter Cook did a cruel impression of Macmillan's patrician accent, exaggerating the upper-class drawl. His replacement as prime minister, Alec Douglas-Home, was a gift to the satirists. He was an earl who became the last premier to sit in the House of Lords before renouncing his earldom to win a seat in the House of Commons. He was a surprise appointment. There was no leadership contest within the Conservative Party, and critics saw his choice as a stitch up by a 'magic circle' of leading Conservatives who, like Douglas-Home, had been to Eton College. Satirists lampooned his wooden, uncomfortable manner on television, and caricatured him as a 'grouse moor' aristocrat who was hopelessly out of touch with the common man and the modern world. Labour leader Harold Wilson enjoyed these attacks on a man he branded an anachronism, but was far from happy when the satirists turned their acid wit against him during his two spells as prime minister (1964–70 and 1974–76). Wilson always tried to present himself as a common man, in touch with youth culture and technological advance. He smoked a pipe, wore an affordable raincoat and claimed to prefer tinned to fresh salmon. He enjoyed inviting celebrities such as the Beatles to 10 Downing Street and made the most of the resulting photo opportunities. *Private Eye* ridiculed this shameless populism with exaggerated examples in its regular column 'Mrs Wilson's Diary'.

The importance of *Beyond the Fringe* and *TW3* is reflected in the way they bracket the start and end of the satire boom. August 1960 was when the stage show was launched and December 1963 was when *TW3* was cancelled after its second series.

SOURCE 2

Academic and novelist Malcolm Bradbury recalls his impression of the satire boom during his time as an English lecturer at the University of Birmingham (1961–65).

TW3 caused enormous euphoria, as if the great British logjam was being broken at last. All my age group was carried away by it, week on week, and it did have an important impact in changing views of – and deference towards – politicians and institutions generally.

The satirical role of the press: *Private Eye* and the Profumo scandal

Between 1951 and 1970, newspaper circulation fell from 16.8 million to 14.6 million; five national daily newspapers were forced to close after 1960. In a bid to boost sales and attract some of the huge amount of advertising revenue that had gone to commercial television since 1955, newspapers tried ever more populist tactics. News headlines became punchier and a growing share of the front page was given over to images rather than words. Driving many of the changes were Cecil King and Hugh Cudlipp, director and editor at the *Daily Mirror*, respectively. Cudlipp believed that it was crucial to get the story out before rival newspapers, no matter what the later comeback might be. In the wake of the 1960–63 satire boom, tabloid newspapers such as the *Mirror* became more scathing in their treatment of politicians and political scandal. A good example of this is the press treatment of John Profumo, Conservative Minister for War, in June 1963.

Whereas in the past politicians had benefited from a 'gentleman's agreement' with newspaper proprietors who kept their private lives out of the media (for example, David Lloyd George, prime minister 1916–22, had had an affair with his secretary for years), this was increasingly no longer the case. Not only had Profumo had an affair with a call girl, Christine Keeler, but there were rumours she was simultaneously having an affair with a Soviet spy – hardly good for national security. Even so, the national press only ran the story after Profumo's resignation on 5 June, and he might have escaped their attention had it not been for the satirical stories run by *Private Eye* magazine. The *Eye* was founded by Richard Ingrams, Christopher Booker and Willy Rushton in October 1961. It did not target one political party in particular, but wanted to poke fun at whoever held power. Although it only had 10,000 readers at the time, its exposé of the Profumo scandal in March 1963 led Labour politicians to demand that Profumo deny the allegations in parliament, and that a Commission of Enquiry be set up to investigate the affair. Profumo did deny the rumours on 4 June, which made his resignation the next day all the more scandalous as he had lied to parliament.

As a result of the Profumo scandal, Prime Minister Harold Macmillan asked Lord Denning to lead the Commission of Enquiry. When Denning's report was published on 26 September 1963, it became a bestseller. When the *Daily Telegraph* published the report in full, readers were amazed by the scandalous stories about the political elites, such as 'The Man in the Mask'. This was about a member of the Cabinet who had served dinner at a private party while naked except for a mask, a small lace apron, and a card around his neck reading 'If my services don't please you, whip me'. The publication of the report did a great deal of damage to the reputation of the Conservative Party. Although Macmillan had been ill for some time, the scandal contributed to his resignation in October 1963. Without the satirical, investigative work of *Private Eye*, it is doubtful that the Profumo scandal or the subsequent enquiry would have emerged.

ACTIVITY
KNOWLEDGE CHECK

Satire and changing attitudes to government

1 Give examples of satire directed against politicians in the 1960s.

2 In what ways, and to what extent, did satire change popular attitudes to government?

3 Assess the value of Source 3 for revealing the impact of the satire boom on changing attitudes to government in the 1960s.

SOURCE 3

A Gerald Scarfe cartoon of Harold Macmillan, Conservative prime minister (1957–63), which copies a pose made famous by a photo of Christine Keeler. The cartoon was published in *Private Eye* in 1963.

Satire and changing attitudes to the monarchy

The rise of parliamentary authority since the late 17th century and the rise of prime ministerial power since the mid-18th century meant that the British monarchy had lost its political importance before the start of the 20th century. George I (1714–27) in particular set the precedent of allowing a prime minister (Robert Walpole) to exercise power on the monarch's behalf, because he spent a good deal of time in his original German homeland and failed to speak good English for most of his reign. Walpole built up so much power in parliament that it was impossible for George II (1727–60) to regain monarchical control. Yet the monarchy retained a national and social significance in that it represented order, stability and continuity. The monarchy, partly thanks to its determination to stick to rationing and remain in London during the Blitz, remained hugely popular with all classes of people in the 1950s and 1960s. Some 20 million people gathered around 2 million TV sets to watch Elizabeth II's coronation in 1953. Although the queen did not reveal anything of her lively character in public, her husband Prince Philip and sister Princess Margaret endeared themselves to the public through their warmer, more outgoing public personas. The life cycle of the royals retained huge public interest. The births of Prince Charles (1948), Princess Anne (1950), Prince Andrew (1960) and Prince Edward (1964), the queen's birthdays and anniversaries (silver wedding in 1972 and silver jubilee in 1977) and marriages such as Princess Margaret's (1960) and Princess Anne's (1973), were all covered extensively on television and in the popular press.

Although the satirical climate of the 1960s meant that the royal family was not totally immune to criticism, it fared far better than politicians. Republicans were in a tiny minority at the start of the decade, in part thanks to the personal popularity of the young queen, but also due to the legacy of Elizabeth's father George VI. His calm, fatherly radio broadcasts, tours of bombed cities and choice to remain in London during the war earned the respect of the nation. Elizabeth II became increasingly adept at using media attention to remain a relevant part of British society. The queen allowed BBC cameras to broadcast live images of her coronation on 2 June 1953. From 1956 onwards, she also began to invite selected members of the public to informal lunches and, later, garden parties at Buckingham Palace. By 1983, 35,000 people enjoyed this honour each year. Her first television broadcast of the Christmas message in 1957 attracted 16 million viewers. A photograph of the queen with her new baby, Prince Andrew, was released in 1960. It portrayed Elizabeth as a mother rather than a monarch, with none of the regal trappings that had featured in earlier royal portraits. The public were allowed a glimpse inside Windsor Castle after its chapel was opened as an art gallery in 1962. In June 1970, the queen went on her first domestic 'walkabout' in Coventry. She had already gone on foreign walkabouts in the USA (1957), Malta (1967) and New Zealand (1970). Mass media coverage of such stories helped to boost loyalty and affection for the monarchy. This popularity automatically undermined the bite of satirical sketches.

EXTRACT

1 From Leonard Freedman's *The Offensive Art: Political Satire and its Censorship around the World from Beerbohm to Borat* (2008). Here, Freedman describes a *TW3* sketch performed by David Frost, and the view of its writers in 1962.

> The 1960s ushered in the era of declining deference and inevitably brought the royals into the sights of the disrespectful young performers of *The Establishment* and *TW3*:
>
> 'The Royal Barge is, as it were, sinking. The sleek, royal-blue hull of the barge is sliding, gracefully, almost regally, beneath the waters of the Pool of London... and now the Queen, smiling radiantly, is swimming for her life. Her Majesty is wearing a silk ensemble in canary yellow.'
>
> The writers of this piece admitted that 'none of our items dealing with the Royal Family had the cutting edge that those with political or religious content sported'.

Paul Moorhouse, curator of an exhibition to celebrate the queen's 2012 diamond jubilee, noted a clear turning point in royal public relations in 1966. The Aberfan disaster, where 116 children and 28 adults were killed when a coal slag heap collapsed onto Pantglas Junior School, prompted the change. It was commented on in the press that she was slow to respond to the Aberfan disaster, fuelling the feeling that she was distancing herself from her subjects. The queen's advisers realised there needed to be a change of strategy and set about portraying her as more approachable. A documentary at the very end of the decade hinted at the rather different relationship that was to emerge between the public and the royal family by the end of the century.

Royal Family, screened on both the BBC and ITV in 1969, was the first glimpse of the royal family in a domestic setting, away from the formality of occasions such as Charles' investiture as the Prince of Wales in the same year. The queen commissioned the film to show the public that the royals were a family like any other, through an unprecedented chance to look behind the scenes at Buckingham Palace, Sandringham, Balmoral, Windsor and even the royal yacht and train. Around 66 percent of the public saw either the BBC or ITV broadcast. The royals increasingly had to balance the need to satisfy popular expectations of more personal public relations with their desire for privacy. Concerns that the documentary portrayed the royals as too ordinary (it shocked posh viewers that the queen stored food in Tupperware containers) led the queen to forbid repeat screenings, but a few clips were re-released to celebrate her diamond jubilee in 2012. The queen regretted her decision to commission the documentary as it did not have the impact on the royal image that she had intended. The balance between dignified privacy and a more personal rapport with the public was difficult to achieve and had not been successfully accomplished by the start of the 21st century.

SOURCE 4

A still photo from the filming of the 1969 documentary *Royal Family*. The photo shows Queen Elizabeth II, her husband Prince Philip and two of her children, Prince Charles and Princess Anne.

ACTIVITY
KNOWLEDGE CHECK

Satire and changing attitudes to monarchy

1 Give reasons why the monarchy appeared to be more immune than politicians to the satire boom in the 1960s.

2 For what reasons other than satire did the public image of the royal family begin to change in the 1960s?

Satire and changing attitudes to the Church

For a brief period between the end of the Second World War and the start of the 1960s, it appeared as if the Church of England would make a steady recovery. Although the 1950s had witnessed a resurgence of intellectual confidence, it had also seen the continuation of a pre-war numerical decline in attendance. The **Free Churches** were in steady decline and the Roman Catholic Church received a major boost from Irish immigration in the 1950s and early 1960s. Yet the sixties saw the start of greater **secularisation**, which accelerated in the final quarter of the century. The causes of this profound shift are a matter of much debate. While satire on TV and in the press helped to undermine the moral authority of religious figures, it is clear that the problems that faced all churches were longer term and deeper rooted than the influence of the satire boom.

There were some famous comedies that satirised the Church in the 1960s, and in many ways they were clearly building on existing popular stereotypes of clergymen. *All Gas and **Gaiters*** (BBC, 1966–71) was a highly popular sitcom (situation comedy) whose farcical plot lines centred on the scheming rivalry of the clergy at the fictional St Ogg's Cathedral. Its star, Derek Nimmo, went on to play an inept monk in *Oh Brother!* (BBC, 1968–70) and its sequel *Oh Father!* (BBC, 1973). The depiction of senior members of the clergy as silly and incompetent led to some angry letters to the press, but even these churchmen generally enjoyed the gentle satire. The success of such humour indicates that this was a clergy stereotype already familiar to British audiences (bumbling priests featured in Anthony Trollope's popular novels a century earlier). In 1963, Peter Sellers starred as a prison chaplain in the comedy film *Heavens Above!*, which was one of the top 12 most popular films that year. His performance mixed a form of naïve piety with an attempt to be modern and trendy. There had been several famous instances of 'trendy vicars' in the late 1950s and early 1960s, such as the Reverend William (Bill) Shergold (Source 5), who wore black leathers and led a bikers' youth club, and who had appeared on mass media in an attempt to make religion seem cool and relevant.

KEY TERM

Gaiter
A cloth covering for the ankle and lower leg, worn over the shoe. It is part of the traditional dress of bishops and archdeacons.

SOURCE 5

Reverend Bill Shergold, who became the most famous leader of 'the 59 club', a Christian motorcycle group founded in East London in 1959 by Canon John Oates.

Beyond the Fringe and *TW3* had also satirised religion, in particular the Church of England. Writer and comedian Alan Bennett's most popular character lampooned Anglican vicars' dreary sermons in the stage show, while David Frost, in a famous *TW3* sketch, compared religions as if they were products in a consumer goods magazine. Religious figures were regular sources of humour for the surreal comedy sketch show *Monty Python's Flying Circus* (BBC, 1969–74). One sketch had 'The Bishop' running a tough vigilante gang, while another had a group of cardinals claiming to be the Spanish Inquisition while ineffectually torturing an old woman with soft cushions. However, the impact of such comedy must be set against the profound changes that were taking place within the Church itself.

In his 1963 book *Honest to God*, Bishop of Woolwich John Robinson called for a less supernatural and more personal interpretation of God and Christianity. Although theologians such as Rudolf Bultmann in the 1930s and Paul Tillich in the 1950s had already put such ideas forward, Robinson popularised the ideas among the British public. The book received a lot of press attention and went through three editions in its first month of publication; by the end of the sixties over 100,000 copies had been sold. Robinson had written the book in response to the high levels of indifference to religion in parts of London, such as Battersea, where just three percent of residents regularly attended church. He argued that in an increasingly secular and individualistic society, the Church needed to reform itself to remain relevant.

Such a questioning approach to traditional religious practice was also found within the Roman Catholic Church. Pope John XXIII unexpectedly emerged as a reforming Pope when he summoned the Second Vatican Council (Vatican II) in 1959, which met in 1962. He wanted a process of *aggiornamento* or 'bringing up to date', to equip the Church to thrive in the modern world. The Council, the first in almost a century, sat for three years and made some dramatic changes to Catholic worship. The most immediate change as far as congregations were concerned was the celebration of Mass in the vernacular rather than traditional Latin. Controversial issues were discussed, but there was no effective resolution of some of the most divisive ones. For example, John's successor, Pope Paul VI, ruled that all forms of artificial contraception were forbidden, but by this time many British middle-class Catholic families had begun to use the Pill for family planning (Anglican bishops had approved the use of artificial contraception in 1930). The compromise agreements of Vatican II pleased almost no one: the changes unsettled those with a firmly traditional faith, while the failure to achieve more significant reforms disappointed progressive Catholics. Catholic congregations and the number of men who entered seminaries to train as priests fell steadily after 1965. The date suggests a far stronger correlation between the impact of Vatican II and this decline than the satire boom, which had subsided by 1964.

These internal reforms were clearly a response to wider and longer-term social change that could not possibly have resulted from the satire boom.

Historians have disagreed over the most significant cause of secularisation. In his 2009 book *The Death of Christian Britain*, Callum Brown sees the 1960s as the key decade when Britain became secularised. He particularly notes the impact of girls' and women's magazines on average Sunday church attendance, which declined from 2.16 million in 1960 to 1.63 million in 1970. This was by far the steepest rate of decline during the 20th century. Attendance had grown from 1.85 million in 1950 and experienced a far more gentle decline after 1970, from 1.55 million in 1980 to 1.16 million in 2000. Brown rightly points out that women were more likely to attend church than men, and he argues that the rise of secular, consumerist values undermined a commitment to regular public worship.

Historian Adrian Hastings agrees with Callum Brown that all churches had been far more comfortable in a culture with clear gender division. He argues that the rise of sexual equality as a practical possibility in the 1960s posed difficult questions for the all-male church hierarchy. He notes that the whole intellectual climate favoured a more scientific, secular approach to the world, and that this even affected some influential theologians. While there might have been an outcry in the 1940s or 1950s, there was no scandal when anthropologist Desmond Morris suggested in his book *The Naked Ape* (1967) that religion has caused a great amount of unnecessary suffering. Indeed, when the *Daily Mirror* serialised the book, sales of the newspaper were boosted. Hastings also agrees that the 1960s represent a decisive turning point for British religiosity. He even narrows it down further to the decade after 1963 due to the impact of *Honest to God* (see page 116) and the subsequent questioning of traditional religion.

EXTRACT

From Adrian Hastings' *A History of English Christianity 1920–1990*, published in 1991.

Sexual equality, like racial equality, became in the sixties a practicable ideal... A strongly sexual segregated pattern of life had been the norm, particularly for the English upper class from school to club. Now even the House of Lords was to admit women. The Church had fitted well into the old sexually divided world and, of all institutions, would now find it most difficult to adapt to the new mode. Intellectually there was a massive shift away from the religion towards the establishment of secularism as the ruling orthodoxy, noticeable particularly at the BBC. For these, and many other reasons, after a rather too comfortable ride through the fifties the churches found the sixties at once challenging and, as time went on, extremely disturbing.

However, many historians have criticised Hastings' view as it ignores the pre-1960s decline. Numbers attending church once a week had already fallen before 1945, from 35 to 13 percent of the population. *Puzzled People*, a Mass Observation report in 1947, concluded that the majority of Britons were either deeply confused about religion or simply did not think about it much at all. This shift helps to explain the overall lack of success of those who wished to restore British public morality back to a perceived golden age of the late 1940s and early 1950s. Social historian

James Obelkevich sees the rise of industry and urbanisation as the most significant long-term factors. He argues that the traditional rural calendar and holidays were strongly linked to Christian festivals, but the introduction of bank holidays in 1871 and the commercialisation of the remaining festivals of Easter and Christmas severed this link. The process was perhaps completed in 1994 when the Keep Sundays Special campaign failed to stop supermarkets opening on 'the Lord's day'. The significance of such long-term trends, and the important internal developments within the Roman Catholic Church and Church of England, strongly suggest that satire mirrored changing attitudes to the Church rather than moulding them in anything other than a superficial sense.

HOW FAR DID FILM AND TELEVISION MOULD OR MIRROR BRITISH ATTITUDES TO SOCIAL ISSUES?

Introduction: the decline of British cinema and the rise of television

A number of factors have affected the impact of film on the British. The first is the shift in its overall popularity – the greater the total audience for a film, the more likely it is to affect popular views. Cinema exploded in popularity during the First World War. *The Battle of the Somme* (1916) was seen by 20 million people in the first six weeks, and it remains one of the most viewed films in British cinema history. However, after record-high ticket sales of 1,635 million in 1946, attendance fell steadily throughout the 1960s to 343 million in 1964 and 220 million in 1970. Reductions in the size of cinema audiences, largely due to the rise of television, meant that over half the cinemas in the country were forced to close between 1955 and 1963. The impact of film was also affected by who went to the cinema most often. There were large variations in cinema attendance. The typical profile of a regular cinema-goer was young, urban, working class and, for those over the age of 19, female. Sixty-nine percent of 16–19-year-olds went once a week compared to 11 percent of over-60s. People in the North of England went on average almost twice as often as those in the South. This was probably because of income differences that enabled southerners to undertake more expensive activities such as participatory sport. Despite such differences, British audiences enjoyed remarkably similar films: comedy, musical romances and crime drama.

Television had become the dominant medium for news and entertainment by the 1960s. In 1955, 40 percent of households had a TV set, and this rose to 80 percent in 1960 and 95 percent in 1969. The Central Statistical Office recorded that watching television was one of the most popular leisure activities among all social groups. Men and women spent around 23 percent of their free time in front of the small screen. Following the launch of commercial television (ITV) in 1955 and the 1964 launch of BBC2 there were three television channels. The limited choice of channel meant large potential audiences for popular programmes. As so many people saw the same programmes, the content of these shows formed an important part of the next day's conversations at school, work or at home. The impact of television was further enhanced by the spread of broadcasts and reception in colour. BBC2 began colour broadcasts in 1967, with BBC1 following in November 1969. The **ubiquity** of television ownership and viewing in Britain gave the medium a huge potential to affect popular perceptions of a range of contemporary issues.

KEY TERMS

Ubiquity
The state of being everywhere all at once.

Americanisation
The adoption of American styles, values and patterns of speech in British cultural products and especially in younger Britons. Examples included music and dance crazes such as swing jive, and slang such as 'Oh yeah?'

Social realist
An artistic style that portrays ordinary people going about their everyday lives. It often focuses on working-class hardship and struggle.

Television, the *Wednesday Play* and attitudes to homelessness

In 1955, the BBC monopoly on television was ended when 14 independent companies were allowed to begin broadcasting, funded by advertising. There were concerns among cultural critics that commercial television would promote vulgar materialism and the **Americanisation** of British culture. One such critic, Richard Hoggart, strongly influenced the 1962 Pilkington Report on the impact of television, which insisted on the safeguarding of a public service ethic. Although the Conservative government, reluctant to interfere in a successful commercial sector, ignored the Report's recommendations that ITV broadcast more programmes that promoted decent public tastes and attitudes, the incoming Labour administration largely based the Television Act 1964 on the Report.

- ITV companies were compelled to screen two plays and two current affairs programmes in addition to the news each week in order to fulfil their public service obligation.

- BBC2 was launched in April 1964 to screen programmes to build knowledge as well as original comedy, drama and arts programmes.

The Report's emphasis on the need for quality drama on television led to a demand for new plays from British playwrights. The *Wednesday Play* (BBC, 1964–70) helped to launch the career of influential writers Dennis Potter and Nell Dunn, and director Ken Loach. Producers and directors were hugely innovative in this period. At the start of the sixties, plays on television, such as those of *Television Playhouse* (ITV, 1955–67), were broadcast live and were essentially the same as plays at the theatre. By the mid-1960s, Loach and others had begun to shoot many scenes on location and 'vision mix' them with live studio footage. This made the films much more realistic – many viewers were unsure whether the scenes shot on location were fiction or news clips. The BBC Board of Governors was so concerned about this that in 1965 it banned *The War Game*, a play about a nuclear attack on Britain. It was not broadcast until 1985. Sydney Newman, the head of drama at the BBC at the time, insisted that powerful art has to reflect the era in which it is created. Writers responded with hard-hitting, **social realist** plays such as *Up the Junction* (1965), which contained a powerful home abortion scene, and *Cathy Come Home* (1966) about homelessness.

Cathy Come Home, the only notable film about homelessness made in the 1960s, follows the story of a young couple with a child who lose their home after Cathy's husband loses his job through ill-health. Social services end up taking Cathy's children as a result of her homelessness. The play had a tremendous impact on the 6–10 million people who saw the first screening of it in November 1966. It significantly raised the profile of homelessness and some viewers were unsure whether it was a play or a documentary about real people. In his 1974 book *Housing: The Great British Failure*, Fred Berry argued that the whole issue of homelessness had been ignored by the British public for years. With *Cathy Come Home*, the public's concern changed almost overnight, and homelessness became a matter that generated profound national sympathy and concern. Berry went on to add, however, that this sympathy only lasted until new television programmes were made that focused on different issues and diverted the public's attention away from homelessness once more. *Cathy Come Home* did have some impact due to the public outrage it generated. Birmingham City Council relaxed its rules about husbands and wives staying together in their shelters, and the homelessness charity Crisis was launched in 1967 following a publicity campaign inspired by the play. However, it was a sheer coincidence that another homelessness charity, Shelter, was launched just two weeks after the first screening of the play. Shelter was founded in response to the publication of studies, such as *The Poor and the Poorest* (1965), about the persistence of poverty despite the rise of the Welfare State. Social historians Susan Hutson and David Clapham (1999) have persuasively concluded that there was no clear sign that the play had any subsequent effect on government policy. Similarly, the passage of the Abortion Act 1967 was possibly eased by the popular reaction to *Up the Junction*, but clearly it had far more to do with backbench MP Dr David Steel's sustained campaign.

While the BBC's *Wednesday Play* discussed controversial topics, the programme did not portray or inspire a rebellion of working-class opinion against their social superiors. On the contrary, the working classes generally held the most conservative opinions about liberal reforms. The programme that working-class viewers identified with the most was the soap opera *Coronation Street*. Launched in December 1960, it had a twice-weekly audience of 20 million within its first year. Northern viewers in particular identified with the ordinary backdrop to the drama: the home, the shop, the pub and the strong female characters, such as Elsie Tanner, who evoked a feeling of nostalgia for wartime community. Yet the show was not exclusively popular with working-class viewers and had many middle-class devotees.

ACTIVITY
KNOWLEDGE CHECK

Mass media and popular attitudes to homelessness

1 In what ways could film and television be said to have had any impact on attitudes to homelessness?

2 What evidence is there that the impact of film and television had only a limited impact on attitudes to homelessness?

How far did film and television change attitudes to racial minorities?

The demographic, legal and international context

Racism can be understood as an ideological viewpoint that compares the 'characteristics' of different ethnicities and ranks them in a hierarchy. Such views, informed by experiences of **imperialism** and a poor understanding of human biology, were common in Europe during the first half of the 20th century and helped to inform negative stereotypical views of black people that persisted into the 1960s. Racism can also be viewed as derogatory, degrading or discriminatory attitudes and actions towards individuals with different skin colour. It is this second definition, with its focus on individual action and expression, that film and television could more easily reflect and perhaps shape.

Although non-white people had lived in Britain since Roman times, they only made up 0.2 percent of the population in 1945. There was no 'colour problem' in the UK until large numbers of West Indians and South Asians began to settle there in the 1950s and 1960s. The British Nationality Act 1948 made all people living in the Commonwealth British citizens and many were encouraged to migrate to Britain to fill shortages in the labour market. Following the disembarkation of 493 West Indian passengers from the SS *Empire Windrush* at Tilbury Docks on 22 June 1948, around 3,000 black immigrants settled in Britain each year for the next five years. Many expected a warm welcome thanks to the stories or direct experience of volunteers in Britain during the Second World War. But the reality for many was racial prejudice, poor housing and manual labour not befitting their prior training or education. The failure of local efforts to integrate racial minorities and the eruption of violent race riots in a few areas in 1958 forced government legislation to curtail unrestricted immigration with the Commonwealth Immigrants Act 1962 and 1968. The Race Relations Acts 1965 and 1968 banned incitement to racial hatred and racial discrimination in public places, housing and employment. This made illegal the use of restrictions such as 'no coloureds' and 'Europeans only' by landlords and employers. The Race Relations Board was set up in 1966 to deal with complaints about

KEY TERM

Imperialism
The domination of one area and people by another. European imperialism expanded in the Americas, Africa and Asia from the 16th century and led to the carving up of almost the whole of Africa between 1880 and 1900. Britain lost control of almost all of its colonies between 1947 and 1980.

racial discrimination. However, many saw it as a waste of time. Complaints could not be made about the police, and only about ten percent of complaints to the Board were ever upheld.

Britain had no tradition of the strong political civil rights movement that emerged in the USA between 1956 and 1968. In part, this was because racism took the form of individual prejudice rather than the visible system of discrimination that existed in the USA (or indeed the apartheid system in South Africa). This situation is also reflective of the more fragmented background of the free black people who arrived in Britain from a range of different countries and settled in local communities with other people who had emigrated to Britain. Yet black Britons were inspired by, and borrowed ideas from, American activists. In 1963, in direct imitation of Martin Luther King's 1955–56 actions in Montgomery, Alabama, a Bristol bus boycott was organised when the local company refused to hire black workers. The four-month boycott, organised by local youth worker Paul Stephenson, made national headlines and succeeded in ending the **colour bar** for bus conductors. Dr King's flying visit to London on 5 December 1964 inspired the formation of the Campaign Against Racial Discrimination (CARD). This group was one of several, such as the Coloured Peoples' Progressive Association and the Association for the Advancement of Coloured People, which put pressure on the government to pass and then improve anti-discrimination laws. Journalist Claudia Jones was born in Trinidad but raised in Britain. In 1958 she launched the *West Indian Gazette*, the first newspaper made by and for black people in London, and this also signified greater assertiveness in the demand for more equal treatment. Jones had worked as a political activist for communism and black empowerment in the USA before her deportation to Britain in 1955 for 'un-American activities'. The American civil rights movement became more violent in the mid-1960s due to the 'black power' messages of Malcolm X and then the Black Panthers. Although this influenced some American films, it had a marginal impact in Britain. One black power activist, Michael de Freitas, changed his name to Michael X and was arrested in 1967 for promoting racial violence against whites.

KEY TERM

Colour bar
This was an unofficial policy adopted by many British employers to refuse jobs to ethnic minority applicants. Paul Stephenson demonstrated the colour bar in Bristol when his 'colour neutral' application led to an invitation for interview, which was cancelled when he informed the bus company that he was black. The unofficial colour bar prevented all but a handful of ethnic minorities gaining professional jobs until the 1990s.

EXTEND YOUR KNOWLEDGE

Immigration and legislation in the 1960s

Ironically, the most significant cause of mass immigration from the New Commonwealth (the non-white parts of the Empire) was the initial legislation which was meant to curtail it. In 1956, 47,000 people entered Britain from the New Commonwealth; by 1961 this had increased to 136,000 with a further 94,900 in the first six months of 1962. The cause of this huge increase was the fear among potential black and Asian migrants that Britain would close its doors to further immigration in the near future. The Commonwealth Immigrants Act 1962 allowed immigrants to settle provided they had been awarded a voucher that proved they had a job lined up. The Act also allowed the dependents (usually wives and children) of pre-1962 immigrants to join them in Britain. Rather than slowing New Commonwealth immigration, the Act enabled existing Asian and black UK residents to organise vouchers and establish unofficial chains of migration from their original homes. The vast majority of Indians came from the Punjab and Gujarat, while most Pakistanis came from a handful of places in Sylhet (which later became part of Bangladesh). Fear of not being able to return to the UK if they went home encouraged more immigrants to settle and bring their families to Britain. Between 1962 and 1968, while 77,966 vouchers were issued, 257,220 dependents settled in the UK. Between 1968 and 1971, 318,521 people from the New Commonwealth arrived; of these only 58,875 were male workers. Despite the surge in numbers caused by the 1962 Act, opinion polls claimed that nearly three-quarters of the British public supported these new controls on immigration.

The Commonwealth Immigrants Act 1968 sought to close these unintended chains of migration from India, Pakistan and the West Indies through a 'grandfather clause': would-be immigrants needed, in addition to an employment voucher, a British-born, adopted or naturalised parent or grandparent in order to allow them to enter the country. By the early 1970s, Britain had some of the toughest immigration laws in the world, and virtually all black and Asian primary immigration had stopped.

Film and racism

The relationship between film, television and racism is complex. As cultural theorist Stuart Hall (2011) has argued, media images of race determine (or construct) for the viewer notions of how race is defined, understood and, indeed, recognised as problematic. There were very few black scriptwriters or directors in Britain in the 1960s, so the portrayal of black people in film and television was overwhelmingly shaped by white perceptions and priorities. As a result, a modern analysis of such productions shed more light on white, male, liberal thoughts on racial issues than the reality of life in Britain in the 1960s. White males also dominated film-making in the USA until the early 1970s. The impact of white American racial stereotypes is significant in a British context because of the popularity of Hollywood films. A further problem when considering the impact of film and television on racism is also persuasively highlighted by Hall. He argues that the audience is not a passive recipient of the meaning intended by programme or filmmakers. Individuals 'decode' the images on screen and 'encode' them into their own meaning. A clear example of this is discussed with regard to the 1965 TV play *Fable* on page 122.

The opportunities for black British actors and directors were extremely limited in the 1960s. Short films such as *Ten Bob in Winter* (a 1963 comedy about class snobbery within the black community, directed by Jamaican-born Lloyd Reckord) and *Jemima and Johnny* (1966 silent film about the friendship of a Caribbean girl and the son of a white racist father, directed by South African-born Lionel Nyakane) are rare examples of black-directed films. The first full-length feature film directed by a black Briton was *Pressure* in 1975.

Although white writers and directors generally held liberal attitudes and usually sought to portray black people in a positive fashion, British films with black characters invariably made race a problematic part of the story that had to be resolved. Hall refers to such 'racial problem' films as examples of *inferential* racism: no matter how positively individuals are portrayed, blacks are the source of the problem. A clear example of this is the 1959 film *Sapphire*, about the investigation of the murder of a Notting Hill girl (Sapphire) thought to be white until her black brother (Dr Robbins) turns up. The film portrays a successful black barrister and doctor, but it is Sapphire's relationship with a white man that is the source of the problem. Her boyfriend's sister murdered Sapphire because of her hatred of black people, something she keeps hidden until she explodes in disgust when Dr Robbins touches her children's toys. There is also *overt* racism in the film. In one scene, a white observer realises that another apparently white girl is of mixed blood when she starts to dance, saying 'you can always tell… once they hear the beat of the bongo'.

Three 1961 films derive their drama from the problems caused by an interracial relationship.

- *Flame in the Streets* was based on Ted Willis' 1959 play *Hot Summer Night*, inspired by severe race riots in Nottingham and Notting Hill in 1958. The story centres on Jack Palmer, a trade unionist who opposes racism in the workplace but is forced to deal with the vicious racism of his wife when their daughter announces her intention to marry a black man.

- *The Wind of Change* is about a Teddy Boy obsessed with violence and couples from different racial backgrounds.

- *A Taste of Honey*, adapted from Shelagh Delaney's play of the same name, tells the story of 17-year-old white schoolgirl Jo who falls pregnant after a brief but happy relationship with a black sailor, leading to tension with her alcoholic mother.

Cultural historian Maggie Andrews has astutely commented that such storylines follow the widely known 'Romeo and Juliet' format: the audience is predisposed to see interracial relationships as problematic and doomed to failure, unhappiness or even death.

SOURCE

 From an interview with Earl Cameron in 1997. Cameron was born in Bermuda but lived in Britain from 1939 to 1979. He featured in many films and television programmes in the 1950s and 1960s, including the films *Sapphire* and *Flame in the Streets*.

Maybe *Sapphire* happened because of the racial tensions in Notting Hill in 1958. But I knew Janet Green, who wrote the screenplay, and I don't think she was influenced in any way by what happened in Notting Hill. The film is not about that. It's a whodunit thriller with a race angle. *Flame in the Street* dealt with racism in a contemporary setting. Like *Sapphire* it gave cinema audiences an opportunity to see black people as real people. John Mills, who played the union leader whose daughter wants to marry a black man, was absolutely brilliant in it. I am sure commercial films like *Sapphire* and *Flame in the Streets*, which reached mass audiences, helped raise their consciousness. They knew racism existed, but they didn't see it exposed. And when they did, certain people felt ashamed about it. So, to an extent, those two films helped make people aware of what life was really like for black people in this country at that time. I remember chatting to Roy Baker, the director of *Flame in the Streets*. He said, 'Look, I'll be very honest, I don't know many of your people,' as he put it, 'and I'd be grateful for any tips you can give me.' I had read the script by then, and there was a lot of domestic stuff in the film, and some directors didn't know how working-class black people lived, and they showed their houses with twenty people living in one room. I told Roy this didn't happen. I told him that films and television plays tended to show people from the Caribbean or Africa being dirty, which was just not true either. I advised him to visit some of the homes in the area where we were filming, and see for himself how black people lived. I wanted him to give some reality to the story, rather than the stereotypical view.

A Level Exam-Style Question Section A

Study Source 6 before you answer this question.

Assess the value of the source for revealing the depiction of black people in mass media and their role in the British media industry in the 1960s.

Explain your answer, using the source, the information given about its origin and your own knowledge about the historical context. (20 marks)

Tip
Try to move beyond the obvious points that are raised by the source content. A careful reading of the source will almost always enable you to make valid inferences for you to support or challenge with your own knowledge.

The context of the US civil rights campaign is significant for the relationship between film and racism in the UK, because British cinema, due to a lack of domestic funding, became increasingly dominated by Hollywood in the 1960s. Until the 1940s, black characters in US films were limited to stereotypes derived from the historic slave-owning culture in the southern states: gentle, subservient 'Uncle Tom' types, 'Mammy' female domestic servants or musical, comical slave caricatures. Recognition of black sacrifices in the Second World War against ideologically racist enemies led to the on-screen portrayal of 'noble blacks' and black heroes. Sidney Poitier was *the* black star of the 1950s and 1960s. His films sum up the peaceful, integrationist solution to the 'race problem' offered by Dr King and hoped for by white liberals. In *Lilies of the Field* (1963) Poitier played a travelling handyman who helped a group of nuns to build a church, while in *Guess Who's Coming to Dinner* (1967) he used his considerable charm to win over a white girl's parents to the prospect of their interracial marriage.

Poitier also starred in an important film set in a school in the East End of London. The 1967 film *To Sir With Love* was based on the part-autobiographical novel by British Guianese-born E.R. Braithwaite, but it had some notable differences from the book. The film tells the story of Rick Braithwaite, who, following his demobilisation from the RAF, is forced to become a teacher when deemed by employers to be overqualified and too 'black' to get an interview for any other line of work. While the book details several examples of racism, these are downplayed in the film. Neither his outbursts against the real British way of life nor an incident where a white waiter spits in his food are mentioned. His rejection by a range of employers is only fleetingly inferred, while his marriage to a white woman is changed to a friendship. American financial backers who wanted to ensure the film's commercial success in the US enforced these changes.

The dominance of the 'racial problem' plot line for black characters in film is representative of white concerns about **miscegenation** in the 1960s. The Reverend Clifford Hall stated in a radio interview that he would have no objection to his sister or daughter marrying a black man. As a result of this statement, he suffered abusive letters, death threats and even a **Ku Klux Klan**-style burning cross in his front garden. This experience led him to conduct a poll of white people in north London asking, 'Would you approve of your sister or your daughter marrying a coloured man?' Ninety-one percent of those who replied said that they would not approve. Interracial marriage remained rare in the 1960s and couples had to overcome a great deal of casual racism.

Television and racism

The same lack of opportunity for black writers and directors existed in television as well as film. Programmes were exclusively made by white-dominated, in-house production teams at the BBC and ITV rather than commissioned from independent companies, as Channel 4 was to pioneer in the 1980s. As a result, the first comedy show (*The Fosters*, ITV) and drama (*Empire Road*) by a black writer were not screened until 1976 and 1978, respectively. Until the start of the 1960s, the black presence on television was largely limited to musicians and singers such as Shirley Bassey, Cleo Lane and Sammy Davis Jr on variety shows such as *Sunday Night at the Palladium* (ITV, 1955–69). In TV dramas, racial issues were presented from a white person's perspective. Black roles were rarely central to the drama, as white writers lacked the necessary knowledge of black British culture to create convincing characters. In 1967, Huw Wheldon, controller of BBC1, wrote to a viewer concerned by the lack of positive representation of black and Asian characters by explaining that casting coloured actors in professional roles simply because of their colour did not reflect real life and as the main aim of BBC plays was to do just that then it would be against BBC policy to represent a world that did not exist.

An important exception was the six-part drama *Rainbow City* (BBC1, 1967) by John Elliot (co-written with Trinidadian-born writer Horace James). It was about John Steele, a Jamaican-born lawyer who dealt with a convincing range of issues that affected the black population of Birmingham. One such issue was poor housing, something that the British public had been made aware of by the Rachmanism scandal in 1963. Peter Rachman was a landlord who used intimidation to force out white tenants in the Notting Hill Area and then charged high rents to black tenants, knowing they would not find even poor accommodation elsewhere. *Fable*, a 1965 *Wednesday Play* about a dystopian black-dominated authoritarian Britain, was another drama that put black characters in central roles. Its broadcast was delayed by several weeks because of fears it would result in heightened racial tension in Leyton, East London, where a by-election was due to take place involving a Labour candidate who had lost his seat to a racist Conservative in Smethwick, Birmingham, in 1964. *Fable* was written by John Hopkins, who was pessimistic about its impact. He reported how he received a letter from a viewer that said, 'I really enjoyed [*Fable*]. Boy, you showed them what would happen if they ever came to power, if they had the authority.' Despite positive reviews in the *Guardian*, BBC audience research suggests that Hopkins was right to be sceptical about the positive impact of the play on race relations. It concluded that the play served to incite the prejudice that it was trying to warn against.

It was far more common for black actors to make occasional and sometimes longer-lasting appearances in roles where race played a problematic part of the storyline. Joan Hooley played Dr Louise Mahler for 47 episodes of *Emergency Ward 10* (ITV, 1957–67) in 1964. Hooley's character was killed off (by a snakebite in Africa!) when the writers became uncomfortable with a developing romance with a white male doctor – a kiss that had been scripted to take place in her bedroom was moved to a garden so as not to upset the audience. The *Daily Express* carried a photo of the kiss the next day but reported that no viewers had complained about the scene. *Coronation Street* was the most popular soap of the decade but only had a handful of small parts for black actors until 1993. Thomas Baptiste played a bus conductor wrongfully sacked for lying, while Cleo Sylvestre (who went on to star in another soap, *Crossroads*, in the 1970s) played a raincoat factory worker for six episodes in 1966. Perhaps the only example of a non-problematic black character in a white TV drama was Horace James' role as a magazine photographer for 26 episodes in *Compact* (BBC1, 1962–65).

There were also examples of overt racism on British television in the 1960s. The most famous example was Jonny Speight's *Till Death Do Us Part* (BBC, 1965–68 and 1972–75). Speight wanted to expose the stupidity of chief protagonist Alf Garnett's racist views. But he was saddened to find that the 18 million-strong audience laughed along with Garnett's outbursts more than they did at his final comeuppance, and he was amazed that the ignorant Garnett could become such a well-loved television character. *The Black and White Minstrel Show* (BBC, 1958–78) attracted audiences of between 16 and 18 million throughout the 1960s. The show, with white performers in black face makeup, was highly offensive to black Britons, yet the racist caricature of black people was clearly not a problem for its white audience.

The public reaction to Conservative MP Enoch Powell's 1968 'Rivers of Blood' speech suggests that liberal scriptwriters failed to have a significant impact on white fears about black immigration. Powell argued that there was a 'gulf between the overwhelming majority of the country on the one side, and on the other side a tiny minority, with almost a monopoly hold upon the channels of communication'. He warned of a violent future for British multiracial society if the numbers of immigrants continued unchecked. Conservative leader Edward Heath sacked Powell from the Shadow Cabinet the next day. Powell never held a senior government position again. A petition to stop him being sacked gathered over 30,000 signatures, and opinion polls suggested that 75 percent of the British public agreed with his speech.

ACTIVITY
KNOWLEDGE CHECK

Mass media and popular attitudes to racial minorities in Britain

1 Explain the difficulties of using film and television to explore the nature of race relations in the 1960s.

2 In your opinion, is there more evidence for film and television reflecting or moulding race relations?

3 Give examples of factors other than film and television that affected race relations in Britain in the 1960s.

How far did film and television mould or mirror attitudes towards women?

Film and sexism

Film and television are important media for the social construction of gender. Although sex is almost always determined by birth, gender refers to behaviours, attitudes and feelings that are associated with the male or female sex. Gender 'norms' of behaviour are dictated by culture rather than biology and can change over time. For example, it has become far more acceptable for men to cry or for women to smoke in public, yet both behaviours were once considered as gender nonconformist. The question is the extent to which film and television preserved more traditional patriarchal, patronising or even sexist social attitudes towards women, or whether they played an important role in changing men's perceptions and the self-image of British women in the 1960s. The same problems that emerged in the assessment of film, television and race apply to the consideration of gender issues. Despite women playing a central role in the early history of British cinema, there were very few female writers and directors in the 1960s. The media image of women was largely filtered through male perceptions.

A number of female directors who had worked on films in the 1940s and 1950s quit because of their frustration with the increasingly patriarchal film industry. The move away from smaller, independent studios to larger ones reduced the opportunities for women such as Mande Kay and Jill Craigie. From the late 1950s through to the 1970s, there were very few female voices reflecting on female issues for a female audience. Muriel Box had worked as a director since 1941 and directed *Too Young to Love* (1960) and *Rattle of a Simple Man* (1964) in the 1960s. *Too Young to Live* was adapted from a play about abortion, teenage sex and sexually transmitted disease. *Rattle of a Simple Man* was a comedy about the gulf in goals and understanding between men and women, and the distance between dreams and real life for women. The lukewarm reception that *Rattle of a Simple Man* received led Box to leave the film industry and become a publisher. Jane Arden wrote and starred in the 1968 film *Separation*, which dealt with the preoccupations of a middle-aged recently divorced woman. Contemporary reviews suggest that the film told audiences more about Arden's favourite films than about the issues affecting a number of British women. Arden also directed the radical feminist 1972 film about female mental illness *The Other Side of Underneath*, the only film solo directed by a woman in the 1970s.

Several films in the 1960s were written and directed by men and dealt with women and gender issues; these reflected male concerns about the changes they perceived. Women in such films tended to be stereotyped either as 'madonnas', chaste and worthy of male admiration, or 'whores' who had loose morals and found that female sexual liberation came with a price. The biggest box-office hit of the 1960s, *The Sound of Music* (1965), starred Julie Andrews as very much a madonna. The 1963 film *That Kind of Girl* told the story of a formerly prim, upright woman who decided to explore her sexuality by working in a brothel. She committed adultery, fell pregnant, contracted venereal disease and ended the film in a miserable state. The 1969 film *A Nice Girl Like Me* also focused on the negative consequences of female free love. In the film, the central character had a series of short, doomed relationships, which ended in an unwanted pregnancy. The director, Desmond Davis, was also responsible for two films that presented a more positive view of female sexual empowerment. *Girl With Green Eyes* (1964) and *Smashing Time* (1967) both concerned naïve country girls who went to the city to find freedom and self-discovery. The girls escaped strict moral constraints at home and revelled in fashion, food, gossip, dancing and sex, through which they were portrayed as adventurers rather than victims. Perhaps the most famous 1960s film that dealt with female sexuality was director John Schlesinger's *Darling* (1965). The film reduced femininity to a commodity used to sell material items in a wholly uncritical fashion. In this highly moralistic film, Diana Scott, a model, relates the story of her life via a soundtrack while the film tells the truth of her harsh life. She is portrayed as selfish and shallow and doing whatever it takes to succeed in her career. She ends up lonely and trapped in a loveless marriage miles from home in an empty palace.

One only has to compare the turmoil of most sexually liberated female characters with the heroic framing of James Bond's inevitable sexual conquests to perceive the dual standards that applied to gender roles in 1960s films. Sean Connery starred in five hugely successful Bond films in the sixties, and scantily clad Bond girls, such as Ursula Andress as Honey Ryder in *Dr. No* (1962), contributed to the films' success. Bond films, together with the *Carry On* comedy franchise, were the most popular films with British audiences in the 1960s. At least one, and sometimes two, *Carry On* films were made every year between 1958 and 1976, with 15 released in the 1960s alone. Especially after the arrival of scriptwriter Talbot Rothwell in 1963, female characters were stereotyped according to their attractiveness to men. For example, overweight Hattie Jacques played fearsome battleaxes, while blond, busty Barbara Windsor played the giggly object of male desire. It must be concluded that film in the 1960s did very little to discuss or advance issues such as family life or employment that mattered to women, and did rather more to reflect male concerns and male ideals of femininity.

Television and sexism

Cultural historians see the 1960s as a decade when television became 'masculinised'. The frivolous, trivial nature of television in the 1950s, that was so criticised in the Pilkington Report, was associated with femininity by male critics. There was a decline in the number of women employed in television, both in front of, and behind, the camera, and this was true in current affairs and in drama. Joan Bakewell's work as presenter of discussion programme *Late Night Line-Up* (BBC2, 1965–72) is one exception to this trend (although her nickname 'the thinking man's crumpet' is indicative of male views of a female presenter). In a meeting of the BBC drama department, the Head of Serials commented that women were feared by young writers. This comment could be interpreted as suggesting that the Head of Serials thought all writers were male.

EXTRACT

3 From Janet Thumim's book *Inventing Television Culture: Men, Women, and the Box*, published in 2004. Thumim was head of the University of Bristol's department of drama, where she taught film and television studies.

In general it seems that representations of women and the feminine on television by and large demonstrate collusion by women in their disempowerment... However, by the mid-sixties it is the proto-feminist challenge to women's assumed collusion with male dominance which formed the pretext for many popular fictions – much of the sparkling dialogue of *The Avengers*, for example, turning precisely on this point... Outside the ghettos of women's and children's programmes, women appeared as entertainers – invariably and clearly subject to a male host or compere – or as 'light relief' included as visual or aural balance in discussion programmes, quiz shows, or current affairs magazines. They were primarily utilised as decorative and hence demeaned as frivolous. The one place where this schema breaks down, however, is the arena of popular drama which, as the decade progressed, occupied an increasingly important place in the schedules. Here not only was a simply female presence more likely to be offered, but her appearance was typically in scenarios in which the routines of daily life were the subject of a drama or comedy foregrounding female experience... Not that these images or performances were necessarily progressive in their definitions of the feminine, but their nightly presence did nevertheless assert a female experience, acting as a counter to the masculinist dominance of most of television's output.

Despite the overall context of 'masculinised' television, there were a few notable female writers who presented a more authentic notion of women's lives and concerns in the 1960s. Nell Dunn rose to fame for *Up The Junction*, adapted for television and directed by Ken Loach as a *Wednesday Play* in 1965. Carla Lane began her highly successful career in television at the very end of the sixties with her Liverpool-based comedy *The Liver Birds* (BBC, 1969–79). The rise of the women's liberation movement contributed to a more overt focus on independent women (although usually based on their relationships with men) in *The Bed-Sit Girl* (BBC, 1965–66). Jane Arden was a Welsh writer, actress and director who became increasingly interested in feminism in the 1960s. In 1965, she wrote and starred in the TV play *The Logic Game*, which presented the private lives and difficulties of a married couple.

There were also a number of programmes written by men that presented a more progressive view of women in the 1960s. *The Rag Trade* (BBC, 1961–63), based on a female shop steward in a garment factory, *Compact*, set in a women's magazine office (BBC, 1962–65), and *Crossroads,* set in a hotel (ATV, 1964–88), all centred on the female experience of women in the workplace. *The Avengers* (1961–69) was one of the most popular drama series of the sixties. It starred Honor Blackman as Catherine Gale and then Diana Rigg as Emma Peel who worked as elite secret agents who were as tough as they were intelligent. They worked on an equal basis with the main male star and regularly overcame male criminals without any assistance. Both characters dressed practically for fighting, but Blackman's tight leather outfits and Rigg's figure-hugging jumpsuits attracted a lot of male and female attention. This ingredient of the show's success is reflected in Rigg's character's name (Emma Peel) – press officer for the show, Marie Donaldson, said that whoever replaced Blackman had to have 'M-appeal' or man appeal. Even in this show, which was regularly cited as the first major example of heroic, emancipated female lead characters, attractiveness to males was deemed essential to its popularity with British audiences.

Other popular television programmes, not to mention advertising, regularly presented women as far from emancipated or the equal of men. There is no question of divorce or paid employment for Alf Garnett's wife Elsie, regularly called a 'silly moo' by her husband in *Till Death Do Us Part*. With the exception of the *Wednesday Play*, in the most popular shows of the decade women were either inferior companions (as in *Doctor Who*, BBC, 1963–89), the love interest of heroic male secret agents (*Danger Man*, ITV, 1960–68 and *The Saint*, ITV, 1962–69), suffering wives and girlfriends (*Dad's Army*, BBC, 1968–77) or purely sex objects (*The Benny Hill Show*, BBC/ITV, 1955–91). It was not until the 1970s and 1980s that second-wave feminism began to make more inroads into this male-dominated portrayal of women on British television. Despite this, women began to make strides in their domestic and working life, as demonstrated in Chapter 1.

ACTIVITY
KNOWLEDGE CHECK

Mass media and attitudes to women in British society

1 How far did British television challenge sexist views towards women in the 1960s?

2 Which would you argue had the greater impact on British women in the 1960s: film or television?

Mary Whitehouse and the NVALA

Mary Whitehouse initially became concerned about modern morality after talking to students in her first job as an art teacher. She joined a group called Moral Rearmament, originally an American evangelical movement whose aim was to 'remake the world'. In 1963, she decided to focus specifically on the damage done to British morals by film and television. She blamed Hugh Carleton-Greene (director-general of the BBC from 1960 to 1969) for the growth of liberal, permissive values on television. She was so concerned with the slide of on-screen morality that on 27 January 1964 she set up her own campaign, called Clean-Up TV. The first meeting, held on 5 May that year in Birmingham Town Hall, attracted 2,000 like-minded supporters, mostly middle-aged women. She launched a manifesto and asked for people to sign a petition in support of its key statements and demands.

SOURCE

7 From Mary Whitehouse's *Manifesto*, written for the Clean-Up TV campaign. The *Manifesto* was launched as a four-page booklet on 27 January 1964.

After the renewal of the BBC Charter earlier this year it seemed clear that neither the Board of Governors nor Parliament intended to come to grips with a situation which had developed wherein a Public Service was propagating ideas entirely contrary to the philosophy on which our civilisation has been built; and the attitude of the BBC to criticism on this point appears so insensitive as to approach contemptuous indifference. Nothing seemed left but for the ordinary women of Britain to take matters into their own hands and to make it quite clear to the BBC that we were prepared to fight for the right to bring up our children in the truths of the Christian faith, and to protect our homes from exhibitions of violence. We therefore drew up the following manifesto and issued it to the press:

1. We WOMEN OF BRITAIN believe in a Christian way of life.

2. We want it for the children we bear and the country we love.

3. We deplore present day attempts to belittle or destroy it and in particular we object to the propaganda of disbelief, doubt and dirt that the BBC projects into millions of homes through the television screen.

4. Crime, violence, illegitimacy and venereal disease are steadily increasing, yet the BBC employs people whose ideas and advice pander to the lowest in human nature, accompanying this with a stream of suggestive and erotic plays which present promiscuity, infidelity and drinking as normal and inevitable.

5. Wherefore your petitioners pray that the BBC be asked to make a radical change of policy and produce programmes which encourage and sustain faith in God and bring Him back to the heart of our family and national life.

Whitehouse managed to gain 500,000 signatures for her Clean-Up TV petition, which she sent to the queen. In 1965, this campaign was merged into the National Viewers' and Listeners' Association (NVALA). The NVALA was popular with Christian organisations. It was a major inspiration for the Nationwide Festival of Light staged in Hyde Park in September 1971 and at 70 regional rallies. The Festival, designed to promote Christian morality and prevent what the organisers saw as the spread of 'moral pollution', attracted over 100,000 people. However, more progressive elements of the media were highly critical of Whitehouse's prejudices against racial minorities and especially homosexuals. Hugh Carlton-Greene replied to a large number of her complaint letters but he refused to meet Mary Whitehouse and consistently defended the BBC's output rather than pander to her objections. It would be fair to conclude that Whitehouse had no impact on British television despite the media attention her campaigning attracted.

ACTIVITY
KNOWLEDGE CHECK

Mary Whitehouse and the NVALA

1 Summarise the reasons why Mary Whitehouse launched Clean-Up TV and the NVALA.

2 In what ways and to what extent do Whitehouse's campaigns shed light on the importance of television in engaging with social issues and prejudices?

TO WHAT EXTENT WERE THE 'SWINGING SIXTIES' MORE IMAGE THAN REALITY?
The sixties' icons and media image

Film, television and the press all played a part in the promotion of the 'swinging sixties'. Consumerism, new fashions, sexual liberation and empowerment for women, youthful energy, and an apparent classlessness that broke with traditional values were the vital ingredients of the 'swinging' image. While only a small number of people based in a few wealthy parts of London actually lived the swinging lifestyle, the image was popular with British and American audiences.

SOURCE
8

From John Crosby's article 'London, the Most Exciting City in the World', published in the *Weekend Telegraph* on 16 April 1965. Crosby was an American journalist who first coined and popularised the phrase 'swinging London'.

In Soho, at the Ad Lib, the hottest and swingingest spot in town the noise is deafening, the beat group is pounding out *I Just Don't Know What to Do with Myself*, on the floor, under the red and green and blue lights, a frenzy of the prettiest legs in the whole world belonging to models, au pair girls or just ordinary English girls, a gleam of pure joy on their pretty faces, dancing with the young blonds, the scruffy, very hotshot photographers like David Bailey or Terry Donovan, or a new pop singer – all vibrating with youth... These are for the rich and famous but London's throbbing nightlife has room for everyone... Ronnie Scott's in Soho is a classless place – the sons of dukes and working men rubbing elbows in mutual appreciation of jazz... [The girls are] more than pretty; they're young, appreciative, sharp-tongued, glowingly alive. Even the sex orgies among the sex-and-pot set in Chelsea and Kensington have youth and eagerness and, in a strange way, a quality of innocence about them... Young English girls take to sex as if it's candy and it's delicious... Behind the swing and gaiety there's a steady pulse of serious purpose in these young ones. In Chelsea young Mary Quant and a bunch of other pretty Chelsea birds, fed up with the stuffy and expensive dresses in the shops began stitching their own dresses – simple, dashing, clean-limbed clothes more suited to their good looks and youth and they didn't give a damn what anyone thought about them. There's a revolution in men's clothes here that is very much part of the London swinging scene, partly because it's adding so much dash to the London street scene, but also as a sign of deeper social turmoil that is transforming England. English men's clothes were almost uniform: staid, sober and, above all, correct, advertising your precise rung on the social ladder. Today the working-class boys – their pockets full of money, are splurging on suede jackets, skin-like tweed trousers... The impact of Carnaby Street is becoming worldwide... In Paris they dance now to the records of the Beatles or Cilla Black or the Rolling Stones where only a year ago the music came from Frank Sinatra, Tony Bennett and Dean Martin – all Americans.

A Level Exam-Style Question Section A

Study Source 8 before you answer this question.

Assess the value of the source for determining the impact of mass media on the 'swinging sixties' and on attitudes towards women in the 1960s.

Explain your answer, using the source, the information given about its origin and your own knowledge about the historical context. (20 marks)

Tip
In addition to using the source content to make judgements, use the existence and nature of the source itself to inform your overall assessment of its value.

Such themes were exciting and popular with British audiences between 1964 and around 1968. From February 1962, colour sections in Sunday newspapers helped to promote new fashions (such as the miniskirt) that blossomed in the boutiques of London's King's Road and Carnaby Street. These fashions played a key part in the classless element of the swinging sixties image. The mass production and sale of such designs in high streets nationwide meant it became almost impossible to tell a young woman's class from the way she dressed. Barbara Hulanicki's fashion company Biba sold cheap clothes from her shops in London and across the country via mail order. The media interest in fashion led to the rise of photographers such as David Bailey, Brian Duffy and Terence Donovan, and models such as Jean Shrimpton, Twiggy and Veruschka, as sixties icons.

SOURCE
9 One of the photographs that helped to establish Twiggy (Lesley Hornby) as 'the face of 1966'.

Radio, television and especially film also promoted the 'swinging' image in order to attract young consumers with larger disposable incomes. *The Avengers* clearly captured the spirit of the swinging sixties, as did the 1966–67 BBC series *Adam Adamant Lives!*, which told the story of an Edwardian gentleman who disappeared in 1902 only to wake up amazed at life in mid-1960s London. Lord Hill, head of the Independent Television Authority (1963–67) and then the BBC (1967–72) talked of Britain being on the cusp of a gulf in attitudes towards sex, religion and art suddenly opening between the older and younger generations. However, the vast majority of British television did not promote swinging sixties imagery. Its higher profile in British cinema was largely due to the investment of US financial backers, who profited from its popularity with American audiences – three-quarters of British films in 1966 were US-financed, a figure that rose to 90 percent in 1967 and 1968. While the social realist 'New Wave' films had depicted life familiar to an average British audience, the films of the mid-1960s sold a distorted version of British life to Americans, which most Britons were happy to have exported.

The 1963 film *Tom Jones* was the first to capture the zeitgeist of the swinging sixties. Based on Henry Fielding's 18th-century novel, it followed the eponymous hero's womanising adventures on his path from rags to riches. It was the highest grossing film of the year and won four Oscars. Its success inspired a break from the gritty social realist films that had dominated British cinema between 1958 and 1962. Albert Finney's portrayal of Tom Jones was described as a rural James Bond, a highly popular franchise that also depicted casual sexual relationships purely for pleasure. *From Russia With Love* (1963) and *Goldfinger* (1964) followed *Dr. No* and continued to promote a chic, sexy, technologically advanced vision of Britain. *Darling* centred on the fashion scene and on the ability of a modern woman to use her sexuality to promote her career. *The Knack... and How to Get It* (1965) ostensibly told the story of a young man who set out to learn how to seduce women, but it was essentially a celebration of Carnaby Street fashions and the pop music played by pirate radio stations such as Radio Caroline. *Blow-Up* (1966) was about the possible discovery of a murder, but it was inspired by the swinging lifestyle of real, London-based fashion photographers.

The Beatles, the Rolling Stones and the swinging sixties

The Beatles remain one of the most famous icons of the 1960s. The band first entered the charts in October 1962 with 'Love Me Do' and went on to have 17 number one hits in Britain between 1963 and 1969. The quality of their songs, together with their smart, iconic look, ensured that 'Beatlemania' had spread across the country by mid-1963. The Rolling Stones, fronted by singer Mick Jagger, had a far more rebellious image, with long hair and scruffy clothes. In March 1964, journalist Maureen Cleave wrote a famous article in the *Evening Standard* called 'This Horrible Lot – Not Quite What They Seem', questioning whether you would let your daughter marry a Rolling Stone. Her answer: certainly not! In 1964, the Beatles and the Rolling Stones led the 'British invasion' of the American charts. In April 1964, the Beatles had no fewer than 12 records in *Billboard* magazine's Hot 100. In 1965, the Beatles were awarded MBEs for their services to British exports. They remained in the vanguard of popular music for the remainder of the 1960s, and the band finally broke up in 1970. In his 1981 book *Shout! The True Story of the Beatles*, Philip Norman estimates that by 1970, in addition to the huge sales of singles and albums, Beatles merchandise, including hats, bags, badges, shirts, jackets, socks, handkerchiefs, tea towels, mugs, ashtrays and jigsaw puzzles, had sold for more than £100 million. The Beatles also starred in two popular films that contributed to the swinging sixties scene: *A Hard Day's Night* (1964) and *Help!* (1965). Both celebrated and capitalised on Beatlemania.

EXTEND YOUR KNOWLEDGE

In addition to the fashion icons mentioned in the main text, the following lists contain a range of key sixties icons whose backgrounds, careers and impact you may wish to research further.

- Actors and actresses: British stars such as Julie Andrews, Michael Caine, Julie Christie, Sean Connery, Cary Grant, Audrey Hepburn and Elizabeth Taylor, and foreign stars such as Brigit Bardot, Doris Day, Rock Hudson, Steve McQueen and Paul Newman.

- Sportsmen and women: Olympic medallists Anita Lonsbrough and Dorothy Hyman; American boxer Muhammed Ali and golfer Arnold Palmer; Australian tennis player Rod Laver; cricketers Ted Dexter and Fred Trueman; footballers Pele, Bobby Charlton, George Best and Jimmy Greaves; and motorsport stars Stirling Moss and John Surtees.

- Musicians: Shirley Bassey, The Beatles, Cilla Black, Bob Dylan, Aretha Franklin, Janis Joplin, The Kinks, Lulu, The Rolling Stones, Dusty Springfield, The Supremes, Dionne Warwick.

The reality of the swinging sixties: economy and society

A large majority of the British population experienced the swinging sixties second-hand through mass media. A poll published by the *Sunday Times* in 1966 suggested that most people were bored with hearing about new fashions and pop music. Although young people with disposable income could buy into the trendy image, life for many British people continued to be shaped by traditional family values.

Many ordinary Britons suffered from the effects of a range of economic problems that both Conservative and Labour governments seemed unable to solve. The economy grew at a slower rate than that of Britain's competitors (2.3 percent per year compared to 5.6 percent in Italy and 5.1 percent in Germany). A key reason for this was a lack of investment in research and development in areas other than defence. By the mid-1960s, the spectre of 'stagflation' (economic stagnation and inflation) hung over Britain. The most damaging economic failure concerned the value of sterling. In November 1967, having attempted (and apparently failed) to borrow his way out of economic trouble, Prime Minister Harold Wilson was forced to cut the value of the pound from £1/$2.80 to £1/$2.40. Although he went on television to explain that the 'pound in your pocket' was worth the same within the UK, he suffered a huge loss of credibility.

Despite the sexual liberation portrayed in many films, two major contemporary surveys suggest that notions of a 'sexual revolution' in the sixties were greatly misleading. Michael Schofield's *The Sexual Behaviour of Young People* (1965) found that only 18 percent of girls and ten percent of boys in his sample of 2,000 teenagers had had sex with more than three people, and that 17 percent of girls and 33 percent of boys had had sex by the age of 19. He concluded that while promiscuity existed among teenagers, this was far from normal behaviour. Geoffrey Gorer's *Sex and Marriage in England Today* (1971) revealed that 96 percent of women and 95 percent of men were married by the age of 45, and that the average age of marriage for women had fallen from 25 in 1946 to 22 in 1970. It was not until the Divorce Reform Act 1969 that the percentage of dissolved marriages began to increase significantly. British people lived far more monogamously than the swinging sixties imagery suggests.

Despite the modern, progressive attitudes depicted by sixties icons, the liberalising laws passed between 1959 and 1969 were introduced after pressure from backbench MPs rather than the British public. David Steel's Abortion Act 1967 was not the result of pressure from his constituents, but his anger at the high number of deaths and injuries that resulted from dangerous 'backstreet' abortions (about 40 deaths and 100,000 injuries in 1966). Many Labour Party leaders feared that liberal legislation would alienate traditional voters, yet Roy Jenkins, Home Secretary (1965–67), saw such changes as the measure of a 'civilised society' and unofficially encouraged Labour support for liberal legal reforms. Therefore, while celebrities and powerful television plays such as *Up The Junction* (1965) attracted a lot of popular attention, it is more persuasive to see them as the occasion rather than the cause of liberal legislation that helped to shape British social attitudes from the 1960s onwards.

A Level Exam-Style Question Section B

'The most significant impact of film and television in the sixties was on attitudes to homelessness.'

How far do you agree with this statement? (20 marks)

Tip
Remember to compare the impact of film and television on social attitudes to homelessness with their impact on social attitudes to other areas such as racism and sexism.

THINKING HISTORICALLY · Cause and consequence (7c)

The value of historical explanations

Historical explanations derive from the historian who is investigating the past. Differences in explanations are usually about what the historians think is significant. Historians bring their own attitudes and perspectives to historical questions and see history in the light of these. It is therefore perfectly acceptable to have very different explanations of the same historical phenomenon. The way we judge historical accounts is by looking at how well argued they are and how well evidence had been deployed to support the argument.

Approach A	Approach B	Approach C
Changes in what is deemed acceptable in modern societies are largely driven by images and messages carried by mass media.	Changes in acceptable behaviour are due to the impact of legislation, which sets down what is and what is not allowed.	Changes in acceptable behaviour are a by-product of increased wealth and technological change.

Work in groups of between three and five (you will need an even number of groups in the class).

In your groups, devise a brief explanation of the increased permissiveness of British society of between 200 and 300 words that matches one of the approaches above. Present your explanation to another group, who will decide on three things:

1 Which of the approaches is each explanation trying to demonstrate?

2 Considering the structure and the quality of the argument and use of evidence, which is the best of the three explanations?

3 If you choose a 'best' explanation, should you discount the other two? Explain your answer.

ACTIVITY · SUMMARY

Media in the sixties: satire, image and social change

1 Create a graph with the vertical axis labelled 'Extent of traditional views' and the horizontal axis labelled 'Time', with years stretching from 1960 to 1970. For each of the following categories plot a line that you feel best charts the change in British attitudes in that area: the government; the Church; the monarchy; racism; sexism; sexuality. Pay particular attention to changes in the plot of each line. Try to explain why the line changes at a particular rate and why rapid changes took place at certain points.

2 Compare your graph with that of another student. Where there are differences, justify why you feel your summary is more accurate.

WIDER READING

Laffin, D. *British Society Since 1945*, Hodder (2013)

Sandbrook, D. *White Heat: A History of Britain in the Swinging Sixties*, Little Brown (2006). Provides an engaging account of key social developments, with lots of cultural and media material.

The National Archives – www.nationalarchives.gov.uk

Waller, S. *A Sixties Social Revolution? British Society 1959–75*, Nelson Thornes (2008)

3.6

The Thatcher governments and the media, 1979–90

KEY QUESTIONS

- What principles underpinned Thatcherism and what was its significance for the mass media industry between 1979 and 1990?

- How effective was the government's promotion of competition in broadcasting?

- How far did the Thatcher governments attempt to control the way mass media reported significant events between 1979 and 1990?

INTRODUCTION

Margaret Thatcher was the most divisive prime minister of the 20th century. To some, she saved Britain from economic ruin and restored national pride; to others, she promoted greedy individualism and condemned whole communities to hopeless poverty. At the time of her death in April 2013, sympathetic obituaries paid tribute to her as the greatest British peacetime prime minister. At the same time, an internet campaign saw the song 'Ding Dong! The Witch is Dead' reach number two in the pop charts. These extreme reactions, dictated by political conviction or personal experience of life under Thatcher, continue to be held by many people even after her death. Passionate supporters and critics would both agree that Thatcher, and her legacy, have strongly shaped 21st-century Britain. However, this interpretation should not be taken as fact. It is the historian's task to see past emotional responses and to analyse both the impact of Thatcher's government on contemporaries and the extent of her legacy since 1990.

Although Thatcher's principles did not evolve with mass media in mind, it is important to understand the origins and key elements of 'Thatcherism' because she clearly tried to apply them to the media industry during her time as prime minister.

WHAT PRINCIPLES UNDERPINNED THATCHERISM AND WHAT WAS ITS SIGNIFICANCE FOR THE MASS MEDIA INDUSTRY BETWEEN 1979 AND 1990?

What is 'Thatcherism'?

The origins of Thatcher's principles

Margaret Thatcher had a clear, unshakable sense of what was right and wrong for Britain. Her strong moral values were rooted in her Methodist upbringing and respect for her father's hard work, self-reliance, thrift and determination. As an adult, she embraced political views

---

1979 – Margaret Thatcher becomes prime minister

Bernard Ingham appointed as Thatcher's chief press secretary

1982 – Launch of Channel 4 and of satellite television in Britain breaks duopoly of ITV and BBC

Hunt Report into the provision of cable television

Government censorship of Falklands conflict

| 1979 | 1980 | 1981 | 1982 | 1983 | 1984 |

1980 – Broadcasting Act establishes Channel 4

1984 – Cable and Broadcasting Act sets up the Cable Authority

Miners' strike

that resonated with her personal experiences – she wanted government to promote the positive moral values from which she had benefited. More than this, she felt that too much state interference in people's lives had been a major reason for British decline. In her opinion, the welfare state had become a 'nanny state' and turned potentially upright, productive citizens into lazy dependents. She thought that state ownership of industry crushed innovation, choice and competition, and led to inferior, uncompetitive products that people did not want to buy. Even worse for her were the high levels of taxation required to pay for large state interference. This drained the wealth of successful individuals who could have used this money for private entrepreneurship. She hated the 'creeping socialism' of the **post-war consensus** and wanted the Conservative Party to break out of the centre ground. A key part of this shift would require the party to stand up to trade union power rather than give in to their demands for higher pay as previous Conservative governments had done.

A number of key influences shaped Thatcher's instinctive moral stance on political policies intended to 'roll back' the overbearing state apparatus (i.e. reverse the growing interference of the state in what should be private matters). More than anyone else, it was 'new right' Conservative Keith Joseph who inspired Thatcher with his brand of free-market liberalism. He introduced her to the ideas of Austrian economist Friedrich von Hayek who, in his 1944 book *The Road to Serfdom*, argued that government should provide the conditions of liberty within which individuals can make their own choices, not provide welfare that leads to dependence. Such ideas had been around since the Second World War but had made little impression. Too many people associated the free market with the dark days of the Great Depression. Thatcher rose to prominence at exactly the right time for many Conservatives to finally give these '**neoliberal**' ideas a chance. By the mid-1970s, government planning and interference seemed to be responsible for a stagnant economy, high inflation and rising unemployment. The Labour government's application for an IMF bail-out and, above all, the impact of trade unions holding the government to ransom during the **Winter of Discontent**, led a large swathe of the British public to agree that something different had to be tried. The acronym TINA, short for 'There Is No Alternative', was frequently used to defend Thatcher's controversial policies in the early 1980s.

KEY TERM

Post-war consensus
This phrase is commonly used to describe the many similarities between the policies of Conservative and Labour governments between 1945 and 1979. Political commentators during this period found that both parties shared near identical economic policies in particular. Thatcher wanted the Conservatives to move further to the right in their economic policies, with tax cuts, reduced state spending and reduced state ownership of industry.

KEY TERMS

Neoliberalism
The belief that the free market is better than the state at allocating goods and resources. Neoliberals recommend that the state does not interfere in the economy or in people's lives. They argue that government regulations should be relaxed, state services replaced by private provision and state assets sold off.

Winter of Discontent
The phrase, originally from Shakespeare's *Richard III*, was used by journalists to describe serious industrial relations problems during the bitterly cold winter of 1978-79. Around 1.5 million public sector workers went on strike to protest against the Labour government's attempt to cap (limit) public sector pay increases at five percent. Rubbish piled up in many cities as dustmen stopped work; 225 corpses had to be stored in a factory in Liverpool as gravediggers in the city went on strike. Eventually the government backed down and awarded pay increases of 10-15 percent.

1985 – Peacock Committee formed to investigate future funding arrangements for the BBC

1987 – BBC forced to stop programme about Zircon spy satellite

1988 – Government ban on live interviews with members of the IRA

1989 – Debates in the House of Commons televised for the first time
Sky TV begins satellite transmissions

1985	1986	1987	1988	1989	1990

1986 – Thatcher supports Rupert Murdoch moving his printing operations to Wapping, thus breaking a printers' strike

Launch of British Satellite Broadcasting (BSB). The company was bought by Rupert Murdoch's Sky Television in 1990

1990 – Broadcasting Act abolishes Independent Broadcasting Authority (IBA), allowing expansion of satellite channels and causing shake up of the ITV franchises

The Press Complaints Commission sets up as self-regulatory body with Code of Conduct for journalists

An overview of Thatcher's career

Margaret Thatcher (née Roberts) was born in Grantham, Lincolnshire, where her father Alfred owned two grocery shops. He was very active in local politics and used to take his daughter to many meetings.

Margaret was brought up with a Christian faith that informed a strongly held set of conservative moral values throughout her life. Having studied chemistry at Oxford University, she worked for a few years as a research chemist, but later she trained to be a barrister. In 1951, she married Denis Thatcher, a wealthy businessman.

She never lost her interest in politics, and she served as president of the Oxford University Conservative Association while a student. She joined the University Graduate Conservative Association in 1948 before putting herself forward as candidate MP in 1950. She lost in the 1950 and 1951 elections and was not selected as a candidate in the 1955 election, but she won the seat of Finchley and became a Conservative MP in 1959. She gradually rose through the ranks of the Party, until in 1970 she was made Education Secretary. In this role, she became notorious as 'Margaret Thatcher, milk snatcher' for stopping the free provision of milk for 7–11-year-olds. In 1975, she became leader of the Conservative Party, which was then in opposition, and when her party won the 1979 election she became the first female prime minister.

Once in power her first priority was the economy, starting with inflation. As soon as this was reduced she aimed to reduce government interference in the economy and use the law to greatly reduce the power of the trade unions. Manufacturing output fell by 30 percent, and unemployment doubled between 1978 and 1983, with 3.6 million out of work. Many commentators felt that it was only success against Argentina in the 1982 Falklands War that saw Thatcher re-elected in the 1983 general election.

Her second term in office gave her the confidence to expand the privatisation of state-owned assets that had begun tentatively before 1983. Thatcher centralised more power in Whitehall at the expense of local authorities and promoted unelected 'political advisers' from the world of business to advance her policies. She took a tough line against a year-long miners' strike in 1984, against the Provisional IRA throughout the 1980s and against the Soviet Union in the last years of the Cold War. These stands were very popular with many British people, who saw her as an almost Churchillian patriot.

In 1987, she was re-elected for a third term, the only prime minister to achieve this in the 20th century. However, a number of policies in her third term, most notably the introduction of the 'Poll Tax' in 1989–90, were very unpopular. She resigned in November 1990.

In 1992, she entered the House of Lords as Baroness Thatcher. She was occasionally critical of the Conservative leaders who followed her, especially of their pro-European stance. Although she died in April 2013, many would argue that Thatcherism, or at least her belief in the liberating power of the free market, remains the new consensus in British politics.

The practical application of Thatcher's principles

Thatcher sought to roll back the state in order to leave Britain with a smaller state bureaucracy, less government interference in people's lives, less government spending and a cheaper tax bill for the British public. The ways in which she sought to achieve this all had an impact on the media industry. Such policies included the following:

Contracting out
Offering contracts for government-funded work or projects to private companies in order to reduce costs.

- **Privatisation**: Thatcher saw the sale of state-owned companies, the removal of government monopolies and the '**contracting out**' of services as key parts of her crusade to cure Britain's economic stagnation. She would cut government expenditure on loss-making industries and reduce the number of civil servants by replacing them with private employees. More than this, privatisation would reinvigorate the British economy by promoting competition and innovation. The revenue generated by the sale of state assets would also fund a reduction in tax, allowing entrepreneurs to invest more wealth in job-creating ventures. Lastly, the sales would help to create wider share ownership. Ordinary people would have a greater incentive to work harder, knowing that they owned a slice of the company for which they worked. While there is no doubt that Thatcher was successful in terms of the pace and extent of privatisation, historians are divided over the long-term success of this policy.

- **Deregulation**: Thatcher was keen to remove the rules and regulations that she believed stifled innovation and competitiveness. The first example of this was the removal of exchange controls in October 1979. Before 1979, there were limits to how many pounds people could convert into foreign currencies and spend abroad. The end of this restriction fuelled greater overseas investment (which returned profits to Britain) but also led to a huge increase in consumer spending on foreign goods, which drained wealth from Britain. Perhaps the most significant example of deregulation was 'Big Bang', unveiled in October 1986. This relaxed the rules on the ownership and trading operation of banks. The City of London rapidly grew to become one of the major financial centres in the world as financial institutions took advantage of the more relaxed rules to offer riskier **financial products** that returned huge profits. It also contributed to a huge rise in private household debt (from £16 billion in 1980 to £47 billion in 1989) and in mortgages (from £43 billion to £235 billion in the same period). By 2003, personal debt, including mortgages, stood at £1.3 trillion, by far the highest in Europe.

- **Cutting taxation and government spending**: Thatcher was willing to risk a temporary period of higher unemployment to tackle inflation. In 1978, inflation stood at 11 percent; by 1980 it had doubled to 22 percent, largely due to spiralling pay demands. Thatcher refused to print money to cover inflation as it punished careful savers and rewarded reckless borrowers. She placed her trust in the economic theories of a few experts. Chicago-based economist Milton Friedman argued that inflation could only be effectively tackled by restricting the amount of money in circulation. '**Monetarism**', as this theory was called, was given a prominent role in the 1980 budget Medium Term Financial Strategy (MTFS), but was never fully understood by Thatcher or the British public. A key problem was that no one was quite sure how best to measure how much money was in circulation. Should this just mean the total value of notes and coins, or should it include money in bank accounts? By 1983, even fans of monetarism such as Chancellor Nigel Lawson began to give up on the idea of setting targets for money supply. A range of **supply-side** policies was introduced to replace monetarism. These included cuts to income tax, cuts to welfare payments where possible and a wide range of deregulation.

The removal of government subsidies for struggling older industries saw a decline in the percentage of the labour force employed in manual labour, from 47 percent in 1974 to 36 percent in 1991. The 1980 and 1981 budgets in particular slashed government spending with negative consequences for British manufacturers and for vulnerable people in many cities. There were riots in several cities, the most severe of which were in Toxteth (Liverpool) and Brixton (London). While these were partly sparked by racial issues, the poverty in such areas heightened tensions. The riots occurred in areas where it was difficult to tell whether the damage was due to the violence or permanent neglect and poverty. Between 1980 and 1981, manufacturing production fell by 14 percent. By 1982, unemployment had risen to over three million, the highest figure since 1930. Ironically, the scale of unemployment benefit payments forced government spending up. Despite this, inflation was reduced to single figures by 1982, and it did not rise above nine percent for the rest of the 1980s.

Thatcher reduced the size of state bureaucracy where this was politically possible but failed to cut overall government spending. This spending made up 43 percent of the value of all wealth produced in Britain in 1977–78. It rose to 47 percent in 1983–84, fell to 39 percent in 1988–89 but rose again to 44 percent in 1994. The total tax bill also rose throughout her time in office, from 38.5 percent of total wealth produced in 1979 to almost 41 percent in 1990. The tax on an average person rose from 31 to 37 percent of their income.

Thatcher's assault on the trade unions

Thatcher also sought to reduce trade union power as part of her overall aim to attack socialism and promote competition. She had been part of Conservative Prime Minister Edward Heath's government that had lost power in 1974 largely due to the impact of a miners' strike that year. She was keen to reduce the power of the trade unions but was prepared to bide her time and avoid the mistakes made by her predecessor. In her view, trade unions bullied individual workers into joining them, forced them into strike action they often had no wish to take part in, and acted irresponsibly with no regard for democratically elected government. Their power was undermined gradually through a series of Employment Acts.

- The 1980 Act meant that workers did not have to join a union when they joined a particular firm. It also meant unions could only organise strikes against their direct employers and were not allowed to strike in sympathy with other workers.

- The 1982 Act meant the unions could be sued for illegal strike action.

- The Trade Union Act 1984 meant that a strike had to be approved by a majority of union members in a secret ballot before it was legal. Thatcher also built up energy reserves (such as stockpiled coal) that would enable the government to resist a miners' strike without resorting to Heath's three-day week emergency measure.

EXTEND YOUR KNOWLEDGE

The 1984–85 miners' strike

Thatcher was highly successful in her stand against the National Union of Mineworkers (NUM). One reason for this was that she was fortunate in her enemy – the NUM President Arthur Scargill made several tactical errors that undermined the miners' strike. For example, the strike began on 6 March 1984, just as the UK emerged from winter and demanded less energy. Scargill did not ballot NUM members about strike action, choosing instead to launch the strike with 'flying pickets' (groups of workers transported to form a picket line at mines or distribution centres other than those in which they worked). This caused miners in Nottinghamshire to leave the NUM and set up their own union, which voted to keep their mines open. Lastly, Scargill lost public sympathy due to what were seen as provocative methods. The level of public disapproval in relation to Scargill never fell below 79 percent throughout the year-long strike.

The strike was finally defeated on 3 March 1985, almost a year to the day after it began, although miners in Kent held out for a further two weeks.

The coal industry had become increasingly uncompetitive since the war and pit closures had led to large-scale redundancies since the 1960s. It is likely that the coal industry would have been scaled back at a slower pace had it not been for the strike. The number of miners fell from 200,000 in 1974 to 10,000 in 1990. Mining was not the only industry to be affected by cuts in government subsidies and the reduced power of trade unions. Many local communities were hugely affected by the decline of a major local industry, such as ship building in Sunderland, and steel manufacturing in Sheffield (as depicted in the 1997 film *The Full Monty*).

SOURCE

A cartoon by Michael Attwell published in the *Sun* on 6 February 1982. The cartoon was inspired by a performance of the Naked Balloon Dance by comedy group 'The Greatest Show on Legs'. The group used Thatcher masks instead of balloons to cover their nudity when entertaining delegates at a TUC conference in Blackpool that year.

Trade unions became far more willing to work with government legislation following the defeat of the NUM in March 1985. A series of Employment Acts in 1988, 1989 and 1990 built on the earlier Acts to weaken the power of the trade unions. Although the main target of all this legislation was the NUM, the Acts affected all trade unions, including those related to the media industry. The total number of trade union members fell from 13.5 million in 1979 to under 10 million in 1990. The total number of working days lost to strike action fell from 10.5 million between 1980 and 1984 to 0.8 million between 1990 and 1994. The impact of Thatcher's anti-union legislation and action is a source of emotional disagreement. Critics argue that she caused unnecessary suffering to whole communities who relied on mining, and that not enough was done to encourage other forms of employment in former mining areas.

ACTIVITY
KNOWLEDGE CHECK

Thatcherism

1 Summarise the key aims of Thatcherism.

2 Explain how Thatcher hoped to achieve these aims.

3 Consider the likely consequences of Thatcherism for mass media.

The significance of the Thatcher government's policies for the media industry

How far did Thatcherism affect the press?

Both Thatcher and Thatcherism affected the press in a number of ways. Firstly, the tough line taken against trade unions allowed newspaper owners to modernise their printing operations. In 1983, newspaper owner Eddy Shah defeated the attempt by the National Graphical Association (the print workers' union) to stop the introduction of new print machines for his chain of local newspapers in the Manchester area. The greater efficiency and profitability of the new system allowed him to set up one of only two new national daily newspapers since the 1960s. The first colour newspaper, *Today*, set a trend, but it folded in 1995 after poor circulation figures. Shah's 1983 victory emboldened Rupert Murdoch (owner of the *Sun*, the *News of the World*, *The Times* and *The Sunday Times*) to move his printing operations from Fleet Street to a new complex at Wapping in 1986. The move meant that journalists could put together the newspaper and print it electronically without having to use specialist print workers. Whereas print strikes between 1976 and 1986 had stopped the production of 296 million copies of the *Sun*, Murdoch was now able to sack the printers who went on strike. For a whole year, many of these workers demonstrated outside the Wapping plant. Murdoch enjoyed the full support of the government with the protection of a sizeable police presence. The demonstrations occasionally turned violent and over 1,000 arrests were made.

Partly because of this assistance, and partly because of his political views, the Murdoch press strongly supported Mrs Thatcher. It is clear that Thatcher had to set aside her promotion of competition to allow Murdoch to buy *The Times* and *The Sunday Times* in 1981 in order to secure his highly influential support.

EXTRACT

 From the *Independent*, Saturday 17 March 2012. Letters between Murdoch and Mrs Thatcher overturned official history to show that the tycoon briefed the prime minister at Chequers before he was allowed to expand his empire.

Rupert Murdoch has been on better terms with more prime ministers than anyone else alive. He had so much to offer by way of influence and contacts the world over – at least until the hacking scandal flooded his empire – and if a politician wanted to meet him in private he did not let his love of news get the better of discretion.

On 12 February 1981, Mr Murdoch was allowed to double the number of national newspapers he owned, by adding *The Times* and *The Sunday Times* to *The Sun* and the *News of the World*. It was normal practice for any bid for a national newspaper to be held up while the Monopolies Commission investigated, but in this case Margaret Thatcher's government overrode objections from Labour and waved it through. Mrs Thatcher reaped the political rewards for the remainder of her time in office.

It could have been embarrassing for the Prime Minister if there had been any suggestion she had privately colluded with Mr Murdoch to ease his bid – but that was specifically denied in *The History of the Times: the Murdoch Years*, written by a Times journalist, Graham Stewart, and published in 2005 by Mr Murdoch's company, HarperCollins. There was it was asserted: "In 1981, Margaret Thatcher and Rupert Murdoch scarcely knew one another and had no communication whatsoever during the period in which The Times bid and referral was up for discussion." Documents being released on Monday by the Margaret Thatcher Archive demonstrate that they did indeed meet. In fact, Mr Murdoch secretly met Mrs Thatcher for lunch at Chequers, on Sunday, 4 January 1981, with the specific purpose of briefing her about *The Times* bids, at a time when other potential buyers were showing an interest and *Times* journalists were hoping to organise a staff buyout.

Mrs Thatcher's advisers were acutely aware that the meeting had to be secret. A formal record was kept, and submitted to Mrs Thatcher the next day with a note from her press secretary, Bernard Ingham, vouching that "in line with your wishes, the attached has not gone outside No 10." The record notes that "the main purpose of Mr Murdoch's visit was to brief the Prime Minister on his bid for Times Newspapers." Mr Murdoch told her that it was "a firm bid" for all the titles, not just the potentially profitable *Sunday Times*. In a hint of the dispute that tore apart the East End of London five years later, when Mr Murdoch sacked 5,000 print and ancillary staff to facilitate the move to Wapping, he also told the Prime Minister that he was gambling on his ability "to crack a particularly tough nut" in the form of the highly organised print unions.

Mr Murdoch also speculated on who his rival bidders might be. They included the tycoon Robert Maxwell, who later bought the *Daily Mirror*, and Sir James Goldsmith, father of the current Tory MP Zac Goldsmith. The note records that Mrs Thatcher "thanked Mr Murdoch for keeping her posted" but "did no more than wish him well in his bid." Mr Murdoch wrote to her on 15 January, to inform her that "The Times business is proceeding well", adding: "See you in New York on 28 February." By then, the deal had been clinched.

Mrs Thatcher needed the media mogul's support because she was so desperately unpopular. Her subsequent success has obscured the extent to which her government was peering over the abyss in 1981. Chris Collins, editor of the Margaret Thatcher Foundation website, describes the documents, which will be accessible at margaretthatcher.org as "the personal archive of a person under great stress".

EXTEND YOUR KNOWLEDGE

Rupert Murdoch (born 1931)

Rupert Murdoch was born in Melbourne, Australia. His father Keith had been a journalist and, on his death in 1952, left shares in a number of Australian newspapers. Rupert was at Oxford University at the time, but returned home in 1953 to take over as managing director of his father's company, News Limited.

He was highly ambitious and an extremely shrewd businessman. Over the next few years, he bought a number of newspapers across Australia. In 1964, he launched Australia's first national newspaper and bought his first newspaper outside Australia: *The Dominion* in New Zealand.

His major ambition was to get into the British media. He achieved this in 1969 when he bought the *News of World* (then one of the highest-selling newspapers in the world) and the *Sun*. He soon began to interfere in editorial decisions at both newspapers, explaining that he hadn't come all the way from Australia not to get involved.

With the revenue from the *Sun*, he was able to found his company News Corporation, and to purchase *The Times* and *The Sunday Times* in 1981. The previous owners of the newspaper had been forced to sell because of the increased cost of printing in the 1970s. Murdoch overcame these costs with the move to Wapping in 1986.

Murdoch had begun to acquire newspapers in America in 1973, but, having obtained American citizenship in 1985, he moved into television through the establishment of the Fox Network. In addition to Fox News and the other Fox Channels, News Corporation also owns Sky, Star TV, Twentieth Century Fox film studios and Myspace, among many other firms. *Private Eye* (see Chapter 5) regularly draws attention to Murdoch's cross-media ownership with a column called 'I-Sky'. It charts occasions when the *Sun* or *The Times* promote Sky television. Murdoch is now estimated to be the 132nd wealthiest person in the world, with assets of over $4 billion.

In Chapter 3 we saw how press ownership could affect the content of British newspapers. Throughout the 1980s and 1990s, around 70 percent of newspapers in circulation backed the Conservative Party, with only the *Daily Mirror* backing the Labour Party on a large scale. However, in 1997, the *Sun* switched allegiance from the Conservatives to Labour. Labour leader Tony Blair had met Murdoch on several occasions and had made a favourable impression. Blair was happy to continue with many Thatcherite policies as part of his 'Third Way' between socialism and free market capitalism, and in particular promised not to impose controls on cross-media ownership. Such was the size of the *Sun*'s circulation (3.8 million copies daily in 1997) that only 33 percent of newspapers sold now backed the Conservative Party.

Television: the promotion of Thatcherism?

The major impact of Thatcherism on television broadcasting (the promotion of competition) is considered in the section on Channel 4 below. Thatcherism also affected the cultural products of the television industry. Although Thatcher never directly said that 'greed is good', she certainly encouraged people to make as much money as they could. Many television shows in the 1980s, and into the 1990s, could be seen as promoting and glamorising wealth and materialism. Many drama series imported from America, such as *Knots Landing*, *Dynasty*, *Falcon Crest*, and most famously *Dallas* (with a peak audience of 21 million in November 1980), focused on the lives of rich, selfish characters. Television also increasingly catered for viewers with large disposable incomes who wanted to improve their lifestyles. The trend began with celebrity chefs such as Delia Smith (whose *Cookery Course* ran for three series between 1979 and 1981) and Keith Floyd (whose *Floyd on Fish* made him a national celebrity in 1984). But this really took off in the 1990s, a decade dominated by Thatcherism if not Thatcher herself. Television programmes catered for people's aspirations for their personal appearance and for their home interiors (in homes that were increasingly privately owned). Programmes included *The Clothes Show* (BBC, 1986–2000) and *Space Craft* (Channel 4, 1987). Gardening was also extremely popular, and television shows such as *Gardeners' World* encouraged people to improve their gardens. All of these programmes suggested that ordinary people could attain greater sophistication or luxury and may be seen as a democratising force. A large number of out-of-town garden centres opened to cater for the demand for products. Shopping itself became a leisure activity, with cafes in garden centres. Critics would argue that lifestyle programmes and quizzes have mushroomed on daytime and early evening television because they are cheap to produce.

How far did Thatcherism affect cinema?

It is sometimes claimed that the Thatcher years saw a renaissance in British cinema. There is some truth to this, as audience figures increased after the mid-1980s for the first time since the 1950s. This recovery, however, had nothing to do with Thatcher, who did much to undermine the British film industry. In part, interest in the cinema may have been rekindled by the rise in popularity of television shows about cinema, such as Barry Norman's *Film* (shown on BBC1 from 1972) and Alex Cox's *Moviedrome* (shown on BBC2 from 1987 to 1994). However, the increased audiences were primarily driven by the popularity of American **blockbusters** and their sequels, which made up around 85 percent of all films shown in British cinemas between 1979 and 1990.

Thatcher wanted film-making to be treated like any other British industry, to remove government subsidies and promote the free market. The Film Act 1985 scrapped the Eady Levy that had subsidised British studios from the total takings at box offices since 1957. Domestic investment in British films also fell after Thatcher privatised the National Film Finance Corporation and removed a 25 percent tax break on investments in film. British filmmakers were forced to become Thatcherite entrepreneurs in order to get their films made. Many, such as director Ridley Scott, went to work in America, where he made films such as *Alien* and *Aliens* (1979 and 1986) and *Blade Runner* (1982). Those who stayed in Britain worked with independent production companies such as Handmade Films (founded in 1978), Merchant Ivory Productions (founded in 1961) and Working Title Films (founded in 1983). In order to produce films with a very high production quality (like those made by the Hollywood studios), these companies often sought American financial backing. They increasingly received this backing, especially after the success of Working Title's *A Room with a View* (1985), which made $4.4 million at the US box office in its first 12 weeks of release. Domestic investment mainly came from television companies such as Film On Four (which produced its first film in 1982) and BBC Film (founded in 1990).

British films reacted to Thatcherism in two divergent ways, which can be referred to as 'us' and 'them' films. 'Us' films were produced by smaller, domestically funded companies and were primarily intended for a domestic audience. These films presented Britain 'as the British saw it'. They overwhelmingly attacked Thatcherism, either through the realistic depiction of social tension that resulted from the increased gap between rich and poor, or through satire and allegory. Film Four funded several such films, including *The Ploughman's Lunch* (1983), *My Beautiful Laundrette* (1985) and *High Hopes* (1988). 'Them' films depict a romanticised, historical image of Britishness to appeal to American perceptions of Britain and maximise profits from US filmgoers. The result of this was the growth of American-financed 'heritage' films such as *Gandhi* (1982), *A Passage to India* (1984) and *A Room with a View* (1985). Thatcherism clearly affected the productions and nature of the British

KEY TERM

Blockbuster
This was originally American slang used to describe a successful play, possibly because of the large numbers of people who would go to the 'block' (a mass of buildings between two streets) where the theatre was. The term was then taken to mean a very successful film. Nowadays it has come to mean a film with very high production and marketing costs geared towards huge audiences and merchandising.

film industry, but its renaissance owes more to National Lottery funding since 1994 and the establishment of the UK Film Council in 2000. The Council distributes around £17 million of Lottery funds to British filmmakers each year, and helps to distribute independent films in cinemas across the country.

ACTIVITY
KNOWLEDGE CHECK

The impact of Thatcherism on cinema and the press

1 Give examples of the ways in which Thatcherism affected the British press and film industry.

2 For what reasons might these changes be celebrated or criticised? Consider the view of the Thatcher governments, those working in the press and film industry and the general public.

3 How useful is Extract 1 to a historian who wants to understand the impact of Thatcherism on the media industry?

HOW EFFECTIVE WAS THE GOVERNMENT'S PROMOTION OF COMPETITION IN BROADCASTING?

The promotion of competition in broadcasting: the launch of Channel 4 in 1982

Thatcher's views on industry, the economy as a whole, and the relationship between the state and private sector had clear implications for the media industry. Until 1973, the BBC had maintained a monopoly on radio broadcasting, and in 1979 a 'duopoly' of the BBC and ITV still persisted in television broadcasting. Thatcher wanted to promote greater competition, particularly to force the BBC to become more responsive to the demands of the free market. She saw the BBC as a wasteful organisation, producing left-leaning 'liberal' programmes that the British public did not want or like. She resented the licence fee as an unfair and undemocratic tax which people had no choice but to pay if they wanted to watch television. Her feelings of animosity increased during the 1980s, due to what she saw as the unpatriotic reporting of conflict in Northern Ireland and the Falklands (see page 147).

However, Thatcher was not entirely responsible for reforms that led to greater competition in the media industry. There was momentum for change from before her tenure of office and there was also pressure bubbling up from below. The Broadcasting Act 1972 had led to the launch of Independent Local Radio in 1973. In the same year that the Act was passed, a highly influential article was published in the *Guardian* by broadcaster and academic Anthony Smith. Smith argued that the persistence of the 'duopoly' in television meant that too much talent was going to waste and that not enough voices were represented on television. He constructively built on frustrations raised by the Free Communication Group founded in 1968, and the 76 Group (so called because the BBC Charter and ITV licence were due to expire in 1976) formed by backbench MPs in 1969, to call for a Royal Commission into the future of broadcasting.

No new channel had been created since the launch of BBC2 in 1964. But the broadcast system had the capacity for a fourth channel, a fact that automatically generated debate and speculation. It was unlikely that this would be awarded to the BBC as it already had two channels. In the early 1970s, the postmaster general Christopher Chataway had come close to awarding it to ITV in the interests of balance and fairness. It was in part due to the points raised by Smith's article that the creation of an 'ITV 2' was not a done deal. Smith advocated what he called an 'Open Broadcasting Authority', an entity that would not produce programmes in-house like the BBC or ITV, but would rather commission them from a range of independent production companies. Only such a system would ensure that broadcasting became more responsive to social change and more democratic.

Although Smith did not have an official role in the creation of the 1977 *Annan Report on the Future of Broadcasting*, he exercised a good deal of influence on the members of the Royal Commission who researched and put together the proposals. Chief among these proposals was the establishment of a fourth television channel along the lines advocated by Smith. While the Labour government was prepared to accept the recommendations of the report, Thatcher's victory in the May 1979 general election meant that the future of the fourth channel was once again in doubt.

SOURCE
2

From an interview with Anthony Smith, conducted by leading media journalist Maggie Brown in November 2006. Until 1982, only the BBC and ITV could broadcast television programmes in Britain. Smith was highly influential in the creation of an independent Channel 4.

You have to understand the role of the duopoly and why it became a tremendous vexation for thousands of people. The point was that society was no longer homogenous. There were a great many different interest groups – the 1960s had shown that – but the screens were not catching up. People had begun making films and videos in the 60s. There wasn't an easy domestic recording system as now, but there was a desire to use the moving image among people coming through the underground movements, and they had causes they wanted to express – everything from taking drugs, having sex, changing the laws about sex, the whole gay-rights thing, the homelessness issue, the beginning of the feminist movement. All these things were bubbling around here and abroad and at the same time the capacity to make messages was growing in the population. Meanwhile, we were all made to believe the broadcasting we were getting was very good. I suppose it was by international standards; but it was all in the hands of this rather well-paid, superior civil-service class. They drove around in big cars. They drank rather a lot and, like all drunks, they didn't listen. They couldn't hear, literally and metaphorically, what was going on around them, what demands were really being made – demands that their comfortable duopoly was able to frustrate.

A few weeks after the election, Smith went to see Keith Joseph (then Secretary of State for Industry) in a bid to save the Open Broadcasting Authority idea. Together with like-minded associates he had noticed that the Conservative manifesto had made much of a 'free market in ideas': the encouragement of competition, enterprise and small businesses. Smith played down the public service and democratising elements of his proposal and instead framed it in the language of the free market. It worked. In a speech on 14 September 1979, Home Secretary Willie Whitelaw made it clear that the fourth channel would not be controlled by ITV and instead an independent body, regulated by the Independent Broadcast Authority (IBA), would use independent producers for a lot of programmes. It was this speech that paved the way for the Broadcasting Act 1980, which established Channel 4. The Act also established the Welsh language channel S4C, but only after this clause was reinstated into the Act when 68-year-old Plaid Cymru leader Gwynfor Evans pledged to go on hunger strike if it did not happen.

Channel 4 launched on 2 November 1982. Thatcher's dislike of the programmes broadcast in the first weeks and months are a clear indicator of the lack of influence she had over the development of the channel. She sympathised with Mary Whitehouse (see page 126) and the National Viewers' and Listeners' Association's attack on swearing in *Brookside* (1982–2003), a soap opera set in Liverpool that tackled socially challenging storylines such as the effects of rape and drug abuse. In 1986 and 1987, Whitehouse also publicly backed two private members' bills to bring television broadcasts within the jurisdiction of the Obscene Publications Act. Whitehouse was particularly outraged by the screening of two films, *Sebastiane* (1976) and *Jubilee* (1978), by gay filmmaker Derek Jarman (other notable programmes for a gay audience included *One in Five*). In addition to such liberality, there were serious concerns over the political balance of Channel 4 programmes. Board member and ex-Labour minister Edmund Dell was concerned that while there was a *Union World* programme, there was no equivalent platform for employers. *The Friday Alternative* was a partly satirical current affairs programme that overtly opposed the government on many issues. This challenged the notion that broadcasts should be balanced and impartial. The driving force behind this development of Channel 4 was its first chairman, Jeremy Isaacs.

Isaacs initially claimed to want only 15 percent of programming to be produced by independents. In the event, the figure was 61 percent. The number of independent production companies doubled from 220 in 1981 to 440 in 1983. He passionately believed in creative freedom rather than imposing a strong editorial line from the top. He wanted the new channel to be different, even if this meant a loss of quality or coherence in the early days. He was empowered to take such a gamble because Channel 4 was funded by an initial levy of £200 million on ITV (in return, ITV was allowed to sell advertising on Channel 4). To a degree, Isaacs was merely fulfilling the Channel 4 Terms of Reference set out by its regulator, the IBA.

Jeremy Isaacs (born 1932)

Jeremy Isaacs was born in Glasgow. He studied Classics at Oxford University and completed his National Service, after which he worked as a producer for Granada Television based in Manchester. He established a strong professional reputation through his work on programmes such as *What the Papers Say* and *All Our Yesterdays*, and he went on to work for the BBC on the long-running current affairs programme *Panorama*. The work that really made his reputation was the 1973 26-episode *The World at War*. This combined extensive archive footage with a wealth of eyewitness interviews and the narration of Laurence Olivier to produce a series that continues to amaze audiences throughout the world. The most important break with previous war programmes was that it was not British-centred and explored the full theatre of combat.

As director of programmes for Thames Television between 1974 and 1978, Isaacs became a natural, if not stand out, candidate to become the first chairman of Channel 4. The position was first offered to film director Richard Attenborough, but he declined due to his work on his latest film *Gandhi*. Isaacs was seen as something of a maverick, particularly after allowing the BBC to use controversial material on Northern Ireland that had been banned by the commercial regulator (the Independent Broadcast Authority) in 1978. His vision for Channel 4 and his determination to push ahead with that vision were the driving forces behind the initial character of the new channel. It was only when viewing figures did not match up to his self-imposed target of ten percent that he finally accepted the need for some compromises to that vision.

He stood down as chairman in 1987 and, having failed to be selected as director-general of the BBC, went on to become general director of the Royal Opera House, Covent Garden. In 1998, he produced another landmark television series, *Cold War*.

SOURCE 3

From the Fourth Channel Programme Policy Statement issued by the IBA to the Board of Channel Four upon its incorporation in December 1980.

The Fourth Channel as a whole is expected to reflect the continuing debate on a wide range of issues of social policy... The additional hours of broadcasting made available by the Fourth Channel increase opportunities for programmes directed to different kinds of minority groups within the community, whether ethnic, cultural, or occupational distinctions mark them off from their neighbours. There should be a place for an increase in the making of such programmes from within the group rather than from outside... These are not times when high ideals are fashionable. Survival rather than expansion and development, may seem to have priority. But that cannot be a lasting mood.

Isaacs' faith in independent producers and in commissioning editors with no experience in television, such as former *Guardian* women's page editor Liz Forgan, meant that a number of films and shows were broadcast that would not otherwise have made it to screen. For example, *Black on Black* and *Eastern Eye* were produced by ethnic minorities for their communities. *In the Pink*, *Twenty Twenty* and *Broadside* were produced by women for women. *The Tube* was a live pop and rock music programme aimed at the youth audience that gave many bands and alternative comedians their big break.

However, the earnest, factual nature of many programmes, together with irregular scheduling, quickly led to a loss of audience share. From an initial 6.6 percent it fell to a low of 3.3 percent in February 1983 before recovering to nearer ten percent in 1985. Three weeks after the launch, the *Daily Mail* branded the station 'Channel Bore'. Isaacs recognised the need for more entertainment programmes to lure viewers to tune in, and he approved the rerun of ITV hits such as *Brideshead Revisited* and *The Jewel in the Crown*. By 1987, advertising revenue exceeded the ITV levy by £19 million. It was the eventual financial success of Channel 4 that led to its independence being suggested in the 1986 Peacock Commission Report and enshrined in the Broadcasting Act 1990.

Television: the promotion of competition

To critics of the BBC such as Thatcher, the success of Channel 4 served as evidence of the Corporation's waste and reliance on public money. The Peacock Committee, named after its chairman Professor Alan Peacock, was set up in 1985 to review BBC financing. The committee's report in July 1986 did not entirely please Thatcher (as it recommended the retention of the licence fee), but its recommendations did have some important consequences for broadcasting. In particular, its call for 40 percent of all BBC and ITV programmes to be commissioned from independents, for ITV franchises to be awarded by competitive tender, and for Channel 4 to sell its own advertising had a profound effect on the Broadcasting Act 1990. Even before the Act became law, the Cable and Broadcasting Act 1984 had increased competition. This allowed **cables** to carry as many new television channels into the homes of subscribers as possible. By 1990, cable television was available to 15 million out of 22 million homes in Britain. The Cable Authority only loosely regulated new television companies such as Sky Channel.

The Broadcasting Act 1990

The most significant introduction of competition in television broadcasting stemmed from the Broadcasting Act 1990. The terms of this Act meant:

- that every terrestrial channel had to commission 25 percent of its programmes from independent production companies (negotiated down from the 40 percent recommended by Peacock)

- the launch of a fifth terrestrial channel (Channel 5 eventually started in 1997)

- the growth of satellite television

- the replacement of the Cable Authority and the IBA with the Independent Television Commission (ITC), a 'light touch' regulator

- that companies had to bid for the 15 regional ITV broadcast contracts. The sums of money required for a successful bid varied from region to region. Carlton TV Ltd bid £43,170,000 to replace Thames Television as the weekday broadcaster in London, while Channel Television only had to bid £1,000 to secure the contract for the Channel Islands. The successful companies were awarded contracts that lasted for ten years

- that acquisitions and mergers were allowed between ITV franchises. These mergers had a number of impacts on television production in Britain after Thatcher's fall from power in 1990. Perhaps the most significant is that the need to make profits in order to survive has, according to critics, led to a 'dumbing down' of programmes to sell advertising to as many viewers as possible.

> **ACTIVITY**
> **KNOWLEDGE CHECK**
>
> **The impact of Thatcherism on television**
> 1 Summarise the reasons why the launch of Channel 4 is attributable to the impact of Thatcherism.
>
> 2 Which would you argue had the greater impact on the British television industry: the launch of Channel 4 or the Broadcasting Act 1990? Explain your answer.

The growth of local and commercial radio

The period 1979–90 saw a steady increase in the number of BBC local radio stations and commercial radio stations. The number of commercial stations, collectively known as **Independent Local Radio,** increased from 20 in 1979 to 58 in 1990 (although the total number of stations was higher than 58 as some had begun to offer different broadcast schedules on the AM and FM frequencies allocated by a single licence). In theory this meant a good deal of competition for BBC local radio. In practice, the target audiences tended to differ, with the commercial FM stations chasing younger listeners and the BBC stations serving the over-50s.

The Broadcasting Act 1990 affected commercial radio to a great extent.

- It led to the launch of three Independent National Radio stations, with licences issued to the highest bidders who met the new Radio Authority regulatory conditions: Classic FM, Virgin (now Absolute) Radio and Talksport.

- It led to the establishment of many more local and regional commercial stations. (However, by 2004, most of these were no longer 'independent' or 'local' – groups associated with the three independent national stations had bought almost all of them.)

- The allowance of acquisitions and mergers led to significant cross-media ownership in radio.

> **KEY TERMS**
>
> **Cable**
> Cable had been laid since the 1920s to transmit radio signals in areas with poor reception. In 1951, Gloucester became the first town to receive television signals via cable. For many years both the BBC and ITV argued against allowing commercial cable operators to bring in signals from other regions or even abroad. Ironically, when this was finally allowed to happen in 1985, the expansion of cable television was small because of the rise of satellite television.
>
> **Independent Local Radio**
> This should not be confused with BBC local radio, launched in November 1967, which had almost 40 stations by 1990. Commercial stations were allowed to broadcast under the Sound Broadcasting Act 1972 and the Independent Broadcasting Authority Act 1973. London Broadcasting Company (LBC) Radio was the first of 19 commercial operators to receive its licence from the IBA between 1973 and 1976.

> **A Level Exam-Style Question Section B**
>
> 'The launch of Channel 4 in 1982 was the most significant promotion of competition in British mass media between 1979 and 1990.'
>
> How far do you agree with this statement? (20 marks)
>
> **Tip**
> *Although there were important changes in mass media competition before 1979 and after 1990, it is important in the exam that you focus **firmly** on the dates in question.*

HOW FAR DID THE THATCHER GOVERNMENTS ATTEMPT TO CONTROL THE WAY MASS MEDIA REPORTED SIGNIFICANT EVENTS BETWEEN 1979 AND 1990?

Attempts to control reportage on issues of national security

Thatcher used a number of methods to restrict or shape the reporting of sensitive political issues or issues of national security far more than previous governments. The most overt method was the attempted use of the law.

SOURCE 4

From Howell Raines' article 'British Press Freedom Erodes Under Thatcher, Critics Say', printed in the *New York Times*, 19 December 1987 © 1987 The *New York Times*. All rights reserved. Raines is an American journalist who joined the newspaper in 1978 and worked as the London bureau chief from 1987 to 1988.

The Thatcher Government's legal actions against newspapers and broadcasters have resulted in a significant erosion of freedom of the press in Britain in 1987, in the view of journalists, civil libertarians and the handful of politicians interested in the issue. Throughout the year, the Government pursued its efforts to inhibit British publication of and news reporting about 'Spycatcher,' an account of misconduct in the British security services by Peter Wright, a former intelligence agent. At the same time, in less publicized cases, it has used the Police and Criminal Evidence Act to look for evidence in the news and photo libraries of newspapers. ...These actions are among nine areas of legal activity directed against the press that have been identified by the Press Council, an ombudsman group financed by the newspaper industry. 'With all these, Britain is sinking further into that league of nations where press freedom is barely understood, let alone protected,' said Kenneth Morgan, director of the council.

Experts differ on whether the rash of litigation represents a coordinated Government effort to bring the press to heel. But they agree that the plight of the financial journalist, Jeremy Warner of *The Independent*, illustrates the fragility of press freedom in Britain and the vulnerability of journalists to Government pressure in this country. Mr. Warner could become the first British journalist in 25 years to go to jail to protect a source of information if he continues to refuse to tell police inspectors how he got information about purported insider trading by civil servants in the Department of Trade and Industry. ...For her part, Prime Minister Margaret Thatcher very early on condemned investigative reporters as 'people who use freedom in order to destroy freedom.' ...When the courts bridled at enforcing the catch-all Official Secrets Act, she turned to the 'law of confidence,' a civil statute designed to protect business secrets, to stall journalistic inquiry into MI-5 and MI-6, the security services. And she has kept up the pressure. The BBC and *The Independent*, for example, are each tied up in litigation with the Government on three fronts. The result of such entanglements has been a marked decrease in the areas open to unrestricted inquiry.

A Level Exam-Style Question Section A

Study Source 4 before answering this question.

Assess the value of the source for revealing the extent and nature of government attempts to control reportage on issues of national security.

Explain your answer, using the source, the information given about its origin and your own knowledge about the historical context. (20 marks)

Tip

Aim to use this background knowledge to expose the limitations of Source 4.

Thatcher did not just promote competition to undermine the BBC. She also tried to directly intervene by banning some programmes and appointing governors of the board who sympathised with her political views. In February 1987, as part of the *Secret Society* series, the BBC planned to broadcast six programmes made by the investigative journalist Duncan Campbell. One of the shows was about a secret new spy satellite, code-named Zircon. The BBC, on the advice of the government, banned the programme. Even after the programme had been pulled, the police raided BBC offices in Glasgow and removed all material from the series. The liberal director-general Alasdair Milne was forced to resign in favour of the much more compliant Sir Michael Checkland. The fact that the governor of the board was the Conservative Marmeduke Hussey made the BBC more compliant with government wishes.

Thatcher also disliked the 'neutral' way in which the BBC reported about Northern Ireland. In 1988, a government White Paper led to a ban on all interviews with members of Sinn Fein. The BBC was forced to disguise the voice and face of Sinn Fein leaders such as Gerry Adams if they wanted to get around the law. Such intrusion led to the formation of Charter 88, a civil liberties pressure group that opposed such censorship.

ITV was not immune from this attempted interference into its news broadcasting. On 28 April 1988, ITV screened an episode of *This Week* entitled 'Death on the Rock'. The show investigated the killing of three members of the Provisional IRA earlier that year on Gibraltar by the SAS. The SAS were authorised to use lethal force if the suspects made any move to detonate a bomb. The SAS claimed that the three suspects did make such moves, while eyewitnesses said that the SAS shot them 'in cold blood'. Thatcher's Home Secretary, Douglas Hurd, tried to ban the show from being broadcast. However, the IBA refused, stating that free speech and free inquiry were the issues at stake and in a democracy were essential for individual liberty.

The role of Bernard Ingham

Bernard Ingham (born 1932)

Bernard Ingham was born on 21 June 1932 in Hebden Bridge, Yorkshire. He began his career as a journalist at the *Hebden Bridge Times* before progressing to the *Yorkshire Evening Post* and then the *Guardian*. He was a Labour voter and even stood as a Labour councillor in 1965. He was also an active trade unionist, serving as vice-chairman of the Leeds branch of the National Union of Journalists. While writing for the *Guardian*, he also published a column in the *Leeds Weekly Citizen* under the pseudonym 'Albion' in which he savaged Conservative values. In 1967, he joined the civil service where he worked as a press and public relations officer for Labour politicians Barbara Castle and Tony Benn. He also worked as a director of information at the Department of Energy from 1974 to 1977.

He got his big break five months after Thatcher won the 1979 general election: she fired her press secretary and hired Ingham after a two-minute conversation. He served as her press secretary for the next 11 years. As a civil servant, he was meant to be politically neutral, but it was clear to everyone how loyal and dedicated he was to Thatcher personally. Although this might seem strange from a former Labour man, he saw himself and the prime minister as 'radicals' who were prepared to take on the vested interests of 'the establishment'. He often said how he admired her 'guts'. Thatcher in return gave great support to Ingham when others were out to attack him, referring to him as the greatest after one of Ingham's press briefings had caused the value of the pound to drop 3 cents against the dollar in January 1985. Ingham increased his power in February 1989 when he became Head of Profession for all Government Information Officers. This power was, however, short-lived, as he stood down when Thatcher resigned in November 1990.

Ingham as Thatcher's press officer

Bernard Ingham became an important part of the Thatcher administration, even though he was not an MP, let alone a member of government. Between 1979 and 1990 he served as Thatcher's chief press officer. The role, part of the prime minister's office, had been created in 1931 by Prime Minister Ramsay MacDonald to help him deal with the media. The press officer's job was to advise the prime minister how they should respond to national events or respond to stories that directly concerned them. The exact nature of the press officer's job has varied according to the personalities involved, but there were four key aspects to it:

- acting as an intermediary with the media: this involved meeting key media figures about political television and press interviews. It also involved a twice-daily meeting with '**the Lobby**'. Ingham insisted on being present at all interviews with Thatcher. Thatcher also requested Ingham to put together a select digest of the daily press for her to read mid-morning. Thatcher rarely watched television and only glanced at *The Times* or the *Telegraph* at the weekend

- advising the prime minister on the best way to present government policy to the media

- co-ordinating the work of all information officers in every government department to ensure they do not give conflicting stances on recent events or forthcoming policies. Ingham presided over a Meeting of Information Officers (MIO) every Monday evening in the Cabinet office

- acting as a spokesperson. Before Ingham, some press officers had spoken for the Cabinet as a whole; as discussed below, Ingham spoke only for Thatcher.

Unlike his predecessors, Ingham became a well-known public figure in his own right and a controversial one at that. There are a number of reasons for this. He himself was an opinionated and often abrasive character. He revelled in his no-nonsense, gruff Yorkshireman persona when dealing with journalists, whom he distrusted and often disliked. Although he was strictly meant to present the prime minister's thinking, at times he expounded his own views. He regularly upbraided Lobby journalists for writing 'bunkum and balderdash'. He was also ambitious for more power and stayed in his post longer than any previous officer. He made a point of working closely with the best new recruits at Downing Street before promoting them to positions of influence within the Government Information Service at different government departments.

KEY TERM

The Lobby
This was a system that was set up in 1884 to allow leading political journalists regular and reliable access to the latest developments in government. It was in the interests of government to provide such access in a bid to cut down on speculation and rumours. The key to its effective functioning has been the non-attributable 'off the record' nature of information given at Lobby briefings. In theory, this allows the government to speak as a whole without creating destabilising divisions that could occur if information was attributable to a particular individual. In 2002, the Labour government scrapped the weekday morning meeting at 10 Downing Street.

In 1995, historian Colin Seymour-Ure argued that the most serious issue was Ingham's **partisanship**. As a civil servant he should have been politically neutral, yet there were a number of occasions when Ingham used the deniability of his non-attributable Lobby briefings to attack members of Cabinet who had displeased Thatcher. For example, while Thatcher publicly continued to support Leader of the House Francis Pym following a pessimistic speech about the economy in February 1982, Ingham made sure the newspapers reported Thatcher's dismay at his relentless pessimism. The *Sun* branded him 'Mr Misery'. This clearly served as a warning to other '**wets**' in government. In a television interview in May 1986, Pym's replacement, John Biffen, discussed the possibility of Thatcher standing down before the next election. The following day, Ingham's briefing led the newspapers to describe Biffen as a 'semi-detached' member of the Cabinet. Again, Thatcher never attacked Biffen directly, but she ignored him thereafter. He was sacked from the Cabinet in the reshuffle that followed the 1987 election.

KEY TERMS

Partisanship
In a political context, this refers to someone who is strongly committed to their party and is reluctant to compromise with rivals. It also suggests an emotional attachment to their party that leads to biased decisions and judgements.

'Wet'
This was Thatcher's term for a member of her government who was not in favour of her neo-liberal agenda. She included several 'wets' in her first Cabinet to preserve the unity of the party but gradually replaced them with her favoured 'dries'.

The Westland affair, 1985–86

Perhaps Ingham's most controversial use of non-attributable information came during the 1985–86 Westland affair. Westland was a British helicopter company that was earmarked for sale. Thatcher, and her secretary of state for trade and industry Leon Brittan, favoured the bid of American firm Sikorsky. The defence secretary Michael Heseltine put together a consortium of European firms to make a counter bid. Both Heseltine and Brittan then used the media to secure support in parliament and in the City for their side. Thatcher, via Brittan, asked the solicitor-general to investigate the wording of a letter that Heseltine had printed in *The Times*. He did so and wrote in his report that there was one section that required a bit more evidence to support one claim. This was duly provided by Heseltine. However, one section of the report taken out of context was leaked to the press. The newspapers the next day all led with the 'material inaccuracies' of Heseltine's letter and the *Sun* simply accused him of lying. Although Ingham denied responsibility for the leak, it is highly unlikely that the information would have emerged without his influence. Heseltine resigned from the Cabinet a few days later and Brittan's resignation was forced for his part in approving the leak.

SOURCE 5

From Robert Harris' *Good and Faithful Servant: The Unauthorized Biography of Bernard Ingham*, published in 1990. Harris gained first-hand experience of Ingham's Lobby briefings as political editor of the *Observer* from 1987 to 1990.

Mrs Thatcher's declaration – that it was not Ingham's 'job to try to persuade the press to boost the Government' – seems at first sight to be so palpably false, it is a wonder it can have been made with a straight face. Only if one studies her reply more closely can one, perhaps, detect behind it the slippery hand of the civil service drafter. Technically, it was correct to state that persuading the press to boost the Government was not his *job*: in so saying she was not denying that this was what he *did*. Why was it necessary to go through these linguistic contortions? What was wrong with seeking to manipulate the press? Why not admit what everyone on the inside track knew for a fact: that Ingham devoted himself, body and soul, twelve hours a day to boosting the Government; that he used the MIO not as a channel for ensuring the smooth transition of facts from rulers to ruled, but as an instrument for even more high-octane Government boosting? The answer was simple. If it was once admitted that Ingham's job was to procure for the government the most favourable press coverage possible, and hence to increase its popularity, he could no longer be regarded as objective. If he was not objective, he was not acting in accordance with his duties as a professional civil servant. And if his behaviour was deemed improper, what of the MIO, whose members were instructed by Ingham to 'encourage' their ministers to do this, that or the other? Ingham's alleged neutrality, in other words, was the rock on which the entire edifice rested. Remove it, and the theory of a Government Information Service whose sole function was to dispense objective facts would have come crashing down. It is hard to think of any other public official whose duties were so hedged around with half-truths and evasions. He was there, but he was not there; he managed the news, but he did not manage the news; he was neutral, but he was not neutral... What had happened [his appointment in February 1989] was without precedent. Ingham now had four separate functions. He was the Prime Minister's personal media advisor. He was the non-attributable spokesman for the entire government. He had responsibility for the 'recruitment, training and career development' of 1200 information officers. He co-ordinated an advertising and publicity budget of some £168 million. In any other country he would have been given the proper title: Minister of Information.

A Level Exam-Style Question Section A

Study Source 5 before answering this question.

Assess the value of the source for revealing the role of Bernard Ingham and the relationship between the Thatcher governments and mass media in the 1980s.

Explain your answer, using the source, the information given about its origin and your own knowledge about the historical context. (20 marks)

Tip
You must base your judgements purely on the merits and limitations of the source in the question. Do not waste any time or words on a wish list of sources that might be 'more useful'.

SOURCE
6

Punch cartoon of Bernard Ingham with Margaret Thatcher in the late 1980s.

'*From now on, Bernard, we skip the Opinion Polls and switch to Ladbrokes.*'

ACTIVITY
KNOWLEDGE CHECK

Control and compliance within mass media in the 1980s

1 Summarise the ways in which Thatcher attempted to control the reportage on issues of national security in the 1980s.

2 Explain why Bernard Ingham became a controversial figure in his role as chief press secretary.

The reportage of the Falklands conflict, 1982

The Falkland Islands lie 300 miles off the coast of the southern tip of Argentina, 7,500 miles from Britain. The islands possibly have untapped oil reserves beneath them, but it was the lucrative seal trade and whaling that first brought Europeans to the uninhabited land. The French, Spanish, Argentines and British had all laid claim to the islands before the British established permanent control from 1833. In 1945, the Argentinians began to press their claim to the islands at the UN. The British said that they would only withdraw once the inhabitants of the island had voted for this to happen. As the population were descendants of the original British settlers, this was never likely to happen.

On 2 April 1982, the Falklands conflict began when Argentinian forces occupied the islands. They had invaded upon the orders of General Galtieri, who led the military **junta** in charge of Argentina. He wanted to gain a swift military victory to draw attention away from domestic economic problems and to bolster his own power. While diplomatic negotiations continued with the Argentinians, a British Task Force was dispatched. British ships arrived on 19 April and began to land troops on the islands. On 2 May, Margaret Thatcher, acting on advice from Admiralty experts, ordered the submarine *HMS Conqueror* to attack an Argentinian cruiser called the *General Belgrano*. The *Belgrano* was torpedoed and sunk with the loss of 368 crew members. This divided opinion in Britain: while some approved of Thatcher's action to protect British troops, reports came back that the *Belgrano* was not in the **Total Exclusion Zone (TEZ)** and was sailing away from the islands. Some critics, notably the Labour MP Tam Dalyell, suspected that Mrs Thatcher had ordered the attack to boost her popularity and to stop any possibility of success for a new diplomatic settlement announced by the Peruvians 14 hours earlier. Thatcher insisted that she did not learn of the Peruvian settlement until after the *Belgrano* had been sunk. On 21 May, British troops began to land on the islands, and after some tough fighting they recaptured the airstrip at Goose Green. By mid-June they had recaptured the capital, Port Stanley, and taken almost 10,000 Argentinian prisoners.

KEY TERMS

Junta
A political or military faction that has seized power following a revolution or coup.

Total Exclusion Zone (TEZ)
An area of 200 miles around the Falkland Islands within which, on 30 April 1982, the British declared they would attack any Argentinian vessel.

The Falklands conflict resulted in the deaths of 649 Argentinians and 255 British men and cost the British government almost £3 billion. It led to a surge of pride and patriotism among the British, and contributed to the success of Mrs Thatcher in the 1983 election. However, disputes over the sinking of the *Belgrano*, and the way the media had reported the Falklands conflict, dragged on into the mid-1980s. In particular, scandal erupted in 1984 when Clive Ponting, a civil servant at the Ministry of Defence, leaked two key documents to Tam Dalyell that confirmed that the ship was outside the TEZ and heading away from the Falklands, and that the government had misled a select committee enquiry into the *Belgrano* case. The government had Ponting arrested and charged with breaking the Official Secrets Act 1911. He was found not guilty by the jury because they felt the documents were in the public interest.

Reporting the Falklands conflict

The Falklands conflict was the last major international conflict in which newspapers provided news more quickly than television. There was no satellite coverage that far south, so signals could not be instantaneously beamed to the UK, as was the case during the Gulf War of 1990–91. Instead, tapes had to be sent by boat to Ascension Island in the mid-Atlantic from where the footage could be transmitted to London. This process took around 23 days, by which time radio and print news had already covered the events. The Navy was initially determined not to have any journalists on board the task force. But Bernard Ingham played a decisive role in forcing the Navy to change its mind, and 21 reporters (16 newspaper, three TV, two radio) and two photographers were embedded in the task force. No foreign journalists were permitted, something that may have undermined international sympathy for the British cause. The journalists had no option but to use the navy's ship-to-shore communication to file reports. This allowed their stories to be scrutinised four times before publication a few days later. The government read a daily report of recent events in parliament, but this lacked any detail about numbers or locations of casualties.

In the absence of concrete information, domestic media took to reporting rumours gleaned from Argentinian as well as British sources. For example, the number of casualties on three ships attacked

SOURCE

The front cover of the *Sun*, published on 4 May 1982. This front cover was only published in the early edition; the headline was replaced with 'Did 1200 Argies drown?' in the later edition.

by Argentine planes on 8 June was reported as over 900 before official reports eventually confirmed the number at 49. The BBC began to refer to 'Argentine claims' and 'British claims', something which enraged Thatcher, who saw the corporation as 'not one of us'. At times, the government misled the media to report misinformation. For example, Sir Frank Cooper, under-secretary at the Ministry of Defence, briefed reporters that the Army forces would make smash-and-grab raids around the coast when he knew that a single beachhead strategy was to be deployed. The BBC received huge criticism for a World Service broadcast about Army preparations for an assault on Goose Green, 18 hours before the attack was launched. The criticism was unfair as the BBC only reported information that had emerged from the Ministry of Defence. The Argentinians heard the broadcast but did not act upon it – they possibly assumed it was deliberate misinformation. Newspapers were naturally more partisan, with the left-wing *Mirror* and the *Guardian* against the whole operation, the *Financial Times* against the defence of an 'anachronism', and the right-wing *Telegraph*, *The Times* and, most stridently, the *Sun* in support of the war.

SOURCE

From an interview with *Observer* journalist Patrick Bishop, shortly after the war in 1982. Bishop was one of the 16 newspaper reporters who travelled to the Falklands with the Navy task force.

The situation was that you were a propagandist; that's how it turned out. So there wasn't any need to put pressure on anyone to write gung-ho copy because everyone was doing it without any stimulus from the military. And that's how most of the reporters felt. They were all very patriotic and 'positive' about the whole thing. So the military didn't have to lean on them.

EXTRACT

2

Article by Julian Barnes, 'The worst reported war since the Crimean', published in the *Guardian* on 25 February 2002.

In April 1982 I took over as the *Observer*'s television critic. I anticipated a cosy period of acclimatisation: a new American soap called Dynasty was soon to start, followed by the year's main event, the stirring quasi-warfare of the World Cup in Spain. Instead, at coffee time on the Monday morning of my second week, ITV brought us the real thing live: the departure of a British military force to recapture a piece of colonial territory 8,000 miles away... Little did we guess that these were the last sunny, honest, unspun images we were likely to get for some time; or that the Falklands war would turn out to be the worst-reported war since the Crimean... All the significant news, good or bad, was announced or leaked from London. Reporters in the south Atlantic had the sour experience of hearing 'their' news being broken for them on the World Service. Reports were censored, delayed, occasionally lost... In the age of image, the Falklands war remained image-free for much of its length – no British pictures for 54 of the 74 days the conflict lasted – and image-weak thereafter... when the action on land began, the images were limited and controlled...

The fact that we'd been trying for decades to offload the islands, with the ardent Thatcherite Nicholas Ridley presenting a leaseback solution to the House of Commons only two years previously, was forgotten. The fact that we'd traded with the junta, welcomed its leaders and sold arms to them, but now realised that it was a filthy dictatorship after all, was swallowed without a burp. The fact that there were a mere 1800 islanders, and that their way of life was preserved at the cost of 1000 British casualties and 1800 Argentinian ones did not seem a grossly stupid and expensive way of conducting foreign policy.

EXTRACT

3

From Lyn Gorman and David McLean's *Media and Society into the 21st Century*, published in 2009.

Britain took account of the perceived lessons from Vietnam during the war with Argentina in 1982, the Falklands War. This was Britain's 'first taste of a campaign fought in the full glare of modern media attention.' The remoteness of this war... facilitated media management. Places on Royal Navy taskforce ships were limited, and the government and military leadership decided which organizations should be allowed to report the war at first hand, excluded non-British correspondents, and controlled communications from the war zone. The Falklands war highlighted the conflict between, on the one hand, the perceived public right in any democratic system to be informed and, on the other, government and military needs to withhold information for reasons of operational security. The British government... practised a policy of 'deception, misinformation, disinformation and media manipulation through denial of access, control of communications and politically based censorship'.

A Level Exam-Style Question Section B

To what extent did the government play a decisive role in the reportage of the Falklands War? (20 marks)

Tip
Aim to focus on the particular wording of the question in your answer. Here you might draw attention to the word 'decisive' when making your judgements.

THINKING HISTORICALLY | Evidence (6b)

The strength of argument

Answer the following questions about reportage on the Falklands conflict.

1 Read Source 8.

   a) What is weak about this claim?

   b) What could be added to it to make it stronger?

2 Read Extract 2.

   a) Is this an argument? If yes, what makes it one?

   b) How might this argument be strengthened?

3 Read Extract 3.

   a) How have they expanded their explanation to make the claim stronger?

   b) Can you explain why this is the strongest claim of the three sources?

4 What elements make a historian's claims strong?

Reportage of the miners' strike, 1984–85

Those who sympathised with the miners' cause (see pages 135–7 for a reminder of the events) resented what they saw as media coverage hugely favourable to the government and biased against Scargill and the NUM. One way in which this bias was manifested was the personalisation of events. For example, television news increasingly referred to 'Scargill's pickets', when in reality they were usually organised by local NUM committees. Scargill was certainly a divisive figure on the left and within the mining community (he never received the support of Labour leader Neil Kinnock) he was the target of bitter personal criticism – 'experts' from within the labour movement, such as former communist and trade unionist Jimmy Reid, were used to provide exaggerated claims of the malign influence of 'Scargillism'. Nicholas Jones, the BBC political correspondent who covered the strike, later reflected that the media fed on each other to promote anti-Scargill feelings. Simon Jenkins, who was then political editor of the centre-right magazine *The Economist*, said that the coverage was strongly biased as a result of Fleet Street's distaste for Scargill. The public were only told of his idiocy and not about the support he was receiving so it grew increasingly baffled by his survival. It was an example of the worst kind of propaganda. The *Sun* even attempted to print a photo of Scargill appearing to give a Nazi salute with the front-page headline 'Mine Führer' before the typesetters refused to print it. In response to MP Tam Dalyell's demand for a statement on the actions of MI5 during the strike, the government confirmed that Scargill's phone had been tapped since 1973. It is clear that the government would have been pleased with this character assassination of what they saw as a dangerous enemy.

Further evidence of media bias is found in the disproportionate attention drawn to violence during the strike. It is true that over 10,000 strikers were arrested and there were 20,000 injuries as a result of clashes with police and attacks on 'scabs' (those who crossed picket lines in order to work), but the pickets were not constantly the scene of 'mob fury', as depicted by several mainstream papers. In 1991, the Glasgow University Media Group investigated the effect of media coverage on popular memories of the strike. A leading initial response was that it was violent. In particular it recalled scenes from the infamous Battle of Orgreave. The focus on violence diverted popular attention away from the underlying issues that drove the strike towards a discussion of 'law and order' issues such as the effectiveness of the Employment and Trade Union Acts. A local Yorkshire paper, *Leeds Other Voice*, captured far more positive stories about the strike, such as the provision of soup kitchens by miners' wives, the loading of coal for hospital use and diary-style reports of life on the pickets. Historian Tony Harcup, who worked for the newspaper during the strike, analysed the stories printed and found that 68 percent of the 281 sources used came from people who were usually 'voiceless' in the mainstream media. Film director Ken Loach had programmes perceived to be biased towards the miners pulled from broadcast on Channel 4 and LWT. *Which Side Are You On?*, a film about the songs and writing produced at the pickets, was eventually screened early in 1985, but Loach concluded that 'it is clear that only approved people can make comments about a struggle as decisive as the miners'.

EXTEND YOUR KNOWLEDGE

The Battle of Orgreave, 18 June 1984

Orgreave was the site of a British Steel coke works near Sheffield (coke is a form of coal that is treated for use in steel production). The plan was to blockade the plant and stop coke getting to steelworks such as the huge Ravenscraig steel mill near Motherwell. Without coke, the steel furnaces would grow cool and cause costly damage to the steel production facilities.

Government preparations for the strike included the establishment of the National Reporting Centre. This was a system to co-ordinate large numbers of policemen to respond to strike areas. Since the experience of urban rioting in 1918, many policemen (organised into 'short shield squads') had been trained to use riot gear, shields and truncheons to deal with protests. Around 6,000 policemen from ten counties were assembled to protect lorries coming in and out of the works. As the empty lorries arrived on the morning of 18 June, the pickets swarmed forward in a bid to break the police cordon. The line held, and mounted police and short shield squads were used to drive the pickets back. The pickets retreated to the other side of a steeply banked railway line and threw bricks, bottles and metal at the approaching officers. It took the police two hours to capture a small bridge across the track and scatter the pickets with further charges.

The mounted police and short shield squads were captured on film and in photographs beating pickets with truncheons. ITN footage that evening appeared to show one officer beating an unconscious miner. Fifty-one pickets and 72 policemen were injured. South Yorkshire Police subsequently paid £425,000 compensation and £100,000 in legal costs to 39 injured pickets. No officers were ever charged with misconduct. Following a 2012 BBC documentary into police conduct at Orgreave, the force referred itself to the Police Complaints Commission. No action was taken due to the length of time that had elapsed since the events in question.

SOURCE

9 A photo capturing the moment that picketing miners attempted to push through a police cordon to stop lorries delivering coal to the coking plant at Orgreave, South Yorkshire on 18 June 1984. The Orgreave plant converted coal into coke, which was vital for the steel industry.

It was also felt that the media played an active part in the defeat of the strike. In particular, the 'back-to-work' movement was given a great deal of support. Miners who braved picket lines to work were portrayed as victims of the strike itself rather than of the government actions which forced such a return to work. The *Sun* exaggerated the numbers involved, with a few returning miners turned into a story about a 'flood back to work'. The Nottinghamshire miners were portrayed as patriotic heroes throughout the strike. It is clear that the government did not have to directly control the reportage of the miners' strike in the way it had the Falklands conflict. The majority of the British press, reflecting the majority of public opinion as well as the political sympathies of their owners, approved of the government's stand against the NUM. The more sympathetic local reportage was never a cause of concern for Thatcher or her government.

ACTIVITY
KNOWLEDGE CHECK

Reportage of the Falklands conflict of 1982 and the 1984–85 miners' strike

1 Explain how the Thatcher government sought to control the reportage of the Falklands conflict.

2 Explain why the Thatcher government had to take action to control the reportage of the Falklands conflict but not the miners' strike.

EXTRACT

From Simon Jenkins' book *Thatcher & Sons – a Revolution in Three Acts*, published in 2006. Jenkins is a journalist who mainly writes for the left-of-centre daily newspaper, the *Guardian*.

Attention thus fastened on a group of services whose leadership was at some remove from the heart of government, notably the health service, housing, schools and universities, urban renewal and local government. In most democracies these activities were either constitutionally protected or were regional or municipal in responsibility... To Thatcher these were just the services most afflicted by socialism, since they were in the grip of such incorrigibly socialist institutions as elected local councils and trade unions. They had to be purged by being brought within the penumbra [shadow] of her office. Aspects of their delivery might be subject to private-sector discipline but never with loss of control... Private sector disciplines were a success in local government... But she brought to public service ceaseless upheaval, blood-letting and top-down reorganisation. This was informed not by public inquiry or consensus but by consultancy out of ideology. The outcome was always contentious. Almost all the public services... never settled down under later prime ministers. They have remained at the top of the league table of public dissatisfaction ever since, demanding ever more money with no diminution of central control.

EXTRACT

From Shirley Letwin's book *The Anatomy of Thatcherism*, published in 1993. Letwin had been taught by a leading free-market thinker at the University of Chicago and worked for a Conservative think tank.

In taking such 'tough' measures on trade unions, the Thatcher Government was answering a widespread and deeply felt public demand to be liberated from a tyranny which, apart from its effects on employees, had made it impossible for Britons to know from one day to the next what stoppage would produce chaos in their daily lives... The legislation was designed to remove obstacles to the thriving of Britain and to the freedom needed by individuals to be independent, efficient and honest workmen... In 1979, socialism, in the sense of dependency of the individual upon the state in a series of vital areas including industry, education, health and housing, was regarded by Britons as 'here to stay'... When Mrs Thatcher proclaimed the need to drive back the tide of socialism, to let freedom of choice and the vigorous virtues flourish, in short to change the course of British history, few if any commentators believed she could do it... Next to the trade unions, Thatcherism's greatest bugbear has been 'local government'. The picture of the Thatcherite relationship to local councils is usually painted in vivid colours: Mrs Thatcher is portrayed as a 'centralist' dictator mounting an all-out attack on ancient bastions of local autonomy and liberty... The reason why the usual picture of the relation between the Thatcher Government and local government poses such problems is that it is a radically false picture. Local government was not an ancient bastion of local autonomy and liberty; and the Thatcher Government's attack on it was the very opposite of an attempt to centralize. Indeed, once the history of British local authorities themselves and of the Thatcherite war on them is properly understood, it becomes apparent that – whether sensibly or utterly misguidedly – the motives for the policies were precisely those that one would expect if one identified Thatcherism with the promotion of the vigorous virtues and the paradigm shift.

THINKING HISTORICALLY Evidence (6c)

Comparing and evaluating historians' arguments

Read the Extracts 4 and 5 and then answer the following questions.

1　Compare the two accounts above and identify factual statements or claims that they both agree upon. Make a list of these points.

2　Look carefully at how the historians use language. Do they both use equally cautious language in making their claims or is one more confident and assertive than the other? Is one (or both) of the historians over-claiming?

3　Do both historians appear to have made equally effective use of evidence?

4　Are both of the historical accounts equally credible or are there reasons to prefer one account more than another?

ACTIVITY
SUMMARY

The Thatcher governments and the media, 1979–90

1　Imagine that you are writing a school-style report on the Thatcher governments of 1979–90. You will award a grade with a letter from A down to E for 'achievement', and a number from 1 (highest) down to 5 (lowest) for 'effort'.

2　You should judge achievement based on how far Thatcher would have been pleased with the changes that took place in mass media during her time as prime minister. Judge effort based on the time and energy that Thatcher's governments spent trying to change mass media.

3　Treat the following areas as separate 'subjects' for which you must award a grade (for example, C3 or D1):

- television

- radio, cinema

- the press.

4　As with most school reports, you must justify your grade with an explanatory paragraph.

　WIDER READING

Brown, M. *A Licence to be Different: The Story of Channel 4*, BFI (2007)

Evans, E.J. *Thatcher and Thatcherism*, Routledge (2004)

Harris, R. *Good and Faithful Servant: the Unauthorized Biography of Berhard Ingham*, Faber & Faber (1990)

Harris, R. *Gotcha! The Media, the Government and the Falklands Crisis*, Faber & Faber (1983)

Stewart, G. *Bang! A History of Britain in the 1980s*, Atlantic Books (2013)

The Margaret Thatcher Foundation – www.margaretthatcher.org

3.7

The Labour government versus the media: the problem of the Iraq dossiers, 2002–04

KEY QUESTIONS

- What was the impact of the initial challenges to the accuracy of the dossiers?
- In what ways and to what extent did Dr David Kelly's death affect relations between the government and the BBC?
- What were the key implications of the Hutton Inquiry for the relationship between mass media and the government?

KEY TERMS

Whistle-blower
A person who comes forward with information about corruption or malpractice within an organisation. The information, usually obtained through first-hand experience, would otherwise remain hidden from people inside or outside the organisation who might be able to help remedy the abuses.

Foreign affairs select committee
A body appointed by the House of Commons to investigate the running and operation of the Foreign and Commonwealth Office and other bodies associated with the Foreign Office.

INTRODUCTION

The events and issues of this chapter are so complex and controversial that they have been the subject of four separate government-appointed inquiries and a colossal amount of media reportage and speculation. Before investigating the controversies, it is worth studying the timeline of events. The central event is the Iraq War of 2003; the key controversy surrounds the government's justification for launching the war in March 2003. The government experienced a great deal of press and popular criticism in the run-up to the war, not least for the release of its February 2003 'dodgy' dossier (see the Timeline). However, the dispute between the BBC and the government concerned the September 2002 dossier. Until 29 May 2003, this government document had not been widely seen as 'dodgy'. However, in a series of broadcasts that morning, BBC correspondent Andrew Gilligan alleged that, during the week prior to its publication, the government had 'sexed up' a draft dossier approved by British intelligence. Although he refused to name his source, the Ministry of Defence confirmed to journalists on 9 July that Dr David Kelly, a renowned biological weapons inspector who had helped to prepare information for the draft dossier, had been the **whistle-blower**.

By 'sexed up' Gilligan, paraphrasing Dr Kelly, meant that the government had selectively edited the intelligence in the draft report before publishing the final dossier to lead parliament and the British public to believe that Iraq posed a greater, more immediate and more certain threat than the intelligence reports supported. The way Gilligan phrased his first report that morning allowed the government to assert that the BBC had broadcast an accusation that the prime minister had *lied* to parliament, a very serious charge. The broadcast and the accusation prompted a **foreign affairs select committee** investigation into the decision to go to war. Alastair Campbell, director of communications and strategy, used his appearance before the committee to strongly attack the BBC. Sections of the press hostile to the war backed the BBC; sections that regularly attacked the BBC sided with the government's outrage at the accusation.

1990–91 – Gulf War: US- and UK-led coalition invades Iraq after Hussein invades Kuwait. Iraq is defeated. UN imposes economic sanctions

1998 – October: US President Bill Clinton secures Iraqi Liberation Act; it makes removal of Hussein's regime official US policy
December: Operation Desert Fox. US and UK airstrikes to 'degrade' Iraq's capability to produce WMDs

1999 – December: UNMOVIC replaces UNSCOM

1990–91	1991–99	1998	1999	2000	2001

1991–99 – UNSCOM tasked to ensure that Hussein regime complies with destruction of CBWs and does not develop nuclear weapons

2001 – 11 September: Al Qaeda attack on USA kills nearly 3,000 people.
20 September: Bush declares 'War on Terror' through pre-emptive action against states harbouring/supporting terrorist groups ('the Bush Doctrine')

In the midst of this tension, Dr Kelly was also summoned to appear twice before the committee. He admitted to having met Gilligan and having spoken to another BBC journalist as well, but, based on what Gilligan had asserted in his report, felt that he could not be the only source for his story. Two days later, on 17 July 2003, Dr Kelly was found dead in the woods near Gilligan's home in Oxfordshire. Clearly there was a connection between his role in the 'sexed up' dossier story, the enquiry into the decision to go to war and his untimely death. A coroner recorded a verdict of suicide, but such was the strength of public mistrust that suspicions of murder emerged almost immediately. The government appointed judge Lord Hutton to investigate the circumstances surrounding the death of Dr Kelly. His January 2004 report heavily criticised the BBC for its part in the 'sexed up' story, while the government was acquitted on all counts. Far from silencing the row, critics of the inquiry immediately labelled it a **whitewash** and called for a more effective inquiry. It is largely due to the deficiencies of the Hutton Report that the Chilcot Inquiry into British involvement in the Iraq War was convened in November 2009.

KEY TERM

Whitewash

This is another term for a cover-up, usually applied to official reports that gloss over details or only investigate the issues in a superficial manner. The term comes from a cheap white paint that can quickly hide the dirt and imperfections on the surface it is applied to.

WHAT WAS THE IMPACT OF THE INITIAL CHALLENGES TO THE ACCURACY OF THE DOSSIERS?

On 3 February 2003, a second dossier was released by the government to help the public understand what it saw as the threat posed by Iraq under Saddam Hussein. The dossier, *Iraq: Its Infrastructure of Concealment, Deception and Intimidation*, had three sections:

- 'How Iraq's security organisations operate to conceal Weapons of Mass Destruction from UN inspectors'

- 'Up-to-date details of Iraq's network of intelligence and security, whose job it is to keep Saddam and his regime in power, and to prevent the international community from disarming Iraq'

- 'The effects of the security apparatus on the ordinary people of Iraq'.

Reportage in the media

The dossier claimed to have drawn upon 'a number of sources, including intelligence material', yet three days later Channel 4 News broadcast a report that comprehensively exposed how dodgy the report was.

2002 – 24 September: The September dossier sets out government's case for necessity for war if Iraq does not comply with UNMOVIC

8 November: UN Security Council Resolution 1441 states 'serious consequences' if Iraq fails to comply with UNMOVIC. Bush and Blair are isolated when they say no further resolution is needed for war

2004 – 28 January: Hutton Report published

February–July: Butler Review investigates intelligence on WMDs

2002	2003	2004

2003 – 27 January: UNMOVIC chairman Hans Blix tells UN Iraq is complying with weapons inspections and no WMDs found

19 March–1 May: Iraq War. US and UK armed forces overthrow Saddam Hussein but find no WMDs

29 May: Andrew Gilligan asserts on BBC radio that British government 'sexed up' September 2002 dossier. Government immediately issues denial

30 June: Dr David Kelly tells MOD he was Gilligan's source; MOD confirms this to press on 9 July

17 July: Dr Kelly found dead two days after appearing before the foreign affairs select committee

1 August: Hutton Inquiry launched

SOURCE 1

A transcript of the report broadcast on Channel 4 News on 6 February 2003.

Jon Snow (news anchor): The government's carefully coordinated propaganda offensive took an embarrassing hit tonight after Downing Street was accused of plagiarism. The target is an intelligence dossier released on Monday and heralded by none other than US Secretary of State Colin Powell at the United Nations yesterday. Channel 4 News has learned that the bulk of this 19-page document was copied from three different articles, one written by a graduate student.

Julian Rush (defence specialist): On Monday... Downing Street published its latest paper on Iraq. It gives the impression of being an up-to-the-minute, intelligence-based analysis and Mr Powell was fulsome in his praise: 'I would call my colleagues' attention to the fine paper that the United Kingdom distributed yesterday which describes in exquisite detail Iraqi deception activities'. Published on the Number 10 website... it outlines the structure of Saddam's intelligence organisations; but it made familiar reading to one Cambridge academic. [Glen Rangwala, lecturer on Politics and International Studies at Cambridge University, then discusses examples of plagiarism (see below).] Academics take plagiarism seriously; it's intellectual theft. Downing Street didn't ask for permission to reproduce the work, which is not current but actually an historical analysis of the occupation of Kuwait before the last Gulf War. [Rangwala explains how the information is 12 years old.] In several places Downing Street edits the original to make more sinister reading... editing to make Saddam's apparatus look more terrifying, raising questions about the way Number 10 is spinning the justification for war.

Rangwala is an expert on politics in the Middle East and noticed the overwhelming similarity between the central ten pages of the dossier and 'Iraq's Security and Intelligence Network: A Guide and Analysis', a paper published in September 2002 by Ibrahim Al-Marashi, a postgraduate student at the Monteray Institute of International Studies in California. Rangwala highlighted several examples of direct cut and paste from the paper into the dossier, the most notorious being 'Saddam appointed, Sabir 'Abd al-'Aziz al-Duri as head' (note the incorrect use of the comma after 'appointed'). A quick internet search revealed that the majority of the rest of the dossier had also been plagiarised from two articles in *Jane's Intelligence Review*: 'Can the Iraqi Secret Service Save Saddam' by Ken Gause and 'Inside Iraq's Security Apparatus' by Sean Boyne.

In addition to plagiarism, Rangwala identified a number of instances of the original information being 'sexed up' before its use in the dossier:

- 'aiding opposition groups in hostile regimes' became 'supporting terrorist organisations in hostile regimes' in the dossier

- the dossier omitted the last three words from an original description of part of Saddam's troops as 'some 10,000–15,000 bullies and country bumpkins'

- Boyne estimated the number of men in this section of Saddam's force at 18,000–40,000, Gause at 10,000–40,000, while the dossier, on the basis of no intelligence whatsoever, put the estimate at 30,000–40,000.

As Rangwala noted, the inclusion of the phrase 'country bumpkins' would certainly have undermined the serious tone

that the government hoped to convey. In the same article, he also expressed alarm at the way the government presented the information as being based on up-to-date intelligence.

SOURCE 2

From Glen Rangwala's article 'Intelligence? The British Dossier on Iraq's Security Infrastructure', posted on the Campaign Against Sanctions on Iraq website on 5 February 2003.

Apart from the obvious criticism that the British government has plagiarised texts without acknowledgement, passing them off as the work of its intelligence services, there are two further serious problems. Firstly, it indicates that the UK at least really does not have any independent sources of information on Iraq's internal politics – they just draw upon publicly available data. Thus any further claims to information based on 'intelligence data' must be treated with even more scepticism.

Secondly, the information presented as being an accurate statement of the current state of Iraq's security organisations may not be anything of the sort. Marashi – the real and unwitting author of much of the document – has as his primary source the documents captured in 1991 for the Iraq Research and Documentation Project. His own focus is the activities of Iraq's intelligence agencies in Kuwait, August 1990–January 1991 – this is the subject of his thesis. As a result, the information presented as relevant to how Iraqi agencies are currently engaged with UNMOVIC is 12 years old.

Julian Rush's report on Channel 4 News (see Source 1) set out Rangwala's criticisms with great clarity. Some journalists picked up on the news story the following day, but by no means all of the national press.

Given that the plagiarised articles were found so easily with a quick internet search, the key question is why the government was prepared to release such a document. Some reasons relate to the broad background to the build up to war in Iraq, others go to the heart of the relationship between the Labour government and the media.

The impact of the September 11 attacks

There would have been little prospect of an invasion of Iraq in 2003, and therefore no need to justify the war with a dossier, had the World Trade Center not been destroyed, with the loss of almost 3,000 lives, by Al-Qaeda terrorists on 11 September 2001 ('9/11'). Al-Qaeda had been formed in 1988 by a Saudi Arabian, Osama bin Laden, and had been largely based in Afghanistan. US intelligence failed to establish any connection between Al-Qaeda and Iraq, yet the two were deliberately linked in the mind of the American public by President Bush. On 20 September, he declared a 'war on terror' which would use pre-emptive action against states that harboured or supported terrorist groups. Bush's logic was informed by a think tank to which he and his closest advisers had given public endorsement from its launch in 1997: Project for the New American Century (PNAC). PNAC sought to promote democracy throughout the world and argued that the USA, as the sole superpower, had a duty to act against unstable dictatorships. In its view, such regimes automatically sought validation through attacks on neighbouring countries. Between 1997 and 2001, PNAC urged President Bill Clinton to approve the removal of Saddam Hussein. This was due to his lack of co-operation with the United

Nations Special Commission (UNSCOM – an inspection team that was checking whether Iraq was following UN orders to destroy its chemical and biological weapons), his threat to oil reserves in the Gulf region and to stability in the Middle East more generally. From January 2001, these PNAC views remained central to Bush as president. He was determined to remove Saddam even before 9/11, but the attacks, in the context of a 'war on terror', provided a justification for invasion of Iraq.

The role of Prime Minister Tony Blair

There would also have been no dossiers had Prime Minister Tony Blair not requested them to be drawn up. He agreed with Bush's view that it was the duty of the civilised world to deal with 'rogue states' for the good of mankind. The speech shown in Source 3 was given against the backdrop of Blair's first successful international intervention. Kosovo is an ethnic Albanian region that was struggling for independence from a Serbian-dominated Yugoslavia in 1999. Britain played a leading role in **NATO** airstrikes against Yugoslav forces and in subsequent ground troop deployment in Kosovo. Despite not being cleared by the UN, NATO intervention was widely praised for averting a repeat of earlier episodes of **ethnic cleansing** in that region.

KEY TERMS

NATO
The North Atlantic Treaty Organization was formed in 1949 to promote the collective security of its members – an attack on one member would be regarded as an attack on all. It originally had 12 members, including the USA, Canada and the UK. Membership expanded chiefly through the admission of central and eastern European countries. By 2003 there were 19 members, and there were 28 members as of 2016.

Ethnic cleansing
The deliberate effort to drive out an ethnic group from a particular area, to ensure that only people from the dominant ethnic group remain resident there.

Blair pressed for further armed intervention in Sierra Leone (2000) and Afghanistan (2001). As he put it in his 2010 autobiography *Tony Blair: A Journey*, British intervention in Kosovo did not weaken his resolve to take action where he felt a solution was required and where he felt a moral case for action could be made. The apparent success of such intervention, despite a range of opposition, together with the logic set out in Blair's 1999 Chicago speech (Source 3), are highly significant when attempting to understand why Blair was so resolute in his desire for regime change in Iraq. The dossier would not have existed had Blair not adopted this interventionist stance on foreign affairs. Although Blair was determined to stand shoulder to shoulder with the USA, he was also keen that UK intervention in Iraq would not be perceived as him acting as 'Bush's poodle'. The dossier was meant to establish the justification for invasion independent of the US position.

The findings of UNMOVIC and Bush and Blair's plans for war
The timing of the dodgy dossier was determined by the ongoing work in Iraq of the UN Monitoring, Verification and Inspection

SOURCE

3   From 'Doctrine of the International Community', a speech made by Tony Blair in Chicago on 24 April 1999. The speech was made just before Blair attended a NATO summit in Washington.

Many of our problems have been caused by two dangerous and ruthless men – Saddam Hussein and Slobodan Milosevic. Both have been prepared to wage vicious campaigns against sections of their own community. As a result of these destructive policies both have brought calamity on their own peoples. Instead of enjoying its oil wealth Iraq has been reduced to poverty, with political life stultified through fear...

Now our actions are guided by a more subtle blend of mutual self-interest and moral purpose in defending the values we cherish. In the end, values and interests merge. If we can establish and spread the values of liberty, the rule of law, human rights and an open society then that is in our national interests too. The spread of our values makes us safer. Looking around the world there are many regimes that are undemocratic and engaged in barbarous acts. If we wanted to right every wrong that we see in the modern world then we would do little else than intervene in the affairs of other countries. We would not be able to cope.

So how do we decide when and whether to intervene? I think we need to bear in mind five major considerations. First, are we sure of our case? War is an imperfect instrument for righting humanitarian distress; but armed force is sometimes the only means of dealing with dictators. Second, have we exhausted all diplomatic options? We should always give peace every chance, as we have in the case of Kosovo. Third, on the basis of a practical assessment of the situation, are there military operations we can sensibly and prudently undertake? Fourth, are we prepared for the long term? In the past we talked too much of exit strategies. But having made a commitment we cannot simply walk away once the fight is over; better to stay with moderate numbers of troops than return for repeat performances with large numbers. And finally, do we have national interests involved?

I am not suggesting that these are absolute tests. But they are the kind of issues we need to think about in deciding in the future when and whether we will intervene. Any new rules however will only work if we have reformed international institutions with which to apply them. If we want a world ruled by law and by international co-operation then we have to support the UN as its central pillar. But we need to find a new way to make the UN and its Security Council work if we are not to return to the deadlock that undermined the effectiveness of the Security Council during the Cold War.

Commission (UNMOVIC). Its chairman Hans Blix made a report to the UN on 27 January 2003 in which he stated that Iraq was complying fully with the weapons inspection team but that no weapons of mass destruction (WMDs) or evidence of current production of chemical and biological weapons (CBWs) had been found. Between November 2002 and February 2003, 550 inspections had been made at 350 different sites. Blix reported that the inspection team had virtually no problems accessing the sites despite the lack of prior warning given to Iraqi authorities. It is clear that he felt Iraq was fulfilling UN Security Council Resolution 1441 (see below) and that Saddam posed no conceivable threat to the UK, let alone his neighbours. However, the whole thrust of the dodgy dossier was to discredit the work of UNMOVIC by drawing attention to how effective the Iraqi regime was at deceiving and misleading the inspectors.

KEY TERM

Unilateral
A country takes action unilaterally if it acts without reference to, or the agreement of, any other country. It is more usual for countries to act in a multilateral fashion; that is, with the co-operation and agreement of other countries.

Bush and Blair believed that Saddam had only agreed to co-operate with UNMOVIC because of the steady build up of US and British armed forces in the region. Bush had initiated plans for an invasion of Iraq soon after 9/11 and was determined to push through with this strategy, **unilaterally** if necessary. Blair tried to persuade Bush to at least go through the motions of using UN diplomacy to pursue regime change and, if armed force must be used, to build a 'coalition of the willing' rather than act in isolation.

In November 2002, the USA and the UK secured UN Resolution 1441, which stated that Iraq would face 'serious consequences' if it failed to co-operate with UNMOVIC. The French and Russians were clear at that time that this did not include the use of military force, as it did not use the usual UN wording for such permission: to force compliance 'by any means'. Blair pursued a 'second resolution' that would unequivocally allow the use of force. The British dossier was designed to strengthen US Secretary of State Colin Powell's petition for such a resolution at the UN on 5 February 2003. At the same time, Blair withheld from his own Cabinet the original view of Lord Goldsmith, the Attorney General, that an invasion without a second resolution would be illegal. Therefore the dodgy dossier was meant to bolster the case for the legality of the forthcoming invasion of Iraq.

Popular opposition to the plans for war

The dossier was also published against a huge amount of popular anger and opposition to war in Iraq. It was released to the press in an attempt to dampen such feelings. On 15 February 2003, around a million people marched in London to protest against the war (it is estimated that between six and ten million marched in 800 cities worldwide that day). The Labour government knew about preparations for the march and had been concerned about the depth of public opposition for some time. The February dossier was part of an ongoing project to make the war more palatable to the public. On 19 July 2002, one of Blair's closest advisers and Downing Street chief of staff, Jonathan Powell, wrote him a memo stating that 'We need to make the case. We need a plan and a timetable for releasing papers we have on human rights abuses, WMDs, etc. We need to have the sort of Rolls Royce information campaign we had at the end of Afghanistan before we start in Iraq.' Clearly the more of a threat Iraq was perceived to be to Britain, the fewer people would oppose the war. However, the media campaign had limited impact: two polls on 12 and 18 February put public support for landing British troops in Iraq at just 24 percent. It was only after British troops had started fighting that the public got more behind the war: a poll in April put public support at 54 percent.

SOURCE

4 From an article in the *Sunday Telegraph* entitled 'One million march against war', published on 16 February 2003.

Britain witnessed its largest demonstration yesterday when an estimated one million protesters took to the streets of London to oppose the looming war against Iraq. The centre of the capital was paralysed by noisy but peaceful people from many political backgrounds. Former members of the Armed Forces, clergymen and young children all joined the march to Hyde Park... Large peace protests were also held all over the country and around the world. Up to 60,000 protesters gathered in Glasgow and up to 90,000 in Dublin... Some organisers from the Stop the War Coalition claimed that two million people had taken part in the protest. Officially, the police said that there were at least 750,000 demonstrators, but this did not include those who had gone direct to Hyde Park.

Outside the Ministry of Defence in Whitehall, a group of Gulf war veterans joined the march. Brian Matthews, 40, a former sergeant in the Parachute Regiment, said he believed the last Gulf war had been justified because Saddam had invaded Kuwait.

This time, however, he said he could see no reason for declaring war other than a quest for oil. 'We chose not to finish the job last time when we had a chance. This time we are going in there to save the world economy, not the people of Iraq,' he said. Jonathan Callow, 57, a businessman from Chelsea, west London, said he... decided to demonstrate against Mr Blair's plans for a war because of his belief that President Bush was misguided and dangerous: 'We are being rushed into a war. The British people are being dictated to by a small minority that support Bush in middle America. We are our own people and should choose for ourselves.'

Mary Chillingford, 48, a housewife from Guildford, Surrey, said that she was demonstrating because she did not believe this was a just enough war for her son, a serving soldier, to die in. 'Saddam is not threatening us. The Government should spend the money on British jobs, hospitals and the rural economy,' she said.

Some marchers were chanting 'Tony Blair: murderer. George Bush: murderer.' Others shouted, 'One, two, three, four, we don't want your bloody war.'

SOURCE

The anti-war march in London, on 15 February 2003. The police estimated a crowd of 750,000; the march organisers claimed that three million people marched. It was almost certainly the largest popular demonstration in British history.

The role of Alastair Campbell and the CIC

The content and wording of the dodgy dossier was ultimately the responsibility of Alastair Campbell. At the foreign affairs select committee in June 2003 he described the dossier as his idea. As director of communications and strategy and chairman of the Iraqi Communications Group, Campbell was present at almost every key meeting about Iraq, both official and informal, and had a central role in the way the mass media was briefed about the government's position. It was Campbell who commissioned the Coalition Information Centre (CIC) to write the dossier. There were a number of other groups and individuals that could have been used to write the dossier, but the CIC was chosen because it was directly answerable to Campbell. It was, in essence, a propaganda unit to undermine anti-American and anti-British stories and put a positive gloss on events in an attempt to control media coverage of the Afghanistan War and later the Iraq War. The information that the CIC released had a poor reputation among journalists who had covered the Afghanistan War. With the exception of Blair, no one was consulted about the compilation or release of the dossier, something which was criticised by the Ninth Report of the foreign affairs select committee. The dodgy dossier is evidence of Campbell's desire to control the story, or – as his critics would more pointedly put it – 'create the truth' about Iraq in Britain.

EXTEND YOUR KNOWLEDGE

The Iraq War of 2003 and the media
The Iraq War was officially fought from 19 March to 1 June 2003. US and British troops made up the vast bulk of the 'coalition of the willing' who undertook the invasion. Although 'mission accomplished' was declared after only seven weeks, widespread violence plagued Iraq for the next decade and the last British troops did not leave until May 2011. During that time 179 British service personnel were killed; estimates of the number of Iraqi deaths vary considerably, but the most respected commentators give figures of around 500,000. The violence and instability in Iraq has been of critical importance to the rise of the Islamic State of Iraq and the Levant, better known in Britain as ISIS.

Most people relied on either the BBC or ITN News for up-to-date information about the war. Audiences for the evening news averaged between five and six million, rising as high as eight million during coverage of key events. The key difference between coverage of the Iraq War and the Gulf War in 1990–91 was the rise of 24-hour news channels: 40 percent of UK households could receive at least three such channels. The most popular of these was Sky News, with an average audience of 250,000 but as high as 1.23 million during the initial bombardment of Iraq. Forty-six percent of households had access to the internet during the war, and numbers accessing the BBC News website increased by 40 percent. The war also saw the increased popularity of alternative sources of news such as www.instapundit.com and www.iraqbodycount.net. The war saw an initial increase in newspaper circulation figures, but this was only sustained by the *Independent*, the *Guardian* and the *Financial Times*. Tabloid readers grew bored of war coverage after the initial bombardment, with daily sales of the *Daily Mail* and the *Mirror* falling by around 40,000.

The impact of the Channel 4 investigation into the accuracy of the dossiers

The revelations of the Channel 4 News investigation cannot be said to have influenced the overall tone of newspaper reporting in the build up to war. Those who supported the need for war (the *Express, Daily Mail, Sun, Daily Telegraph, The Times* and *Star*, with a combined circulation of 9.4 million) continued to offer general support for the war, despite some severe attacks on Campbell himself. They tended to publish stories that justified the war in terms of the threat posed by Saddam Hussein and defended the armed intervention, even when WMDs were not immediately found. Only the *Mirror, Guardian, Observer* and *Independent* (combined circulation 2.7 million) opposed the war. They published stories that questioned the legality of the war and the intelligence that was used by Britain and the USA to make the case for war. The *Guardian* and *Observer* made no reference to the online posting of the February dossier but did publish an article that summarised Rangwala's criticisms. The *Sun, The Times* and the *Daily Mail*, more sympathetic to the need for war, contained nothing about the February dossier or Rangwala's criticisms between 3 and 7 February. The *Mail* and *The Times* reported on US threats to Saddam Hussein and Tony Blair's acknowledgement of public opposition to war in Iraq. They focused far more attention on US Secretary of State Colin Powell's speech in favour of war at the United Nations on 5 February. It was no secret that Rupert Murdoch, owner of the *Sun* and *The Times,* was a keen supporter of Tony Blair and New Labour. This might help to explain the absence of contemporary reporting on the February dossier in his newspapers.

The Channel 4 News investigation did, however, lead to an investigation by the foreign affairs select committee. Although the committee generally conducts interviews in public, this is optional; several examinations that provided evidence for the Ninth Report were conducted in private. The Committee can invite people to give evidence but does not have the authority to summon them. Alastair Campbell, like Tony Blair, initially refused to accept the invitation before changing his mind. During his appearance before the committee, Campbell apologised for not acknowledging all of the sources of information prior to the publication of the dossier, and admitted that it would have been better had the **joint intelligence committee** been able to scrutinise the document prior to its release. He did not apologise for in any way attempting to mislead anyone about the nature of the 'intelligence' in the dossier.

In its Ninth Report findings, the committee concluded that 'the effect of the February dossier was almost wholly counterproductive. By producing such a document the government undermined the credibility of its case for war and of the other documents which were part of it'. The foreign affairs select committee also concluded that 'the degree of autonomy given to the Iraqi Communications Group chaired by Alastair Campbell and the Coalition Information Centre which reported to him… were contributory factors to the affair of the "dodgy dossier".'

The Ninth Report was not published until 7 July 2003, the day before it emerged that Dr Kelly was Gilligan's source and ten days before Dr Kelly's death. The impact of the report in the press was rather lost in speculation about the source of the 'sexed up' dossier story. Newspapers did report information given at public hearings throughout the Committee hearing, with many headlines centring on Campbell's role in the creation of both the September 2002 and February 2003 dossiers.

ACTIVITY
KNOWLEDGE CHECK

The dodgy dossier

1 Summarise the information released to the press in the February dossier.

2 Summarise the reasons why the Channel 4 investigation had such an impact on the popular response to the February dossier.

3 How useful is Source 3 in helping to understand why the February dossier came to be written and released to the press? Explain your answer.

4 How useful is Source 4 in understanding how the popular press covered the impact of the February dossier?

IN WHAT WAYS AND TO WHAT EXTENT DID DR DAVID KELLY'S DEATH AFFECT RELATIONS BETWEEN THE GOVERNMENT AND THE BBC?

The reaction of the media to the New Labour government

The struggle for the daily news agenda

Relations had been tense between the BBC and the Labour government even before the run-up to the Iraq War. Kevin Marsh, editor of the flagship Radio 4 morning news programme *Today* (2001–03) argues that the tension was ultimately due to two competing attempts to set the daily British news agenda: that of the *Today* programme and that of Alastair Campbell. Like Bernard Ingham, Campbell's chief advantages in this contest were access to the full, undisclosed situation, and the use of the Lobby (see page 145) to control the release of non-attributable information to the press. Campbell, a **special adviser**, gained a further advantage in the summer of 1997 when an **Order in Council** was used to give him the power to 'co-ordinate' the work of the Government Information Service (GIS). The GIS press officers were civil servants attached to government ministries whose job was to liaise between that branch of government and the media. Campbell saw the GIS as unprofessional and wanted to ensure that all press officers were 'on message' with a planned communications strategy. There were to be no contradictory messages, and no clashes with the release of important government information. In effect, as Marsh (2012) puts it, 'Campbell acquired a power that no unelected, unaccountable, part-political appointee should ever have in a democracy. The power to give orders to impartial, apolitical civil servants and to ministers… Campbell was given the authority to command civil servants to create and tell the New Labour story.'

This attempt to control the news agenda became known as 'spin'. Campbell along with minister without portfolio Peter Mandelson were labelled 'spin doctors'.

KEY TERM

Joint intelligence committee (JIC)
The JIC advises the prime minister and the Cabinet on intelligence and sets the priorities for the three UK intelligence services: the Secret Intelligence Service (MI6), the Security Service (MI5) and Government Communications Headquarters (GCHQ). It also sets the priorities for Defence Intelligence, part of the Ministry of Defence. The JIC is made up of the heads of these intelligence groups, together with representatives from the Ministry of Defence and the Foreign Office.

A Level Exam-Style Question Section B

To what extent was Alastair Campbell to blame for the dodgy content of the February 2003 dossier on Iraq? (20 marks)

Tip
Examiners will expect you to focus on the stated factor in your first main paragraph and to dedicate around a third of your essay to assessing its significance. You must offer comparative judgements with other factors to access the highest levels in the mark scheme.

KEY TERMS

Special adviser
Unlike a permanent civil servant, this 'temporary' civil servant is a political appointee who owes their allegiance to the governing party. They are unelected and usually have a background in the area of expertise they draw upon to advise ministers.

Order in Council
This is a rule passed by the Privy Council (in effect the Cabinet) backed by the accepted executive powers of the queen. The Civil Service (Amendment) Order in Council allowed the prime minister to give management authority over civil servants to as many as three political (special) advisers.

- In an interview with the *Guardian* in August 1997, Peter Mandelson admitted to managing what news was leaked to the press in an attempt to show government policies in the best possible light.

- Another example of spin was an email sent by Jo Moore to the press officer of the Department of Transport at 9.55 a.m. on 11 September 2001: 'It's now a very good day to get out anything we want to bury. Councillors' expenses?' This was after two aeroplanes had struck the World Trade Center but before either tower had collapsed.

A clear example of the use of spin was the leak of two stories on 2 August 1997 – one about a last-minute reprieve for the royal yacht *Britannia*, which had been earmarked for scrapping, the other about an MI6 investigation into the last governor of Hong Kong, Chris Patten – both of which proved to be false a few days later. The stories dominated the weekend papers, and the MI6 investigation became the focus of the BBC news coverage, which meant that news of foreign secretary Robin Cook's affair with his secretary made little impact.

The previous Conservative government has suffered from persistent press stories about 'sleaze' and New Labour had promised an end to such disreputable behaviour. The BBC news programme *The World At One* broadcast a story about how the government had deliberately leaked non-stories to keep sleaze off the news agenda, something that greatly irritated Mandelson and Campbell. The government response to any BBC story that was not in line with the Party version of events was to issue demands for 'corrections' and 'rebuttals'. Every complaint had to be dealt with, even when it was clear that the BBC's information was watertight. Campbell often accused the BBC of having Conservative sympathies when such stories were broadcast.

The role of Andrew Gilligan

Andrew Gilligan began his career in journalism at Cambridge University, where he rose to become editor of *Varsity*, the student newspaper. He had a brief stint at a local newspaper before moving to the *Sunday Telegraph*, where he began work as a defence correspondent. When the Iraq War broke out, he had held the same role on the *Today* programme for almost four years. In that time he had proven himself to be a determined and relentless investigative journalist. The row between the BBC and the government might not have escalated to the extent it did had he not been both tenacious and unorthodox. It was Gilligan who broke the story about the 'sexed up' September 2002 dossier, on 29 May 2003. Although the story was based on a single source, *Today* editor Kevin Marsh felt that the details of the story and the profile of the source were of sufficient quality to allow the story to be broadcast. Gilligan submitted a script that was approved the day before going to air. Unfortunately for Gilligan and the BBC, he did not stick accurately to his script in the initial 'two-way' (a brief introduction to a news item that follows later in the show) at 6.07 a.m. (You can find the transcript of the two-way or original script in the Hutton Inquiry report; see Wider reading on page 173.)

EXTRACT

1 From Kevin Marsh's book *Stumbling Over Truth: the Inside Story of the 'Sexed Up' Dossier, Hutton and the BBC*, published in 2012. Marsh was editor of the *Today* programme at the time of the broadcast.

It was another exasperating performance from an exasperating reporter. I listened to Andrew Gilligan's live two-way, his first shot at reporting Dr Kelly's allegations about the September dossier, while I was on my way into the office... Gilligan's live performances were always clumsy, his delivery halting. Peppered with 'ums' and pauses as he searched for words. This morning was not one of his best. He sounded barely awake, struggling to make sense. He seemed unable to get his story out. And not much of it sounded like the script I'd read before leaving the office barely an hour earlier... His source, he said, was 'in charge' [rather than merely 'involved' in writing the dossier]. It got worse. Most reporters, if they lost their thread in a live two-way as Gilligan clearly had, would take a deep breath and just read from their script... You have to be precise about the exact words and about the difference between what it was the source said and what you inferred from them. Gilligan had lost control of that precision [he said the government had 'put in' the 45-minute claim and that they knew it was 'wrong' before doing so]. I didn't remember 'wrong' being in the script... And the phrase 'put in' hadn't been in the script... It sounded as if Gilligan had got up late and was doing it off the top of his head. Bad call. As I walked in through the door, I saw [assistant editor Gavin Allen] with a phone clamped to his ear. He pointed to the handset and mouthed the words 'Downing Street'. It was about 6.35. It was a long call and once he'd put the phone down, he told me they'd said 'the Gilligan story is 100 per cent untrue... They want us to broadcast a denial in the news bulletin at seven'... That was never going to happen. The story wasn't 'completely untrue'. Gilligan's performance had been less than 100 per cent. He certainly hadn't followed his script. But I wasn't going to put out a misleading non-denial on air. The government would have the chance to rebut the allegations at ten past eight. That's the way we always handled contentious reports.

The key aspects of Gilligan's story were that some parts of the intelligence community were unhappy with the final dossier because it did not reflect the more tentative wording supported by the available intelligence. In particular, the '45-minute' claim was used to make Iraq sound more threatening than the available intelligence could reasonably support.

However, Gilligan's slips in the 'two-way' at 6.07 a.m. gave Campbell the chance to issue what *Today* editor Kevin Marsh has referred to as a 'non-denial denial'. That is, denying something that was never meant to be alleged in the first place to avoid having to respond to the real accusation. Campbell knew that those 'in charge' of writing the dossier were himself and Sir John Scarlett, head of the JIC, and that neither of them had spoken to Gilligan. In the 7.32 a.m. broadcast, Gilligan accurately stated that the source was merely 'involved' in the discussions that helped to prepare the dossier. A further slip was his statement that *his source had told him* that the government had 'put in' the 45-minute claim and that they knew it was 'wrong' before doing so. Dr Kelly never explicitly said this when he spoke to Gilligan; the inference was Gilligan's own and was misattributed to Dr Kelly. This slip also made it sound as if the government had *made up* the '45-minute' claim, whereas the later script made it clear that the claim had been part of the original intelligence, but that it was not deemed reliable enough to use in the way it was presented in the final dossier. It was these slips, and the final one in particular, that led to a serious and sustained clash between the BBC and the government. Gilligan further increased the tension provoked by his broadcast in an article he wrote for the *Mail on Sunday* the following weekend. In that article, he named Alastair Campbell as the key figure responsible for sexing up the dossier.

Most of the national press adopted a fairly neutral stance during the escalation of tensions, merely reporting what Campbell or the BBC had said in relation to the ongoing allegations. However, the *Sun* was noticeably partisan in its support for the government and hostility towards the BBC. This became even more apparent in the *Sun*'s reporting of the Hutton Inquiry (see pages 167–71).

ACTIVITY
KNOWLEDGE CHECK

Tension between the government and the BBC between 1997 and the end of May 2003

1 Explain why tension existed between New Labour and the BBC even before the Iraq War.

2 Summarise the role of Andrew Gilligan in igniting the open row between the government and the BBC on 29 May 2003.

3 How useful is Extract 1 for understanding the role of Andrew Gilligan in the confrontation between the government and the BBC in 2003?

The role of Alastair Campbell

Between the 6.07 a.m. two-way and the 7.32 a.m. report, the government wrote to the BBC demanding a denial of the story in the 7 a.m. headlines. They complained that 'These allegations are untrue. Not one word of the dossier was not entirely the work of the intelligence agencies. The suggestion that any pressure was put on the intelligence services by No. 10 or anyone else to change the document are [*sic*] entirely false'.

Although the newspapers mostly led with the story of the 'sexed up' dossier for the best part of the following week, the story had died down in the public sphere before Campbell made two highly robust performances: one on 25 June 2003 at the foreign affairs select committee, and one two days later on Channel 4 News. The committee, appointed by and answerable to parliament, was investigating the process by which the dodgy dossier had been created. Campbell was clearly heavily implicated in its failings but was determined that the headlines the following day would not drag his name through the mud. It was surely no coincidence that he chose this moment to reignite his anger over the '45-minute' claim: 'I find it incredible and I mean incredible that people can report based on one single anonymous uncorroborated source – and let's get to the heart of what the allegation is – that the prime minister, the Cabinet, the intelligence agencies, people like myself connived to persuade parliament to send British forces into action on a lie. That is the allegation. I tell you, until the BBC acknowledge that is a lie, I will keep banging on, that correspondence file will get thicker and they had better issue an apology pretty quickly.' Campbell reiterated his anger with the BBC's 'accusation of lying' during his appearance on Channel 4 News (available to see online). The BBC continued to respond by pointing out that Campbell was denying things that they had never alleged in the first place.

SOURCE 6 Dr David Kelly giving evidence at the Foreign Affairs Select Committee on 15 July 2003.

As well as reigniting the public row, Campbell played a large part in the public naming of Dr Kelly as Gilligan's source. Kelly came forward to the Ministry of Defence (MOD) on 30 June to admit that he had met Gilligan, but that he did not think he could be the sole source referred to in Gilligan's story. On 8 July, a statement was released to the press that the source was not 'in charge of drawing up the dossier'. The next day further clues were provided, stating that the source was an expert on WMDs. The MOD press office was instructed that if a journalist came to them with Dr Kelly's name as the source then they could confirm it. On 9 July, Dr Kelly's name was confirmed to three journalists. Although the BBC continued to refuse to name the source, in an email to three members of the foreign affairs select committee Gilligan himself gave away Dr Kelly as the source for a similar story by a different BBC journalist, Susan Watts. Dr Kelly appeared before the committee twice on 15 and 16 July. He received a tough interrogation from MPs but consistently denied that he could have been Gilligan's only source. In a voice so quiet it could barely be heard over the air-conditioning, Dr Kelly also denied that the '45-minute' claim could have come from his talk with Gilligan. Dr Kelly was not under oath and it is clear that he did not tell the whole truth to the committee – he admitted to having met Susan Watts but denied meeting any other BBC journalists when he had in fact also met Gavin Hewitt. Susan Watts recorded her second meeting with Dr Kelly, and the information he provided was substantially similar to that which Gilligan claimed he had received from Dr Kelly at their meeting on 22 May.

SOURCE 7

From Alastair Campbell's diaries between 4 and 20 July 2003. Campbell had always intended to publish his diaries once he and Tony Blair stepped down from their respective positions. These entries are taken from *The Blair Years*, a condensed version of the diaries published in 2007.

Friday 4 July: I spoke to Hoon, who said a man had come forward who felt he was possibly Gilligan's source... Yes he said intelligence went in late, but he never said the other stuff. It was double-edged but GH and I agreed it would f*** Gilligan if that was his source.

Monday 7 July: TB was meeting Kevin Tebbit, Omand and others re 'the source'... It was agreed he should be interviewed again, and then we should get it out that the source was not in the intelligence community, not involved in drawing up the dossier. Agree we should be saying the source was misrepresented by Gilligan... I felt we should get it out through the papers then have a line to respond...

Wednesday 9 July: The biggest thing needed was the source out. We agreed that we should not do it ourselves, so didn't, but later in the day the *FT*, *Guardian*, and *The Times* got the name... Andy Marr led the news, massively ramped across all channels, with a story about senior sources saying we were unlikely ever to find WMD. It transpired the source was Jack Straw. JS apologised to me later saying he thought he was just chatting for background, not that Marr was going to do a big story. It was an outrage the way the BBC was now using its reports and outlets to promote its line on the issue.

Tuesday 15 July: We were looking forward to Kelly giving evidence to the FAC but... I predicted it would be a disaster and so it proved. Despite MoD assurances he was well schooled... by the end of the day, we were down as usual.

Friday 18 July: I was the story and that was that even though it was unfair... Things quietened down but then I wept because of the pressure I was under, and the sadness I felt for Kelly's family... I said to journalists who got through on the phone that I was shocked and felt dreadful, it was about our media culture, but I had done nothing wrong...

Saturday 19 July: The papers, as expected, were totally grim, the *Mail* needless to say the worst, pictures of TB, Hoon and me and 'Proud of Yourselves?'... The only person who came out well was Kelly. There was not nearly enough directed towards the BBC.

A Level Exam-Style Question Section A

Study Source 7 before you answer this question.

Assess the value of the source for revealing the tensions between the Labour government and the BBC between 2002 and 2004, and the role of Alastair Campbell in these developments.

Explain your answer, using the source, the information given about its origin and your own knowledge about the historical context. (20 marks)

Tip
It is important to take note of the specific words and phrases that are used to convey information in each source: why is one particular word used rather than a different one? Quote these words or phrases in your answer to support your judgements on how far the tone of the source affects its credibility. Judgements on tone can often be usefully linked to the purpose behind the source.

The impact of the death of Dr Kelly

The most tragic impact of Dr Kelly's death was on his immediate family. In the same way that Lord Hutton accepted the Oxfordshire coroner's verdict that Dr Kelly had committed suicide, the Kelly family never challenged this conclusion publicly. However, various individuals, mostly journalists but also one prominent MP, have challenged the suicide verdict. Their concerns about the validity of the investigation of Dr Kelly's death centre on three key areas: the treatment of the crime scene, the actions of the government in the immediate aftermath of the death, and decisions made by Lord Hutton during his inquiry. Although their concerns, and their presentation of their case for murder rather than suicide, were quickly dismissed by some as merely fuelling conspiracy theories, it is likely that the weight of evidence they assembled in support of their case did serve to undermine public trust in the government and the Hutton Inquiry. The treatment of the crime scene is discussed below, while the actions of the government and Lord Hutton are dealt with in the next section (page 167).

Dr Kelly's wife called the police several hours after he had failed to return from his regular walk. A huge police search operation was undertaken and local volunteers were drafted in to help with the search. Louise Holmes and Paul Chapman were the volunteers who first found his body, sat up and slumped at the foot of a tree. They went to fetch the main police search team but almost immediately bumped into three different officers. These men stayed with the body and sent Louise and Paul to get the other police. When they returned, the body was lying down away from the tree. Two of the three men were identified at the Hutton Inquiry as Detective Constable Graham Coe and DC Colin Shields, but the third man's identity was not revealed and Hutton asked no questions about him during the inquiry. Coe and Shields were members of **Special Branch,** whose assistance was highly unusual in a missing person or suicide case.

The coroner's post-mortem report (made public in 2010) stated that 'the main factor involved in bringing about the death of David Kelly is bleeding from the incised wounds to his left wrist. Had this not occurred he may well not have died at this time. Furthermore, on the balance of probabilities, it is likely that the ingestion of an excess number of co-proxamol tablets [painkillers] coupled with apparently clinically silent coronary artery disease would both have played a part in bringing about

KEY TERM

Special Branch
Section of the police force that is concerned with issues of national security, usually relating to national and international terrorism. It works closely with, and in support of, the Security Service (MI5).

death more certainly and more rapidly than would have otherwise been the case.' However, it was revealed through a Freedom of Information Request in 2007 that no fingerprints (not even Dr Kelly's) were found on the knife, pill packets, a water bottle, mobile phone or glasses found next to the body.

Although experts have argued over whether Dr Kelly could have died from the wounds sustained to his left wrist, there is no doubt that the way in which the suicide verdict was recorded was unusual. In virtually every case of 'violent or unnatural death' a coroner's inquest is held. This has the legal authority to summon and examine witnesses under oath in order to establish the facts. The inquest is held in public – the press and members of the public are allowed to attend the proceedings. However, in Dr Kelly's case, the Lord Chancellor, Charlie Falconer (who used to be a flatmate of Tony Blair when they were training to be barristers) adjourned the coroner's inquiry. Within three hours of the discovery of the body, it was replaced by a public inquiry. These are usually held in cases of multiple deaths, such as a natural disaster, mass murder or a transport crash. The use of such an inquiry into the death of one person was highly unusual. Unlike a coroner's inquiry, witnesses do not have to give evidence under oath at a public inquiry.

Dr Kelly's wife stated that her husband became terribly withdrawn and quiet the day before his disappearance and death. However, the reasons for this change in his mood are not entirely clear and have provided plenty of scope for conspiracy theorists. In particular, they draw attention to two emails he sent on the morning of his death. One was to a friend in which he stated 'It has been difficult. Hopefully it will all blow over by the end of the week and I can travel to Baghdad and get on with the real work'. The other was to *New York Times* journalist Judith Miller in which he wrote, replying to her hopes that it was all going well, 'I will wait until the end of the week before judging. Many dark actors playing dark games.' The identity of these 'dark actors' has been the subject of much speculation.

The national press focused its attention on the circumstances of Dr Kelly's death and the personal tragedy for his family. Initial coverage also hinted at the apportioning of blame that would become far more intense following the publication of the Hutton Report. The *Sun* reported how Andrew Gilligan made no comment, while Tony Blair immediately took action with the approval of his senior ministers in appointing an independent judicial inquiry. However, even newspapers that had given general support to the Iraq War clearly pointed the finger of blame at the government. The *Daily Mail* was typical of this reaction when it highlighted the government's role in the release of Dr Kelly's name to the press and his subsequent thrust into the media spotlight.

SOURCE

8

From Barry Shelby and Sarah Colman's 'Suicide and Suspicions over War in Iraq', posted on www.worldpress.org on 13 August 2003. Worldpress.org was founded in 1997 to provide chiefly American readers with an objective account of the way foreign media report current news events.

In the aftermath of the suicide, British commentators were divided as to whether the lion's share of blame for Kelly's suicide rested with the government or the BBC. Some blamed the news agency for refusing to release Kelly's name sooner; other fingers pointed at the MoD for violating its normal rules of secrecy by telling reporters that it would confirm the mole's name if they submitted it to the ministry. For its part, the government accused the BBC of having an anti-war bias that had led to sensationalist reporting. Britain's conservative tabloids were eager to point fingers at the BBC. 'Are the BBC to blame?' asked the conservative, mass-circulation *News of the World* (July 20). 'Maybe... It is the reputation of the BBC that will be covered in Kelly's blood.' The *Sun* (July 21) was even more damning in its rhetorical questions: 'The BBC is in the gutter... How can we ever trust them again?' But others argued that it wasn't clear exactly what the BBC could have done to save Kelly. Writing in the liberal *Guardian* on July 21, Jackie Ashley offered an explanation for the conservative attacks on the corporation. 'The attacks on the BBC have been led by two groups – Rupert Murdoch's newspapers and New Labour spin-doctors – which have been closely intertwined in recent years. The covert Murdoch message is clear enough: Tony, we are your real, reliable supporters, not the dodgy lefties of the BBC.' Others cautioned against making too much of the battle between the BBC and press secretary Alistair Campbell, saying that they were simply actors in a larger drama. 'Blair went to war arguing that Iraq posed an imminent threat,' said an editorial in London's liberal *Independent on Sunday* (July 20). 'It is not scientific advisors, or Campbell, or the BBC... who should be in the dock but the prime minister... We need [an inquiry] into the real reasons why this country was taken into a war that has claimed not only too many lives as its victims but the nation's trust in its leaders as well.'

ACTIVITY
KNOWLEDGE CHECK

The '45-minute' claim and the death of Dr Kelly

1 Who would you argue was more to blame for the public naming of Dr Kelly as Andrew Gilligan's source: the government or the media? Explain your answer.

2 Summarise the media's reasons for doubting the suicide verdict in Dr Kelly's death. Take care to differentiate between information that was available before and after 2004.

3 How useful is Source 8 in understanding the media reaction to the news of Dr Kelly's death?

WHAT WERE THE KEY IMPLICATIONS OF THE HUTTON INQUIRY FOR THE RELATIONSHIP BETWEEN MASS MEDIA AND THE GOVERNMENT?

The role of Lord Hutton

The British public had first heard of Dr Kelly as Andrew Gilligan's source, as the whistle-blower on the government's use of intelligence reports in a way not supported by members of the intelligence community. Following Dr Kelly's death, it was inevitable that huge press coverage would not only report the circumstances of his death, but also speculate on the possible connections between his death and his role in undermining the dodgy dossier. For some commentators, the government appointment of Lord Hutton to lead a public inquiry just three hours after Dr Kelly's body had been found was, at best, understandable given the sensitivity of the case and the likelihood of such speculation. However, even before the inquiry got underway, some eyebrows were raised at the very unusual decision to appoint a public inquiry in place of the usual coroner's inquest, and the haste with which this was enacted. They were raised further by the choice of Brian Hutton, a judge who had a reputation for the respect and support of government authority. That the secretary of state for constitutional affairs made the appointment should not have been controversial – Lord Falconer had this power within his remit. However, it was known that Charles Falconer only became a lord because he was Tony Blair's first recommendation as prime minister. The implication is that Lord Falconer selected Lord Hutton as a favour to the government, as his previous judgements suggested that he would be unlikely to deliver a report that was critical of the government.

EXTEND YOUR KNOWLEDGE

Lord Hutton (born 1931)

Brian Hutton was born in Belfast, the city where he lived and worked as a barrister and then a judge, having completed his education. He developed a reputation as a judge who showed respect for institutions and figures of authority and little sympathy for whistle-blowers. He was also known for his tendency to focus on key details in his judgements rather than consider broader generalisations about the case in question.

He first came to prominence when he represented the MOD at a 1973 inquest into the shooting of 26 unarmed civilians by British troops in January 1972 ('Bloody Sunday'). The judge at that inquest cleared the troops of wrongdoing. Hutton criticised both the coroner and jury for expressing 'wide-ranging views, particularly when a most eminent judge has spent twenty days hearing evidence and come to a very different conclusion'. The inquiry was widely criticised, and in 1998 a fresh inquiry was ordered into the events. In light of the final report in 2010, Prime Minister David Cameron apologised for 'the unjustified and unjustifiable' killing.

Hutton was also one of four Law Lords who rejected the appeal of David Shayler in March 2002. Shayler had worked for MI5, but a year after he left he sold stories about his work to a newspaper. He argued that he was acting in the public interest by revealing details of illegal activity by the state, but Hutton rejected this defence as Shayler had broken the Official Secrets Act. The Inquiry into the Circumstances Surrounding the Death of Dr David Kelly was the first (and only) occasion Hutton had led such a public inquiry.

The media had high hopes for a thorough report that would settle all of the arguments in an authoritative manner. In the event, the report was roundly criticised by virtually the whole press. Even before its contents were held up to scrutiny, there was widespread condemnation of the fact that a copy of the Hutton Report had been leaked to the *Sun* the day before its official release on 28 January 2004. The *Sun* was vitriolic in its condemnation of Andrew Gilligan and the BBC, stating that they should be ashamed of their role in Dr Kelly's suicide. It was also fulsome in its praise for the government's conduct and for the *Sun* journalists themselves, who now stood vindicated in their earlier criticisms of the BBC. *The Times* was far more measured and even published a poll that suggested two-thirds of the public still trusted the BBC while only 31 percent trusted the government. The *Independent* led with a historic almost totally blank front cover to emphasise its view that the Report was an official 'whitewash', covering up the truth to spare the government's blushes rather than delivering a just verdict. However, it was arguably the *Mail on Sunday* columnist Peter Hitchens who went the furthest in his condemnation of the Report (see Source 9). While the *Mail on Sunday* had been broadly sympathetic to the Iraq War, it was critical of New Labour and used the occasion of the Report to direct public anger against its use of spin.

A Level Exam-Style Question Section A

Study Source 9 before you answer this question.

Assess the value of the source for revealing the causes of tension between the government and the BBC, and the media reaction to the Hutton Report.

Explain your answer, using the source, the information given about its origin and your own knowledge about the historical context. (20 marks)

Tip
Remember to pay careful attention to the authorship of the source. It is useful to consider a range of questions about the authorship of the source when considering its overall value. Would this person have been in a position to know the details or have an overview of the issue in question? Would this person have a vested interest in the events being discussed? Might they have a motive to distort the details or present a particular angle? Above all, carefully consider the purpose that lies behind their authorship of the source in question.

SOURCE 9

From Peter Hitchen's article 'Hutton: the Verdict', published in the *Mail on Sunday* on 1 February 2004 in response to the publication of the Hutton Report.

Lord Hutton is a deluded booby who understands modern British politics about as well as Saddam Hussein grasps the laws of cricket. He simply cannot believe that a British Prime Minister could ever behave in an underhand manner, or that he would deliberately surround himself with Stalinist gangsters. And so, rather than see the truth that glares and gibbers before his face, he has turned the whole world upside-down to fit his comical prejudices. The guilty are exonerated, the innocent condemned and poor David Kelly himself is given a post-suicide ticking off for failing to follow non-existent Civil Service rules... We have all seen exactly the same evidence that he has seen but I have yet to meet a single person who thinks that he came to the right conclusion. His verdict is complete tripe. If Alastair Campbell is so innocent of everything, why exactly did he resign all those months ago? It must be the first case of a man resigning because he did his job with perfect propriety. Why, even the Prime Minister admitted his post was 'at risk' last weekend, before he and his friends at The Sun newspaper had been given their advance copies of the report. Why would that be, if he is so guiltless? But what really baffles me is the way that our society's leading figures have responded, for this week the essential truth of Andrew Gilligan's report has become clearer and clearer... If the Blair Government can get away with this, then it will swell still further in power and arrogance. From being a general, vague threat to liberty and democracy it will become an infant tyranny, for if it is now a punishable offence to tell the inconvenient truth about what Mr Blair does, who is next after the BBC?

Do not forget that, for the most part, the BBC has been a fawning servant to New Labour since before it was elected, conducting a war of scorn against the Conservative Party and its supporters, excluding Labour's opponents from the national debate where possible, treating them with sneering unfairness when it had to let them on the air. But for our new rulers, that is not enough. Nothing short of total obedience will do, for the truth that Lord Hutton cannot acknowledge is that our Government thinks it is so good and virtuous that it can do no wrong.

One key reason for such a negative media response was the narrow frame of reference that Hutton gave himself when conducting his inquiry.

SOURCE 10

From the introduction to the Hutton Report, published on 28 January 2004. Here Lord Hutton sets out his frame of reference for the report.

In my opinion [my] terms of reference required me to consider the circumstances preceding and leading up to the death of Dr Kelly insofar as (1) they might have had an effect on his state of mind and influenced his actions preceding and leading up to his death or (2) they might have influenced the actions of others which affected Dr Kelly. There has been a great deal of controversy and debate whether the intelligence in relation to weapons of mass destruction set out in the dossier published by the Government on 24 September 2002 was of sufficient strength and reliability to justify... military action [against Iraq]. This controversy and debate has continued because of the failure to find weapons of mass destruction in Iraq. I gave careful consideration to the view expressed by a number of public figures and commentators, that my terms of reference required or, at least, entitled me to consider this issue. However, I concluded that a question of such wide import, which would involve the consideration of a wide range of evidence, is not one which falls within my terms of reference. The major controversy which arose following Mr Andrew Gilligan's broadcasts on the BBC *Today* programme on 29 May 2003 and which closely involved Dr Kelly arose from the allegations in the broadcasts (1) that the Government probably knew, before it decided to put it in its dossier of 24 September 2002, that the statement was wrong that the Iraqi military were able to deploy weapons of mass destruction within 45 minutes of a decision to do so and (2) that 10 Downing Street ordered the dossier to be sexed up. It was these allegations attacking the integrity of the Government which drew Dr Kelly into the controversy about the broadcasts and which I consider I should examine under my terms of reference. The issue whether, if approved by the Joint Intelligence Committee and believed by the Government to be reliable, the intelligence contained in the dossier was nevertheless unreliable is a separate issue which I consider does not fall within my terms of reference... At the outset I state... that I am satisfied that Dr Kelly took his own life by cutting his left wrist and that his death was hastened by his taking Coproxamol tablets. I am further satisfied that there was no involvement by a third person in Dr Kelly's death.

Hutton, persuaded of the suicide verdict, failed to ask questions that could have helped to clarify issues with the evidence from the scene of Dr Kelly's death outlined above. He also failed to explore the role of the government in affecting Dr Kelly's state of mind, despite the fact that Kelly had been subjected to several interviews by the MOD after he had come forward as the potential source. The MOD did receive a mild rebuke for not informing Dr Kelly about the release of his name as the source. Instead, Hutton focused on the alleged failings of the BBC and was heavily critical of the way in which Gilligan's story had made it on air. His key conclusions were as follows.

- Gilligan's allegation that the government probably knew that the 45-minute claim was wrong or questionable was unfounded.

- The editorial system at the BBC was defective, as Gilligan was allowed to broadcast his report at 6.07 a.m. without editors having seen his script.

- The BBC management was at fault for failing to investigate properly the government's complaints that the report in the 6.07 a.m. broadcast was false. They should have made a more thorough investigation of Gilligan's notes to see whether they supported his allegations.

- The BBC governors were at fault for not making their own more detailed investigation into the extent to which Mr Gilligan's notes supported his very grave allegations.

The implications of the Hutton Report

The Hutton Report had remarkably little impact on the long-term relationships between the government and the media. This was largely because it was so roundly condemned for being an official whitewash. The fact that Hutton's conclusions were so one-sided in favour of the government meant that it lacked credibility from the outset. The release of more evidence after the inquiry further invalidated its findings and led to pressure for a second inquiry. The result was the appointment of the Iraq Inquiry under Lord Chilcot in November 2009.

The Hutton Report had some limited influence on the BBC but failed to affect relationships between the government and media more generally to any significant extent. The damaging conclusions of the Report led to the resignation of Gavyn Davies (chairman of the BBC board of governors), Greg Dyke (BBC director-general) and Andrew Gilligan. The deputy chairman Lord Ryder apologised unreservedly for the BBC, and the acting director-general (Mark Byford) stated the BBC would 'learn lessons'. An internal review was announced called 'the Process'. In the end this did little other than confirm the existing BBC editorial guidelines. *Today* editor Kevin Marsh set out in exhaustive detail how those guidelines were adhered to in the decision to broadcast Gilligan's story. The story was single sourced, but the source sounded serious and credible and the details he gave chimed with information previously gathered. A script was written and approved, but Gilligan failed to stick to it in his 6.07 a.m. two-way. All of this could have come to light had Marsh been summoned to appear before the Hutton Inquiry, but remarkably he was not.

The fact that the BBC was prepared to take action in light of the Report (despite severe individual criticism of the Report from Greg Dyke and Andrew Gilligan) helps to explain why relations between the BBC and the government recovered significantly from the near total breakdown experienced during the Gilligan affair. Since 2004 there have been only minor tensions, and these were nothing to do with the Hutton Inquiry (they centred on the rate of licence fee increases in the run-up to the BBC Charter renewal in 2006). The BBC has been largely exonerated of its alleged failings in the Report, and of New Labour accusations of bias. Academics at Cardiff University compared 1,534 evening news reports taken from the BBC, ITV, Channel 4 and Sky News during the period from 20 March to 11 April 2003. They found that the BBC was far less unfavourable towards the government than Channel 4 News. The BBC emerges from the study as fairly impartial in its war coverage. Despite some contemporary fears to the contrary, the BBC was not cowed by the Hutton Report and has continued to broadcast news, interviews and documentaries that, where deserved, are sharply critical of government.

From Andrew Gilligan's resignation speech on 30 January 2004.

[T]he BBC collectively has been the victim of a grave injustice. If Lord Hutton had fairly considered the evidence he heard, he would have concluded that most of my story was right. The government did sex up the dossier, transforming possibilities and probabilities into certainties, removing vital caveats; the 45-minute claim was the 'classic example' of this; and many in the intelligence services, including the leading expert in WMD, were unhappy about it... This report casts a chill over all journalism, not just the BBC's. It seeks to hold reporters, with all the difficulties they face, to a standard that it does not appear to demand of, for instance, government dossiers. I am comforted by the fact that public opinion appears to disagree with Lord Hutton and I hope this will strengthen the resolve of the BBC. I repeatedly said also that I did not accuse the government of fabrication, but of exaggeration. I stand by that charge, and it will not go away. I love the BBC and I am resigning because I want to protect it. I accept my part in the crisis which has befallen the organisation. But a greater part has been played by the unbalanced judgments of Lord Hutton.

A further reason for the lack of the Hutton Report's impact on government relations with the media is that this relationship was already in a process of change, which the Report did little to alter. New Labour had been fairly successful in its attempt to manage the release of potentially damaging news during its first few years in power, but a series of embarrassing stories made this increasingly difficult. Jo Moore (special adviser to the Secretary of State for Transport) and Martin Sixsmith (press chief for the Transport Department) both resigned after it came to light that they had recommended that Transport Minister Stephen Byers use the 9/11 terrorist attacks on the World Trade Center as a 'very good day to get out anything we want to bury. Councillors' expenses?' Alastair Campbell was also embarrassed by accurate reports that he had tried to secure a more prominent role for Tony Blair during the Queen Mother's funeral on 9 April 2002. Such stories provoked a rising sense that trust had broken down between the government, media and the general public. A parliamentary investigation was held into the role of special advisers in government and, following on from this, an independent review of government communications was also appointed under Bob Phillis, chief executive of the Guardian Media Group. The Phillis Report (2004) was specifically tasked to 'conduct a radical review of government communications' with an examination of 'the roles played by... special advisers who have a responsibility for communications'.

The Phillis Report was published at almost exactly the same time as the Hutton Report, in January 2004, and condemned the role of spin in the breakdown of trust between the government, the media and the public. It was critical of New Labour's use of the Lobby to release news through a privileged 'inner circle' of reporters, and it recommended that lobby briefings be televised to make the system more transparent. It criticised the use of Order in Council powers that had enabled special advisers to give orders to civil servants, and recommended the break up of Alastair Campbell's dual role as the prime minister's spokesperson (a civil service role) and director of communications (a political appointment). Campbell had resigned as director of communications and strategy on 29 August 2003, during the Hutton Inquiry. In his diaries he stated that he had intended to resign before the dodgy dossier or Dr Kelly's death. Following his resignation, the job he had held was broken up into two clearly distinguished political and civil service roles in the government media service.

Since his report was published, it has become clear that Hutton's conclusions regarding the use of the '45-minute' claim, and some other alarming pieces of intelligence in the September dossier, were too lenient on the government. It is also clear that Gilligan's allegations were substantially true. The 24 September dossier presented to parliament was the final version of the document that had been six months in gestation. The original internal report from February 2002 was called *WMD – Programmes of Concern*. This gave an analysis of the threat posed by North Korea, Libya, Iran and Iraq. In March 2002, another report was written that focused on Iraq only. The reason for this was that comparisons with the other three countries made Iraq seem far less of a threat. There was little new intelligence to add to the internal reports until 29 August, when a trusted Iraqi source reported he had heard the '45-minute' claim from someone else. The JIC-approved draft of the dossier stated that 'Intelligence also indicates that chemical and biological munitions could be with military units and ready for firing within 20–45 minutes'. The final dossier (which only Sir John Scarlett rather than the full JIC approved) changed this to 'Recent intelligence... indicates that Iraq attaches great importance to the possession of weapons of mass destruction and that Saddam Hussein is committed to using them if necessary; it envisages the use of weapons of mass destruction in its current military planning, and could deploy such weapons within 45 minutes of the order being given for their use.'

Although the Defence Intelligence Service expressed concern over the prominence and weight given to the '45-minute' claim, and the JIC felt that the intelligence was limited, sporadic and patchy, Blair's foreword to the report 'based in large part on the work of the JIC' referred to the intelligence as 'extensive, detailed and authoritative'. The title of the dossier was also changed at the last minute from *Iraq's Programme of Weapons of Mass Destruction* to *Iraq's Weapons of Mass Destruction*. Alastair Campbell, together with Jonathan Powell, recommended several of the changes that 'sexed up' the dossier. It is clear that the dossier put before parliament and the public was misleading. It took tentative intelligence and presented it in a way that was designed to support the case for war against Iraq. On the same day that Hutton delivered his report, the head of the USA's Iraq Survey Group, which had been searching for WMDs, told the Senate 'I don't think they existed... we were all wrong'.

EXTEND YOUR KNOWLEDGE

Where did the intelligence behind the September 2002 dossier come from?

The '45-minute' claim emerged on 29 August 2002. The immediate source was the Iraqi National Accord (INA), a political party based in Jordan who used disgruntled officers within Iraq to gather information. They got the information from Colonel al-Dabbagh, an artillery commander in Western Iraq. While the INA had provided reliable intelligence in the past, this single source was untried, hence the tentative reception of the information by the JIC.

It was never clear what weapons and in what circumstances the '45-minute' claim pertained to, but it seemed to the JIC to relate to battlefield weapons. The Butler Inquiry ruled that the use of the '45-minute' claim in the September dossier was 'sloppy'. It was included on the strength of two new sources of evidence that seemed to corroborate the claim. While the details were never made public, one of the sources was known as 'new source on trial', the other as 'Red River'. The claims of the first source were later dismissed and the second failed a lie-detector test after the war.

A further claim in the dossier was that Saddam had tried to obtain 500 tonnes of uranium for his nuclear weapons programme from Niger. Brian Jones, head of the WMD section of Defence Intelligence, was dismissive of the evidence for this claim, and rightly so. The documents on which the claim was based turned out to be poor forgeries.

The 'best' source for Saddam's renewed weapons programme was codenamed 'Curveball'. He fled Iraq and claimed asylum in Nuremburg. His real name is Rafid al-Janabi, a chemical engineer who made up stories of mobile biological weapons facilities in Iraq in order to gain a better life in Germany. The German intelligence service and the Secret Intelligence Service both provided warnings about Curveball, but his lies nevertheless became a key component in the justification of war by Britain and the US.

EXTRACT

 From James Stanyer's article 'Politics and the Media: A Crisis of Trust?', published in *Parliamentary Affairs* in April 2004. Stanyer is Professor of Communication and Media Analysis at the University of Loughborough.

The consequences of the Inquiry were felt before the final report was delivered. The first casualty of the Inquiry was Alastair Campbell. Before it had finished taking evidence he announced that he was resigning, although he claimed to have been contemplating leaving for some time. The second casualty was the news-management system he had created. His August announcement was used to make a symbolic break with the 'Millbank model' developed while in opposition. Seeing effective communication of government policy as central to electoral success, it led to a radical shake-up of government communication, greater centralisation of control in Downing Street and widespread obsession with dominating the news agenda. However, constant revelations about spin and attempts to control the news by government spin-doctors, culminating in the Hutton Inquiry, discredited this type of news operation. The interim findings of the Phillis Committee, formed in February 2003 to review government communications, provided the blueprint for Downing Street media operations post-Campbell. The major change has been that a senior civil servant (at Permanent Secretary level) is in overall charge of strategy and coordinating government media operations, not a political appointee. Responsibility for the day-to-day operations has been split between the director of communications – a political appointee – and a civil servant. The political appointee, David Hill, a former head of Labour Party media operations, is responsible only for party political matters; his role is to provide the political perspective on behalf of the Prime Minister and assist cabinet ministers with the political context for departmental communications. The civil servant is the Prime Minister's official spokesperson in charge of communicating on non-party-political matters. Importantly, David Hill will not enjoy the powers that Campbell had to direct civil servants. This can be seen not as the end of spin but as a return in spirit to the way media operations were run before Blair's election in 1997, with civil servants back in control.

ACTIVITY
KNOWLEDGE CHECK

The Hutton Inquiry

1 Summarise the key judgements of the Hutton Inquiry.

2 Give reasons why the Hutton Report failed to have a significant long-term impact on relationships between government and the media.

3 How useful is Source 11 in understanding the media reaction to the Hutton Report?

A Level Exam-Style Question Section B

To what extent would you agree with the view that the Hutton Inquiry had a highly significant impact on relationships between the government and the media? (20 marks)

Tip

The key to a strong answer is sustained judgement. In order to offer persuasive conclusions you should carefully consider the criteria you will use to inform your judgement. With regard to this particular question, in what ways could you consider whether the Hutton Inquiry had a significant impact on relationships between the government and the media?

 THINKING HISTORICALLY Interpretations (6a)

Ever-changing history

Our interpretations of the past change as we change. This may be because our social attitudes have changed over time, or perhaps a historian has constructed a new theory, or perhaps technology has allowed archaeologists to discover something new.

Work in pairs.

Make a timeline that starts with the Iraq War and ends 50 years from now. Construct reactions that illustrate the point that time changes history. In the future box you can speculate how people might react to the event in 50 years' time. Below is an example.

19 March 2003	1 May 2003	28 January 2004	2015	2066
Event: Outbreak of Iraq War: US and UK forces invade and overthrow Saddam Hussein	President George Bush: 'Mission Accomplished' Iraqi man: 'Thank you for toppling Saddam Hussein!'	Lord Hutton: 'Not in my terms of reference' The *Independent*: 'Whitewash' Iraqi man: 'I thought the fighting would be over! Please stop the insurgents.'	Tony Blair: 'The Iraq War is not to blame for the rise of Isis.' Lord Chilcot: 'My Report will be more than 2 million words long.' Iraqi Man: 'How will the government defeat Isis?'	?

Answer the following questions.

1 Identify three factors that have affected how the Iraq War is interpreted over time, or might affect it in the future.

2 If a historian was to write a book proposing a radically new interpretation of the Iraq War, how might other historians react? What would affect their reaction?

3 How will the future change the past?

ACTIVITY
SUMMARY

The Labour government versus the media: problem of the Iraq dossiers, 2002-04

1 Construct a table like the one below.

2 In the first column, set out the key events of the confrontation between the government and the BBC between 2002 and 2004.

3 In the second column, give a mark out of 5 for the degree of impact, where 1 indicates only a minor impact and 5 is a very serious impact on BBC-government relations.

4 In the third, fourth and fifth columns, give a percentage value for the extent of blame. (The three percentage figures should add up to 100.)

5 In the final column, explain as concisely as possible the values you have chosen for columns 2 to 5.

Event or development	Degree of impact on relations between the government and BBC	Extent to which the BBC was to blame	Extent to which the government was to blame	Extent to which other agents were to blame	Explanation

---

WIDER READING

Campbell, A. *The Burden of Power: the Countdown to Iraq*, Hutchinson (2012)

Marsh, K. *Stumbling Over Truth: the Inside Story of the 'Sexed Up' Dossier, Hutton and the BBC*, Biteback Publishing (2012)

Rogers, S. *The Hutton Inquiry and its Impact*, Politico's Publishing Ltd (2004)

The Chilcot Inquiry evidence – www.iraqinquiry.org.uk

The Hutton Inquiry report – http://webarchive.nationalarchives.gov.uk/20090128221546/http://www.the-hutton-inquiry.org.uk/

Preparing for your A Level Paper 3 exam

Advance planning

Draw up a timetable for your revision and try to keep to it. Spend longer on topics that you have found difficult, and revise them several times. Aim to be confident about all aspects of your Paper 3 work, because this will ensure that you have a choice of questions in Sections B and C.

Paper 3 overview

Paper 3	Time: 2 hours 15 minutes	
Section A	Answer 1 compulsory question for the option studied, assessing source analysis and evaluation skills.	20 marks
Section B	Answer 1 question from a choice of 2 on an aspect in depth for the option studied.	20 marks
Section C	Answer 1 question from a choice of 2 on an aspect in breadth for the option studied.	20 marks
	Total marks =	60 marks

Section A questions

There is no choice of question in Section A. You will be referred to a source of about 350 words long, printed in a Sources Booklet. The source will be a primary source or one that is contemporary to the period you have studied, and will relate to one of the key topics in the Aspect of Depth. You will be expected to analyse and evaluate the source in its historical context. The question will ask you to assess the value of the source for revealing something specific about the period, and will expect you to explain your answer, using the source, the information given about its origin and your own knowledge about the historical context.

Section B questions

You will have a choice of one from two questions in Section B. They will aim to assess your understanding of one or more of the key topics in the Aspect of Depth you have studied. Questions may relate to a single, momentous year, but will normally cover longer periods. You will be required to write an essay evaluating an aspect of the period. You may be asked about change and continuity, similarity and difference, consequences, significance or causation, or you may be given a quotation and asked to explain how far you agree with it. All questions will require you to reach a substantiated judgement.

Section C questions

You will have a choice of one from two questions in Section C. Questions will relate to the themes of the Aspects of Breadth you have studied, and will aim to assess your understanding of change over time. They will cover a period of no less than 100 years and will relate either to the factors that brought about change, or the extent of change over the period, or patterns of change as demonstrated by turning points.

Use of time

- Do not write solidly for 45 minutes on each question. For Sections B and C answers, you should spend a few minutes working out what the question is asking you to do, and drawing up a plan of your answer. This is especially important for Section C answers, which cover an extended period of time.

- For Section A, it is essential that you have a clear understanding of the content of the source and its historical context. Pay particular attention to the provenance: was the author in a position to know what he or she was writing about? Read it carefully and underline important points. You might decide to spend up to ten minutes reading the source and drawing up your plan, and 35 minutes writing your answer.

Preparing for your A Level exams

Paper 3: A Level sample answer with comments

Section A

These questions require you to analyse and evaluate source material with respect to its historical context. For these questions remember to:

- look at the evidence given in the source and consider how the source could be used in differing ways to provide historical understanding
- use your knowledge of the historical context to discuss any limitations the source may have
- use your historical understanding to evaluate the source, considering how much weight you would give to its argument
- come to a judgement on the overall value of the source in respect to the question.

Study Source 10 (Chapter 7, page 168) before you answer this question.

Assess the value of the source for revealing the impact of the Hutton Report and the circumstances surrounding Dr David Kelly's death on relations between the government and the BBC between 2002 and 2004.

Explain your answer, using the source, the information given about it and your own knowledge of the historical context. (20 marks)

Average student answer

The source is very useful because the Hutton Inquiry was all about the death of Dr Kelly. Lord Hutton heard loads of evidence about the death of Dr Kelly from many witnesses, so many that the Inquiry went on for months. He heard from people who worked at the BBC, such as Greg Dyke, and he heard from people who represented the government's side of things, like Alastair Campbell. In this way he must have got both sides of the story to allow him to make his report. Therefore the source must be useful when looking at the impact of Dr Kelly's death on relations between the BBC and the government.

> This is a weak opening paragraph despite some accurate detail. The detail is used to describe the Report rather than to interrogate any of the claims made by the source in relation to the question.

The content of the source also backs up my claim that the source is very useful. As it says right at the start, his 'terms of reference' were to investigate the circumstances surrounding the death of Dr Kelly, so we know it's all about the exact point we are looking at. Later on it also mentions 'Andrew Gilligan's broadcasts' and his 'allegations' that the government 'probably knew' about the 45-minute claim. Once again, this is all about the BBC and the government. The 45-minute claim refers to Saddam Hussein's weapons of mass destruction (WMDs). It is true that they looked for his WMDs in Iraq in 2003 but they didn't find any at all. This is accurate and further backs up the usefulness of the source.

> This paragraph demonstrates understanding of the source by drawing attention to relevant sections. However, the judgements about its use are asserted rather than justified: it is about the BBC and the government, but what does the source tell us exactly?

However, the source is also not useful because it doesn't go into the cover-up or conspiracy theories about Dr Kelly's death. Who was really responsible: the government or the BBC? Although the report simply admits the idea he committed suicide, some people think he might have been murdered. There are rumours that the government might have even played a part in organising the murder. Lots of the evidence at the so-called suicide did not stack up and definitely looked dodgy to some eyewitnesses. Therefore the report is not useful because it doesn't actually tell us everything that it could have done about the actual death. This is important because obviously the nature of the death affects the relationship of the government and the BBC.

> Avoid direct contradiction. Use relative rather than absolute judgements to discuss the strengths and limitations of the source. Words such as 'partially', 'superficially' or even 'more useful' add greater subtlety to your judgements.

The source is also not useful because of who wrote the report, when he wrote it and for what audience. The tone is pretty neutral here so that's not an issue. It was written by Lord Hutton who as a judge might have been biased to the government. After all, he gets his job from them so why would he attack them? It was published on 28 January 2004. This is almost a year after the actual events and so things might have died down by then between the BBC and the government (although the report did stir things up again between them). It was written for the government who had asked Hutton to do the Inquiry in the first place. Once again, this suggests that his report will probably be biased to the government. He even says that he is not going to consider whether the intelligence on Iraq was dodgy, clearly letting the government off the hook as we now know.

> Try to avoid this formulaic listing of provenance points. It is a clear sign to the examiner that you are going through the motions of assessing the position of the author rather than actively using this information to make informed judgements about the usefulness of the source.

Overall, yes, the source is useful to a certain extent because it is actually about the exact thing we want to know about and it has lots of points specifically on this issue. However, no, the source is not useful because of the clear bias of Lord Hutton to the government because of how he was asked to write the report in the first place by them and did not even investigate some of the things that the government might have done that maybe led to the suicide, or even possibly murder, of Dr Kelly. It would have been better to have had another source, possibly from Andrew Gilligan telling his side of the story, or someone else from the BBC like Greg Dyke who could have said what the impact on his relationship with the government was. Alastair Campbell would not have been useful in this way because he was a spin doctor and so his job was to 'make the truth up'.

> This concluding paragraph is not strong because it repeats some of the underdeveloped statements made in earlier paragraphs and it does not stick to the source in question. Your overall judgements must stick to the specific source rather than offering a 'wish list' of potentially more useful sources.

Verdict

This is an average answer because:

- it does not always explicitly develop points or judgements
- it uses vague rather than precise evidence to expand, confirm or challenge points raised by the source

- it only superficially analyses the provenance of the source in a rather formulaic fashion.

Use the feedback on this essay to rewrite it, making as many improvements as you can.

Paper 3: A Level sample answer with comments

Section A

These questions require you to analyse and evaluate source material with respect to its historical context. For these questions remember to:

- look at the evidence given in the source and consider how the source could be used in differing ways to provide historical understanding
- use your knowledge of the historical context to discuss any limitations the source may have
- use your historical understanding to evaluate the source, considering how much weight you would give to its argument
- come to a judgement on the overall value of the source in respect to the question.

Study Source 10 (Chapter 7, page 168) before you answer this question.

Assess the value of the source for revealing the impact of the Hutton Report and circumstances surrounding Dr David Kelly's death on relations between the government and the BBC between 2002 and 2004.

Explain your answer, using the source, the information given about it and your own knowledge of the historical context. (20 marks)

Strong student answer

The source presents the crux of the dispute between the BBC and the government but fails to apportion blame or go into any detail about how the death of Dr Kelly specifically affected relations between the two parties. This is understandable given that this is the introduction to a report, but it might also be explained by Lord Hutton's relationship to the New Labour government.

> This is a strong opening paragraph because it offers a clear initial judgement and definite criteria to assess the source.

The source correctly suggests that the major cause of the dispute between the BBC and the government started before the death of Dr Kelly with Andrew Gilligan's broadcasts on 29 May 2003. Hutton states that his broadcasts were the 'major controversy' that drew Dr Kelly into the dispute. It is true that Gilligan did make a series of broadcasts that morning where he discussed allegations that the September 2002 dossier had been 'sexed up'. Gilligan had met with Dr Kelly on 22 May to discuss his unease with the strength of conviction the government was due to place on evidence Dr Kelly did not consider merited such confidence. However, the source fails to capture the differences between the reports Gilligan made that morning. It is true that he said the government 'probably knew' the 45-minute claim was wrong in his 6.07 'two-way', but in his 7.32 broadcast Gilligan more accurately reflected the truth which was that members of the intelligence community were unhappy with the emphasis being placed on the 45-minute claim when it was only singly sourced. In this way the source subtly supports the government position that the BBC was at fault for inaccurate and unedited live broadcasts when, in fact, it was Gilligan himself who was at fault for not following a prearranged script because he had just woken up. This gets to the crux of the dispute between the government and the BBC because the government, Alastair Campbell in particular, claimed that the BBC had accused the government of lying. This is not what Gilligan's original report implied, only the mistake in the 6.07 'two-way' referred to by the Hutton Report.

> These paragraphs use well-selected evidence to confirm and challenge the representation of the key issue put forward by the source. This supports a highly convincing interrogation of the source content.

The source also correctly reveals that Gilligan's report set in motion the events which led to his death where it says 'these allegations… drew Dr Kelly into the controversy'. Tensions between the BBC and the government did grow more intense during the period when the BBC refused to name Dr Kelly as a source and following his death on 17 July 2003. However, the source underplays the role of the government in proceedings by directing all attention at Gilligan. In reality, while Gilligan refused to name his source, the government gave a series of clues to the media about the identity of the source, culminating in the confirmation of his name to three journalists on 9 July 2003. Alastair Campbell was keen to get Dr Kelly's name in the public arena because Kelly was not in charge of the report as Gilligan's 6.07 'two-way' had alleged: he was only involved in the discussion of the intelligence as Gilligan correctly stated in his later reports. The source is therefore limited in that it fails to present the degree of government involvement in the circumstances surrounding Dr Kelly's death.

The source gives reasons why it might not offer the most impartial guide to the growing dispute between the BBC and the government: Hutton specifically rules out any investigation into government wrongdoing in the lead-up to the war on Iraq, choosing instead to limit himself to the events in the immediate run-up to Dr Kelly's death. This ruled out investigation into the intelligence on weapons of mass destruction that Dr Kelly raised concerns about. It also ruled out any investigation into the nature of Dr Kelly's death where it simply accepts a suicide verdict. Both of these things suited the government and directed blame towards the BBC for accusing the government of wrongdoing. Hutton was chosen to lead the inquiry just three hours after Dr Kelly's body had been found; from previous cases, he was known to sympathise with authority and to focus on particular details rather than the broader points of a case. His terms of reference and his judgements were rejected by the majority of the media as a whitewash. This reaction strongly undermines the weight that can be placed on the uncontroversial view of Dr Kelly's death presented by the source.

> This paragraph integrates an analysis of the source provenance and content. A strong answer will generally analyse the strengths and limitations of a source in this fashion rather than bolting on a separate paragraph on the provenance.

Overall, the source presents the central elements of the dispute between the BBC and the government but fails to draw attention to the government role in the death of Dr Kelly. In focusing attention on faulty reporting from the BBC the source gives a misleading account of how the events surrounding Dr Kelly's death soured relations between the government and the BBC. It was for this reason that the Report was condemned as a 'whitewash' by many media commentators and, ultimately, a further Inquiry into the whole affair was launched under Lord Chilcot.

> This is a strong conclusion because it offers a clear substantiated judgement that uses the criteria set out in the introduction. It clearly distinguishes between the parts of the source that can be relied on with certainty and those that lack such credibility.

Verdict

This is a strong answer because:

- it uses well-selected, accurate evidence to interrogate the source

- it clearly points out areas of the source that are more valid and useful than others
- it reaches persuasive conclusions based on a range of well-substantiated points.

Paper 3: A Level sample answer with comments

Section B

These questions require you to show your understanding of a period in depth. They will ask you about a quite specific period of time and require you to make a substantiated judgement about a specific aspect you have studied.

For these questions remember to:

- organise your essay and communicate it in a manner that is clear and comprehensible
- use historical knowledge to analyse and evaluate the key aspect of the question
- make a balanced argument that weighs up differing opinions
- make a substantiated overall judgement on the question.

How accurate is it to say that the launch of Channel 4 in 1982 was the most important change in British television under the Thatcher governments 1979–90? (20 marks)

Average student answer

Channel 4 was launched in November 1982, three years into Margaret Thatcher's 11-year rule. It was such an innovative channel that even the programmes were not timetabled in the way they were on BBC and ITV. It massively affected British television with its new programmes and also how it was different to the three existing channels: BBC1, BBC2 and ITV. Channel 4 was different, but how different and what would this mean for British television?

Channel 4 was launched because Thatcher hated the BBC. She thought it was like the socialism she wanted to get rid of in Britain: forced on people and undemocratic with its licence fee charge. Thatcher hoped that Channel 4 would change British television because the BBC would have to compete with a new channel that offered different programmes to the older programmes that had been offered to the British public. The BBC had dominated television since the 1920s. Although television broadcasts were stopped during the war, only the BBC was allowed to broadcast television after the war. ITV joined them in 1955 and this was different because it was commercial television rather than funded by the licence fee. The BBC and ITV kept most viewers throughout the 1980s so Channel 4 did not change this much. In this way Channel 4 did not affect the BBC or ITV because they just kept going the same as before. Things really didn't change until the satellite channels came along a bit later: suddenly there were hundreds of channels to choose from, and not just BBC, ITV, Channel 4 or even Channel 5. Thatcher got some choice in the end, but much later with the rise of the satellite channels like Sky. Channel 4 was basically another channel like BBC or ITV and was not that different in this respect.

Channel 4 was new and so it was bound to offer new programmes that could have made a big difference to what was already out there on British television. Channel 4 launched new show after new show and some of these had so much swearing that Mary Whitehouse wrote letters in protest at Channel 4. Mary Whitehouse had protested at other programmes before Channel 4 came along so this is not necessarily a big change for British television. But then again, she complained about really small things in our eyes. Channel 4 was a bit of a change with shows like Brookside but change had happened before with the growth of ITV in the 1950s so it was not that big an impact. BBC and ITV did not really change their shows and they continued to broadcast huge favourites like Coronation Street and EastEnders. The shows on these channels did not really change so it's not like Channel 4 forced them to add any new programmes.

Other things were changing in the 1980s that might have affected British television. Thatcher was very popular after the Falklands War and lots of people liked the way she encouraged people to buy their own homes. She also tried to shake up the world of business. Thatcher

This is a weak opening paragraph despite some accurate detail. The detail is used to describe when Channel 4 was launched, setting the scene rather than providing a guide to the criteria that will be used to offer judgements throughout the essay.

The points in these paragraphs are linked to the topic but not to the question in hand. This is largely due to a lack of chronological focus on the period stipulated by the question. You must stick to the years set out in depth study questions.

The points in these paragraphs are not always supported by accurate evidence. Even though there is some evidence, it is too generalised to offer effective support to any judgements that might have been reached. Aim to use precise examples to support key points.

hated socialism and wanted Britain to be more like America with lots of competition between businesses and people trying to make as much money as possible. In a way she introduced this American greed in Britain and people tried to do whatever they could to make lots of money. This helped promote sales not only of houses but of things to go in houses and even in gardens. Some programme makers must have realised what was going on because there were more television programmes about homes and gardens. And this just got more and more in the 1990s until we get to today with Saturday Kitchen and Nigella Bites and Great British Bake Off to name but a few. This was obviously a big change because there had only been a few cookery programmes before the 1980s and almost no home improvement programmes.

In conclusion, Channel 4 was an important change in British television in the 1980s. It helped shake things up with a big change from just the BBC and ITV – it was a new channel after all. There were new programmes too and these also made a difference to British television. Other changes had happened before, like the launch of ITV in 1955 or even the launch of the BBC in the 1920s, but things hadn't changed for a while by the 1980s. New programmes came along too, more so on Channel 4 than on the BBC and ITV. We can thank Channel 4 in a way for the range of programmes we have today – without it we might not have them at all.

The concluding paragraph lacks clear judgements. Some conclusions are offered, but they are too general and lack a real grounding in the period in question. It is important to answer the question as directly as possible in the conclusion with clearly justified judgements.

Verdict

This is an average answer because:

- it does not stick to the period stipulated by the question
- it uses a lot of vague rather than precise evidence to back up points
- it offers general conclusions rather than judgements precisely focused on the question.

Use the feedback on this essay to rewrite it, making as many improvements as you can.

Paper 3: A Level sample answer with comments

Section B

These questions require you to show your understanding of a period in depth. They will ask you about a quite specific period of time and require you to make a substantiated judgement about a specific aspect you have studied.

For these questions remember to:

- organise your essay and communicate it in a manner that is clear and comprehensible
- use historical knowledge to analyse and evaluate the key aspect of the question
- make a balanced argument that weighs up differing opinions
- make a substantiated overall judgement on the question.

How accurate is it to say that the launch of Channel 4 in 1982 was the most important change in British television under the Thatcher governments 1979–90? (20 marks)

Strong student answer

The launch of Channel 4 was a significant part of government efforts to increase competition in broadcasting although there are other more important examples of this between 1979 and 1990. The new channel also contributed to a greater range of broadcast programmes that represented a wider range of British interests and identities. However, the limited audience for such new shows undermines the overall impact of Channel 4 on British television in the 1980s.

> This is a strong opening paragraph because it clearly focuses on the time period and the major focus of the question: the impact of the stated factor on British television.

The launch of Channel 4 was a significant part of government efforts to boost competition within the media industry in the 1980s but was not the only important measure in this respect. The whole purpose of the Broadcasting Act 1980 in giving the fourth terrestrial channel to a new company was to break the duopoly of BBC and ITV control of television broadcasting that had prevailed since 1955. The terms of reference stipulated by the Independent Broadcasting Authority called on Channel 4 to commission far more programmes from independent production companies, especially from minority groups, rather than create shows 'in house' as the BBC and ITV had done. This was a clear reflection of the Conservative Party's 1979 election manifesto which promised an 'open market in ideas'. It also dovetailed with Thatcher's broader strategy to promote competition through privatisation and deregulation; she hoped increased media competition would force the BBC to offer better value for money and more popular programmes. The first Channel 4 Chairman, Jeremy Isaacs, delivered 61 percent rather than the expected 15 percent of shows commissioned from independent production companies, the number of which doubled from 220 in 1981 to 440 in 1983. This clearly undermined the previous control of the BBC–ITV duopoly and democratised access to television production.

> It is important to remember to consider both sides of the argument: the ways in which the stated factor did have a significant impact, but also to recognise any limits to that impact. Try to avoid direct contradiction when you set out both sides of the argument.

However, it is important not to overstate the significance of Channel 4 in the promotion of competition. First, the independently produced programmes were often of poor quality and seen as dull. Channel 4's audience share halved from its initial 6.6 percent in the few months. Second, the BBC did not use independent production companies in large numbers until the Broadcasting Act 1990 compelled it to do so. This hardly represents the introduction of 'contracting out' in British television in the 1980s as Thatcher had envisaged. Much to Thatcher's annoyance, the 1986 Peacock Report backed the retention of the licence fee, a break on the impact of Channel 4's competition. Her demand for more competition is reflected in the call for a fifth channel in the 1990 Act. Third, media competition had received a significant boost from the Cable and Broadcasting Act 1984. This enabled new channels such as Sky to broadcast to 15 million of the 22 million homes in Britain by 1990. Competition did therefore increase in television, although Channel 4 played a comparatively limited role in this process.

Channel 4 offered an important new broadcast platform to minority groups in the 1980s but the overall impact was limited by small audience share. A range of minority voices were represented on television for the first time, such as Black on Black and Eastern Eye made by and for members of racial minority communities. Homosexually themed films and shows by filmmaker Derek Jarman were also screened. While the most popular programmes such as Brookside, with stories about drug abuse and rape, pushed the boundaries of what was acceptable on prime-time television, viewing figures were tiny compared to rivals Coronation Street (ITV) and, from 1985, EastEnders (BBC). Channel 4 soon copied the larger channels in importing shows from the USA to attract larger audiences: where the BBC had Dallas and Dynasty, ITV had Falcon Crest, Channel 4 imported Cheers from 1983, a move which helped its audience share recover to almost 10 percent by 1985. Such American shows chimed well with the Thatcher government's promotion of material aspiration. Channel 4 also contributed to the origins of what became 'lifestyle television' in the 1990s: Space Craft (1987) was an early programme dedicated to interior design. The growth of cookery and gardening programmes on BBC and ITV also reflected an increased desire to attain greater sophistication and luxury at home in the 1980s. This was far more due to the growth of disposable incomes than the impact of Channel 4 programming.

> Precise examples of programmes are clearly used here to support the judgements made in relation to the question. Make sure you use a range of examples to substantiate your key point in every paragraph.

While Channel 4 clearly did promote competition within British television, that the Broadcasting Act 1990 was so comprehensive in setting out even greater competition highlights the limits of the channel's overall impact. The channel can be judged as significant in terms of the new boundaries it pushed in its programming, but the limits of its audience share must dilute the strength of even this impact on British television.

> The concluding paragraph offers a strong clinching argument to justify the overall finding that Channel 4 had a limited impact on the main area it was meant to affect: competition in television production.

Verdict

This is a strong answer because:

- it puts both sides of the case in terms of competition

- it consistently uses relevant evidence to support judgements
- it considers the nature of British television products as well as the structure of the industry.

Paper 3: A Level sample answer with comments

Section C

These questions require you to show your understanding of a subject over a considerable period of time. They will ask you to assess a long-term historical topic and its development over a period of at least 100 years, and they require you to make a substantiated judgement in relation to the question.

For these questions remember to:

- organise your essay and communicate it in a manner that is clear and comprehensible
- use historical knowledge to analyse and evaluate the key aspect of the question covering the entire period
- make a balanced argument that weighs up differing opinions
- make a substantiated overall judgement on the question.

To what extent was the launch of Butlin's holiday camps in 1936 the key turning point in British holidaymaking in the years 1882–2004? (20 marks)

Average student answer

Billy Butlin opened his first camp at Skegness in 1936. By 1966 he had opened another nine camps. Butlin's was not the only new luxurious holiday camp and there was a lot of competition from rival chains such as Pontin's and Warner's. Holiday camps were very popular in the 1950s and 1960s but less popular after this because of foreign package holidays.

Butlin's camps were not the first holiday camps in Britain. Camps had been set up for over 30 years before Billy Butlin opened his first camp in Skegness in 1936. Although Butlin's only had two camps open by 1939, there were over 200 around the UK coasts by this time. Holiday camps were not popular with everyone because although they offered healthy fresh air and countryside the facilities were not all that good. It was a bit more like camping in the modern sense of the word than holiday camping like a modern Centre Parcs. Centre Parcs was originally a Dutch company but opened its first centre in Sherwood Forest in 1987. With its impressive facilities under huge domes it was way more popular than Butlin's.

Butlin's entertainment was all about getting together to have fun. The Redcoats would sing, dance, tell jokes and get all the campers to get involved with competitions like 'glamorous granny' or 'knobbly knees' or even tug-of-war. There were massive dining rooms where everyone ate together: the mums could go for a dance afterwards because there were people to check on the children left in bed in the chalets. This was a huge breakthrough for British women as they didn't have to just look after the kids like they always had to at home. This type of entertainment was alright in the years after the Second World War as people didn't know any better, but it simply wasn't good enough as popular entertainment got better and better in the 1960s and 1970s.

Before Butlin's camps most people went to the seaside for their holidays. The working class were able to get to the coast by train and later by coach (few people had cars before the 1950s). Sometimes they were able to stay overnight in B and Bs but these were not great because landladies were very strict about things like: you had to be a married couple and you had to get out of the house during the day even if it was raining loads outside. The really poor people did not even get to stay overnight and just had a day trip. People liked the seaside because of the amazing things to do there like piers or the Blackpool Tower. There were even naughty postcards which made everyone laugh a lot.

After the 1960s the foreign package holiday grew hugely and seaside holidays went down. Horizon Holidays was the first and soon people could afford to go for a whole week to Spain

This is a weak opening paragraph despite the accurate detail. The detail is used to describe the popularity of holiday camps themselves rather than set out criteria by which the impact of Butlin's camps can be judged in the rest of the essay.

The points in these paragraphs are not always supported by evidence. Even though there is some evidence, it is not explicitly used to answer the question: a discussion of holidays before and after 1936 is offered, but the significance of Butlin's in this change is not directly addressed.

Try to avoid slang terms or colloquial English such as 'loads of'. Also consider the chronological range of the supporting evidence: these paragraphs focus almost exclusively on the 1960s.

and even Greece. This was a huge change for the British holidaymakers because they were in a country with a different language and different food. In fact, they found this so disgusting that all they wanted was what they had at home: cooked breakfast and lots of chips. Some foods did come back with these holidaymakers: pizza, lasagne and spaghetti were not really known of before the package holidays but soon everyone loved them in Britain. Butlin's did not open any camps in Spain or Greece so it's just not relevant here.

There were lots of other things happening with holidays apart from Butlin's. Transport for one thing. As mentioned above, package holidays grew hugely in the 1960s but this would never have happened if planes had not got much better: jet engines were quicker than old propeller planes and these old planes did not even have pressurised cabins! This is just like the rise of cars because all of a sudden people could go to loads of places in the UK they had not thought of before, like Cornwall. Even safety bicycles were important because you could use it to get out of the town or city and get some fresh air. This was important for women in particular.

Overall, Butlin's holiday camps were an important change in their own way and in their own time but looking back from today they do not seem as important. Going to Spain or even Greece was much more of an impact than just going to Skegness which you could have done before Butlin's anyway. Butlin's offered fun entertainment, like tug-of-war, but this simply wasn't good enough as modern entertainment grew in the 1960s and 1970s.

> Every paragraph should offer clear comparative judgements with regard to the significance of the stated factor. Try to avoid 'bolt on' paragraphs that could just as easily be cut and pasted into any general question related to the overall topic.

> The concluding paragraph lacks precise focus. It attempts to make judgements, but these are vague and not well justified. It is important to avoid simply restating everything you have said in the rest of the essay in your conclusion.

Verdict

This is an average answer because:

- it does not directly address the question but discusses the topic more generally
- it does not always use evidence to back up points
- it does not come to a strong reasoned judgement
- it does not address the whole period.

Use the feedback on this essay to rewrite it, making as many improvements as you can.

Paper 3: A Level sample answer with comments

Section C

These questions require you to show your understanding of a subject over a considerable period of time. They will ask you to assess a long-term historical topic and its development over a period of at least 100 years, and they require you to make a substantiated judgement in relation to the question.

For these questions remember to:

- organise your essay and communicate it in a manner that is clear and comprehensible
- use historical knowledge to analyse and evaluate the key aspect of the question covering the entire period
- make a balanced argument that weighs up differing opinions
- make a substantiated overall judgement on the question.

To what extent was the launch of Butlin's holiday camps in 1936 the key turning point in British holidaymaking in the years 1882–2004? (20 marks)

Strong student answer

Butlin's camps became an enduring and iconic part of British holidays following their launch in 1936. Although they raised average expectations about the quality of holiday accommodation and represented the pinnacle of communal holiday experiences for Britons, they cannot be said to have been a turning point in terms of who took holidays, where they went and for how long.

The launch of the first Butlin's camp in Skegness in 1936 was certainly a turning point in terms of meeting and fuelling raised expectations about the quality of holiday camp accommodation. Holiday camps had existed since the 1890s, but these 'pioneer' camps were basic, lacking sanitation and privacy. The camps expected guests to enjoy 'roughing it' and often had a political or religious affiliation. Billy Butlin marketed his camps as the height of modernity and luxury: posters depicted swimming pools, tennis courts, and chalets with electric lights, running water and clean, comfy beds. These improvements contrasted with poor alternative holiday accommodation. The 1938 Amulree Report criticised the overcrowded and unsanitary nature of seaside boarding houses. However, there was no sudden shift in the quality of holiday accommodation. The Development of Tourism Act 1969 aimed to improve British hotels to attract more foreign tourists. Therefore, while Butlin's dramatically changed the holiday camp experience itself, its broader impact on British holidaymaking was more limited.

The launch of Butlin's camps did not represent a key turning point but rather benefited from earlier changes in terms of who went on holiday and for how long. After 1945, Billy Butlin delivered on his aim to offer a week's all-inclusive holiday for less than the average working man's weekly wage. However, before 1939, at £3 10s for the week, a Butlin's holiday was beyond the means of blue collar workers who continued to stay in cheap boarding houses or just took day trips to the seaside as they had done since the 1880s. The Holidays With Pay Act 1938, because of the numbers affected, was more significant than Butlin's camps in enabling workers to take extended holidays. Even at its height of 1 million guests in 1963, Butlin's only catered for five percent of domestic holidaymakers. The rise of car ownership, cheap Sprite caravans and self-catering holidays were more important in terms of wider access to affordable longer holidays. Although Butlin's, with its communal dining and entertainment, benefited in popularity due to positive communal experiences during the austere war years, this was an exception to British holidaymaking rather than a turning point. The rise of caravanning in the 1960s, and the

This is a strong opening paragraph because it clearly focuses on the question and provides criteria by which the stated factor can be judged in terms of its impact as a turning point.

It is important to remember to consider both sides of the argument: the ways in which the stated factor did have a significant impact, but also to recognise any limits to that impact. The student has clearly done this in this paragraph where changes are acknowledged, but limits to change in this particular context are also highlighted.

decline of package tours and rise of independent holidays after the 1997 deregulation of flights within the European Union are clear examples of the British preference for individualism in their holidaymaking.

Butlin's camps cannot be seen as a turning point in terms of where Britons spent their holidays. Beach holidays had been popular since Victorian times because of the health benefits of sea air. Throughout the 20th century, even after Butlin's decline from the 1960s, Britons were drawn to the seafront by the coast itself and by resorts' attractions, such as Blackpool's Pleasure Beach. Between 1921 and 1923, Blackpool spent £1.5 on its promenade to keep Lancashire workers coming each August. Butlin's camps failed to prevent a slump in seaside holidays in the 1970s and 1980s due to the rise of foreign package tours. Companies such as Horizon, Clarksons and Thompson, perhaps inspired by Butlin's all-inclusive price, offered flights, food, drink and accommodation in Greek or Spanish resorts with virtually guaranteed sun at affordable prices. While the number of Britons who took a week's holiday in the UK remained at 25 million between 1951 and 2003, the number who went abroad increased from 1.5 million to 32.5 million in the same period. This dramatic change in British holidaymaking took place despite Butlin's best efforts to fight it.

Overall therefore, the success of Butlin's camps between 1936 and the 1960s is explained by earlier turning points in the growth of lower middle- and working-class holidays to the seaside. Even in those areas where Butlin's can be said to have made a difference, changes in communalism and standards of accommodation were limited in timescale and scope of their impact. Butlin's, limited by UK weather, was unable to compete with the growth of foreign package holidays which must be deemed a far greater turning point in the nature of British holidaymaking.

> The points in these paragraphs are supported by detailed, relevant evidence. The examples and statistics lend weight to the judgements made relating to the question.

> The concluding paragraph is clearly focused on the question. It does not merely repeat previous points but offers reasoned judgements that build on those offered throughout the essay.

Verdict

This is a strong answer because:

- it puts both sides of the case
- it consistently uses relevant evidence to support judgements
- it builds to a strong reasoned judgement in the conclusion.

Index

Acknowledgements

The authors and publisher would like to thank the following individuals and organisations for permission to reproduce photographs and text in this book.

Photographs
(Key: b–bottom; c–centre; l–left; r–right; t–top)

Alamy Images: Amoret Tanner 46, Mary Evans Picture Library 105, National Geographic Image Collection 6, Trevor Smith 151, Trinity Mirror / Mirrorpix 32, 73; **BBC Photo Library:** 93; **Birmingham Museums Trust:** 51; **D. C. Thomson Co., Ltd:** Red Star Weekly © DC Thomson & CO Ltd 23; **Getty Images:** Hulton Archive 115, Popperfoto 128, SSPL 18; **Mary Evans Picture Library:** Marx Memorial Library 80, Onslow Auctions Limited 82, Retrograph Collection 101, The National Army Museum 48; **Mirrorpix:** 98, 136, 159, 98, 136, 159; **Press Association Images:** PA Archive 164; **Punch Limited:** 78, 147; **Reproduced by kind permission of Private Eye magazine:** 8, 113; **Rex Shutterstock:** Associated Newspapers 116; **The Sun Newspaper:** 148.

Cover image: Getty Images: Duffy

All other images © Pearson Education

Figures
Figure 2.2 after *Britain 1914–2000* Collins Educational (Murphy, D. 2000) p.360, Reprinted by permission of HarperCollins Publishers Ltd © D. Murphy 2000.

Tables
Source 2 p.13 from Office for National Statistics, licensed under the Open Government Licence v.3.0; Source 7 p.22 adapted from *Britain 1914–2000*, Collins Educational (Murphy, D. 2000) p.350, Table 14, Reprinted by permission of HarperCollins Publishers Ltd © D. Murphy 2000; Source 15 p.36 from *Britain 1914–2000*, Collins Educational (Murphy, D. 2000) p.344, Table 6, Reprinted by permission of HarperCollins Publishers Ltd © D. Murphy 2000; Source 5 p.49 from *British Tourism: The remarkable story of growth*, Middleton, V.T.C and Lickorish, L.J., pp.191–92 Copyright © 2005 Elsevier Ltd. Reproduced by permission of Taylor & Francis Books UK; Source 9 p.53 from the Department of Transport, licensed under the Open Government Licence v.3.0; Source 10 p.54 from *British Tourism: The remarkable story of growth*, Middleton, V.T.C and Lickorish, L.J., pp.190, 197. Copyright © 2005 Elsevier Ltd. Reproduced by permission of Taylor & Francis Books UK.; Source 11 p.57 adapted from Office for National Statistics, *Social Trends* 41, 2011, p.3, licensed under the Open Government Licence v.3.0; Source 8 p.104 from *Hamburg Broadcast Propaganda: The Extent and Effects of its Impact on the British Public during mid-winter 1939/40*, 8 March 1940 (BBC WAC R/9/9/4, LR/98) © BBC, with permission from the BBC Written Archives Centre.

Text
Source 4 p.16 from *Married Love: A New Contribution to the Solution of the Sex Difficulties* Oxford University Press (Stopes, M. 1918), © The Galton Institute London; Extract p.17 from Stated aim of the Family Planning Association (FPA) in 1939, with permission from the FPA (www.fpa.org.uk); Source 6 p.19 from *Working-Class Wives: Their health and conditions*, Penguin Books (Spring Rice, M. 1939) pp.102–3, 105, 106 copyright © Margery Spring Rice, 1939. Reproduced by permission of Penguin Books Ltd.; Extract 1 p.20 from Bruley, S., *Women in Britain Since 1900*, 1999, Palgrave, p.138 reproduced with permission of Palgrave Macmillan; Extract p.25 from *A Woman's World* Heinemann (Summerskill, E. 1967) p.61; Source 11 p.30 from a letter to the *Liverpool Echo* in 1911 reproduced with permission from the Liverpool Echo; Source 13 p.32 from The Guardian Archive, http://www.theguardian.com/theguardian/2014/jun/20/dagenham-women-ford-strike-equal-pay 20 June 1968: Women strikers at Ford Dagenham sense victory, Copyright Guardian News & Media Ltd 2016; Extract 2 p.37 from *Women in Britain 1900–2000* Hodder & Stoughton (Mayer, A. 2002) p.148 with permission from Dr A. Mayer; Extract 3 p.37 from Bruley, S., *Women in Britain Since 1900*, 1999, Palgrave, p.178, reproduced with permission of Palgrave Macmillan; Extract 4 p.37 from *Finding a Role: The United Kingdom 1970–1990*, Oxford University Press (Harrison, B., 2010) pp.238–9 by permission of Oxford University Press; Extract 1 p.42 from *Seeking a Role: The United Kingdom*

1951–70, Oxford University Press (Harrison, B., 2009) p.334 by permission of Oxford University Press; Extract 2 on page 48 from *British Tourism: The remarkable story of growth*, Middleton, V.T.C and Lickorish, L.J., p.71 Copyright © 2005 Elsevier Ltd. Reproduced by permission of Taylor & Francis Books UK; Source 7 p.50 from Monty Python Travel Skit, *Monty Python Just the Words* Methuen Publishing Ltd (Graham Chapman) 11 October 1999; Source 14 p.60 from *Walking in the Shade* Flamingo (Lessing, Doris 1997) p.16, Reprinted by permission of HarperCollins Publishers Ltd © 1997 Doris Lessing; Source 15 p.62 from *The Internet in Everyday Life* by Wellman, Barry; Haythornthwaite, Caroline. A. (Anderson, Ben and Tracey, Karina 2002) pp.149–50, Reproduced with permission of Blackwell Publishing, Incorporated in the format book via Copyright Clearance Center; Source 16 p.62, statistics from *ONS Statistical bulletin: Internet access- Households and Individuals 2014*, Office for National Statistics licensed under the Open Government Licence v.3.0; Extract 1 p.73 from Boyce, D. George, 'Harmsworth, Alfred Charles William, Viscount Northcliffe (1865–1922)' in *Oxford Dictionary of National Biography*, Oxford University Press (Matthew, H. C.G. and Harrison, B. (eds), 2004, online 2016) by permission of Oxford University Press; Extract 2 and quote 'gave the wheel another shove' on p.74 and quote 'I shall go back to New Brunswick' on p.76 from *Beaverbrook* Hamish Hamilton (Taylor, A.J.P. 1972) pp.102, 111, 112, 250, with permission from David Higham Associates Limited; Source 1 p.92 from Report by the BBC Listener Research Section, Programme Division, late July 1940, http://www.bbc.co.uk/archive/battleofbritain/11432.shtml © BBC, with permission from the BBC Written Archives Centre; Extract p.92 from *Listener Research Survey,* February 1941 © BBC, with permission from the BBC Written Archives Centre; Source 3 p.96 from *Diaries and Letters: 1930–1964* Penguin (Nicolson, H. 1980) p.188 Reproduced with permission of Curtis Brown Group Ltd. London on behalf of The Beneficiaries of the Estate of Harold Nicholson, Copyright © Harold Nicolson, 1940, 1980; Source 4 p.96 from http://hansard.millbanksystems.com/ commons/1940/jun/18/war-situation#S5CV0362P0_19400618_HOC_260, Contains Parliamentary information licensed under the Open Parliament Licence v3.0.; Extract p.98 'Ministry of No Comment' from http://www.moidigital.ac.uk/blog/ministry-worth-exploring/, author of post Dr Henry Irving, used with permission; Extract p.99 from *Print for Victory: Book Publishing in England 1939–1945* The British Library (Holman, V. 2008) p.91, ©The British Library Board; Source 9 p.104 from a broadcast by William Joyce on 29 August 1940 cited in *Nazi Wireless Propaganda: Lord Haw-Haw and British Public Opinion in the Second World War,* Edinburgh University Press (Doherty, M. 2000) p.76; Winston Churchill quote on page 111 from SC House of Commons Debates, 23 February 1955, vol. 537, cols 1276–7 http://hansard.millbanksystems.com/commons/1955/feb/23/parliamentary-debates-broadcast, Contains Parliamentary information licensed under the Open Parliament Licence v3.0; Source 1 p.112 from *The News Interview: Journalists and Public Figures on the Air*, Cambridge University Press (Clayman, S. and Heritage, J. 2002) pp.50–51; Source 2 p.112 from *A Great, Silly Grin: The British Satire Boom in the 1960s* Da Capo Press (Carpenter, H. 2003) p.242, Reproduced by permission of Felicity Bryan Literary Agency and Curtis Brown, London on behalf of the Estate of Malcolm Bradbury; Extract 1 p.114 from *The Offensive Art: Political Satire and its Censorship around the World from Beerbohm to Borat.* Praeger Publishers Inc (Freedman, L. 2008) p.71, Reproduced with permission of Greenwood Publishing Group, Inc. in the format Republish in a book via Copyright Clearance Center; Extract 2 p.117 from *History of English Christianity 1920–1990* SCM Press (Hasting, A. 1991) p.518; Source 6 p.121 © Stephen Bourne, 2001, *Black in the British Frame*, p.109, Continuum UK, by permission of Bloomsbury Publishing Plc; Quote p.122 from *How Colour Prejudiced is Britain*, Victor Gollancz Ltd (Hill, C.S. 1965) p.19 © Clifford S. Hill 1965 Survey Questionnaire (Sociological Survey of Attitudes to Racial Difference) Part III Question 3, with permission from Rev. Dr Clifford Hill; Extract pp.122–3 from John Hopkins quoting a letter he received about the film *Fable*, http://www.screenonline.org.uk/tv/id/476259/, article author Mark Duguid, used by permission of BFI; Extract 3 p.125 from *Inventing Television Culture: Men Women, and the Box,* Oxford University Press (Thumim, J. 2004) p.175 by permission of Oxford University Press; Source 7 p.126 from *Manifesto* (written for the Clean-up TV campaign), NVALA (Whitehouse, M. 1964), over 50 years on the campaign is still thriving under the name of Mediawatch-UK, reproduced with permission; Source 8 p.127 from 'London, the Most Exciting City in the World' *Weekend Telegraph*, 16/04/1965 (Crosby, John) © Telegraph Media Group Limited 1965; Headline p.129 'This Horrible Lot – Not Quite What They Seem', *Evening Standard*, 21/03/1964 (Cleave, M.), used with permission; Extract 1 pp.137–8 from Revealed: Murdoch's secret meeting with Mrs Thatcher before he bought The Times, *The Independent*, 17/03/2012 (McSmith, A.), http://www.independent.co.uk/news/media/press/revealed-murdochs-secret-meeting-with-mrs-thatcher-before-he-bought-the-times-7575910.html; Source 2 p.141 from *A Licence to be Different: the Story of Channel 4,* British Film Institute (Brown, M. 2007) p.16, reproduced with permission of Palgrave Macmillan; Source 4 p.144 from 'British press freedom erodes under Thatcher, critics say', *The New York Times*, 19/12/1987 (Raines, H.) © 1987 The New York Times. All rights reserved. Used by permission and protected by the Copyright Laws of the United States. The printing, copying, redistribution, or retransmission of this Content without express written permission is prohibited www.nytimes.com; Source 5 p.146 from *Good and Faithful*

Servant: The Unauthorized Biography of Bernard Ingham, Faber and Faber Ltd (Harris, R. 1990) pp.116, 170, Reprinted by permission of SLL/Sterling Lord Literistic, Inc. Copyright by Robert Harris; Source 8 p.149 from an interview with Patrick Bishop in 1982 used by kind permission of Patrick Bishop; Extract 2 p.149 from 'The worst reported war since the Crimean', *The Guardian*, 25/02/2002 (Barnes, Julian), Copyright Guardian News & Media Ltd 2016; Extract 3 p.149 from *Media and Society into the 21st Century: A Historical Introduction*, Wiley Blackwell (Gorman, L. and McLean, D. 2009) pp.215–16, Reproduced with permission of Wiley-Blackwell in the format Book via Copyright Clearance Center; Extract 4 p.152 from *Thatcher & Sons – A Revolution in Three Acts* Penguin Books (Jenkins, S., 2007) p.110. Copyright © Simon Jenkins, 2006. All rights reserved. Reproduced by permission of Penguin Books Ltd.; Extract 5 p.152 Republished with permission from Transaction Publishers, from *The Anatomy of Thatcherism*, Letwin, S., 1993, p.310; permission conveyed through Copyright Clearance Center, Inc.; Source 1 p.156 from a transcript of a report broadcast on Channel 4 News, 6 February 2003, with permission from Channel 4 News; Extracts p.156, left-hand column, bullet points from *Select Committee on Foreign Affairs Written Evidence*, Memorandum from Dr Glen Rangwala, Prepared 7 July 2003 http://www.parliament.the-stationery-office.co.uk/pa/cm200203/cmselect/cmfaff/813/813we18.htm, © Parliamentary copyright 2003, Contains Parliamentary information licensed under the Open Parliament Licence v3.0; Source 2 p.156 from Glen Rangwala's article 'Intelligence? The British Dossier on Iraq's Security Infrastructure', posted on the Campaign Against Sanctions on Iraq website on 5 February 2003. http://www.casi.org.uk/; Source 3 p.157 from 'Doctrine of the International Community', a speech made by Tony Blair in Chicago on 24 April 1999, http://webarchive.nationalarchives.gov.uk/+/www.number10.gov.uk/Page1297, Contains public sector information licensed under the Open Government Licence (OGL) v3.0; Source 4 p.158 from 'One million march against war', *The Telegraph*, 16/02/2003 (Syalm, R. Alderson, A. and Milner, C.), http://www.telegraph.co.uk/news/uknews/1422228/One-million-march-against-war.html © Telegraph Media Group Limited 2003; Extract p.161 from House of Commons, Select Committee on Foreign Affairs, Ninth Report, para. 136 http://www.publications.parliament.uk/pa/cm200203/cmselect/cmfaff/813/81301.htm, © Parliamentary copyright 2003, contains parliamentary information licensed under the Open Parliament Licence v3.0; Extract p.161 and Extract 1 p.162 from *Stumbling Over Truth* © Kevin Marsh, 2012, reprinted by permission of Biteback Publishing pp.52, 125–9; Extract pp.163 and 166 and Source 10 p.168 from Report of the Inquiry into the Circumstances Surrounding the Death of Dr David Kelly C.M.G. by Lord Hutton, 2004, Contains Parliamentary information licensed under the Open Parliament Licence v3.0; Extract p.163 from Select Committee on Foreign Affairs Minutes of Evidence, http://www.publications.parliament.uk/pa/cm200203/cmselect/cmfaff/813/3062514.htm, © Parliamentary copyright 2003, contains parliamentary information licensed under the Open Parliament Licence v3.0; Source 7 on page 165 from *The Blair Years* by Alistair Campbell, published by Arrow, Reprinted by permission of The Random House Group Limited; Source 8 p.166 from 'Suicide and Suspicions over War in Iraq' (Shelby, Barry and Coleman, Sarah), 13/08/2003 http://www.worldpress.org/europe/1405.cfm, www.worldpress.org; Extract p.167 from Minutes of the Widgery Inquiry, http://cain.ulst.ac.uk/hmso/widgery.htm, Contains public sector information licensed under the Open Government Licence (OGL) v3.0; Source 9 p.168 from 'Hutton: the Verdict', *The Mail on Sunday*, 01/02/2004 (Hitchens, P.), http://www.dailymail.co.uk/columnists/article-207200/Hutton-verdict.html; Source 11 p.170 from Andrew Gilligan's resignation speech on 30 January 2004, with permission from Andrew Gilligan; Extract p.170 from Phillis, An Independent Review, 2004 p.1, www.publications.parliament.uk, contains parliamentary information licensed under the Open Parliament Licence v3.0; Extract 2 p.171 from Stanyer, J., Politics and the Media: A Crisis of Trust?, *Parliamentary Affairs*, 2004, Vol. 57 , by permission of Oxford University Press.